Distant
Provinces
in the Inka
Empire

Toward a Deeper

Understanding of

Inka Imperialism

Edited by

Michael A. Malpass

and Sonia Alconini

University of Iowa Press | Iowa City

University of Iowa Press, Iowa City 52242

Copyright © 2010 by the University of Iowa Press

www.uiowapress.org

Printed in the United States of America

Design by April Leidig-Higgins

The University of Iowa Press is a member of Green
Press Initiative and is committed to preserving natural
resources.

Printed on acid-free paper

Library of Congress Cataloging-in-Publication Data

Distant provinces in the Inka empire: toward a deeper
understanding of Inka imperialism / edited by
Michael A. Malpass and Sonia Alconini.

   p.   cm.

Includes bibliographical references and index.

ISBN-13: 978-1-58729-869-1 (pbk.)

ISBN-10: 1-58729-869-4 (pbk.)

   1. Incas — History.   2. Incas — Politics and
government.   3. Imperialism — History — To 1500.
4. Colonies — Administration — History — To 1500.
5. Regionalism — South America — History — To
1500.   6. Human geography — South America —
History — To 1500.   7. Incas — Social conditions.
8. Elite (Social sciences) — South America — History
— To 1500.   9. Social control — South America —
History — To 1500.   10. South America — Ethnic
relations.   I. Malpass, Michael Andrew.   II. Alconini
Mujica, Sonia.

F3429.D57   2010

985'.01 — dc22   2009030882

Dedicated to three giants
of Andean studies
John Rowe,
Alberto Rex Gonzales,
and Craig Morris

Contents

Preface and
Acknowledgments

The 1993 publication of *Provincial Inca: Archaeological and Ethnohistorical Assessment of the Impact of the Inca State* was a step forward in our understanding of how the Inkas interacted with the people of their conquered provinces. The book's main focus was on comparing the two forms of information and synthesizing the results to provide a more complete picture of the Inka Empire and the variability in Inka rule. The book's conclusion, one that was widely being realized at that time and earlier, was that the Inka Empire was less a homogenous monolithic entity than it was a series of broadly similar yet distinctive sets of provinces governed in a variety of ways.

These results were based on both ethnohistorical accounts and archaeology, but the latter was largely restricted to survey work with some limited excavations of sites. The information was thus general and the conclusions broad. In addition, the coverage of the book was uneven, with one chapter from northern Chile, four from Peru, and one covering broader aspects of the empire. Significantly, there were no chapters from the extreme ends of the empire, from south-central Chile or Ecuador, or from the Bolivian/Argentinean area. Thus, the regions where one could expect that Inka imperial rule might take on different forms due to the recency of conquest or the importance of maintaining a border to the empire were largely underrepresented.

To review the state of research on Inka imperial strategies of control in the far reaches of their empire, the two authors organized a symposium at the 2004 Society for American Archaeology annual meeting in Montreal. The goals of the symposium were to gauge the advances in Inka studies and to look at the information from regions not covered in the first book. Toward that end, investigators from the extremes of the empire were recruited as well as others from the coast of Peru. After the authors decided to publish the results, the essay by Rossen et al. (chapter 2) was added to have data from the southern extreme of the empire. The distribution of the research included in this volume can be seen in figure 1.1, which shows the locations of the investigations from this volume.

In addition to the complementary coverage, the papers presented in Montreal indicated that recent investigations had gone well beyond the survey and testing of earlier research to include excavations reflecting much more fine-grained studies of Inka control, and local resistance to or compliance with it. Excavations at Inka and local sites showed the range of variation in adoption and rejection of Inka material culture and architecture much more clearly than earlier. As a result, the investigations here have deepened our understanding of Inka imperialism and the way that local people confronted the empire.

The authors have chosen to follow the Quechua spelling of terms, especially Inka names, rather than the hispanicized versions. This reflects a shift in the field away from the latter toward the former. Most readers of this volume are already accustomed to the terms, and the non-Andean reader should have few difficulties in translating them.

As any editor of a contributed volume can testify, getting the authors to complete their chapters in a timely fashion can be a difficult and time-consuming task. We are fortunate that we had no such problems with the authors here. Our first acknowledgment therefore goes to the contributors for the quick and thorough completion of their chapters and the subsequent requested revisions. Even more, they provided their figures and tables in like fashion, expediting the completion of the final volume.

The authors would also like to thank Holly Carver, Karen Copp, and the staff at the University of Iowa Press for the ease with which negotiations about the volume were completed and the final version published.

The senior author wants to thank the Provost's Office at Ithaca College for the teaching reduction that allowed him to have the time for completing his part of the final drafts. He also owes a large debt of gratitude to his wife, Susanne Kessemeier, and son, Soren, for bearing with him during the never-ending completion of the work. The second author thanks her colleagues and friends at the University of Texas at San Antonio for their support in this endeavor. She especially wants to thank her family, Vince and Anna Wara McElhinny, for their invaluable support.

Distant Provinces
in the Inka Empire

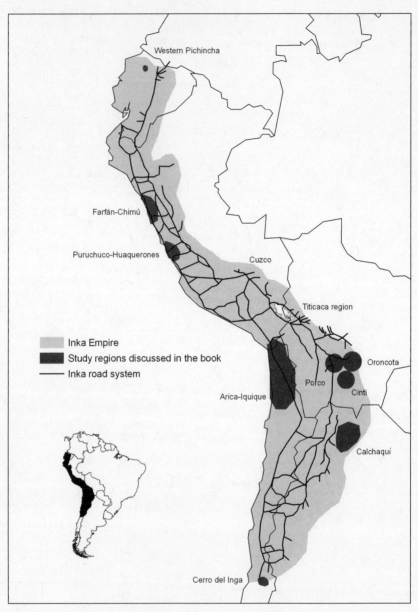

FIGURE 1.1. Location of the different investigation areas presented in the book. Map based on Hyslop 1984 and D'Altroy 1992.

Michael A. Malpass
and Sonia Alconini

Chapter One

Provincial Inka Studies in the Twenty-first Century

This book began as a symposium at the 2004 Society for American Archaeology meetings in Montreal. The purpose of the symposium was to
bring together researchers who had advanced our ideas about the nature
of the Inka Empire, both geographically and in the details of the processes
involved. Geographically, the research presented focused on provinces
of the empire that were far from the capital of Cuzco. The volume here
includes six chapters that cover the southern part of Tawantinsuyu and
three that cover the central or northern part. Particularly exciting are the
two chapters dealing with the Central and North coasts of Peru, areas
where little previous research has been reported. This additional coverage
adds more support to the conclusions that have emerged in the past two
decades that Inka strategies of control were flexible and tailored to the
particular situations faced in different regions.

Another focus of the symposium was to report on studies that added
more details about the specific nature of Inka control of their conquered
provinces. Four chapters in the current volume report on specific excavations and studies of local and Inka sites that give a more nuanced view of
the complex interrelationships that occurred when the Inkas incorporated
conquered groups into their empire. The archaeological research shows

how the particulars of Inka control were manifested in ways that ethno-historical documents do not, and perhaps cannot, address.

Five issues emerged from the original symposium as points of discussion about the Inkas: (1) the various forms of Inka imperial control exercised in the provinces as seen through a range of archaeological indicators (that is, settlement patterns, household analysis, cultural material, architecture, bioarchaeology, and so forth); (2) the nature of the interaction of archaeological and ethnohistorical research seeking to understand the various manifestations of Inka imperialism and provincialism; (3) local reactions to imperial control and institutions, including resistance, colonization, and negotiation of power as seen through archaeology and ethnohistory; (4) the scales of analysis and archaeological correlates used to understand the various forms of Inka provincialism and imperial control (that is, regional-level versus household approaches); and (5) the re-evaluation of marginality and marginal provinces in the Inka Empire, or how archaeologists understand and measure imperial marginality, Inka imperialism, and Inka provincialism.

From these five themes, a salient issue addressed by the different contributors to this book involves imperial strategies of domination exerted by the Inkas across their provinces. In order to provide a theoretical framework for such discussion, we first provide a brief overview of the history of studies involving Inka imperialism and forms of Inka imperial control.

Forms of Inka Imperial Control

Empires can be defined as highly extractive polities controlling a vast territory through a combination of political, economic, military, and ideological strategies of domination (Mann 1986:251, 271). As such, empires are by essence multiethnic, plurilinguistic, and multinational as they expand over large expanses of land incorporating a variety of environments and cultures (Alcock et al. 2001; Barfield 2001; D'Altroy 1992, 2002; Schreiber 1992). The study of ancient empires has benefited greatly from core-periphery models emphasizing the dominance of the imperial core in the asymmetric economic and sociopolitical relations established with its peripheries (Wallerstein 1976). As a response to such metrocentric perceptions of imperial control, many studies have emphasized the importance of peripheral regions and their native elite as important catalysts of imperial expansion (Doyle 1986). More recently, the study of empires has broadened to look at not just empires and how we define them but also the relations between empires and adjacent regions, the worldviews of the societies calling themselves empires, the kinds of data on which empires are defined, and the historical aspects of the descriptions of empires (Alcock et al. 2001).

For the Inkas, the study of imperialism has emphasized the flexibility in the forms of control that they used to maintain compliance in the various provinces. In response to a monolithic view of the Inka Empire portrayed in ethnohistorical documents often magnifying the role of the rulers or the might of the empire, the work of Dorothy Menzel in 1959 first recognized the flexibility of imperial control as a response to existing sociopolitical conditions. On the Peruvian coast, she acknowledged, the Inkas, whenever possible, took advantage of existing administrative facilities and bureaucratic apparatuses to minimize imperial expenditures. Such was the case of Chincha, a South Coast society with a strong centralized authority, where the Inkas did not need to establish their own centers of administration, but exploited those in existing enclaves and also delegated the control to native elites. In comparison, she noted that in nearby coastal valleys, such as Ica, with lesser levels of political centralization, the Inkas had to build an administrative infrastructure from scratch by establishing imperial centers in strategic locations while ruling the region in a direct fashion. Therefore, while indirect control was possible in regions with already centralized governments by delegating the administration to native elites, direct rule was exercised where the Inkas targeted resource extraction in regions that had low levels of political centralization and the absence of a bureaucratic apparatus (Menzel 1959).

In more recent years, such notions of direct and indirect Inka rule were expanded into broader theoretical models. In 1992, the work of Katharina Schreiber on the Wari Empire stressed the varying kinds of imperial control in subdued provinces, ranging from direct territorial control to indirect hegemonic rule as ends of a continuum. She also remarked that it is not only very likely that a combination of both forms of control were common in the Inka provinces but also that the degree of imperial rule was a response to three factors: the availability of administrative personnel, the cost-benefit ratio involving direct rule, and the existing levels of political complexity (Schreiber 1992). Depending on whether the local system was adequate for imperial rule, the administrative structures might be left intact or completely reorganized to better respond to imperial needs. In addition, she recognized that depending on the levels of cooperation of indigenous elites and the associated imperial interests, native leaders might be left in place as provincial rulers. Alternatively, if cooperation was not likely, local elites might be completely replaced or simply displaced in the hierarchical structure by adding a third tier of imperial administrators to overlook the regional affairs (Schreiber 1992).

At about the same time, and inspired by the work of Luttwak (1976) and Hassig (1985, 1992) studying the Roman and Aztec empires, respectively, Terry D'Altroy (1992) laid out the mechanics of territorial and hegemonic rule for the Inkas. Using a cost-benefit analysis, he explained that the degree of imperial control in the provinces was usually determined by the intensity of imperial extraction. Therefore, he stressed that imperial control should be envisioned along a continuum, ranging from direct territorial control to indirect hegemonic rule. At one extreme, direct territorial control entailed a high-control, high-extraction strategy where the empire invested significantly in support infrastructure and military control in the provinces in order to ensure large economic gains for the imperial core. In this case, the provinces fell under direct imperial rule. At the other extreme of the spectrum lies indirect hegemonic control, involving a low-control, low-extraction strategy. In this latter case, the empire ruled indirectly through patron-client ties established with native elites with the consequent low levels of economic revenues. The burden of defense was left to local allies with the promise of military support. One advantage of indirect hegemonic rule was that although the economic gains were low, it allowed the empire to expand over large stretches of land with minimum investment. An important aspect of the territorial-hegemonic model is that it stresses the flexibility of imperial rule both in time and space as a response to varying local conditions, including the existing levels of political organization of the subjects, the kinds of resources available, and the goals of the empire vested in the region. Rather than isolated typologies, the territorial-hegemonic model emphasizes the varying forms of imperial domination falling in between both extremes by combining different scales of political, economic, military, and ideological power (D'Altroy 1992).

An important point brought out by a reviewer of this book is the fact that *all* Inka control was indirect. While governors of provinces were likely Inka elites from Cuzco, *kurakas* of decimal units from 100 to 10,000 were local elites incorporated into the administrative hierarchy (see also D'Altroy 2002:233–234). The significance of this lies in the fact that the dichotomies of direct/indirect and territorial/hegemonic must be reconsidered as absolute categories and not as ends of a continuum of forms of control. What we see in the archaeological record is not so much evidence of Inka officials administering the distant provinces from the top levels to the bottom, but local ones under the control of an imperial official, likely the local governor. What needs to be explained in the archaeological record is why some local officials manifested Inka expressions of power, like house form and imperial ceramics, while others did not — in other words, the degree of Inkanization that regional chiefs had as tools of political self-legitimization, imperial imposition, and inter-elite competition. Therefore, the interface between the local elites and their Inka overlords becomes the critical factor. Clearly, a finer level of analysis is needed to understand this interface, which is provided by four of the essays in this volume (chapters 4, 5, 6, and 9).

Related to the issue of direct versus indirect control is the territorial versus hegemonic continuum. As stated above, a territorial strategy implies direct control over a province with heavy investment by the Inkas for maximum extraction of resources. The control often assumes a large contingent of Inka personnel for managing the activities, since no local organization is present. A hegemonic strategy implies indirect control with a reduced level of extraction of resources. In this latter situation, the Inkas used local leaders to rule indirectly. Of course, a combination of these strategies is likely, depending on the combination of military, political, and ideological forms of control.

The fact that Inka imperial rule was always indirect in the provinces, as suggested by the reviewer, brings up interesting issues involving the different scales of analysis when one seeks to understand the makeup of empires — in this case, the Inka. On the one hand, we have information that Inka *orejones* (members of the Inka nobility, distinguished by their large ear spools) and Inkas-by-Privilege (honorary Inkas from a variety of ethnicities from the Cuzco region) were central in the expansion of the empire (Covey 2006; D'Altroy 2002; Rowe 1946; Rostworowski de Diez Canseco 1988). In fact, the uppermost positions in the army were reserved for them in order to ensure loyalty, whereas the annexation of new territories and tributaries, either through warfare or diplomacy, benefited directly members of the royal elite. New territories and people implied a resource base for the competing *panaqa* elite lineages of the empire (Conrad and Demarest 1984; D'Altroy 2002). On the other hand, we also know that the organization of the provinces was usually delegated to local lords using a decimal form of administration of tributaries and resources (Julien 1987). Of course, this depended on whether the local chiefs sought to preserve and even aggrandize their positions in the emerging power structure or if they resisted Inka conquest.

Whereas top provincial positions were filled with Inka *orejones* as direct representatives of the empire, whether or not they resided in the provinces, intermediate administrative positions were usually filled with low-ranking bureaucrats of native origins. In a way, the assertion that Inka imperial control in the subject provinces was always indirect is true, if one views this from a bottom-up perspective. From a top-down perspective, one can argue that the imperial elites, those from Cuzco and from royal *panaqa* lineages, sought to establish a direct exercise of control through the mediation of intermediate elites (Covey 2006; Morris and Santillana 2007). Other factors being equal, it was in the interest of the imperial elites to maximize their revenues by incorporating midranking bureaucrats from the subject provinces through a range of strategies. That is, the optimally balanced control entailed the combination of indirect and direct forms of control in order to ensure the maximum benefits with the least cost (for more discussion, see Alconini 2008). In this context, the diverse reactions of the local elites, whether they became fully or partially Inkanized, or even remained loyal to their cultural traditions, is an aspect that deserves further exploration.

Therefore, issues that are central in understanding the ways in which the Inkas exercised control in their distant provinces involve a set of related variables. Even though the degree of investment in imperial infrastructure (such as roads, elaborate facilities, temples, administrative centers, extensive agricultural terraces, and warehouses) usually correlates with degrees of control, one needs to be aware of the nuanced politics of imperial control. One can assume that a sustained investment in a region implies a direct form of control and therefore marked economic extraction (and vice-versa). However, depending on the nature of interaction with local leaders, the shifting balance of power, and the imperial interests in the region, this task may be either delegated to native chiefs, to intermediate Inkas-by-Privilege bureaucrats, or even to non-Inkanized trusted ethnicities.

Alternatively, the presence of an existing local infrastructure in conquered regions does not preclude additional organizational changes by the Inkas to develop the decimal administrative system to manage the province. Elevating local elites must have been a tricky thing to do, as there would have been competing factions that could have been appropriate for a given position. While the chroniclers tell us that the Inkas tried to follow local kinship and political norms and existing leadership, in hierarchically organized societies like the Chimú, this could have been problematic.

As will be illustrated in this book, Inka imperial control was more complicated than one would expect from the traditional direct territorial or indirect hegemonic model. To cite a few examples, some provinces evidenced their progressive incorporation from indirect to direct control on a temporal scale (see chapter 3). In other regions with marked levels of sociopolitical complexity, such as the Peruvian North Coast, recent research shows more than expected evidence of direct rule within an otherwise hegemonic circumstance (see chapter 9). In other provinces, such as those in the southern parts of the empire, both indirect and direct rule appear to have been strategically combined, forming a landscape dotted with pockets of direct control, a strategy defined as selectively intense (D'Altroy et al. 2007; Williams and D'Altroy 1998). The question, then, is who is in charge of these pockets — Inkas from the heartland or locals who took on the trappings of their conquerors, either by coercion or acceptance?

Some contributors to this book indicate the importance of analyzing imperial domination and colonization from a bottom-up perspective. Using an agent-oriented approach, Félix Acuto (chapter 5) points to the nuanced ways that local people responded to the Inkas. Taking into consideration inner processes of competition, both in the provinces and the imperial core at the ethnic, class, and faction levels, it is not surprising that the Inkas had to accommodate a range of circumstances in order to exert domination. Indeed, D'Altroy (2001) has noted how even different Inka elite groups would use imperial power to gain private resources both near to and distant from Cuzco, in contrast to the state uses of conquered lands. This provides another intriguing avenue for understanding the complexity of the Inka Empire, though one not discussed by authors in this book.

As presented in this volume, detailed contextual analyses and bio-archaeological research in Inka and elite residences of the distant provinces are useful to evaluate the impact of the empire on the leadership strategies of Inkanized populations, whether they were Inkas-by-Privilege, Inkan-ized *kurakas*, or foreign midlevel administrators from trusted ethnicities.

The Interaction of Archaeological and Ethnohistorical Research

Virtually all the chapters in this book discuss the intersection of archae-ology and ethnohistory. The complementarity between archaeology and ethnohistory as sources of information has almost become a truism in Inka studies, reflected in the research presented here. Of some interest in this volume is the research conducted in the far distant regions of the empire, Ecuador and Chile. The work of Ron Lippi and Alejandra Gudiño (chapter 10) provides new information on the ethnohistorical and archaeo-logical evidence of Inka activities in Ecuador. The works of Jack Rossen et al. (chapter 2) and Calógero Santoro et al. (chapter 3) provide information about poorly known regions of Chile. The latter especially demonstrates how archaeology is changing our views of Inka control that were based on a very fragmentary ethnohistorical basis. The chapters on Bolivia and Argentina by Sonia Alconini (chapter 4), Félix Acuto (chapter 5), Clau-dia Rivera Casanovas (chapter 6), and Mary Van Buren and Ana María Presta (chapter 7) refine the outlines of Inka domination that had already been worked out. In these areas, the detailed archaeological investigations begin to fill in the blanks in our knowledge.

Local Reactions to Imperial Control and Institutions

One new result of the research reported in this volume is the nature of local responses to the Inka presence. While it was certainly never the case that local groups were passive in their reaction to the Inkas, several chap-ters here indicate the different ways those responses were manifest. Acuto (chapter 5) reports on how the northern Calchaquíes resisted Inka influence in some communities by using Inka material culture only in domestic contexts, not sacred ones. In other communities, however, there was the emergence of a new level of local elite who were accepting Inka power and benefiting from it. In this one area, then, different segments of the same society can be seen to respond differently. Alconini (chapter 4) shows that in a context of increasing Chiriguano incursions into the southeastern Inka frontier, Yampara elites benefited from the imperial conquest by enhancing their own status and wealth by becoming effective agents in the implementation of the imperial program. Rivera Casanovas (chapter 6) contrasts those results with her study of the nearby Qaraqara, where little evidence of Inka control is displayed at all. Here, control over major trade caravans was the principal evidence for increased Inka control over local resources. The nature of the political control, either through local elites or by direct Inka bureaucrats, has not been determined through archaeological research.

At the other end of the empire, Lippi and Gudiño (chapter 10) show how the Inka presence at the Yumbo site of Palmitopamba is nearly ubiquitous except for the site summit, which was a sacred Yumbo *tola* (earthen mound), suggesting the Inkas respected the power of the local elites who were important in maintaining access to valued trade goods from the regions west of the empire's frontier.

Carol Mackey's work (chapter 9) is an important contribution to our understanding of the very poorly known incorporation of the Chimú kingdom into the Inka Empire. While previous studies failed to identify much evidence of the Inka impact, her work at Farfán revealed significant and far-reaching effects and modifications directed by the Inkas. The Inkas increased storage and craft production at the site, and new levels of social hierarchy were identified architecturally and in mortuary activities. Her research reveals how the Inkas attempted to accommodate local Chimú and Lambayeque elites into their imperial plans while modifying Farfán to advance their political and economic goals.

Scales of Analysis and Archaeological Correlates

The chapters in this volume provide different perspectives on the Inka impact through different scales of analysis and emphases on different aspects of the archaeological record. Regional surveys and pan-imperial views provide broad-scale analyses of general patterns. The research of Van Buren and Presta (chapter 7) at the mining center of Porco, Bolivia, shows how even preliminary survey can still provide significant insights into a regional center. The nature of the mines at Porco provides a unique view of how the Inkas were able to extract a valued material in a remote, sparsely populated, and agriculturally marginal region. This research is in contrast to the information provided from other regions, where labor and staple goods were more likely the focus of imperial designs.

At the other end of the analytical scale, the fine-grained analysis provided by household archaeology is utilized by Alconini (chapter 4) and Acuto (chapter 5) in their studies of two southern regions. Their work indicates that even within a given ethnicity, the nature of Inka control could be contested by some while embraced by others. In a similar manner, but on an interregional scale, Santoro et al. (chapter 3) indicate that Inka control may have evolved through time, starting as largely hegemonic and changing toward a more territorial form later in the archaeological sequence. These studies provide new views of how involved the Inkas were in the control of these small valleys and coastal zones. Ceramic analyses in particular accentuate how the Inkas may have sent groups or individuals from the altiplano to act as bureaucrats in these regions. The research reported contrasts with other work that has suggested minimal involvement by the Inkas in this area of the southern Andes, which is so poorly known ethnohistorically.

In a different vein, the contributions of Rossen et al. (chapter 2) and Susan Haun and Guillermo Cock Carrasco (chapter 8) indicate the value of archaeobotanical and bioarchaeological studies to our understanding of the Inkas. The former shows that studying plant remains from specific archaeological contexts can demonstrate how the Inkas transformed the landscape, not just conquered people. In contrast to regions in the central Andes, the Inkas brought some plants of their own (quinoa) for food, but also incorporated native plants. This research also indicates a new means for identifying Inka *mitmaq,* or colonists, through their use of nonlocal foods.

Haun and Cock Carrasco show how studies of skeletal populations, coupled with the mortuary objects and the patterning of this data, can reveal new insights into the actual people who occupied the provinces. Their research follows other recent studies in providing new and exciting avenues for understanding how the Inkas controlled their subject populations. When burials of important individuals are identified, they might be able to show whether the administrative elites are local or Inka — therefore, how direct the Inka rule was.

The Reevaluation of Marginality in the Inka Empire

An unresolved issue in Inka studies is whether the northern and southern regions of the empire might have been incorporated differently than those in the core. Since each new conquered group constituted a frontier before its incorporation, some authors have argued that the social organizations and political structures of groups living in northern Ecuador, in the eastern foothills or lowlands of Bolivia and Argentina, and in south-central Chile might have been different enough from central Andean groups to warrant different forms of control. As a concrete example of this, it remains to be explained why the north and south frontiers have the largest numbers of fortresses.

The results here suggest that these regions may not have been any different than those closer to Cuzco. The possible exception to this could be Ecuador, where, Lippi and Gudiño (chapter 10) argue, the significant trade relations that existed with groups outside the frontier might have led to subtle differences in the relationships of the Inkas to those in the transitional regions. The exceptionally fierce resistance of the northern Ecuadorian groups could also have been a factor. In this respect, the same is said of the Araucanian groups just south of the Inka frontier in Chile. Still, this is not so different from many of the groups in the central Andes who also resisted the Inkas to the point of practicing a scorched earth policy in preference to submission.

It is possible that these regions may appear different because they were conquered late, and so the form of control was in flux. As Santoro et al. note for Chile, there is evidence of a transition from hegemonic to territorial control in central Chile through time, so perhaps the same was occurring in Ecuador. The realization that Inka control may have varied over time is a contribution to our understanding of what it meant to be marginal in the Inka Empire.

Conclusion

In many ways, this book is a follow-up to *Provincial Inca: Archaeological and Ethnohistorical Assessment of the Impact of the Inca State*, and indeed it began as a symposium to address where provincial Inka studies were a decade after the publication of that book. *Provincial Inca* filled an important niche in Inka studies, as indicated by the widespread use of and references to the book in the general literature about the Inkas. Its utility stemmed from the specific foci of the book: how archaeological and ethnohistorical data are complementary in assessing the impact that the Inka state had on its subject polities, and how varied were the means of incorporating these polities into the Inka state. As reviewers noted, however, there was one major limitation in the book, and that was its limited coverage. There were no studies north of Huamachuco and only one south of Cuzco. In addition, most of the chapters were based on surveys with little substantive excavation data to discuss. Given the scope of the book and the stage of research on the Inkas at that time, this was not surprising, and it certainly was not a criticism. In fact, the book has served as a catalyst for additional research, much of which will be reported in this volume.

This limitation of the first volume has been substantially overcome by the chapters in the present volume. Chapter 10 provides data on the Inka conquest of a region of Ecuador west of Quito, and six other chapters cover the regions in the southern part of the empire. Two others inform us about the Inka presence on the Central and North coasts of Peru. This coverage reflects the focus on the distant provinces of the title.

Another concern about *Provincial Inca* was the relative lack of detailed studies of the Inka administration of their provinces. Virtually all the studies involved archaeological surveys and limited testing at best. Therefore, there was little specific that could be said about how Inka control was manifest. The focus of the book was on assessment of the ethnohistorical record with archaeological data. Some of the chapters here (chapters 2, 3, 7, 8, and 10) follow that same strategy, while others (chapters 4, 5, 6, and 9) provide more specific data on Inka control that goes beyond anything in the previous volume. The detailed nature of the research done in these latter chapters begins to show how truly varied Inka control of their provinces was. It also sheds light on the way the conquered people interacted with the Inkas, especially the local leaders who were brought into the empire as *kurakas*. These chapters constitute a significant step forward in our understanding of Inka control of the more distant provinces of their realm.

The more detailed studies also focus more particularly on the archaeological research that has been conducted, rather than on the ethnohistorical work. In some regions, like northern Chile, this is due to the relative absence of historical documents that talk about this region. But in several regions, the archaeological work provides details about Inka control that documents do not: for example, how the Inkas utilized existing structures for their own uses or built new ones. They show how conquered people accepted some kinds of Inka material culture but rejected others. These studies begin to provide the specifics of how the Inkas interacted with their conquered people and attempted to meld them into a cohesive empire, and how their subjects responded to those attempts.

The result of these investigations is that this volume provides a richly textured, more detailed view of the reality that was the Inka Empire of the fifteenth and sixteenth centuries.

Jack Rossen, María Teresa Planella,
and Rubén Stehberg

Chapter Two

Archaeobotany of Cerro del Inga, Chile, at the Southern Inka Frontier

Editors' Introduction

This study represents the introduction of systematic water flotation archaeobotany to Chilean archaeology. As such, Rossen et al. provide new lines of analysis for understanding the interaction between the Inkas and their conquered people. Specifically, using archaeobotany to identify the food remains and stored foods at the site of Cerro del Inga allowed the authors to see how the Inkas introduced their own foods into the local economy, yet continued to use the foods of the region. As they state, this analysis goes beyond simple identification of food plants and provides information about social, political, and economic policies.

The archaeobotanical analysis was also able to identify the uses of some of the structures at the site as *qollqas* and others as habitations. The imperial policy of storing only one kind of grain in a storeroom was also corroborated in the research.

An intriguing aspect of the research in this chapter is whether the individuals in charge were local leaders elevated to the status of *kurakas* or whether Inka individuals from other regions were present. Both ethnohistorical information and archaeological work indicate the presence of *mitmaqkuna* in the vicinity of the site. It is suggested they were the ones growing quinoa, probably an introduced plant to the region. However, the identification of quinoa in storerooms at the summit of the site could suggest it was also for the consumption of the individuals in charge. Was it a status food given to the elevated *kurakas*, or food grown for a foreigner who was more accustomed to it than the local foods? While these questions cannot be answered here, they become hypotheses that could be tested with additional research. Regardless, the research also suggests that quinoa was grown to alter the landscape as another strategy of assimilation for the Inkas. It shows how plants can be used as representative of both political aggression and resistance. Acuto (chapter 5) notes how the inhabitants of the northern Calchaquí Valley in Argentina also differentially accepted Inka material culture as an act of resistance.

This chapter also provides new information about the Inkas at the very margins of their empire. The evidence indicates that the Inkas deliberately co-opted this site, fortified it against possible attack, and used it as a visual symbol of their control. The ceramic evidence from different areas of the site corroborates the reuse of the site by the Inkas. Similar locations for other Inka sites along the road network in the south suggest this strategy was common.

This kind of research indicates how archaeobotany can contribute to finer lines of analysis that are presented elsewhere in this volume (see chapter 8 for a bioarchaeological contribution). Applying analytical techniques more typically used in other regions of the world to Inka studies will increase our knowledge of the varying forms of interaction between the Inkas and their subject people.

Introduction

One key concern of this volume is the assessment of new scales of analysis in order to better understand the nature of Inka provincialism (see chapter 1). One finer scale of analysis that has been added to South American archaeology in the last decade is archaeobotany. The analysis of plant remains systematically collected by water flotation of soil samples was developed in the U.S. Midwest in the 1980s and has gradually been adopted in other regions. South American archaeologists were relatively hesitant to adopt water flotation techniques, either because sites contained unusually good plant preservation (such as Peruvian coastal sites) or large architectural sites did not invite the finer excavation and special sample extraction techniques that were necessary.

The first author traveled to Chile in 1993 to teach archaeobotany, including the construction and use of a flotation tank and laboratory analysis, compilation of comparative collections, and controlled carbonization studies to understand shrinkage and deformation that archaeological plant materials experience. The second and third authors had already conducted several field seasons of excavation at Cerro del Inga, located in the Cachapoal Valley in central Chile, 95 kilometers south of present-day Santiago. The site was already recognized as the southernmost known Inka military installation. The goals of the research were varied: to determine whether small circular stone features were, as suspected, the remains of *qollqas*, and to see whether plant remains could be recovered and identified through water flotation, since none had been previously noticed through standard excavation and screening techniques.

As sample extraction and processing developed and it became clear that hundreds of seeds were being recovered, the research goals and questions became more sophisticated. How can we distinguish natural inclusions from archaeological materials? Can we understand the interaction of cultural and natural forces that produces an archaeobotanical assemblage? Perhaps most important, what do the plant remains add to our knowledge of Inka provincialism at the southernmost border of the empire? In the final analysis, we had a botanical collection that included both classic Inka plants usually associated with the highland (southern Peruvian) heartland and local plants known to have been (and still) cultivated by Chilean indigenous groups. The results are part of a general movement within archaeology to include finer scales of analysis, but also to reevaluate the types of information that may be gleaned from plant remains. Rather than representing only a laundry list of plant foods and medicines, or an indicator of paleoenvironmental conditions, plant remains can indicate culture change, sociocultural boundaries, and political aggression and resistance. In the Cerro del Inga case, the presence of certain Inka plants indicated the symbolic power of their plants, while the use of local plants may be viewed as syncretism or even local resistance. The Inkas employed a wide variety of military, technological, economic, and social strategies of control and consolidation. We argue that plants like quinoa represent an attempt to transform the landscape, making it Inka, as one strategy to incorporate and consolidate the people of conquered regions. Even at the empire's farthest reaches, the arriving Inkas utilized resources from their heartland, adopted local resources, and perhaps planned to transform the landscape.

Background

During the late fifteenth and early sixteenth centuries, the Inka Empire became the largest political entity in the New World prior to European contact. The Inkas briefly administered a vast region stretching from southern Colombia to south-central Chile, including portions of present-day Peru, Ecuador, Bolivia, and Argentina. The expanding Inkas encountered an enormous diversity of social situations. Relationships with foreign polities varied from peaceful or violent annexation under direct or indirect rule to resistance and rebellion (Dillehay and Netherly 1988; Hyslop 1988). The fluid dynamics of the Inka frontiers are today represented by a static, differentially preserved archaeological record and contradictory ethnohistorical documents. It is thus not surprising that the limits of the Inka Empire and the nature of those boundaries are debated.

Over the last few decades, scholars have begun to reevaluate the nature and limits of Inka expansion and rule (Dillehay and Netherly 1988; Malpass 1993). In particular, discrepancies exist in the ethnohistorical documents concerning the southern limits of the state. The primary discrepancy covers about 230 kilometers, ranging from the Maipo River 40 kilometers south of Santiago to the Maule River 270 kilometers south of Santiago (Cobo 1979:Book 11; see discussion in Hyslop 1988:44–46). Occasionally, the Bío-Bío River, an additional 200 kilometers south, is discussed as a possible southern limit (see Kauffman-Doig 1983:579). Recent interpretations of ethnohistorical documents have favored the more northern Maipo River (figure 2.1), leaving a buffer zone between that river and the Angostura Pass, where the indigenous province of Promaucae began (Hyslop 1988; Silva 1986:13; Téllez 1990:70).

An explanation for the variation in the documents is that the empire had multiple types of boundaries, both formal and informal, and that each chronicler was considering a different type of frontier. For example, military boundaries represented by fortified outposts may be ephemeral, in

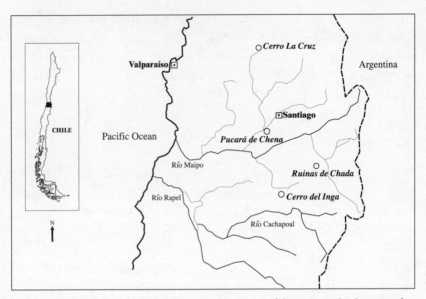

FIGURE 2.1. Map of central Chile showing locations of the principal Inka sites of Cerro del Inga, Cerro La Cruz, Pucará de Chena, and Ruinas de Chada. Map by Jim A. Railey.

the sense that settlement and cultural influences may lag behind a limited military presence. In contrast, socioeconomic frontiers can exist beyond the military presence. In the case of south-central Chile, Dillehay and Gordon (1988) have persuasively argued that a different type of frontier existed with Araucanian groups beyond regions of military occupation, where religious and technological activities and economic and social transactions occurred.

The characteristics of an empire at its frontier may illuminate the fundamental nature of power and how it was formulated and exercised. Formal military presence represents one type of power, yet informal social and economic power, leading to contact and later consolidation and transformation of conquered people and land, may be a truer test of the commitment to rule and administer, not just subdue, a foreign people (Malpass 1993; Schaedel 1988). Finer scales of analysis can lead to new insights into the strategies and commitments that were made at the edge of the empire. For example, by correlating corn, a high-status plant, with other status materials such as textiles and ceramics, Hastorf (1993:226) was able to understand corn as an impetus for pre-Inkan social change and control in the Jauja region of southern Peru, and agriculture in general as a "fulcrum for those changes."

Few studies have attempted to integrate archaeological data with ethnohistorical documents and finer scales of analysis to investigate the locations and nature of Inka frontiers (Dillehay and Netherly 1988; Stehberg 1976). This chapter discusses one Inka site located near the southern extent of the empire. Cerro del Inga, known today as Cerro Grande de La Compañía, was located on the basis of seventeenth-century ethnohistorical documents (Planella 1988). Three archaeological field seasons were conducted there from 1990 to 1993 by Maria Teresa Planella, Rubén Stehberg, Blanca Tagle, Hans Niemeyer, and Carmen del Río. As a result of these efforts, the architecture and artifacts were investigated, and a site chronology was defined (Planella et al. 1991, 1992). In 1993–1994, an archaeobotanical study of the site, including reexcavation of features at the site, was directed by the first author.

Cerro del Inga contains evidence of military presence and organization as well as evidence of strategies designed to consolidate and transform the newly contacted region. The ethnohistorical study shows the influx of settlers (*mitmaq*) into the region, and the architectural and archaeobotanical studies detail how traditional Inka values were syncretized with local influences. Architecture, road construction, and alteration of local agricultural systems may have all been tools of control and consolidation. That is, the buildings and provisions of the frontier fortress of Cerro del Inga contained the means to display power, transform the landscape, and incorporate local populations into the new political reality. Our investigation combined ethnohistorical, archaeological, architectural, and archaeobotanical approaches to explore these themes.

In this chapter, we emphasize the contributions that archaeobotany can make to the understanding of social and political frontiers. The recovery and analysis of archaeological plant remains have traditionally been used to reconstruct ancient diet and understand the origins and makeup of agricultural economies (Ford 1978, 1985). Only recently have archaeobotanists begun to tap the great potential of plant remains to increase our understanding of aspects of social organization and change (Bush 2004; Fuller 2003; Hastorf 1993; Weber 2003). The Cerro del Inga plants give insights into Inka strategies of consolidation at the Inkas' southernmost boundary, as well as evidence of syncretism with the local cultural system.

Cerro del Inga: Site Location and Description

Cerro del Inga is located atop an imposing, isolated promontory in the central plain of the Cachapoal Valley, 55 kilometers south of the Maipo River, 95 kilometers south of Santiago and 2,700 kilometers south of the Inka capital of Cuzco (Peru) (figures 2.1 and 2.2). The hill is positioned within a sector of ancient marshes that is presently a rich agricultural zone. The great agricultural potential of the valleys between the Aconcagua and Cachapoal rivers was noted by early Spanish chroniclers (Bibar 1966; Góngora Marmolejo 1960).

The base of Cerro del Inga covers 60 hectares. The hill is situated along an ancient road connecting the coast and the eastern highlands, and a prehispanic irrigation canal drawing water from the Cachapoal River still runs along its base (Planella 1988). The site strategically commands a view of the entire middle Cachapoal Valley, including the narrow mountain passes to the north (Angostura de Paine) and south (Angostura de Rigolemo) and an east-west panorama from the coastal mountains to the Andean cordillera.

Historic studies suggest that the site was last occupied by a local indigenous group known as the Promaucaes, who, along with other central

FIGURE 2.2. Cerro del Inga as seen from the Pan-American Highway.

Chilean groups, resisted the Spanish Conquest (Bibar 1966:52, 1979:66; Garcilazo de la Vega 1960:Book 7; Planella and Stehberg 1994). Indigenous resistance in the Cachapoal River area was noted by members of Diego de Almagro's expedition in 1536 (Medina 1952:271, 289, 321). Direct ethnohistorical mentions of a Cachapoal fort, organized by a cacique of the same name, date to approximately 1540–1541, when the fort was attacked by a Spanish force led by Pedro de Valdivia (Planella and Stehberg 1994). A generalized memory of the Cachapoal Valley fort is reflected in early-seventeenth-century documents, when local inhabitants called it Cerro del Inga. During this time, the hill was within a farm owned by the Dominican Order (Planella 1988). The farm and surrounding lands later formed the extensive hacienda of the Company of Jesus (La Compañía).

Site Architecture and Ceramics

Defensive stone walls define and delimit the site, forming three distinct perimeters at different altitudes (figure 2.3). They protect the spurs and flats of the hill and the principal plaza, and have several access points or gates. One wall enclosed a specialized area of the site, containing most of the site's rectangular habitation structures with trapezoidal openings and small circular storage units (qollqas) built in the provincial Inka style. Along the interior base of the wall are several piles of round stones probably intended for use as sling projectiles. Excavations in this area produced ceramic sherds of various painted, slipped, and polychrome types, all diagnostic of the Inka-Diaguita period. Based on ceramic styles, Diaguita was an indigenous group in the region beginning about A.D. 1200 that was syncretized by the Inka arrival about A.D. 1470 (Ampuero 1989).

Other walls form a second line of defense at the middle elevation of the hill (625–650 meters). These wall interiors also have regularly placed piles of sling stones brought from the valley floor below. Also found were fragments of burned clay in two wall corners, which suggest the use of torches. A walled battlement and a rectangular turret made of mud mortar and stone defend the south hillside. From the turret, the prehispanic road that passes west along the hill to the Cachapoal River could be monitored.

The hill summit is a natural esplanade or plaza that was flattened during fortress construction (figures 2.4 and 2.5). The plaza interior has 10 simple stone structures, including four with rectangular plans that were

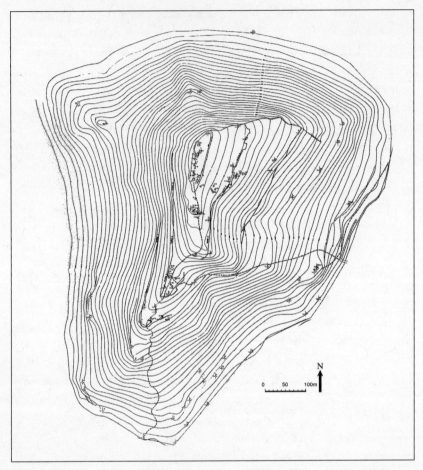

FIGURE 2.3. Topographic and architectural map of Cerro del Inga. Drawing by Jim A. Railey.

probably habitations and guard posts, one in the form of an open wall that may have been a windbreak, and five with circular plans that were probably storage units. The provincial Inka-style summit structures were built using a double row of stones over an adobe base (figures 2.6 and 2.7). Stones were partially cut and smoothed on their exterior faces, and the entrance spaces are trapezoidal. Inside two summit structures were found circular depressions 2.1 to 2.7 meters in diameter, each surrounded by a circle of large stones. The form of these circular depressions is similar to the pre-Inka structures of the lower level of the hill. The features suggest the architectural superpositioning of structures of different architec-

FIGURE 2.4. Aerial view of summit structures of Cerro del Inga.

FIGURE 2.5. Rectangular summit structure, Cerro del Inga.

FIGURE 2.6. Rectangular summit structure, Cerro del Inga.

FIGURE 2.7. Circular thick-walled storage unit, Cerro del Inga.

tural styles. This summit area contains ceramic sherds of various painted, slipped, and polychrome types that are all diagnostic of the Inka-Diaguita period.

Small circular structures, ranging from 3.0 to 3.4 meters in diameter and found on both the hill summit and lower slopes of the site, are aligned storage units. Excavations by the team of Planella et al. revealed massive bases of stone walls filled with mud and small stones. The fill spaces of these walls (80 to 95 centimeters in width) are larger than the central cavities (ca. 75 centimeters in diameter). Excavations also revealed underground ventilation shafts (e.g., Morris 1992). Ceramics in the summit structures have been dated to the Inka period by thermoluminescence, but a series of more than 20 small, massively built circular structures on the eastern slope date to the Late Agroceramic period (A.D. 900–1470) (Durán and Planella 1989:324). In contrast to the Inka ceramics of the site summit, a variety of local ceramic types were recovered in this area, dominated by globular vessels and bowls with a white or cream slip with painted lines of various shades of red or brown (Latcham 1928; Massone 1980).

A group of circular structures is located on the lower south hillside of the site. These are circular depressions 3 meters in diameter with central posts and hearths. Monochrome ceramics from these structures also represent the Late Agroceramic period. These circular structures probably are the remains of conical huts with a sapling or branch framework, either with or without roof supports, a house type used by indigenous groups of central Chile (Guevara 1929; Joseph 2006; Lizárraga 1928).

In summary, Cerro del Inga was an indigenous community 95 kilometers south of Santiago that was conquered and remodeled by the Inkas. The distinctive architectural differences between the pre-Inka and Inka remodeled sectors of the site provided an interesting contrast and basis for adding a finer scale of analysis, that is, the recovery and analysis of botanical remains.

Archaeobotanical Study

An archaeobotanical study was conducted at Cerro del Inga from August 1993 to January 1994. The basic goals of the study were to clarify the nature and contents of stone foundations of varying size and form at the site, and to produce baseline archaeobotanical data in central Chile, where no systematic studies of this type had been conducted. Forty-one soil samples (204.6 liters) were collected, processed, and analyzed. Most important, archaeobotanical remains were used to understand specific archaeological contexts and generate hypotheses concerning the nature of Inka domination and indigenous influence at the farthest edge of the empire.

This section begins with an explanation of the methodologies utilized in the study. Following this is a summary review of some background issues, including a discussion of plant taphonomy. The study was helpful in clarifying aspects of the site and in raising some regional questions of culture history.

General Archaeobotanical Issues

At Cerro del Inga, the shallow fill inside the stone foundations contained numerous tiny seeds that suggest the original contents of the structures. Alternatively, recovered seeds may indicate more recent materials that intruded into the site. A detailed understanding of the particular processes of deposition at a site is crucial to an evaluation of archaeobotanical data and its integration with other site assemblages. The following characteristics of Cerro del Inga as an archaeological site complicated the archaeobotanical study.

The site has generally superficial deposits, rarely more than 30 centimeters in depth. There is thus difficulty in separating prehistoric contexts from noncultural and recent cultural contexts. This problem is particularly acute outside of structures, where samples may represent either cultural contexts with light deposition or noncultural contexts. The shallow nature of site deposits also suggests that more mixing and intrusion of modern botanical elements is possible, an issue discussed further below.

The semiarid environment, with eight extremely dry months annually, potentially allows the archaeological preservation of desiccated (noncarbonized) plant remains mixed with carbonized remains. This apparent preservation advantage may be a complication in a shallow site, where the cultural-natural distinction of certain plant remains is unclear. That is, the desiccated plant materials at this site may be either archaeological or modern intrusions, while at sites with poorer plant preservation, only carbonized materials may be considered archaeological. Fortunately, density comparisons using control samples from nonarchaeological areas can distinguish archaeological from intrusive desiccated plants.

A natural carpet of recent seeds covers the site and intrudes on the archaeobotanical assemblage. As will be explained, some recovered species appear to be both culturally used and deposited prehistorically and naturally intrusive. Further complicating this situation is the possibility that ancient plant use at the site altered the present-day weedy flora of the hill, which later intruded on the archaeobotanical assemblage. In these cases, detailed examinations of spatial distributions and contexts are needed to consider natural versus cultural deposition.

Basic local botanical processes, such as the number of seeds produced by certain plants and the dispersion of seeds by small animals, birds, and ants, have been little studied and remain poorly understood. Studies of control samples — that is, flotation samples taken from noncultural contexts at the site — allowed us to begin to understand these processes.

There is a lack of ashy midden development at the site. Very little evidence of fuel use, such as wood charcoal, ash, or hearths, was found. Refuse may have been tossed down the hillsides.

There was difficulty during the original archaeological studies in determining the function of some site foundations from their architecture, form, and positioning at the site. This was due to the state of the site, with its shallow deposits and spatially constricted hilltop. The situation is different than at many Inka sites, where, for example, storage units (*qollqas*) are apparent by their form and arrangement (LeVine 1992). Rather than beginning the study by using archaeobotany to understand details of residential and storage unit contents (Lennstrom and Hastorf 1992), the study began by attempting to define contexts as either storage or nonstorage.

Modern picnicking still occurs at the site, usually, due to the heat, without campfires. Desiccated remains of introduced species such as grape (*Vitis* sp.) sometimes occur in the first 10 centimeters of the site.

In summary, as archaeologists move toward finer scales of analysis, there are also newly created issues to address and overcome. The above-listed issues are important to recognize. They may complicate but do not prohibit an archaeobotanical study. The methods used to treat these issues are discussed below as they become relevant.

Field and Lab Methods

In the field, we removed 20-cubic-centimeter soil blocks at various site locales. We chose to sample the corners of rectangular structures, and placed blocks along the centerline of circular structures. In this way, we were able to sample unexcavated structure centers while leaving an equal portion of the structure center intact. Control samples were taken from outside structures and from other areas expected to contain little or no cultural deposition. We removed soil block samples by levels (usually 10 centimeters) in order to compare contents of different depths. Approximately 1 liter of soil was taken from control contexts for every 4 liters of soil from cultural contexts.

Soil samples were measured for volume in liters, which allows density studies to be performed, and were processed in a flotation tank built specifically for the project. The tank is of simple design, with a showerhead providing agitation and a weighted plastic frame supporting the 1-millimeter screen that collected nonflotation heavy fraction remains. Floating light fractions were collected in nylon paint strainers. Simple, inexpensive flotation tanks like this one can be built for use at even the most remote sites.

All flotation samples were microscopically examined at magnifications ranging from 8 to 30 and were sorted by species and counted. Botanical identifications were aided by the herbarium at the Museo Nacional de Historia Natural, standard seed catalogs (Martin and Barkley 1973), an environmental special study (discussed below), and the development of new comparative collections.

Environmental Special Study

The hillsides of Cerro del Inga contain a degraded relict forest dominated by native species. Much of the site is now bare due to animal grazing, and most areas surrounding the site are in large-scale agriculture. For this reason, a special study of the relict forest was made to understand the local paleoenvironment. Samples of 23 native species were collected as an indication of the past mixed forest (table 2.1). The species list appears to indicate a mixed Mediterranean-type forest. Bogs with wetland grasses and sedges once were present north of the site (Bibar 1979:97–98; Planella 1988:16).

TABLE 2.1. Native Woody Species in Relict Forest at Cerro del Inga

Scientific Name	Common Name
Acacia caven	Espino
Aristotelia chilensis	Maqui
Azara sp.	Lilén
Chusquea quila	Quila
Colliguaja sp.	Colliguay
Crinodendron patagua	Patagua
Cryptocarya alba	Peumo
Ephedra andina	Pingo-pingo
Escallonia pulverulenta	Corontillo
Eupatorium salvia	Salvia
Lithraea caustica	Litre
Maytenus boaria	Maitén
Muehlenbeckia hastulata	Quilo
Myrceugenia sp.	Arrayán
Peumus boldus	Boldo
Porlieria chilensis	Guayacán
Psoralea glandulosa	Culén
Quillaja saponaria	Quillay
Ribes punctatum	Zarzaparilla
Satureja gilliesii	Oreganillo
Sophora macrocarpa	Mayú
Talguenea quinquinervia	Tralhuén
Trevoa trinervis	Tebo

Collection by first author, assisted by Raúl Peña.

Archaeobotanical Results

The recovered botanical remains are described in functional categories of cultigens and possible cultigens, fruits, a medicinal herb, and miscellaneous wild plants (table 2.2).

CULTIGENS

Seven cultigens or possible cultigens were recovered, including quinoa (*Chenopodium quinua*), maize (*Zea mays*), madi (*Madia chilensis*), sunflower (*Helianthus* sp. cf. *tuberosum*), gourd (*Lagenaria* sp.), and two unidentified legumes (small and large).

Quinoa (*Chenopodium quinoa*) (n = 9 distributed in three samples) is a pseudo-cereal native to the high-elevation altiplano of Peru and Bolivia

TABLE 2.2. Botanical Remains from Cerro del Inga

Species	Frequency	Ubiquity	State
CULTIGENS			
Maize (*Zea mays*)	175	.10	C
Madi (*Madia chilensis*)	27	.05	D
Quinoa (*Chenopodium quinua*)	9	.07	C, D
Sunflower (*Helianthus* sp. cf. *tuberosum*)	6	.02	C
Gourd (*Lagenaria* sp.)	3	.02	C
FRUIT			
Guillave (*Echinopsis chilensis*)	3,253	.80	D, C
Michay (*Berberis* sp.)	50	.27	D
Boldo (*Peumus boldus*)	24	.20	D
Quilo (*Muehlenbeckia hastulata*)	18	.10	C
Grape (*Vitis* sp.)	4	.07	D
Blackberry (*Rubus* sp.)	1	.02	D
Cocito, Palm Nut (*Jubaea chilensis*)	1	.02	C
LEGUMES			
Unidentified, small (*Astragalus* sp.?)	3	.07	C
Unidentified, large	19	.02	D, C
Lupine (*Lupinus* sp.)	1	.02	D
MEDICINAL HERB			
Pata de Guanaco (*Calandrinia grandiflora*)	1,053	.76	D, C
MISCELLANEOUS WILD PLANTS			
Various Grasses (Poaceae)	1,596	.32	C
Colliguay (*Colliguaja odifera*)	90	.22	D, C
Espino (*Acacia caven*)	6	.07	D, C
Lengua de Gato (*Galium* sp.)	6	.05	C
Sedge (*Cyperus* sp.)	4	.07	C
Chenopod (*Chenopodium* sp.)	3˙	.05	C

C = carbonized
D = desiccated

(Cárdenas 1969; Latcham 1934). It is still grown in isolated regions of central Chile (Latcham 1936:148–154; Looser 1943, 1945; Molina 1776:118; Mösbach 1992:75; Reich 1901:9). Quinoa has long been known as one of the agricultural staples of the Inkas (Towle 1961) and has been recovered in Inka qollqas in Peru (D'Altroy and Hastorf 1992; Lennstrom and Hastorf 1992). The recovery of quinoa in both the carbonized and desiccated states at Cerro del Inga indicates the mixed preservation of both ancient desiccated and carbonized remains, since its recent inclusion in the site is extremely unlikely.

The presence of both desiccated and carbonized quinoa seeds gives insight into the use of particular structures (E-14b and E-1) where seeds were present. The seed pericarp of quinoa is bitter and must be removed by washing. It is advantageous, however, to store quinoa without processing the seed, because rodents will not eat the bitter pericarp. For this reason, the recovery of a desiccated seed, complete with pericarp, in association with thick-walled ceramic sherds in Structure E-14b (summit south hill-spur) strongly suggests that the structure was utilized for food storage (figure 2.8). In contrast, the carbonized quinoa seeds, popped and without pericarp, recovered from Structures E-1 (summit) and E-15 (lower south hillside) strongly suggest that those structures were used for some form of habitation, including food preparation (figure 2.8).

In four samples (n = 175) small, carbonized embryos or sprouts of maize (*Zea mays*), along with three maize kernels, were recovered. Maize embryos or sprouts have previously been recovered from other Inka storage units (Lennstrom and Hastorf 1992) and could be the expected form of remains from a storage context where usable maize was removed and embryos represent spoiled or otherwise unusable remnants. Maize is historically reported as having been abundant in the Cachapoal Valley in the year 1541 (Góngora Marmolejo 1960:83).

Madi (*Madia chilensis*) occurred in three samples (n = 27) in a desiccated state (figure 2.9). Madi is a small biennial herb that has long been cultivated by Araucanian groups in south-central Chile for its oily seeds (Latcham 1936:155–159; Molina 1776:118; Mösbach 1992:112; Navas 1979:221–222; Ovalle 1969: 1:75). Two Chilean species of madi are known, including one wild (*Madia sativa*) and one cultivated species (*M. chilensis*). Although the plants of the two species are often difficult to distinguish, the larger wrinkled seeds of the cultivated *M. chilensis* are very different from the smaller smooth seeds of the wild *M. sativa*. Like quinoa, the presence of this desiccated cultigen is indicative of the mixed archaeological preservation of desiccated and carbonized remains.

Sunflower (*Helianthus* sp. cf. *tuberosum*) appeared as carbonized specimens in one sample (n = 6). *H. tuberosum* is a cultigen presently grown for its oily seeds by indigenous Araucanian populations.

Three small gourd rind (*Lagenaria* sp.) specimens were recovered from

FIGURE 2.8. (Left) Recovered carbonized and desiccated quinoa (*Chenopodium quinua*) seeds.

FIGURE 2.9. (Right) Recovered madi (*Madia chilensis*) seeds.

a sample taken near the site summit wall. This area also contained ceramics and a variety of other botanical remains, and may be one of few midden areas present on the site.

A small-seeded legume is present in carbonized form in three samples (n = 23). A much larger legume is present in one sample (n = 19). Legumes represent a special archaeobotanical problem in central Chile that will require future investigations, including controlled carbonization studies on modern legume specimens. The family Leguminoseae contains three subfamilies and 36 genera in Chile (Navas 1976). Several are difficult to identify solely from their seed form, including species like *Astragalus*, which is difficult to distinguish from introduced species like *Medicago* (a genus that includes alfalfa). The archaeologically recovered small specimens resemble *Astragalus*.

Archaeobotanical samples recently analyzed by the first author from other central Chile pre-Inka sites such as Huechún 3, located north of Santiago, indicate that other varieties of unidentified legumes were probably part of both pre-Inka and Inka agricultural systems in the region.

FRUITS

Seeds of the cactus fruit *Echinopsis chilensis* (Hoffmann 1979:84–85), known commonly as guillave or quisco, represent the dominant botanical remain at Cerro del Inga (n = 3,253 distributed in 33 samples). *Echinopsis* occurred primarily in the desiccated state, and because the cactus presently grows in several sectors of the site, much care was taken to attempt to separate recent natural intrusion from ancient cultural deposition. The cactus fruits are sweet and edible. In addition, the stalks were used as torches by indigenous groups of central Chile (Mösbach 1992:94). The latter use at Cerro del Inga may explain the archaeological remains and the present preponderance of *Echinopsis* near the defensive walls.

The total density per liter of guillave seeds in cultural context samples was compared with those in nearby control samples. Although the volume of cultural samples is four times that of noncultural samples, guillave fruits appeared in a ratio of 18.8:1, or more than four times higher than would be expected if guillave was naturally (and equally) intrusive in all samples (table 2.3). Furthermore, a study of guillave conducted as the fruits ripened in January 1994 showed that the fruits open when ripe, exposing their seeds to birds and ants. However, the fruits do not detach or fall to the ground and thus remain inaccessible to small animals that might produce more irregular natural seed distributions. In contrast, birds and ants, eating only small portions of fruits, tend to produce more uniform natural seed dispersions. This premise is further supported by a general consideration of densities per liter of guillave throughout the site. Most samples, including all control samples, display guillave density frequencies of 10 to 19 per liter, which probably represent the natural seed carpet of the site. Much higher seed densities found in samples from inside structures, ranging from 41 to 398 per liter, probably represent cultural depositions (table 2.3). A similar phenomenon of natural versus cultural seed density and distribution is described below for the medicinal plant *Calandrinia*.

The presence of guillave seeds in occasionally high frequencies (n = 741 and 677, respectively, in two samples) also led to a consideration of the potential frequency of seeds produced by a single fruit and, in turn, by an individual cactus. In this case, the botanical observation forces the archaeological evidence of guillave to be downplayed. An individual fruit of typical size examined in the lab contained nearly 4,600 seeds. Larger cactus individuals may produce as many as 30 fruit a year, and thus one cactus may annually produce almost 140,000 seeds. Although the comparative densities and distributions of guillave seeds are convincing of

TABLE 2.3. Density of Seeds per Liter of Soil for *Echinopsis chilensis*

Site Sector	Architecture	Structure	Density/ Liter
Summit South Hillspur	Small Circular	E-14c	398
Summit	Large Rectangular	E-1	79
Summit	Small Circular	E-4	60
Summit	Large Rectangular	E-1	41
Summit	Aisle	E-1, E-2	33
Summit	Defensive Wall	1	30
Summit	Medium Circular	E-4a	25
Summit	Aisle	E-1, E-2	25
Summit South Hillspur	Small Circular	E-13	19
Lower South Hillside	Large Circular	E-15	18
Summit South Hillspur	Small Circular	E-12	16
Summit	Large Rectangular	E-1	16
Summit South Hillspur	Small Circular	E-14b	12
Summit	Large Rectangular	E-1	12
Lower South Hillside	Small Circular	E-16	11

cultural deposition, the intensity of that use is unimpressive in terms of the archaeological frequencies.

Several other fruits appear in low frequency in the collection. Michay (*Berberis* sp.), boldo (*Peumus boldus*), and quilo (*Muehlenbeckia hastulata*), along with nuts of the Chilean palm, coquito (*Jubaea chilensis*), were probably utilized in season. Indigenous use of boldo has been ethnohistorically described in the region (Rosales 1877:1:227).

Other fruits found in samples are clearly intrusive, such as the introduced grape (*Vitis* sp.) and blackberry (*Rubus* sp.). Grapes were introduced quite early in the Contact period (A.D. 1579–1580) to the Cachapoal Valley (Planella 1988).

MEDICINAL HERBS

One medicinal plant, pata de guanaco (*Calandrinia grandiflora*), is common in the collection (n = 1,053 distributed in 31 samples). The plant is well known as a strong medicinal remedy for strike-blow injuries and contains a variety of oxalates, tanins, saponins, resins, and mucilagens (Godoy 1945; Murillo 1889:24; Navas 1976:78). *Calandrinia*, with its December violet flowers, was observed growing on the lower hillslopes of Cerro del

TABLE 2.4. Density of Seeds per Liter of Soil for *Calandrinia grandiflora*

Site Sector	Architecture	Structure	Density/ Liter
Summit South Hillspur	Small Circular	E-14c	64
Summit South Hillspur	Small Circular	E-13	38
East Hillside	Small Circular	J-2	26
Summit	Defensive Wall	1	21
Summit South Hillspur	Small Circular	E-13	12
Lower South Hillside (Hearth)	Large Circular	E-15	11
East Hillside	Small Circular	J-1	11
Summit	Small Circular	E-5	10
Summit	Large Rectangular	E-1	6
Summit	Large Rectangular	E-1	6
Summit	Large Rectangular	E-1	5
Summit	Medium Circular	E-4a	4
East Hillside	Small Circular	J-2	4
East Hillside	Small Circular	J-1	4
Summit	Medium Circular	E-4	3
Summit	Large Rectangular	E-1	3
East Hillside	Small Circular	I-15	3
East Hillside	Small Circular	I-15	3
Lower South Hillside	Control	—	3
Summit	Control	—	3

Inga. At other times of the year, it is inconspicuous or invisible. The plant
grows in mixed communities interspersed with other small flowering
plants whose seeds did not appear archaeologically. Like *Echinopsis, Calandrinia* was analyzed for its density in both cultural and control samples
and found to appear in cultural samples at a ratio of 18.5:1 instead of the
4:1 ratio that would be expected with purely natural deposition (table 2.4).
Furthermore, *Calandrinia* exhibits a natural carpet presence of between
three and six seeds per liter in many samples, while its frequency is many
times greater in a few cultural samples.

MISCELLANEOUS WILD PLANTS

The possible past use of a few additional wild plants at the site may also
be considered. Carbonized grass seeds (Poaceae) appear in large quantity
in certain samples (n = 1,596 distributed in 13 samples). These specimens
appear mostly inside small structures. The remains primarily represent

larger-seeded species and morphologically range from long, thin, triangular seed forms to long, thin, cylindrical and long, broad, flat seed forms.
The seeds are clearly distinctive from the short, broad, flat grass seeds that
dominate the present grasses on the site. It is likely that the carbonized
grass seeds represent the remains of thatched structure roofs that burned.
Broad-bladed grasses from the wet bogs at the base of the hill would have
better served as roofing material than the shorter hilltop grasses. The
bog grasses may thus have been procured for construction, producing
the marked dichotomy between carbonized and desiccated specimens in
the flotation samples. The idea that other wetland plants at the base of
the site were exploited is also supported by the low frequency presence of
the wetlands sedge *Cyperus* in carbonized form (n = 5 distributed in two
samples).

Colliguay (*Colliguaja odorifera*) nutshell appears (n = 90 distributed in
nine samples) in both desiccated and carbonized form. Colliguay contains
albumen (Trujillo 1933), which was historically used as an arrow poison
(Navas 1976:271; Rosales 1877). Excavations at the site also produced 10
projectile points (Planella et al. 1991, 1992). Other remains in the assemblage are either weedy species that could be accidentally carbonized and
deposited (small-seeded *Chenopodium*, *Galium*) or desiccated specimens
that are probably intrusive, such as espino (*Acacia caven*).

The cultigen distributions by site sector and other important archaeobotanical remains are depicted in table 2.5. The large majority of cultigens occur in the Inka-occupied summit of the site, with the exceptions
of quinoa in one sample each from the summit south hillspur and lower
south hillside, and madi and maize, each in one east hillslope sample. This
suggests that the majority of plant-oriented activity occurred on the site
summit. Furthermore, there appears to be some spatial separation of species. Quinoa and maize remains never appear together in the same structure. A similar pattern of cultigen separation has been noted in Peruvian
Inka storage contexts, which may signify a degree of storage specialization
(Lennstrom and Hastorf 1992).

In some cases, the spatial distributions and combinations of botanical
remains allow the functional interpretation of a structure (table 2.6). To
begin, it appears that several structures at the site, both large and small,
had thatched roofs made of wetland grasses and sedges brought from the
hill base. The large amount of carbonized grass seeds in two structures

TABLE 2.5. Distributions of Key Plants by Site Sector

Species	Site Sector(s)
Quinoa (*Chenopodium quinua*)	Summit, Summit South Hillspur, Lower South Hillspur
Maize (*Zea mays*)	Summit, East Hillside
Madi (*Madia chilensis*)	Summit, East Hillside
Sunflower (*Helianthus* sp. c.f. *tuberosum*)	Summit
Legumes, small (*Astragalus?*)	Summit
Legumes, large	East Hillside

strongly suggests these structures burned while empty or nearly empty, an interpretation consistent with historic reports of structure burning during the 1541 Spanish storming of the site (Bibar 1966:80).

The large rectangular summit structure, the large circular lower south hillside structure, and the medium-size circular summit structure contain a greater variety of plant remains than the smaller structures, supporting their interpretation as habitations or multifunctional buildings. In two of these structures (one provincial Inka building and one local indigenous), the presence of carbonized quinoa suggests habitational, nonstorage functions. These botanical observations coincide with other characteristics of the structures, such as the rare presence of a hearth just outside a lower south hillside indigenous structure.

In contrast, the small circular structures of the summit's south hillspur and the east hillslope individually contain less diverse plant remains, suggesting their use as storage facilities. As mentioned above, Inka storage facilities in Peru also display segregated individual plant storage. In one case, a small circular structure with thick-walled foundations contained desiccated quinoa with its pericarp and thick ceramic sherds. These are unprocessed quinoa seeds, stored in their pericarps because the tannins inhibit rodent infestation. Unprocessed quinoa stored in jars was also documented at the Inka installation of Huánuco Pampa, Peru (Morris 1992).

Discussion and Conclusion

This was the first major water flotation–based archaeobotanical study conducted in central Chile. In beginning this finer scale of analysis, the limitations of examining one site assemblage in a vacuum became ap-

TABLE 2.6. Interpretations of Structures Based on Archaeobotanical Contents

Site Sector	Structure	Form	Contents	Interpretation
Summit	E-1	Large Rectangular 4.2 × 3.8 m	Carbonized Quinoa Madi Guillave	Habitation
Summit	E-4	Medium Circular 3.4 m diameter	Guillave Grasses Maize Quilo Colliguay Ceramics	Storage
Summit	E-5	Small Circular 1.7 m diameter	Maize Sunflower Small Legumes	Storage
Summit South Hillspur	E-14b	Small Circular 2.2 m diameter	Quinoa w/ Pericarp Thick Ceramics	Storage
Lower South Hillside	E-15	Large Circular with Hearth 5.4 m diameter	Carbonized Quinoa Sedge Guillave Pata de Guanaco Grasses	Habitation
East Hillside	J-2	Small Circular 2.4 m diameter	Maize Grasses Sedge	Storage(?)
East Hillside	I-7, I-15	Small Circular 2.4 m diameter	Empty	Unknown

parent. Each plant species recovered archaeologically represents its own history and chronology that can only be ultimately understood in terms of comparative archaeobotanical data. Emerging data from new studies will gradually clarify each plant's history. For example, a recent study has documented the Contact period introduction of Old World crops like wheat, barley, and peach at an Inka administrative center in northwestern Argentina (Capparelli et al. 2005). Furthermore, a single site plant collection as a unit represents a set of species related in time and space, but in cases like the briefly occupied Cerro del Inga, removed from long archaeobotanical and prehistoric sequences. More archaeobotanical data from pre-Inka agricultural Llolleo or Aconcagua Culture sites of central Chile (Durán and Planella 1989) will add regional time depth to the Cerro del Inga collection.

Archaeological investigations of Cerro del Inga verified two occupations at the site, a pre-Inka indigenous settlement and an Inka-Diaguita fortress. Excavation and mapping, including an architectural study of the site, demonstrated that the hill was used differently by pre-Inka and Inka people. The earlier indigenous occupation was situated across the hill and concentrated on the lower hillslopes and spurs. The Inkas, in contrast, focused their construction efforts and occupation on the militarily strategic hill summit, where existing structures were remodeled into a provincial Inka style. The superimposed strata from the two occupations in at least one summit structure suggest direct or near-direct contact between the successively occupying groups. Contact between the two groups is also suggested, as discussed below, by the Inka adoption of local economic plants.

The Cerro del Inga research has begun to advance our knowledge of indigenous resistance to the Spanish domination by identifying this site as the Cachapoal Fort that was taken by Pedro de Valdivia in 1541. Although this event cannot be absolutely confirmed by the archaeology, some structures at the site were burned, perhaps during that event. The Spanish storming of Cerro del Inga ended an approximately 140-year sequence of use of the hill as a settlement and fortress, beginning as an indigenous installation from approximately A.D. 1380 to 1430 or 1450, and continuing with its remodeling as an Inka fortress from about A.D. 1430 or 1450, with a possible local reoccupation by the Promaucaes to resist the Spanish Conquest. Since no archaeological materials related to the Promaucaes were recovered, no recovered plant materials are considered to be related to that ethnohistorically documented occupation. Ongoing research should further clarify the cycles of conquest and resistance that occurred during the centuries leading to the Colonial period.

BOTANICAL ISSUES

What did adding a finer scale of analysis through archaeobotany contribute to our understanding of Inka provincialism in this case study? The archaeobotanical study was the first of its kind undertaken in central Chile.

The recovery of cultigens, fruits, and medicinal plants probably used to provision troops, along with grasses probably used as construction material, shows the potential for understanding economic plant use. This study is also an attempt to push archaeobotany beyond the simple reconstruction of diet and agricultural systems to address issues of culture change and contact. The botanical inventories, frequencies, and distributions are in some ways similar to those found in a water flotation study of Inka storage units in the heartland area of Junín, Peru (D'Altroy and Hastorf 1992; Lennstrom and Hastorf 1992). There are, however, key differences. Provincial Inka plant use at Cerro del Inga involved a syncretism of species well known in the Inka heartland with local economic plants. The presence of local plants, including an oily seeded cultigen (*Madia chilensis*), an arrow poison (*Colliguaja*), and a potent medicinal herb (*Calandrinia*), suggests the ability of the arriving Inkas to select and adopt local resources.

Other recovered plants are more difficult to characterize. At Cerro del Inga, quinoa was found more than 2,000 kilometers from its southernmost probable origin area of Lake Titicaca (Peru/Bolivia) (Cárdenas 1969; Erickson 1988; Pearsall 1989:329). Quinoa has also been recovered from Chilean Inka sites north of Cerro del Inga, such as Cerro de la Cruz (Rodriguez et al. 1993). The diffusion of quinoa to the south is an unresolved research issue. The botanical attributes and history of the plant are complex, and archaeobotanical data are emerging to further complicate the issue. A report of quinoa at La Granja site, also in the Cachapoal Valley, dates to A.D. 700–1000 (Planella and Stehberg 1994:73), and thus the plant may have been locally present prior to the Inka occupation.

Whether or not quinoa was locally present prior to the Inka presence, we hypothesize that near Cerro del Inga, the Inkas encouraged intensified use of the plant, which they identified with their heartland. Quinoa cultivation produces strikingly brilliant red and yellow fields that transform the landscape. Today, quinoa is still grown on traditional farms in a circumscribed, isolated region not far from Cerro del Inga. Present-day quinoa cultivation near Cerro del Inga is remarkable because the plant carries no market value and is recognized by farmers as a historical tradition. The same region matches historic accounts of a zone of Inka forced settlers (*mitmaq*) probably associated with the fortress (Planella 1988). The fragility of the quinoa seed, which must be planted annually to preserve fertility, also ties these quinoa growers to their Inka ancestors (Rossen 1994, 1997).

THE CENTRAL CHILE INKA NETWORK

Cerro del Inga is the southernmost manifestation of a network of forts designed to incorporate people and territory into the Inka state. The complete site system included various walled installations like Cerro del Inga interspersed with settlements and Inka-Diaguita cemeteries. In the Aconcagua Valley, the fortified sites of Cerro Mercachas (Sanguinettei 1975), Cerro La Cruz (Rodriguez et al. 1993), and Cerro Mauco (Vicuña Mackenna 1881) have been described. The Maipo Valley, near Santiago proper, contains the sites of Pucará de Chena (Stehberg 1976) and Ruinas de Chada (Stehberg et al. 1997).

Similarities and differences between these sites give insight into the Inka incursion into central Chile. Cerro Mercachas and Cerro Mauco are, like Cerro del Inga, located on isolated hilltop promontories with artificially flattened summits, commanding views of the valley, and multiple perimeter walls. Only Cerro Mercachas, however, has both rectangular and circular structures to suggest a pre-Inka occupation like that of Cerro del Inga. The site of Pucará de Chena shares the trait of multiple perimeter walls, but more specifically like Cerro del Inga, it also has turrets with a central corridor restricting access and a summit plaza. With its three adjoining cemeteries, Pucará de Chena had a much more developed settlement component than Cerro del Inga.

Sites like Cerro La Cruz, Pucará de Chena, and Ruinas de Chada exhibit the rapid development of settlement and industry as the Inka frontier pushed southward (figure 2.1). Among these sites, Cerro La Cruz stands out in representing a stronger establishment of local power and infrastructure. The significance of the metallurgy-smelting operation there and the existence of rich designs of provincial Inka ceramics suggest the site was an Inka administrative enclave of importance. In contrast, Ruinas de Chada lies at a lower elevation and has only the foundations of two perimeter walls, suggesting the site was a settlement instead of a military-industrial installation. Despite this, Ruinas de Chada shares certain architectural traits with Cerro del Inga, such as its entrances through walled balconies. Pucará de Chena, with its three adjoining cemeteries, exhibits greater development for settlement than the frontier outpost of Cerro del Inga, though *mitmaq* populations may have been associated with the latter site (Planella 1988). These sites were all connected by the principal Inka highways of the region, which traversed the low elevation precordillera and central plain, connecting to branches of the Trans-Andean Inka highway and points north through the Maipo and Aconcagua valleys (Stehberg 1995).

Cerro del Inga represents an advance in our understanding of the southernmost Inka expansion into central Chile and the accompanying processes of conquest, contact with ethnic groups, colonization, and annexation. Prior to the work of the second and third authors, the settlement of Pucará de Chena, located in the Maipo Valley 40 kilometers south of Santiago, represented the generally accepted southernmost boundary of Inka architecture and ceramics (Hyslop 1990; Stehberg 1976). The southern Inka military boundary may now be placed in the Cachapoal Valley, 95 kilometers south of Santiago. Historical documents discussing local *mitmaq* populations (Planella 1988) and the present-day enclave of quinoa farmers in the region suggest that substantial social and demographic change occurred concurrently with the military presence. Nonmilitary social and economic boundaries of the Inkas probably extended even farther south than Cerro del Inga (Dillehay and Gordon 1988).

By combining ethnohistorical, architectural, and archaeobotanical approaches at Cerro del Inga, it becomes apparent that the southern Inka frontier was complex and multidimensional. The discrepancies in the historical documents become understandable. The southern frontier was not merely a military outpost in the wilderness, but a layering of various military, social, and economic activities, each with a different scope and intensity. The Inkas, even at the farthest tentacles of the state, were committed to a varied strategy of settlement, consolidation, and transformation of the landscape, instead of just subjugation.

Finer scales of analysis such as water flotation–based archaeobotany add nuance to our understanding of those varied strategies. Fine-grained evidence of the provincial Inka plant-use system displays a combination of local and imperial traits. Soldiers and forced migrants brought their plants with them, but also adopted plants from local peoples. We are just beginning to understand the power of plants, in terms of how they represent imperial power, ethnicity, and, like architecture, a symbolic landscape. We can also now begin to frame research questions concerning how the adoption of local plants represents syncretism and the infiltration of local cultural elements into the Inka world at its outermost fringe.

Acknowledgments

Several seasons of field research, highly condensed here, were supported financially, technically, and logistically by Chilean institutions: Museo Nacional de Historia Natural, Museo Regional de Rancagua, Fondo Nacional de Ciencia y Tecnología (FONDECYT), Instituto de Física de la Universidad Católica de Chile, and Centro Agrícola Experimental Las Garzas. We gratefully acknowledge our colleagues Blanca Tagle, Hans Niemeyer, and Carmen del Río. Field and lab aspects of the botanical study were conducted for a class on theory and method of archaeobotany, and the entire group of 17 Chilean and Argentine professionals is gratefully acknowledged. The archaeobotanical study and class were made possible by a Fulbright Commission grant to the first author, in cooperation with the Museo Nacional de Historia Natural. Raúl Peña, Oscar Matthei, Gladys Fernández, and Luis Faúndes provided crucial assistance to the botanical analysis. We thank Brian Bauer and Tom Dillehay for their helpful comments on the manuscript.

Calógero M. Santoro, Verónica I. Williams,
Daniela Valenzuela, Álvaro Romero,
and Vivien G. Standen

Chapter Three

An Archaeological Perspective on the Inka Provincial Administration of the South-Central Andes

Editors' Introduction

This chapter constitutes an important contribution to the Inka archaeology of northern Chile. In particular, the authors focus on Arica, one of the most distant, and seemingly marginal, regions of the empire. Based on extensive archaeological research, ranging from regional studies, changes in the artifact assemblages, architecture, and dietary patterns from a household scale, this chapter highlights the distinct strategies of Inka control in the coastal valleys in comparison to the highlands of Arica. Against earlier assumptions that Inka control in these regions was uniformly indirect and through highland archipelago populations from the Circum-Titicaca, the authors compare the different historical trajectories of the coastal valleys and highlands in Arica.

Even though in the Arica coastal valleys there was no significant construction of Inka infrastructure compared to that in the nearby highlands, the authors emphasize the important changes generated by the empire. This is reflected in the selected distribution of Inka prestige goods such as decorated pottery, copper objects, *mullu* shells, and *khipus* in elite burials and residences, in addition to major population concentrations, changes in the local architecture, and distribution of *qollqas* between the littorals of Arica and the inner Inka settlements. This may not be a surprise, since these coastal valleys were rich in fish and guano resources. In this context, the Inkas sought to have access to such goods through a prestige-goods economy targeted to coastal elites. In comparison, the highlands of Arica show visible state investment evidenced in the amplification of the Inka road network with associated *tampus*, concentrations of *qollqas* in selected locations, *chullpa* mortuary towers in the altiplanic style, and agricultural intensification. In this case, the investment of imperial infrastructure was directed to ensure a significant economic extraction.

Whereas the authors suggest that the highlands of Arica show evidence of direct imperial involvement in the local socioeconomy, they also emphasize the role of intermediate but nonlocal populations in the consolidation of imperial power in the region. Specifically, their research shows the presence of Pacajes and other altiplanic populations from the Circum-Titicaca basin associated with Inka installations in the sierra of Arica. Such was the case of the *qollqas*, adobe *chullpa* towers, and imperial *tampus* associated with Pacajes-Saxamar and other Inka altiplanic ceramic wares. Taking into account that these altiplanic materials were already distributed in the sierra of Arica even before the arrival of the Inkas, we can hypothesize the important role that these nonlocal Circum-Titicaca populations played in the expansion and administration of the northernmost Inka provinces in this region. This early presence, perhaps in the form of colonies from the Circum-Titicaca, ensured the successful imperial expansion into the farthest northern regions, with Pacajes and other altiplanic groups as the main imperial agents. In all, we consider this chapter to be a significant contribution to understanding the varying ways in which the Inka Empire strengthened its power despite distance limitations. In this case, Inkanized Circum-Titicaca populations were the agents of imperialism and the mechanism to ensure a direct — although delegated — form of imperial control.

Introduction

In 1993, when Michael Malpass edited the volume *Provincial Inca: Archaeological and Ethnohistorical Assessment of the Impact of the Inca State*, the knowledge of the expansion of the Inka state toward the southern Andes rested upon models mostly based on ethnohistory (Dillehay and Netherly 1988; González 1983; Julien 1983; Llagostera 1976; Lynch 1993; Malpass 1993; Silva 1985, 1992–1993; Trimborn et al. 1975). This did not imply a lack of archaeological interest in learning about and explaining the way that the history of this great preindustrial empire unfolded (see D'Altroy 2003:39), but the weight of the chronicles and other written colonial records and the influence of scholars such as Murra (1980), Rostworowski de Diez Canseco (1953, 1988b), Rowe (1944, 1982), and Zuidema (1964) laid out profound trails for Andean history construction. The emphasis of those analyses was on the operation of state political, economic, and ideological structures at the level of the leading elites, leaving aside other segments of the system, or the social processes that took place in communities far away from the principal political centers (see Elson and Covey 2006). Similarly, as most of the archaeological studies tend to be concentrated in the major political centers, the effects of both the local historical processes and the state's policies themselves have received less attention (Bauer 2002; D'Altroy 2003; D'Altroy and Hastorf 2001; Lynch 1993; Romero 2002; Stanish 1997; Williams 1997, 2005).

In recent years, the limitations of the written ethnohistorical records have been under scrutiny as new directions and theoretical frames based on problem-oriented archaeological research are in progress, where the main foci are the processes of emergence, expansion, and domination of the imperial state along the Andes, analyzed as more dynamic rather than monolithic (Alcock et al. 2001; D'Altroy 1992, 2003; D'Altroy et al. 2000; Kaulicke 2002; Schreiber 1992; Silva 1985, 1992–1993; Uribe 1999–2000, 2004; Williams 2005; Williams and D'Altroy 1998; Williams et al. in press). As a result, a more heterogeneous panorama of the ways in which the Inka state interacted with the provinces is being unveiled (Bauer 2002; D'Altroy and Hastorf 2001; D'Altroy et al. 2000; Hyslop 1984, 1990, 1993; Julien 1983, 1993; Kaulicke 2002; La Lone and La Lone 1987; Lynch 1993; Nielsen 1996; Pärssinen and Siiriäinen 2003:128; Uribe and Adán 2004; Williams and D'Altroy 1998).[1] Pärssinen's (2003:128) conclusion about the absence of historical information regarding the Inkas' process of conquest of the coastal territories of southern Peru and northernmost Chile is a good example of the limitations of the ethnohistorical data used without an archeological contextualization. We believe this topic should be approached using techniques and data from both archaeology and ethnohistory, and by considering the cultural context in which architecture, pottery, and other cultural goods are integrated (D'Altroy et al. 1997; Gyarmati and Vargas 1999; Schjellerup 2005). It is important to recognize that differentiated development of the archaeological investigations in the Andes can accentuate or minimize the presence of the Inka state and its effects on local processes.

In this chapter, we examine the expansion of the Inkas into the western territories of the South-Central Andes, and we attempt to support the notion that the imperial state provoked important political, economic, and ideological transformations among local communities in the marginal territories of the Atacama Desert in northern Chile, where no major architectural or infrastructural projects were undertaken by the state (figure 3.1). Particularly, we explore variability in ceramic style preferences in domestic contexts, grave goods, settlement patterns, and health conditions, shown in archaeological records from the coast, low valleys, mountains, and highlands of the Arica region. Based on this data, we show that important transformations took place in the local communities' ways of life as these communities were incorporated into the empire. Thus, we attempt to explain the process of the state expansion into marginal territories of the Inka Empire, which cannot be considered borderland like the eastern side of the Andes, where indirect government was the major state strategy.

Studies dealing with the expansion of the Inka state in different places/ sites of the Andes oppose different motivations and different control strategies where the economic sphere, destined toward the intensification of production to obtain a surplus for the expansion and maintenance of the state, is highlighted. This prime economic urge would have been linked to political concomitants (Bray 2003b; Bray et al. 2005; Burger and Salazar 2004; Covey 2003, 2006; D'Altroy 1992, 2001; D'Altroy and Bishop 1990; D'Altroy and Earle 1985; D'Altroy and Hastorf 2001; D'Altroy et al. 2000; Earle 1994; Gyarmati and Vargas 1999; Hayashida 1998; Morris 1974, 1982; Morris and Thompson 1985; Pärssinen 2003; Stanish 1997, 2001), to coercive military actions (Arkush 2006; Carneiro 1970, 1990), and to the legitimization of ideological processes expressed through symbols of power that have greater archaeological visibility than the military operations that enjoy greater prestige in written documents (Alconini 2004; Aldunate et al. 2003; Bauer and Stanish 2001; DeMarrais et al. 1996; Earle 1990; Morris 1995; Nielsen and Walker 1999; Niles 1992, 1999; Uribe 2004; Van

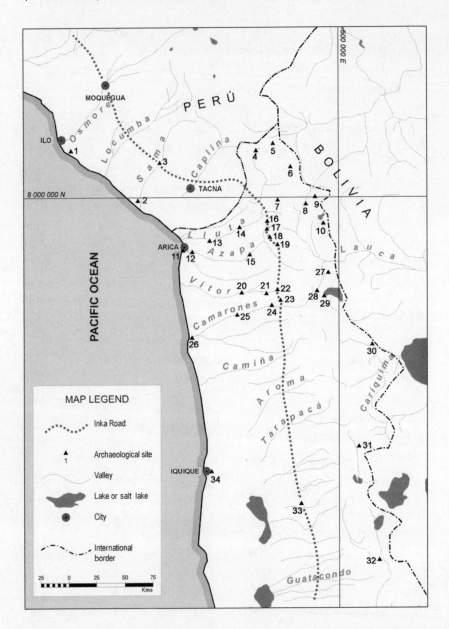

de Guchte 1999). The Inka state, like other preindustrial imperial states, operated as an integrated system of political, economic, and ideological organization, which was carried out to the farthest reaches of its domain, encompassing the most diverse social and cultural polities. However, economic issues were not the only motivation for the expansion. Maintaining

FIGURE 3.1. (Facing page) The western valleys, mountains, and highland of the South-Central Andean region, with major sites mentioned in the study: (1) Tacahuay, (2) Cerro Los Hornos and Morro de Sama, (3) Sama Antigua, (4) Tambos Tacora and Hospicio, (5) Tambo Huayancayane and Pukara Visviri, (6) Chullpas Huacollo, (7) Shrine Tarapacá volcano, (8) Shrine Guane Guane Hill, (9) Tambo Caquena, (10) Tambo Chungará, (11) Playa Miller 6, (12) Az-15; (13) Milluni, (14), Molle Pampa Este and Rosario 2, (15) Achuyo and Pubrisa, (16) Tantalcollo (17) Zapahuira Complex (*qollqas, tampu, chullpas*, Royal Inka road), (18) Caillama, (19) Belén area (Chajpa, Ancopachane, Huaihuarani), (20) Cachicoca, (21) Molle Grande 1 and 2, (22) Incauta, (23) Saguara, (24) Pachica, (25) Hacienda Camarones, (26) Camarones 9, (27) Paquisa, (28) Caracota, (29) Surire 1, (30) Isluga (Citani Chullpas, Pukara Isluga, high mountain shrine) and Cariquima (*tampu*), (31) Collacagua, (32) Collahuasi, (33) Pica, (34) Cerro Esmeralda. Drawn by Álvaro Romero — (58)314904 — Arica Parinacota (Chile).

a peaceful territory, in and outside the frontiers, was also important in order to maintain control over the conquest territories.

Archaeologically, it is important to look at historical processes in local contexts (Dillehay 1987; Dillehay et al. 2006) as a source for understanding the interaction of local communities with the state, based on discrete economic, political, ideological, and military action carried out by the state administration. Recently, there have been several attempts to establish the local social spheres affected by the state administration and how the state then shaped its political, economic, and ideological structures to administer these provinces (Acuto 1999; Alconini 2004; Arkush 2006; Covey 2006; D'Altroy and Hastorf 2001; D'Altroy et al. 2000; Earle 1994; Frye 2006; Nielsen and Walker 1999; Santoro et al. 1998; Santoro et al. 2004; Stanish 1997; Uribe 2004; Uribe and Adán 2004; Wernke 2006).

The presence or absence of Inka prestige goods, such as decorated ceramics, metal objects, feathers, *mullu* shell (*Spondylus* sp.), high-quality textiles, and tools for farming and weaving, should be analyzed in the context of changing patterns in household contexts and in terms of eating habits, health conditions, intensification of production, and so forth. These household contexts are especially sensitive to state-provoked changes in the political, economic, and ideological local systems (Hastorf 1990; Wernke 2006). Conversely, the absence of investment in architectural facilities of greater archaeological visibility does imply that certain state political and economic institutions were linked to other kinds of cultural material. Consequently, the archaeological analysis should be concerned with understanding the political, economic, and ideological context of interaction that provoked certain arrangements of the cultural material.

Household archaeology has proved effective in highlighting the changes among the elites and the commoners in the Mantaro Valley (D'Altroy and Hastorf 2001) and Calchaquí Valley (Acuto, this volume; D'Altroy et al. 2000). This approach was taken in the study here using data from archaeological excavations of households from different villages in the Lluta Valley (Santoro 1995), as well as data from the highlands of Arica. Conversely, archaeological studies of state domination at the provincial level provide an excellent opportunity to look at general principles of administration and its possible variations as a consequence of local, ecological, political, economic, and ideological conditions.

Another topic under debate is the Inka chronology. Using historical data, Rowe (1944), followed by Pärssinen (2003), estimated that the expansion of the Inka Empire occurred in a very short period of time. The archaeological data, however, show a much larger historical process (D'Altroy 2000; D'Altroy et al. 1998; Schiappacasse 1999). However, Pärssinen and Siiriäinen (1997) have pointed out that Inka pottery in context in the Lake Titicaca region predating Rowe's (1944) chronology should not automatically be considered evidence of an earlier Inka conquest of the Circum-Titicaca region. Hyslop (1977) has also suggested that Inka goods are not necessarily evidence of state domination.

The rapid advance was achieved because the political control strategy was based on the conquest — peaceful or military and with the strong support of ideological power — of the heads of the provinces. Responsibility for the administration of the new territorial organizations was then transferred to these leaders or to others imposed by the Inkas. In some cases, the Inkas invested in infrastructure and made substantial changes in the preexisting organizational systems (Eeckhout 2004). This is particularly true for the core provinces in central and northern Peru and the Titicaca region. The incorporation of more distant provinces, like the desert of northern Chile, may have required different strategies, as seen in Ecuador (Salomón 1986) and the eastern border from Bolivia to northwestern Argentina (Alconini 2004; Pärssinen and Siiriäinen 2003; Schjellerup 2005; Williams and D'Altroy 1998). Provinces like the territories of the Atacama Desert in northern Chile show important imperial state impact on the local community economy, political organization, and ideology, despite the fact that no major state investment in infrastructure or major military mobilization is known from the archaeological records, which creates the ambiguous image of an absent state government management. Would this explain the lack of ethnohistorical documentation of the Inka conquest of the coastal desert strip between Ica and Tarapacá, highlighted by Pärssinen (2003:128)?

The Inkas in the Southern Andes

Within Cuntisuyu (or northern Kollasuyu, depending on where one draws the boundary between these administrative units), the territories of the coast, low valleys, mountains, and highlands of northernmost Chile (figure 3.1) encompass low population density and limited ecological potential for stable processes of agricultural and pastoral intensification of production. The opposite occurs in the Circum-Titicaca and the Valluna subareas, where there were more state investments for production intensification. These ecological, geographic, and demographic factors would explain the scarce state investment in northern Chile. Considering these environmental conditions and following Murra's (1972) vertical model, Llagostera (1976) proposed an indirect Inka state dominion derived from political groups in the Circum-Titicaca area (Caranga, Lupaqa, Colla, and Pacaje). It was assumed that, prior to the Inkas, these polities had the demographic and economic capacity to confront the problems of maintaining power over territories outside of their native lands in the highlands (Covey 2000; Santoro et al. 2004; Schiappacasse et al. 1989). Llagostera's (1976) hypothesis stated that the Inkas first removed control over long-distance colonies and the traffic of exotic goods from and toward the highlands from the leaders of the altiplano kingdoms, a strategy applied in other regions of the Andes (Mantaro, northern Ecuador). Second, they used the network of the Circum-Titicaca polities to incorporate the lower territories with the Pacific Coast as well as with the eastern *yunga* by reorganizing the alliances between the Circum-Titicaca region lords and the *kurakas* in these provinces (Cardona 2002; Llagostera 1976; Santoro and Ulloa 1985). This model has been applied — explicitly or implicitly — to most of the studies describing the Inkas in the Pacific valleys of southern Peru and northern Chile (Aldunate 2001; Berenguer 1995; Cardona 2002; Durston and Hidalgo 1997; Gordillo 2000; Hidalgo and Santoro 2001; Llagostera

1976; Muñoz 1989, 1998; Muñoz and Chacama 1993; Muñoz, Chacama, and Espinosa 1987; Muñoz et al. 1987; Núñez 1992; Santoro 1983; Santoro and Ulloa 1985; Santoro et al. 1987; Schiappacasse and Neimeyer 1989).[2] Consequently, although the provinces of northern Chile and southern Peru were not located in the Inka border frontier, it has been postulated that a system of indirect state control over the provinces existed there (D'Altroy 1992; Stanish 1997).

For the Atacama region, indirect state control is also assumed, from political centers in the Circum-Titicaca region, linked to high mountain shrines (Núñez 1992), monumental architecture (Gallardo et al. 1995), and a possible state rock art (Gallardo and Vilches 2001; Vilches and Uribe 1999). In a recent synthesis, Aldunate (2001:20) points out that "metaphorically speaking, the Inka occupied northern Chile disguised in the clothes of the altiplano peoples under their control" (see also Hidalgo and Santoro 2001; Santoro and Ulloa 1985).

This dichotomy between direct and indirect state control has confused distinct levels of state control, which were far from being indirect (D'Altroy 1992; D'Altroy and Hastorf 2001; Schreiber 1987, 1992; Stanish 1997). Archaeologically, the idea of indirect control is supported by the absence of a visible, monumental state architecture for infrastructure, which is reduced to prestige goods. The identification of a small number of cultural material categories, like pottery styles, has been stressed to define direct or indirect control, giving little attention to the mechanism of integration and its consequences among the local communities. For example, the presence of a ceramic component from northwest Argentina, in the Atacama region (that is, Inka-Paya and Yavi Chico Polychrome pottery) and distributed throughout the Circum-Puneña subarea, is mentioned as a feature that accompanied and identified the Inka expansion in the Puna of Atacama as part of imperial equipment (Bray 2004; González and Díaz 1992; Uribe 2004; Williams 2004; Williams et al. 2006). Silva (1992–1993, 1993) and Uribe (1999–2000) have pointed out that the archaeological analysis of the Inka in northernmost Chile is primarily focused on descriptive case studies (Focacci 1981; Muñoz 1989; Muñoz, Chacama, and Espinosa 1987; Muñoz et al. 1987; Muñoz et al. 1997; Romero 2002; Romero and Briones 1999; Santoro 1983; Santoro and Muñoz 1981; Santoro et al. 1987; Schiappacasse and Niemeyer 1997). In this context, Uribe (1999–2000) estimates that both the Atacama oasis and the Loa basin were directly controlled by the Inka state, with the support of a strong ideological apparatus (Cornejo 1995; Uribe and Adán 2004; Uribe et al. 2000). Following this line of argument, it has been emphasized that the Inkas used state symbolic and ideological displays to administer and legitimize their supremacy in the conquered territories and that local cultural patterns were framed within this imperial cultural system (Uribe and Adán 2004). However, these explanations lack well-defined archaeological data to compare the operation of these or other institutions of the Inka state organization, such as the mechanisms of expansion and administration of territories far from Cuzco, which according to Schreiber (1992) encompassed a mosaic of control.

Consequently, by comparing the pre-Inka and Inka sociocultural conditions, we attempt to shed light on the versatility of the imperial policies in the incorporation of new peoples from marginal territories. We believe that the impact of the state should be found at this local community level. The mere identification of state material goods or architecture does not directly describe and explain the kind of interactions between the Inka state and the community. Thus, it is important to look at material culture to identify possible scenarios of acceptance or resistance to the state control policies and their impact on the reproduction of the community's traditional patterns (D'Altroy and Hastorf 2001; Miller et al. 1989; Schreiber 1987, 1992).

The Valleys and Coast of Arica and Tacna

The current archaeological data from the coastal valleys of northernmost Chile (Lluta, Azapa, and Camarones), in this Western Valleys zone of the south-central Andean region (figure 3.1), demonstrate important state intervention, although there is no major Inka state installation (administrative, ceremonial, or productive) on the archaeological landscape, which has been used to support the idea of an indirect government. In a later phase, however, the coastal valley territories show certain architectural features and cultural material of the kind customarily considered signs of direct state control, as observed at Sama (Trimborn et al. 1975), Azapa 15 (Focacci 1981; Santoro and Muñoz 1981), Playa Miller 6 (Hidalgo and Focacci 1986), Camarones 9 (Correa and Ulloa 2000), Hacienda Camarones (Niemeyer 1963), and Cerro Esmeralda (Checura 1977). The archaeological features that characterized the relationship between communities of the coastal Pacific valleys and the Inka state summarized below come principally from the Lluta Valley (Romero et al. 1998; Santoro 1995; Santoro et al. 2004).

Within an architectural scenario of rather scarce Inka architecture, it is worth highlighting three platforms with a rather local architectural style made of roughly cut stone walls set with a blackish hard mortar consisting of a mixture of ashes and other substances. These platforms are located in the central part of Molle Pampa Este, and may have served as *kallankas* (long, one-room halls) or more possibly as *usnus* (pyramid platforms in a ceremonial complex), as suggested by Hyslop (personal communication 1991). The main platform (R-3) is dated at A.D. 1480–1640 (Beta 101497). Other examples of elaborate architecture are found at Pubrisa (Muñoz and Chacama 2006), an Inka-related town in the *chaupiyunga* zone of the Azapa Valley, but certainly not planned with an Inka orthogonal design. It is characterized by a concentration of rectangular large structures that occupied the central part of the hamlet, surrounded on its west flank by semicircular smaller structures, which seem to be part of an earlier phase of occupation. The surface of the domestic area, including storage pits, is about 14,000 square meters. Another architectural feature related to Inka intervention corresponds to a stone wall platform to support a light architecture of cane, reed, and wood posts of Rosario 2, a town of the Lluta Valley dated between A.D. 1410 and 1630 (Beta 101496).

Previous to the Inkas, the architecture in the coastal valleys consisted of nothing more than simple rooms of reed, canes, and wood posts (Santoro 1995; Schiappacasse and Niemeyer 1989). At the heads of the valleys, at an altitude between 2,000 and 3,000 meters (that is, Achuyo, Milluni, Cachicoca; see figure 3.1), the architecture consists of stone wall masonry structures, without an Inka architectural pattern or mode of construction. The stone structures were constructed in accordance with the local topographical and climatic conditions, and the masonry resembles the patterns shown at the altiplano Caranga site of Cchaucha del Kajula Marka (Rydén 1947). Milluni is dated between A.D. 1400 and 1620 (Beta 180800, calibrated) from a charcoal sample obtained at the beginning of its occupation and is associated with decorated pottery of Arica's local style and the Black on Red highland style (figure 3.2).

FIGURE 3.2. Principal pottery styles of the Late Intermediate and Late periods. (a–d) Arica, (e–f) Charcollo from the high Andean valleys, (g–i) Black on Red from the altiplano, (j) Saxamar or Inka Pacaje, and (k–m) Inka.

Another issue related to the Inka intervention is the concentration of the population in much larger towns as seen in the village of Molle Pampa Este, with more than 10 hectares of domestic facilities, and greater complexity compared to Late Intermediate period hamlets, which did not extend more than 2 to 3 hectares (Santoro 1995). As a consequence, there was an alteration of health conditions, evidenced by a significant increase in intestinal parasites such as pinworm (*Enterobius vermicularis*) and fish tapeworm (*Diphyllobothrium pacificum*) during the Inka period in Molle

Pampa Este, compared to pre-Inka conditions. This epidemic seems to be an effect of overcrowded residences, caused by an increase in population density and the close proximity of households (Santoro et al. 2003).

Inka prestige goods such as decorated ceramics; feathers of *suri* and other, more colorful birds; fragments of *mullu* shell (*Spondylus* sp.); copper objects (*tumis*, discs); and small fragments of *khipu* were found in small quantities in tombs and a household context at Molle Pampa Este. These goods have been also reported for funerary contexts at Az-15 in the Azapa Valley, Camarones 9, and Cerro Esmeralda in Iquique (Catalán 2007; Checura 1977; Focacci 1981; Santoro 1995). These kinds of elements may have been administered by communal *kurakas*, who in this case did not have the opportunity to create social inequality on the basis of an advantageous administration of the productive processes demanded by the state from their communities as occurred later with caciques of Codpa, under the Spanish colonial government (Hidalgo and Durston 1998).

There is also evidence of maize production intensification, judging from a large facility of subterranean *qollqas* (storehouses) in Huaylacán (ca. 1.5 hectares, and about 765 *qollqas*). The *qollqas* are stone wall cylindrical subterranean chambers covered by clay (0.50–150 centimeters in diameter and 100–200 centimeters in depth; Barraza 1995). The site is located in the coastal section of the Lluta Valley, a sterile zone of the valley where today farming is difficult because of the salinity of the soil and a high surface water table. This location is about 7 kilometers from the littoral and 11 and 16 kilometers, respectively, from the Inka-related towns of the valley, Rosario 2 and Molle Pampa Este.

There are also signs of intensification of textile production, evidenced by an increase of spindle whorls in domestic contexts, as observed in other parts of the Andes. This productive activity was performed in each household, with no evidence of full-time specialist spinners. This production was possibly part of the labor quota demanded by the state for the textile *mit'a* (Murra 1983), which implied changes in the everyday production activities of these populations (Loyola et al. 2000; Santoro 1995).

The Mountains and Altiplano of Arica

In the highlands of Arica and Tacna, the archaeological evidence shows a more visible state investment via buildings with typically provincial Inka

FIGURE 3.3. Typical local Inka architectural features characterized by double-row stone masonry with clay mortar.

architecture, but not to be confused with the beautifully fitted Inka masonry style of finely cut polygonal stone utilized in the cyclopean building in Cuzco and other conspicuous Inka centers in the Andes. The local Inka architecture in the highlands of Arica is characterized by simple, double-faced, rough stone walls that include both round and flat blocks, in rather uniform rows (figure 3.3). The general plan of the structures is approximately rectangular, with corners that do not always form a precise 90 degree angle, particularly in the interior, a design element that resembles the typical rounded corners of the buildings at Cuzco. These constructions represented an important accomplishment by the local communities, via the state-imposed *mit'a* (corvée) obligation, expressed in infrastructure of *qollqas, chullpas* (aboveground tombs), *tampus*, high mountain shrines and *usnu*, and the Royal Inka road, which are described in more detail below, since most of these data are not known in the literature.

QOLLQAS

The *qollqas* of Zapahuira, known as Tambo Zapahuira 1, Az-140 (Muñoz et al. 1987:71), are typical Inka state storehouses and represent the most

FIGURE 3.4. *Qollqas* of Zapahuira (Az-140) crossed by the Arica–La Paz highway. View toward the west. Note fixed floor and ducts for air circulation and temperature control.

important state investment in production management in the highlands of Arica. They are located in an open pampa (3,226 meters) not appropriate for cultivation because of the absence of water, windy conditions, and the extreme temperature fluctuation between day and night. The location, however, is perfect for storehouses, and they are about 3,500 meters west of the Royal Inka road. The closer farming area is located around Tambo Zapahuira.

The storehouses are composed of one long row of contiguous rectangular structures, with an east-west axis, and another shorter row with a north-south axis, which was placed over the southeast corner of the first row, although there are no clear architectural signs that they were originally joined (figure 3.4). The doors open to the southwest, the direction of the prevailing cold wind in the afternoon — of great help for ventilation and heat control. The shorter row was partially destroyed in the 1950s, when the international highway (Arica–La Paz) and the remaining ruins collapsed due to earthquakes (restored by Universidad de Tarapacá). The complex has a deviation of about 5 degrees to the northwest.

The construction pattern is typical of local Inka architecture. The floor was specially prepared with a layer of pebbles and crossed by longitudinal and transversal ducts (Muñoz et al. 1997), possibly for air circulation, temperature control, or the circulation of water for humidity control. A similar device is described for the Huánuco Pampa *qollqas* to maintain ideal conditions (temperature, humidity) for potatoes (Morris and

Thompson 1985:105–106), one of the products that may have been stored at Zapahuira.

Two thermoluminescence dates — A.D. 1240, from a pottery fragment of Saxamar or Inka Pacaje style (Muñoz and Chacama 1988:23, Lam. 4, figure 3.1), and A.D. 1210, from a fragment of a bowl with "Late Altiplanic" style (Muñoz and Chacama 1988:23, plate 4, figure 2) — suggest a very early state investment in economic infrastructure. However, a radiocarbon date was A.D. 1400–1640 (Muñoz et al. 1997), which is more in line with the process of the Inka expansion over this region.

CHULLPAS

Chullpas, in contrast, represent an important state investment in ideological power, standing near the border of *quebradas* or other prominences on the landscape, with the door facing east. Some of them were made of massive adobe bricks, partially supported by a wooden structure, less than 2 meters tall, with a base of 2.5 by 1.8 meters. Examples of these ceremonial landmarks have been recorded in Zapahuira (Az-122; 3 examples; see figure 3.5), Caillama (27 examples; Santoro et al. 2003), Zapahuira Gentilar,[3]

FIGURE 3.5. *Chullpa* of Zapahuira (Az-122), facing east. Note the trapezoidal small door.

and Copaquilla. A variation of this ceremonial construction corresponds to stone wall structures covered by mud plaster, also used as mortar, as seen in Huacollo (figure 3.1). They were built with large slabs of volcanic rocks (measuring up to 138 centimeters in length by 30 by 20 centimeters), which were specially selected and brought from an unknown, and probably distant, quarry.

The pottery associated with these *chullpas* corresponds to the Inka altiplanic variety, Inka Pacaje, and other local undecorated wares (figure 3.2). The *chullpas* of Zapahuira yielded two early radiocarbon dates: A.D. 1280–1400 and 1300–1450, calibrated (Muñoz et al. 1997). Romero (2003:99) suggests that the mud *chullpas* started to be built in the Late Intermediate period, with no association to Inka features as seen in Caillama, but *chullpas* became an important landmark in the Inka period as seen at Zapahuira, Ancopachane, Incaullo, Huacollo, and Zapahuira Gentilar. This last site has been dated at 400 ± 60 B.P. (A.D. 1400–1520; Beta 201823, calibrated).

In this ideological/political context, we inspected Late period villages in the highland of Arica to look for rock art, a rather unknown feature in relation to the Inkas, but with no positive results. Apparently, rock art was not a significant element used by the state as a symbol of power, which is more evident in architecture, high mountain shrines, and the *chullpas*. This is an important distinction from the low valleys, where monumental architecture was replaced by geoglyphs. This rock art, designed on the slopes of the lowland valleys, has a certain degree of monumentality, great visibility, and durability (Briones et al. 1999; Valenzuela et al. 2004).

TAMPUS

Tampus are the most common and best-known state features found in the highlands, linked to the Royal Inka road. In the high altiplano, above 4,000 meters, there are Tambo Pisarata, Tambo Tacora (Muñoz and Chacama 1993; Muñoz et al. 1997), Tambo Chungará (Chacón and Orellana 1982), and the recently discovered Tambo Huayancayane and Tambo Hospicio. In the sierra zone (ca. 3,500 meters above sea level), we have studied Tambo Zapahuira and Tambo Tantalcollo located along the side of the Inka road, south of Socoroma (figure 3.1).[4]

Tambo Pisarata is composed of a row of 10 contiguous structures that cover a space of 43 by 5 meters, close to the *bofedal* of Caquena, some 2 kilometers from the highland town of the same name (Muñoz et al.

1997). It presents typical double-faced stone wall masonry with clay mortar. Archaeological excavations of shallow deposits yielded limited samples of cultural material consisting of plain and decorated pottery that was complemented by the surface collection. Muñoz et al. (1997) recognized five ceramic styles: Inka regional, Inka Pacaje or Saxamar, Chilpe, and two types of plain wares of red burnished fine paste and yellowish sandy paste. A thermoluminescence date of A.D. 1535 was obtained from a bowl fragment with the Black on Red style (Muñoz et al. 1997:153).

Tambo Tacora, located south of the highland town of the same name, is composed of a row of several rectangular structures, with a north-south axis, plus another parallel row with two structures. The surface collection is composed of prehispanic Inka-related and highland styles, as well as colonial pottery (Muñoz and Chacama 1993). Additionally, we found struck fragments of glass treated as lithic raw material (seen at other sites). In the southeast corner of the shorter row there is a towerlike structure of about 1.5 meters in height, built with double-faced stone wall masonry and clay mortar, which stands out as an anomalous structure, as it does not have the conditions for domestic functions. The walls of the other structures were built combining adobe up to about 1 meter high, upon which the wall was raised with two rows of natural stones, roughly rectangular in shape and filled in with gravel. The facade of these rows resembles the appearance of the walls of Tambo Chungará, discussed below. A thermoluminescence date of A.D. 1590 was obtained from a fragment of an *aríbalo*, defined as "local Inka altiplanic" (Muñoz et al. 1997:155).

Tambo Hospicio, located to the southwest of Tambo Tacora, is currently used as a corral, but its original purpose as a *tampu* is remembered by the local inhabitants. It is characterized by an orthogonal layout of adobe structures; a few of the interior dividers of these have been conserved. Features such as *hornacines* stand out. The surface contained a few fragments of glass with signs of use, pottery with the Black on Red style, and an ovoid-shaped lithic artifact that may have been used as a knife.

Tambo Huayancayane seems to be a facility characterized by massive single-row stone masonry of contiguous structures (north-south axis that spans 530 meters in length), some measuring 8 by 10 meters and others 18 by 20 meters, located at the bottom slope of a stony hill that protects its west-facing side. In the interior of some of the structures, there are smaller constructions that may have served as storage rooms. Similar facilities were inventoried in the district of Surire, southeast of Arica. These constructions resemble the large single stone wall structures on the western side of the Turi Pukara (Aldunate and Cornejo 2001:38), identified tentatively as field camps (Castro et al. 1993:81, 95). The entrances of the barracks face east to a wide prairie covered by *tolar* vegetation, not well suited for camelids (especially alpaca herding). The immediate flat area shows evidence of irrigation canals that may have been used to maintain a *bofedal*. This land is not suitable for farming because of its altitude and cold weather. Originally, the barracks may have served the Inka army parties in the process of conquering the territories south and west of Lake Titicaca.

Tambo Chungará, identified as one of the most important Inka constructions in the area (Aldunate and Cornejo 2001; Chacón and Orellana 1982; Muñoz and Chacama 1993; Muñoz et al. 1997), seems to be of posthispanic origin, according to our own recent excavations. It is characterized by impressive stone wall masonry not seen in other Inka facilities in northern Chile, in particular the first row of structures, numbered 2, 3, 4, and Terrace E on Chacón and Orellana's map (1982). Our own 2.5-meter-square archaeological excavations were located in units 2 and 3 and in Terrace E, and several soil samples obtained with an auger show no stratigraphic evidence to support the notion that the main row of ruins was built in prehispanic times. This does not mean that the site was not used before the European invasion. Inka and other types of pottery are still a common surface finding. The excavations of Chacon and Orellana, as well as those of Ivan Muñoz and his team, yielded some Inka and other prehispanic pottery in their deposits, mixed with glass fragments characteristic of colonial times. Our excavation yielded only fragments of glass with an absolute absence of diagnostic prehispanic pottery.

Other buildings attached to the main row need to be tested stratigraphically for possible prehispanic occupation and construction, as their architecture lacks the complexity of the other ones. There is a towerlike structure, more than 2 meters tall, located on the southeast side of the *tampu*, flanked by a stone stairway on its north side. The facade of the structure does not have the well-fitted stone masonry of the other buildings. Instead, this structure follows the patterns of rough stone masonry of local prehispanic style.

We think that the main line of rooms of the *tampu*, as seen today, was built in colonial times, as a main stop on the "silver road" from Potosí-Arica, where the process of silver production started in the sixteenth century. Coincidentally, a thermoluminescence date of a small cooking pot corresponds to A.D. 1695, well into the Early Colonial period (Muñoz et al. 1997:154). This is confirmed by a radiocarbon date, obtained by us, from Room 3, stratum 5, which places the beginning of occupation in the seventeenth to the eighteenth century (160 ± 50 B.P. [A.D. 1640–1710]; Beta 200947).

The construction of these colonial facilities did not enlarge or obliterate pre-Spanish buildings, as no signs of older buildings showed up in our excavations. The *tampu* may have been built by indigenous people who were familiar with the Inka architecture system, and for that reason the building had that "Inka" appearance, such as the trapezoidal shape of the walls of the structures but not in the doors; the use of natural, rectangular stone — not cut stone — carefully chosen to maintain a regular pattern of superimposed stones; and a rather smooth external facade, as observed in Tambo Tacora.

The main row of structures has also undergone several restorations, including the work of ancestors of the Blanco family, who own the land of the *tampu*. According to one member of the family, "Our grandfathers built this edifice and they lived here until a few decades ago [ca. 1950], but the cold weather and the winter snowstorms, which cover the pastures used for the animals, forced them to build their houses where we live today," about 6 kilometers farther south of the *tampu*, in the same Guallatire basin (story by Ariel Blanco, August 1, 2004, confirmed separately by his wife the next day).

Tambo Zapahuira (Az-124; Muñoz et al. 1987), the most important and complex Inka installation in the highlands of Arica, may have functioned as a local administrative center, integrating the economic activities of the Lluta and Azapa valleys. In contrast to Tambo Chungará, all of its components, the dating of the stratigraphic deposits, and the architectural patterns show a clear link with the Inka period. The *tampu* is located over an open pampa on the southern edge of a ravine, at an altitude of 3,280 meters and about 1,300 meters from the Inka road to the west. The complex possesses a typical Inka rectangular architectural plan, with two U-shaped, orthogonal units originally opening toward the east and separated by about 150 meters, with an east-west axis. The space between the two units includes several circular structures for living, storage, and corral functions, and it covers 8,000 square meters in total.

The two U-shaped structures are composed of three large pairs of buildings of uneven walls, which demarcate open plazas that were fully closed by postoccupation walls of more rustic construction style. Originally, the complex on the east side was integrated by three buildings oriented 5 degrees toward the north, and doors opening onto the plaza. The main structure of the U, with a north-south axis, is 20 by 6 meters, with straight exterior corners and rather round interior corners. Originally, it had two internal subdivisions, which have been completely destroyed. The parallel sections of the U (east-west axis) are about 27 by 6 meters in size and are placed next to the south and north sides of the base, respectively, separated by corridors 2 meters wide and 6 meters long, with an east-west axis. They constituted circulation paths which were later sealed on both extremes for storage or other unknown purposes.

The U-shaped structure on the western section is smaller, although it follows the same general plan and has the same construction characteristics, with three architectural units that open also to the east. As in the other complex, the three units do not have matching walls where they intersect, and two corridors were left for circulation, but with a north-south axis, and they were also closed by later occupants. A difference from the east sector is that the structures of the west group feature a 10-degree deviation to the west.

Both complexes show double row walls made from natural stones, with the stones' flatter surfaces specifically selected for the facades. The rocks are placed transversally, which gives them a width of 80 centimeters, filled in between with mud mortar. The walls are conserved up to approximately 1.7 meters. The fact that the walls were built with the intention of having the two rows be more or less uniform gave them greater stability and a more standardized appearance. The pillars of the doors are made up of larger rock slabs, which are filled in with the smaller blocks from the wall. The perimeter walls of the U-shaped structures feature a stone base foundation, characteristic of this type of architecture.

We obtained a collection of 509 ceramic fragments, 74 of which were decorated. These decorated fragments were distributed as follows: Arica style (4.8 percent, n = 5), Serrano style (that is, Charcollo and burgundy-colored glaze, 28.6 percent, n = 30), Black on Red style (that is, Chilpe and

Vilavila, 23.8 percent, n = 25), Inka style (Inka Pacaje and Inka, 13.3 percent, n = 14) (figure 3.2), and unidentified (28.5 percent, n = 31). Regarding pastes, pastes 210 and 220 stood out in the sample (34 percent, n = 173, compared with a lower number of decorated fragments); these were fine-textured, orange pastes. These types of paste are frequently associated with Inka decoration. The majority of the pastes correspond to standard 400 (48 percent, n = 246), which is of local origin, while 17.7 percent (n = 90) correspond to other paste types (Romero 2002; Santoro et al. 2001).

We excavated structures R-7 (1.0 square meter), R-17 (2.9 square meters), and R-21 (1.0 square meter), and the northeast corner of the west plaza (0.5 square meter). Test pits were placed in R-3 of the east plaza, and several tests in different sectors of the site were made with an auger. These stratigraphic tests allowed us first to realize that the plazas were not artificially sealed with a layer of clay to level them.

The 2-square-meter excavation of Structure 17 revealed a stratigraphy that was about 30 centimeters in depth and showed the best chronological and cultural history of the site. The site clearly possessed a prehispanic occupation that contrasts with Tambo Chungará. Inka ceramics appear in the upper strata associated with glass and other colonial elements. In the subjacent intermediate strata, the hispanic elements disappear completely, and Inka items, such as Inka altiplanic and Inka Pacaje pottery, dominate. A complete copper *tumi* with remains of a leather strap in its distal extreme was found there. These intermediate strata have been dated at 290 ± 50 B.P., or A.D. 1470–1670 (Beta 189245, stratum 3); 330 ± 50 B.P., or A.D. 1440–1650 (Beta 200945, stratum 4); and 420 ± 50 B.P., or A.D. 1400–1490 (Beta 200946, stratum 5). The lower stratum shows no Inka ceramic wares but is clearly associated with the early Pacaje style (figure 3.6), characterized by larger and less-stylized camelids (llamas) than the classic Inka Pacaje, as defined by Albarracín-Jordán (1991:55, figure 18, 1996). Stratum 6 is dated at 590 ± 50 B.P., or A.D. 1280–1420 (Beta 189246). A thermoluminescence date of A.D. 1520 was obtained from a fragment of an Inka altiplanic globular pot that "came from cultural strata of site N° 2" (Muñoz and Chacama 1988:24, Lam. 6, figure 3.2).

Tambo Tantalcollo is located alongside the Inka trail, between Socoroma and Zapahuira, on the northeast edge of the Pampa Tantalcollo. The trail is connected to a natural path that communicates this pampa to the highland valley of Socoroma, at the base of the Andean foothills. Besides

FIGURE 3.6. Early Pacaje style, characterized by larger and less-stylized camelids than the classic Inka Pacaje, as defined by Albarracín-Jordán (1991:55, figure 18, 1996).

the Inka trail, the path is the connecting point for the Vilasamanani-Socoroma transvalley canal, which enters the Socoroma gorge (Osorio and Santoro 1988). Consequently, the site is an important node between the Andean foothills; the intermediate plain of Zapahuira, which includes several Inka facilities; and the entrance to the lowland Lluta and Azapa valleys. The Inka trail descends from the path to Tambo Tantalcollo covering a distance of about 1,000 meters (with an east-west axis), and then it turns to the south, toward Zapahuira, a path that has been obliterated by the international Arica–La Paz highway.

The *tampu* consists of a group of three structures, which are roughly circular but of different sizes,[5] and covers an area of 400 square meters. A platform added on to the northeast edge of the semicircular perimeter wall acts as an entrance to the enclosures. To the south there is another semicircular perimeter wall, which excludes the enclosure that is located in the southern extreme of the *tampu*. This last enclosure is adjacent to a rocky outcropping, and it consists of a large semicircular structure 4.5 by 5.0 meters, plus three attached small ones (two on the outside and one on the inside). These have a total surface area of 400 square meters. The original masonry has been changed by the addition of roughly constructed stone walls, especially in Structure 2. On the surface, we collected fragments of Inka altiplanic, Inka Pacaje, and Black on Red styles.

Drilling excavations with an auger in different parts of the settlement made it possible to locate a dense stratigraphic deposit in the platform, which predates the structures. A 1.5-by-1.5-meter grid was excavated to a depth of 80 centimeters, which included occupations from the Late Intermediate to recent periods. Between strata 1 and 5 (up to 20 centimeters below the surface) there were Inka artifacts with colonial and modern elements that feature glass fragments, some of which were carved as raw lithic materials, as well as indigenously produced colonial and modern ceramic wares. From strata 6 to 11 (up to 75 centimeters deep) there is clear evidence from the Late Prehispanic period, which incorporates Arica, Inka, and Black on Red ceramic styles. This last type of fragment was found exclusively in the deepest strata. Excavations also took place in Structures 2 and 5, covering an area of 3.5 square meters, but, unlike the terrace, they did not yield diagnostic cultural material. A radiocarbon sample from stratum 11 in the platform yielded a date of 490 ± 70 B.P., or A.D. 1280–1440 (Beta 200949). Unfortunately, no charcoal or other material was available for dating the upper stratum. The date fits perfectly with the chronology of the other sites.

Toward the southern foothills of the Andes, in the Belén area (figure 3.1), we have worked on the Chajpa Ancopachane complex, which — along with Incaullo (Dauelsberg 1983) — formed another Inka administrative center, 80 kilometers to the south of Zapahuira.[6] Ancopachane is a large domestic complex, very close to the current village of Belén, characterized by a dispersed population, primarily associated with agricultural *andenes*. The presence of sierra-style (Red Slip and Charcollo style) ceramics stands out (ca. 50 percent), as does the pre-Inka altiplano style Black on Red, although to a lesser degree (24 percent). Much less common are the Inka Pacaje and Inka styles, which together make up 15 percent of the total. Fragments of Arica styles are minimal (figure 3.2).

Chajpa is located on a natural hill at the western edge of the Ancopachane village, where there is an orthogonal state building with internal subdivisions of the *tampu* style. The foundations of large circular structures, which probably correspond to *qollqas*, similar to those at Incaullo, were also detected (Dauelsberg 1983). One of these circular structures corresponds to a semisubterranean cylindrical chamber about 10 meters wide and about 70 centimeters deep. We did not find signs of a fixed floor as seen in Zapahuira. The perimeter is composed of double row stone masonry. The structure was completely filled with postdepositional debris of fluvial origin. Between the domestic and administrative areas, the foundation of a mud *chullpa* was found (Romero 2003).

High Mountain Shrines

High mountain shrines were placed at the Tarapacá and Isluga volcanoes and the Guane Guane, Belén, and Marquez hills (Reinhard 2002).[7] The *usnu* of Saguara, a village in the mountains of Camarones, might represent a similar kind of shrine (Schiappacasse and Niemeyer 1989, 2002). These state installations represented an expression of symbolic power (Uribe 2004).

The Royal Inka Road

The Royal Inka road articulated this as part of the imperial infrastructure and the political, economic, and ceremonial activities that fall under the umbrella of state control. Examples of stone-paved roads are identified in sectors close to Inka towns and on the slopes of several valleys in the mountain range, such as Socoroma (figure 3.7), Zapahuira, Murmuntani, Chapiquiña, and Belén (Dauelsberg 1983; Santoro 1983). These examples correspond to the coastal Inka road, which ends in Tacna (southern Peru), but because of the hyperaridity of the coast and the absence of a marine platform farther south, the road deviated to the sierra of Arica, at an altitude between 2,000 and 3,600 meters above sea level (Santoro 1983). The construction and maintenance of this and other secondary roads that connected the highland and the coast were certainly important tasks for the local communities, achieved via the *mit'a* system.

Chronology

Chronologically, Inka control of the sierra and highlands of Arica could be organized as follows. In Camarones, there is an early period of Inka domination associated with Black on Red and Inka Pacaje pottery styles that dates problematically to A.D. 1320–1400 by thermoluminescence methods. This period is followed by a later phase associated with Inka altiplanic pottery styles, like Black on White bowls or Black/Red on White with geometric motifs, as well as animal representations like *suches* and *parinas*, dated to A.D. 1420–1560, uncalibrated radiocarbon dates (Schiappacasse and Niemeyer 1989; table 3.1).

The same sequence is clear both stratigraphically and chronologically in the revised highland sites of Zapahuira, which have yielded a new set of

FIGURE 3.7.
Royal Inka road at
Socoroma. Note
detail of transversal
stones as stepwise
and water evacuation
of the road.

radiocarbon dates. Four radiocarbon dates fall within the range of about
A.D. 1300–1400 (*chullpas* of Zapahuira and the earlier occupations of
Tambo Zapahuira and Tambo Tantalcollo). The later locus is associated
with early Pacaje and Black on Red styles. This period predates the Inka
process of conquest and control of these territories, but reflects possible
contacts with Inka-influenced groups elsewhere. The following phase,
dated from about A.D. 1400 to about 1535–1600, corresponds to the *qollqas*
of the Zapahuira site and the upper dated levels at Tambo Zapahuira, and
represents the period of Inka rule. It is associated with Inka ceramics from
the highlands.

We would like to propose a transitional phase of the early colonial
epoch, one that is still greatly influenced by prehistoric cultural material,
ranging from A.D. 1535 to 1700, as seen in Tambos Tacora, Chungará, and
Hospicio. This phase integrates early colonial pottery and glass fragments,
and Black on Red and Inka altiplanic pottery. We think that while the core
area of the Inka Empire rapidly collapsed after the Spanish Conquest, iso-

TABLE 3.1. Chronological Chart of the Study Region

Chronology	Period	Cultural Phase	Pottery Styles
1550–1700	Colonial	Early Colonial	Not described
1400–1550	Late	Inka	Inka, Saxamar or Inka Pacaje
1300–1400	Late Intermediate	Pre-Inka	Arica (San Miguel, Pocoma, Gentilar), Black on Red (Chilpe, Early Pacaje), and Charcollo

lated provinces like this region maintained the reproduction of certain activities that were accommodated to the colonial demand.

Discussion and Conclusion

Contrary to previous ethnohistorical and archaeological studies, we conclude that the Inka state established direct control over the Western Valleys zone in the South-Central Andes (17 to 18 degrees south), which included specific loci on the coast, in the coastal and mountain valleys, and in some enclaves in the high plateau, above 4,000 meters above sea level. Consequently, we think that the idea that the Inka state had little or no interest in these territories, based on an apparently minimal archaeological presence and the absence of ethnohistorical documents, should be reconsidered. Similar views are held for other Andean regions (Hyslop 1990, 1993; Lynch 1983).

The archaeological data summarized above support the idea of a much deeper involvement of the state, which means that the Inkas did effectively control populations and territories in the Western Valleys (figure 3.1). In a previous paper (Williams et al., in press), we used Luttwak's (1976) and Hassig's (1985) concept of hegemonic and territorial control, applied by D'Altroy (1992) for the Andes, to show the different grades of the state control observed archaeologically in the coastal valleys compared with the highlands, but considered these forms of government as part of a continuum that may or may not have led to full control of the conquered territories (Stanish 1997).

In the coast and lower valleys, the state government was expressed in the form of prestige goods (textiles, pottery, metal objects, and *mullu*) to create an image of a unified government. These gifts were given away in public ceremonies and feasts financed by the state, which helped to impose the new political and economic order and to appoint or support the new leaders (of local origin or brought in from abroad). The stone wall platform of Molle Pampa Este, the *usnus*, the *chullpas*, the *qollqas*, and the *khipus* seem to be good features to demonstrate the regular reproduction of performance linked to state government. Even along the coast, state control was manifest over certain productive fishing enclaves, guano islands, and the coastal silver mine of Huantajaya, located near the Cerro Esmeralda. These features show a complex and heterogeneous state interaction with local coastal spaces and communities. Particularly for the coastal valleys of southern Peru, Covey (2000) recognizes colonial dwellings of *mitmaqkuna* from the altiplano. The Inka installation at the Los Hornos site, north of Tacna in southern Peru, associated with a well-made Inka road linked to marine guano exploitation in the Morro de Sama, is an important enclave of state control. Local fishermen in the Tacahuay and the Ilo-Ites area seem to have remained outside of Inka control (Covey 2000; figure 3.1). On the coast of Iquique, the Cerro Esmeralda shrine (Checura 1977) and the Los Verdes and Punta Patillos sites show elements (pottery and textiles) of Inka morphology (Moragas 1995). The marine guano deposits identified in the seventeenth century by Vázquez de Espinosa between Majes and Iquique (Julien 1985:189; figure 3.1) allow us to suggest that apparently marginal territories were included in the political and economic sphere of the empire. The state presence, however, is reduced to a limited number of goods (textile, wood, and ceramic) and a few traces of architecture (Muñoz 1989; Schiappacasse and Niemeyer 1989). Schiappacasse and Niemeyer (1989) recorded important socioeconomic changes in Camarones during the Inka period: the establishment of new populations in previously uninhabited areas; reusing settlements in high sectors that were connected to already established highland populations (that is, Pachica and Saguara); and the disappearance of iconographic features typical of the Arica culture. Also, a different use of space is recognized on the coast of Arica (Hidalgo and Focacci 1986; Julien 1985:202–203).

The sierra, in contrast, shows important investments in infrastructure to store and administer the local production and related activities, complemented with the installation of symbols of ideological power. At sites such as Zapahuira-Socoroma, the infrastructure for administration and economic management includes *tampus*, *qollqas*, and roads, along with certain ideological backing, represented by the *chullpas*, which may have been linked to the high mountain shrines of the Tarapaca volcano (Reinhard 2002). In the Chapiquiña Belén zone, on the other hand, the state installations at Chajpa annexed pre-Inka settlements, like Ancopachane, which were oriented toward productive activities, with ideological reinforcement (*chullpas*) and high mountain shrines. This phenomenon has been also verified in the higher part of the Camarones Valley farther south (the Saguara and Pachica sites [Schiappacasse and Niemeyer 1989, 2002]).

These scenarios of the Western Valley zone demonstrate the versatility of the Inka state in terms of its ability to adapt its general policies to local conditions, without losing sight of the state's primary interests (Bauer 1996; D'Altroy 1992, 2003; Hyslop 1993; Morris 1995). As other states, the Inka Empire needed a labor force for activities related to its operations, which in these provinces included different forms of agriculture, terraces, and irrigation canal investment (principally in the highlands); textile, dried fish, and guano production; labor for state service in the army; and maintenance of the roads, *tampus*, and *qollqas* (Murra 2002). These activities would have been financed with local production via the state system of redistribution, which implied important reorganization of the local populations' economies and political systems.

Additionally, it was critical for the state to have self-sufficient and peaceful provinces in order to ensure that the different provinces of the empire functioned properly. Consequently, the actual contribution of the desert valleys zone to the macroeconomics system, in terms of production of precious metals or agricultural supplies taken to the central government storage system, may have been minor. However, as the province functioned self-sufficiently at the microeconomic level, it was a guarantee for the operation of a nondeficit macroeconomics imperial system as a whole. Ultimately, the state needed to avoid the possibility that populations outside of the state's control could turn into hostile groups. Such factionalism, depending on the size and ability of the groups to form alliances with other communities, could eventually result in large uprisings against the state or, on a smaller scale, organized attacks on caravans, military posts, or state storage houses. Physical anthropological analyses of osteological human collections from the Azapa and Camarones valleys show no evidence of bone injury caused by interpersonal violence, a common issue among hunters and gatherers and early farmers (Standen and Arriaza 2000; Standen et al. 2005; Uribe 2004). The same peaceful climate is observed in the Puna de Atacama for the Inka period (Torres-Rouff 2005).

Acknowledgments

This study was funded by FONDECYT grant 1030312 and the Centro de Investigaciones del Hombre en el Desierto, Arica, Chile. Verónica I. Williams was supported by the Fundación Antorchas of Argentina, project 4248-45, FONDECYT grants 7040186 and 103031, and the Mecesup project 9903. We would like to thank Francisca Egaña, Daniella Jofré, and the students of the Magíster in Anthropology of Universidad de Tarapacá and Universidad Católica del Norte — Edna Quispe, Gabriel Cantarutti, Danisa Catalán, Rolando Ajata, and Paula Ugalde — for their help in field and lab work at different stages of the project, as well as field assistants Andres Vilca and Anita Flores. Thanks to Carolyn McKenzie, who did the English translation, and Félix Acuto, who read our paper at the symposium. This manuscript has received critical comments at the Seventeenth Annual Meeting of Ethnology at the Museo Nacional de Etnografía y Folklore, La Paz, August 2003, as well as the twelfth Jornadas de Historia Andina, Universidad de Valparaíso, Viña del Mar, November 2004. We are grateful to Sonia Alconini and Michael A. Malpass for inviting us to participate in this volume, and to the two anonymous reviewers for the University of Iowa Press whose comments helped us in improving the quality of this chapter.

Notes

1. Recent studies published in a special issue of *Chungará Revista de Antropología Chilena* 36(2) (2004) show important improvements in Inka archaeology in the Andes.

2. Indirect control has been suggested for southern Peru (Cardona 2003; Gordillo 2000; Trimborn et al. 1975; Vela 2004), the southern highland of Bolivia, the Lipes sector (Arellano 2000), and the northwest region of Argentina (Earle 1994; Nielsen 1996; Otonello and Lorandi 1987; Williams and D'Altroy 1998). In contrast, González (1983) and Raffino (1981) proposed that the Inkas exercised

a system of direct control in northwest Argentina, due to the state interest in exploiting the riches of the mines, just like in the Norte Chico of Chile.

3. The Zapahuira Gentilar archaeological site, as it is currently known by the local inhabitants of this hamlet, is located on a higher pampa about 500 meters to the south of Tambo Zapahuira.

4. Niemeyer (1962) described the Inka Tambo Collacagua, 3,800 meters, for the highlands of Pica. In the highlands of Iquique, Sanhueza (1986) studied Tambo Cariquima, of Inka affiliation. Cora Moragas (personal communication, January 2005) has identified Tambo Corralones in the Tarapacá ravine.

5. The site has been altered in recent years, due to its use as a temporary camp-site for various workers.

6. Other Inka nodes are located in the Camarones Valley with two important sites, Pachica and Saguara, and in the Codpa Valley with several sites from the Late Intermediate and Late periods, including Cachicoca, Molle Grande 1 and 2, and Incauta, and another one in the highlands.

7. In the highlands of Iquique, Sanhueza (1986) has identified other shrines in the mountains of Tata Jachura, Jatamalla or Mama Wanapa and Cawari. North of Isluga in the Salar de Surire we have inventoried several archaeological sites, a few of them associated with the Inka Empire: Paquisa, Caracota, and Surire 1.

Sonia Alconini

Chapter Four

Yampara Households and Communal Evolution in the Southeastern Inka Peripheries

Editors' Introduction

This chapter presents relevant data to understand the interaction of the Inka Empire with Yampara elites, in a region facing the southeastern Inka frontier. This region, according to colonial narratives, was part of the Inka frontier that witnessed the advances of Chiriguano-Guaraní groups entering from the southeastern tropical piedmonts and Chaco. In this context of Inka imperial and Chiriguano-Guaraní encroachment, the author explores the shifting power relations of Yampara elites vis-à-vis their conquerors. Based on excavations in Yoroma, a local center of the region, Alconini finds important changes associated with the arrival of the Inkas. Prior to the Inkas, Yoroma was a large elite settlement involved with the production of flake artifacts at a communal scale and focused on feasting and redistribution. With the Inkas, Yoroma not only increased in size, but also the elite maintained their status and wealth, as seen in the enlargement of their residences and a modest access to Inka imperial materials. In addition, the site intensified the manufacture of lithic tools, and feasting activities also expanded in public spaces. This aspect is striking, taking into account the proximity of two imperial installations of the region,

Inkarry Moqo and Oroncota. Despite the fine architecture at both facilities, these imperial centers did not become the focus of craft production, redistribution of prestige imperial materials, or population attraction. Instead, the flaking industry in Yoroma, perhaps including weaponry for the eastern fortifications, was a task organized and supervised by the local chieftains. Therefore, in a context of increased conflict in the southern frontiers, the data suggest that Yampara lords were not only important imperial allies but also that they were successful in maintaining their autonomy and status.

The imperial politics in this region echo some of the policies seen in other regions discussed in this volume. Architecturally, the fine Inka architecture in Oroncota resembles that of La Casa Morada, in Guitián, northwestern Argentina, discussed by Acuto in chapter 5. So far, both Inka sites are unique in the southern Andes for their fine architectural elaboration, typical of prestigious constructions of the imperial core. However, the dynamics of local elites show different trajectories. In Yoroma, although the elites maintained their autonomy and leadership in lithic industries, they did not enjoy substantial access to imperial materials. In comparison, the local residents of Guitián saw the insertion of imperial facilities in their own settlement such as the construction of La Casa Morada, important changes in their economy, and the insertion of high-ranking imperial officials, in addition to a significant influx of Inka prestige materials. Comparing both cases, we might argue that the elite in Yoroma were more astute in the kinds of alliances that they established with the empire, although this did not necessarily translate into privileged access to prestige imperial materials. Overall, the kind of work presented in this chapter exemplifies the advantages of studying the Inka phenomenon from a bottom-up perspective. Hopefully, future research at the household and communal scales will continue exploring the kinds of changes that the Inkas generated in elite and commoner economies in the various provinces of the southern Andes.

Introduction

Recent studies focusing on the effects of the Inka Empire in the incorporated provinces have revealed the wide array of strategies of domination used by this empire, tailored to respond to specific local sociopolitical and historical conditions (Costin and Earle 1989; D'Altroy 1992; Malpass 1993; Schreiber 1992; Stanish 2001b). These studies have also revealed the multistranded effects of the empire and the various responses of native leaders and populations to imperial conquest and colonization, ranging from open resistance to opportunistic alliances.

These different forms of local response to imperial expansion were intensified in contexts of imperial frontier interaction. In most cases, the Inka imperial frontier, often established in ecological interfaces that overlapped with cultural boundaries, had varying effects on the local politics and dynamics of the regions. As explained in ethnohistorical accounts, some of these frontier regions were already part of marked internal conflicts by local competing ethnicities who saw the arrival of the Inkas as avenues to advance individual agendas by establishing alliances with the empire. Such was the case of the competing Chiriguano and lowland groups in the southeastern Inka frontier, or the Tucumán and Lules in the southern frontier, now in Argentina (Alcaya[ga] 1961; Lorandi 1988; Pärssinen and Siiriäinen 1998). In other cases, fluid interregional contact was often blocked by the Inkas in order to monopolize the exchange of valued raw materials beyond the borders, by delegating to selected ethnicities the control of such exchange networks. For example, this was the situation of the Yunga Kallawaya groups and the Chuncho groups in the eastern frontier (Meyers 2002). In either case, Inka arrival reshaped the mosaic of local political interactions. Whereas in some circumstances it exacerbated competition among local peer polities, in others it favored the formation of interethnic alliances under the imperial umbrella. Still in other instances, imperial intrusion contributed to the forging of local alliances against the Inkas.

My recent research has revealed that the southeastern Inka frontier — intended to defend the imperial territories against the intermittent invasions of the recalcitrant Chiriguano-Guaraní groups — took the form of a soft military perimeter rather than a line of defensive installations. Instead of true garrisons, these defensive facilities were used as distant warning points placed at strategic nodes of communication, occupied in times of conflict (Alconini 2002, 2004).

Behind this defensive front, the Inkas established in the Oroncota region a small administrative center. Despite its small size, Oroncota was built with fine Inka architecture usually found in high-prestige buildings of the imperial core (Julien 1995; Walter 1959). As discussed in earlier publications, the presence of fine architecture did not generate substantial effects on the local socioeconomy (Alconini 2004, 2005). This is evident in the reduced storage capabilities of the Inka facilities in the Oroncota region, in the continuities in the existing settlement patterns, and in the near absence of a prestige-goods economy based on imperial valuables. Because of these peculiarities, I defined Oroncota as a disembedded center, as a midpoint in the spectrum of territorial-hegemonic forms of control (Alconini 2008a).

In a historical context, the Oroncota region is described as part of the southeastern limits of the Yampara territory in the southeastern Bolivian valleys of Chuquisaca (Barragán Romano 1994:63, 75). It is possible that, prior to the Inkas, Oroncota was part of an earlier confederation of Chicha-Chuy groups, although this topic is still being debated (Pärssinen and Siiriäinen 2003:203–207). In any case, by the time of the Inkas, Oroncota and the nearby valleys were inhabited by the Yampara, along with other *mitmaq* colonies, including the Churumata and Moyo Moyos from Tarija and Cochabamba (Barragán Romano 1994:97, 114). Specifically, Oroncota was part of Hatun Yampara, located in the southern and eastern portion of Chuquisaca, and possibly part of the Ayllu Yamparaez Hanansaya Guaracha (Julien 1995:106–108).

One important aspect is that with the increasing eastern Chiriguano-Guaraní invasions, the Yampara established an alliance with the Inkas, as illustrated in a pact with Francisco Aymoro, a Yampara chief under Huayna Capac's reign (AGI, Charcas 44ff. 151v, cited in Julien 1995:105; Barragán Romano 1994:58; Platt 1999:104).

Based on such alliances, the Yamparas not only benefited from imperial protection but also were part of the mobilization of large contingents of military *mitmaqkuna* aimed at protecting the imperial borders. Therefore, an aspect that I explore in this chapter is the effect of the imperial conquest on the communal- and household-level political economies. If the alliances that the native chiefs established with the Inka Empire were mutually advantageous, with the Yamparas benefiting from imperial protection against the constant attacks and intrusion of the belligerent Chiriguano-Guaranís and the Inkas targeting this region as worthy of investing in the construction of fine architecture rarely found in the peripheries, then how was this interaction between elites crystallized at a microlevel?

Along the spectrum of interactions between local elites and the Inka Empire, ranging from openly cooperative and mutually beneficial to a rather vertical and unequal incorporation into the imperial political hierarchy, one goal of this research is to illuminate the interactional nature of local Yampara leaders with the Inka Empire. On the one hand, we have archaeological documentation that in some regions such as Mantaro, local elites were lessened in status, and Inka control was manifest in the monopoly of long-distance trade networks, imperial appropriation of feasting and redistributive activities once in the hands of native elites, and insertion of a prestige-goods economy based on imperial materials, in addition to leveling mechanisms between elites and commoners in terms of access to valuable materials, food, and storage capabilities (Costin 2001; Costin and Earle 1989).

On the other hand, we know that in other regions such as the Calchaquí territory, marked by a politically fragmented landscape, local leaders benefited differently from such interaction. While most of the populations saw Inka domination as a distant phenomenon affecting their lives, local elites advanced individual agendas differently, as the empire selectively controlled specific aspects of the local economy and settlement areas (D'Altroy et al. 2000; Demarrais 1997). Even though the sponsorship of feasting capabilities remained localized, there was no significant insertion of imperial materials into the region, while existing trade networks and craft industries continued (Gifford 2003). There is also evidence that the empire selectively incorporated sacred spaces into Inka control while promoting the Inkanization of local chieftains (Acuto 2004). In the context of competition, native leaders also emulated and copied Inka cultural materials and architecture to enhance their own status (Gifford 2003).

Distance from the imperial core alone cannot account for the wide range of interaction variations among local elites and the Inka Empire as seen in other regions. Each case constituted a unique challenge to the Inka Empire, which was seeking to maximize access to labor and valuable resources while minimizing conflict and political instability.

Comparing these different local elite and Inka Empire interaction scenarios, my goal in this chapter is to understand the effects of the empire at the communal and household levels and in the local leadership strategies by studying Yoroma, a local center in the Oroncota region. Specifically, I want to know whether local Yampara elites sought to advance their own privileged position in the community through alliances with the Inka Empire, or if this alliance involved their status being lessened in the local political and economic arenas. I also seek to understand the evolution of Yoroma in order to evaluate the changes in the communal economy on a temporal scale. The research questions that guided my investigation were: Did the Inkas affect existing status and wealth relations in the Yoroma settlement? What kinds of activities took place in the different architectural areas of the settlement? How did the activities differ across time? Did the Inkas promote shifts in craft production activities at communal and household levels? Answering these questions called for mapping and recording the spatial distribution of architecture and functional areas in Yoroma; conducting surface collections to document intensity and distribution of artifactual assemblages (ceramics, lithics, worked bones) in the different architectural/activity areas of the settlement; and excavating the different architectural/activity areas to document shifts in the residential patterns, activities, and artifact assemblages over time.

In 2003, my research team and I excavated the site of Yoroma (s-289), one of the largest Yampara centers (15 hectares) in the Oroncota region. Twenty-two units, each 2 by 2 meters, were excavated in the different architectural areas, exposing a total of 88 square meters of the entire Yoroma settlement, until sterile soil was reached. The site is located on top of a mound with access to agricultural areas on the valley floor. To the north runs the Inkapampa River, to the east the Pilcomayo River, and to the south extends the great Pucara mesa rising up about 1,000 meters above the valley (figure 4.1). Judging by its location, the inhabitants of Yoroma enjoyed access to fertile soil for agriculture, while also having access to riverine resources. The site still preserves architectural remains built with local rough stone. Far above my initial expectations, my excavations revealed that the settlement had a long history of occupation dating back to the Early Yampara period (A.D. 400–800), followed by the Classic Yampara (A.D. 800–1300) and Yampara-Inka periods (A.D. 1300–1536) after the arrival of the Inkas. As I have explained elsewhere, these periods are defined on a regional chronology based on the distribution of ceramic assemblages (Alconini 2008b).

This chapter is divided into three main sections. In the first part, I discuss the architectural layout, cultural contexts, and spatial distribution of cultural assemblages in each cultural period. In the second, I highlight the most significant changes in the local lithic production and feasting activi-

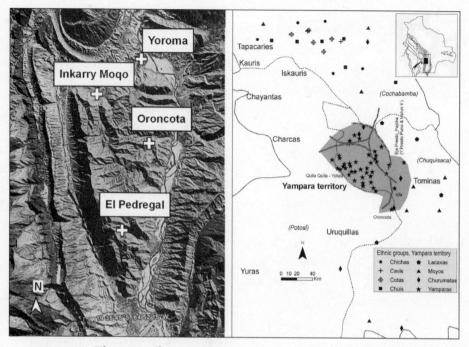

FIGURE 4.1. The center of Yoroma in the Yampara territory, Oroncota, Bolivia. Map based on Barragán Romano 1994 and Ibarra Grasso 1944.

ties in order to illuminate the changes in the elite leadership and economic strategies before and after the Inkas. In the conclusion, I summarize my findings in light of the research questions.

Architectural Layout, Archaeological Context, and Cultural Assemblages

EARLY YAMPARA PERIOD (A.D. 400–800)

During the Early Yampara period, occupation in the Yoroma site was dispersed and scattered. Judging by the artifacts' temporal associations, this occupation took place at the end of the Early Yampara and beginning of the Classic Yampara periods. Excavations revealed two main areas of occupation lying over the sterile soil. The first was focused on the southern segment of the site associated with a funerary and trash area. The second lay in the northern area of the site with evidence of domestic occupation.

Southern Area. In the southern area, a dense layer of trash on top of the sterile soil was identified with no associated architectural features. The remains had a significant density of utilitarian and decorated pottery along with fragmented bones. The dominant component was undecorated serving vessels, followed by decorated serving wares in the Early Yampara and Classic Yampara styles. Imported pottery from the nearby valleys was nearly absent and was restricted to a few Huruquilla-style sherds. Because Early and Classic Yampara styles were both found in association, it is very likely that this occupation was related to a transitional episode between the Early Yampara and Classic Yampara periods.

Despite the relative density of pottery remains in the trash area, the frequency of lithic debris, which included a quartz core and a polisher, was minimal. Taking into consideration the dominance of utilitarian serving vessels and the near absence of lithic remains in the trash, I suggest that their accumulation was due to food consumption activities in an open space.

We identified a group of funerary urns nearby to the east. In the following periods, this area became the focus of intense religious activities and rituals. These funerary urns lacked associated architecture and lay on sterile soil. Although we do not know whether the burials had initial primary depositions, my excavations revealed that the urns held the remains of multiple secondary burials along with Early Yampara pottery. Four funerary urns were identified, holding the remains of partially articulated bones of various individuals, mostly adults. The paraphernalia in the funerary urns included three decorated vessels in the Early Yampara style, including a jar and two bowls. In addition, imported Huruquilla pottery from the neighboring southern valleys was found, suggesting early interregional connections with this region.

Taking into account the proximity of the funerary space to the trash area, I argue that both activities were not just contemporaneous but also part of a broader set of interrelated activities. Both the funerary rituals and public consumption activities might have been part of an emerging cult to the ancestors in the Yoroma settlement.

Northern Area. In the northern part of the settlement, evidence of domestic occupation was found in this early period. We found the remains of an early circular structure on top of the sterile soil. Inside the structure, a compact occupational floor was evident with a complete Early Yampara vessel placed in a horizontal position, a semicircular stone ax, and dispersed sherds. An ash pit was also found, perhaps the remains of a hearth. After the disuse and abandonment of the construction, a light occupation matrix covered the entire area in the following Classic Yampara period, suggesting its abandonment.

CLASSIC YAMPARA PERIOD (A.D. 800–1300)

Before the Inkas arrived during the Classic Yampara period, occupation continued in the northern and southern parts of the settlement, with minimal evidence of residence in the central portion of the site (figure 4.2). During this period, marked changes are observed in the settlement structure, including an expansion of the residential areas and the formation of two extensive trash mounds in the vicinity. Overall, the domestic compounds were formed by a number of circular constructions (about 3–4 meters in diameter) distributed around open patios. These and other structures were built using local rough stones. As will be explained in the next section, architectural and interassemblage comparisons of the domestic compounds did not reveal significant variations in the cultural materials in terms of status and valuable materials, or in the range and intensity of craft production activities that would suggest an elite sector markedly different from the sectors where other Yoroma residents lived.

Northern Area. In the northern ridge of the settlement directly facing the valley floor, a residential compound was found, formed by a cluster of three circular rough-stone structures (figure 4.2). The bad preservation and high levels of erosion prevented extensive excavations. Our excavation efforts focused on a circular construction with evidence of domestic use (Structure 3). In the occupational matrix, a hearth was found, and below it cutting into the floor the remnants of an infant buried in an undecorated funerary urn were discovered. Few preserved bones were deposited in the urn, which was filled with fine sand and sealed with a flat stone serving as a lid. Funerary urns with lids are commonly found in the Bolivian southeastern valley polities and those in northwest Argentina (Acuto 2000; Howard and Willey 1948). The ceramics associated with this occupation level were mostly utilitarian vessels for storage and cooking activities, with a slightly higher proportion of serving vessels in comparison to other areas. The lithic remains were minimal.

To the west of the compound, an occupational matrix was found with no associated architecture, in a space where an earlier domestic structure

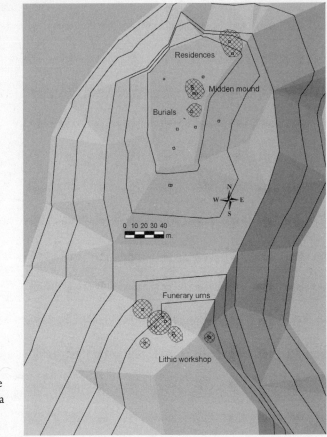

FIGURE 4.2.
Yoroma settle-
ment during the
Classic Yampara
period, A.D.
800–1300.

was built in the previous period. The few remains had a dominance of utilitarian storage vessels. The absence of architecture in this period might suggest the spatial reaccommodation of the domestic architecture into new areas of the site.

Near the center of the settlement, a large refuse mound was formed as a result of the continuous deposition of trash. This midden (about 16 square meters and 1 meter high) contained large amounts of broken pottery along with white quartz flakes, charcoal, and bone fragments, including fish from the Pilcomayo River.

The dominant remains included broken utilitarian storage vessels of all sizes. The serving vessels comprised a variety of decorated cups, small jars, bowls, and tazones in the local Yampara and imported styles (figure 4.3). A considerable number of lithic remains from a knapping technology, in-

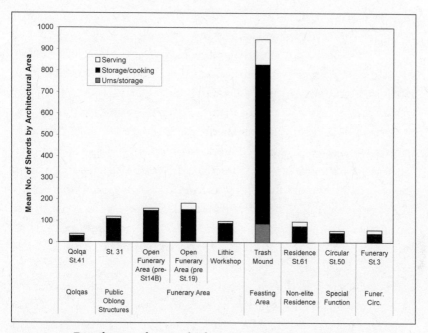

FIGURE 4.3. Distribution of pottery by function in the Yoroma settlement, Yampara Classic period.

cluding quartz cores and flakes in different stages of reduction, were also present.

Overall, the considerably higher density of broken pottery in this area in comparison to other areas of the settlement (figure 4.3) suggests that the discarding of storage and serving vessels was continuous and intense and, most likely, the product of food consumption activities in an open and public space. These activities were tied to the processing of lithic tools on a relatively large scale.

Southern Area. Excavations revealed that the southern part of the settlement also had a consistent occupation during this period. In this area, a concentration of stone circular structures was identified (figure 4.2). Excavation in some of these circular structures revealed a domestic use, while others had more specialized functions. Because of the clustered concentration of these structures and the absence of extensive excavations, it was difficult to establish with accuracy the layout and composition of individual residential compounds.

Excavation of Structure 50, a small circular room, evidenced a cultural matrix associated with the remains of an offering cache. This offering was formed by two grinding stones and a chopper, all carefully covered with a layer of ash. As in similar circular structures, there was a concentration of cultural remains, mostly utilitarian storage and broken cooking pots, along with a minor percentage of serving vessels. The few lithics included quartz flakes.

Excavation of a second circular structure (Structure 41) revealed the construction of a well-prepared orange clay floor and a light cultural matrix with scattered artifactual remains. Although restricted in quantity, the dominant pottery sherds included utilitarian and cooking vessels. Most of the serving vessels were decorated. Because of the construction investment of the clay floor, along with a near absence of cultural remains, this room might represent the rise of special-purpose structures in this period.

To the southeast, the excavations revealed an open mortuary space, as a group of partially dismembered secondary burials placed directly in the sterile soil was uncovered (figure 4.2). The partially articulated bones (including the pelvis, femur, and vertebral column) belonged to two adult individuals, deposited directly in a pit and then covered with ash. On top, a layer of sherds from a utilitarian vessel was found, perhaps part of the funerary paraphernalia. The rest of the remains belonged to utilitarian jars for storage, with a minimum amount of decorated pottery.

East of the cluster of circular rooms rested a group of elaborate funerary urns from the earlier period, still in use in the Classic Yampara period (figure 4.2). Judging by the intentional selection of a large number of teeth and incisors, along with poorly preserved bone fragments, some of these funerary urns held the remains of various individuals who had been deliberately reburied together. The first urn contained the remains of at least three individuals (as seen by the number of teeth and incisors) and included three utilitarian and two decorated vessels (bowl and jar) in the imported Huruquilla style. The second urn lacked human remains, but held two complete vessels, including a jar and a bowl, in the Early Yampara style. The third urn kept the remains of a handful of teeth, molars, and bone fragments, and two ceramic vessels consisting of an Early Yampara bowl and a Yura jar from nearby valleys (figure 4.4). The fourth urn held the remains of a flexed infant about two to four years old. This primary burial contained a decorated Huruquilla vessel with white slip

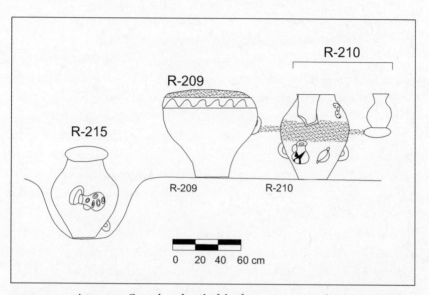

FIGURE 4.4. Ancestors Complex: detail of the funerary urns in the Yoroma settlement (Structure 19).

and a painted bowl combining the Huruquilla and Oroncota White Ware styles as part of the funerary paraphernalia.

Judging by the careful organization of selected human remains in collective funerary urns, including mortuary paraphernalia from the Early Yampara period, these burials — assembled during the earlier period but reorganized and amplified in the Classic Yampara — represent a strong cult to the ancestors evolving in the Yampara society. Despite the remains being rearranged periodically, Yoroma residents were scrupulous in keeping them together rather than spatially separating them, perhaps because they belonged to the same kin group.

This evolving tradition to the ancestors emphasized the use of decorated pottery from the previous Early Yampara period, probably in order to enforce an ideology of antiquity and tradition. Imported vessels from nearby valley polities, including the gray Huruquilla and orange Yura styles, might also have contributed to enhancing the prestige of the deceased individuals, or simply these imported materials were effective in conveying regional ideologies and symbols.

Southeast of the mortuary urn complex, a dense concentration of lithic and pottery remains in an open space started forming in this period (figure 4.2). In comparison to other areas of the settlement, the density of lithic remains, mostly quartz cores and flakes in different stages of reduction, is significant in suggesting that this open space might have been used as a lithic workshop. The absence of finished projectile points (except a few failed samples from the surface) also seems to indicate that after being produced, these artifacts were exported and moved somewhere else for further use. A second possibility is that Yoroma specialized in the collection and production of quartz flakes to be moved to other settlements of the Yampara network for further finishing. Whatever the case, it becomes clear that Yoroma in the Classic Yampara was an important settlement for the procurement and production of quartz materials at a scale beyond the domestic needs.

During this period, a concentration of broken pottery is also evident in the midden. Most of the remains (about 82 percent) belonged to utilitarian storage vessels of all sizes, with a small proportion of decorated and undecorated serving vessels. In comparison to the midden found in the central part of the settlement, there was a similar proportion of serving vessels relative to storage jars (about 10 to 80 percent, respectively) (figure 4.3). The absence of grinding stones or storage structures in the vicinity, including the fact that both middens were in open areas, seems to indicate that rather than being the remains of domestic food processing and storage, both trash areas were the product of large-scale food consumption activities in an open space. Overall, the ratio of serving vessels to storage containers in both midden areas roughly matches the ratio found in feasting activities in the later Inka Oroncota building complex in the region.

Therefore, the combination of specialized lithic production and public food consumption was part of a broader cycle of production-consumption in Yoroma beyond the domestic level, and part of the broader economic strategies used by emerging elites. Taking into account that these activities took place behind a ritual space dedicated to the ancestors, the sponsorship of production and consumption in a religious context was essential in the elite politics aimed at legitimizing the extraction of labor and surplus.

Farther east in the peripheries of the settlement were two medium-size oblong structures, perhaps part of a domestic compound (figure 4.2). Excavations of one room (Structure 61) revealed a light cultural matrix and ash scatters. The remains included a moderate concentration of materials with a dominance of utilitarian pottery, mostly from serving and cooking vessels. However, the proportion of serving vessels was significant in comparison to other areas, and most of them were decorated wares in a variety of local Yampara styles. The lithic remains were minimal.

In synthesis, occupation in the Yoroma settlement during the Classic Yampara period was characterized by five main activities: a domestic occupation represented by hearths and moderate occupational levels; the celebration of consumption activities beyond the domestic scale evidenced by the formation of refuse in the northern and southern segments; funerary practices in the form of burials directly deposited in the soil matrix with no associated paraphernalia, perhaps as markers of low social status; funerary practices related to a strong cult to the ancestors manifested in the continuous redeposition of selected remains in large funerary urns, along with imported and early-affiliated pottery as ritual paraphernalia; and specialized lithic production in the workshop accompanied by public food consumption as part of a broader cycle of labor extraction and reciprocity sponsored by local elites.

YAMPARA-INKA PERIOD (A.D. 1300–1536)

In the Yampara-Inka period, the Yoroma settlement grew in size and complexity as seen in the increase of domestic and public architecture and in the amplification of the earlier range of activities (figure 4.5).

Northern Area. The northern ridge, overlooking the cultivatable area, was the focus of increased domestic residences. In this area, we found the remains of a group of small circular stone structures (n = 5) located on a terraced platform (figure 4.5). Excavations suggested that the circular structures were all part of a residential complex. Two of the five constructions were excavated based on best preservation. Structure 35 was a circular room used as a domestic space. In the occupational surface, remains of a hearth, a grinding stone, two mortars, and a utilitarian bowl lying on the surface were found. The few ceramic remains associated with this cultural level were undecorated and belonged to utilitarian cooking and serving vessels, with a dominance of storage jars. Judging by the emphasis on cooking utensils and the hearth, this structure might have been used as a kitchen area.

Nearby, excavation of Structure 3 (figure 4.5), also used in the earlier period, revealed a specialized use. Two episodes of use were identified in this period. In the earlier episode, a compact yellow clay floor was built,

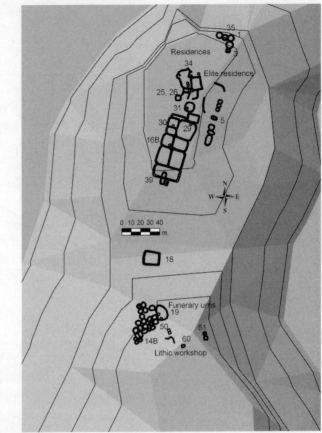

FIGURE 4.5.
Yoroma settle-
ment during the
Late Yampara-
Inka period,
A.D. 1300–1536.

suggesting the renovation of the room. In the cultural matrix, a decorated funerary urn in the Yampara Presto-Puno style, containing the remains of an infant, was found. The urn was sealed with a flat stone as a lid, enclosing the few preserved bones in a sand matrix. The urn was deposited in a pit, with a roughly paved base covered with ash. The mortuary offering included a grinding stone, and below, five complete terrestrial shells were carefully buried.

In the later episode, this structure was the repository of an elaborate ritual offering, including a large utilitarian vessel containing a decorated Yampara bowl (Simple Yampara style) and a utilitarian jar. On the base were the remains of a grinding stone, ash lenses, and 77 finely elaborated shell beads.

The few pottery fragments associated with this occupational level displayed a dominance of serving vessels (60 percent), mostly decorated wares in the local Yampara styles. Therefore, I argue that in this period, this room in the residential compound shifted to specialized functions, as seen in the renovation of its yellow clay floor and use as a funerary repository. As in earlier residences, few white quartz flakes were found in both excavated rooms, suggesting minimum lithic production at a domestic level.

Overall, these findings suggest that a typical Yampara residence would still conform to a cluster of circular structures, formed by a kitchen and special-purpose rooms, including a funerary repository. Even though there is evidence of increased access to prestige materials, such as the complete terrestrial shells and finely elaborated shell beads, the architecture and composition of the household compound remained about the same. A clear shift, however, is the addition of more circular rooms to the household compound, perhaps to compartmentalize different activities or as a response to an increase in household size. The fact that this residential compound enjoyed access to prestige materials, mostly in the form of mortuary paraphernalia, might also be evidence to suggest the increased status of its inhabitants.

Nearby in the northeastern steep slopes of the site, a small group of circular and oval stone structures (n = 7) were still preserved following a linear configuration (figure 4.5). Judging by their marginal location, cluster pattern in steep terrain, and the excavation results, these structures had nondomestic functions, and most likely were *qollqas*. For example, the excavation of Structure 5 revealed a slight occupational matrix, two quartz flakes, and a few sherds from utilitarian storage vessels. It is possible that the construction of *qollqas* in this period was related to Inka conquest as a response to increased storage activities being inserted into the communal economy. Architecturally, the *qollqas* in Yoroma are similar in size and composition to other storage units found in Inka and local settlements of the region, although on a smaller scale (Alconini 2002, 2004).

Central Area. In the central part of the settlement, a group of large oblong stone structures of roughly 12 by 12 meters was built. These structures had a cellular pattern as all shared walls (figure 4.5). Three structures were excavated — Structures 29, 30, and 16B — revealing similar results. All of them were large constructions with a single episode of use, light occupation matrix, and few associated features.

In Structure 16B, a sheet star copper bell, a bone artifact, and a few sherds from undecorated storage vessels were found in the cultural matrix. Systematic surface collections also revealed that Structure 38, a large oblong room next to it, held the remains of two grinding stones on the surface, suggesting grain-processing activities. Structures 29 and 30 both had a few sherds from utilitarian storage jars and serving vessels. The few lithic remains in both structures included quartz flakes, while in Structure 16B they were absent.

We also excavated a small oval room (Structure 16A) attached to a large oblong structure. The cultural level held a well-prepared stone hearth and a relatively low distribution of cultural remains. In this room, the proportion of undecorated serving vessels was significantly higher in comparison to other areas, suggesting an emphasis on consumption activities. This evidence suggests that this small room might have been a support facility for the activities taking place in the nearby large building.

In none of the large oblong structures did we find an earlier level of occupation, suggesting that this central part of the settlement was not inhabited before this period. Judging by the large dimensions of these oblong structures, light cultural matrix, and absence of domestic features, I argue that they had public functions, perhaps associated with the new range of activities taking place beyond the domestic scale in the settlement. The fact that these large structures were built next to each other in the central area of the settlement might also suggest an effort to compartmentalize the range of public activities, perhaps taking place simultaneously. Among others, these activities included grain processing.

Structure 31 was an isolated circular structure of relatively large dimensions (about 7 meters in diameter) built during this period in an area with earlier occupation during the Classic Yampara and Early Yampara periods. This structure held the remains of an intrusive primary burial placed in a flexed position and deposited directly in a pit with no associated paraphernalia. The occupational level revealed no other cultural features. The associated remains came from undecorated storage and cooking vessels, a few serving vessels, and a couple of quartz flakes. Although the function and type of activities that took place within the structure are not clear, they might not have lasted for a long time. At abandonment, the structure was primarily used as a funerary space.

Elite Residences. In the central part of the settlement, an enclosed residential compound was built (figure 4.5). This compound was formed by three medium-size oblong structures aligned on top of an artificial platform built with stone retaining walls, and two large enclosed patios below. The refuse mound accumulated in the previous Classic Yampara period served as the foundation of the terraced platform. Excavations in two of the rooms of the upper platform (Structures 25 and 26) revealed that they were used by local elites, judging by their architecture and preferential access to Inka prestige materials.

In one of the rooms (Structure 25), we identified in the occupational level the remains of a duck head Inka bowl and a sheet star copper bell used as a prestige local marker. Both items had high local value, underscoring the status of the inhabitants. The cultural matrix revealed a relatively high concentration of pottery remains in comparison to other areas, with a dominance of utilitarian storage and cooking vessels. The serving vessels were mostly decorated in a variety of local Yampara styles (Classic Yampara and Oroncota White Ware variants). The relatively high concentration of lithic remains in comparison to other areas, mostly quartz cores and flakes in different stages of reduction, suggests that its inhabitants were involved in the production of lithic tools.

In the second room we identified a hearth pit filled with ash in the occupational level. A collar of stones defined its margins, perhaps as support for the cooking pots. At the base of the pit a copper *tupu* pin of Inka affiliation was identified. The cultural matrix also included a relatively high concentration of pottery sherds, with a clear presence of utilitarian storage and cooking vessels. The serving vessels were minimal, with half of them being decorated in the local Yampara style, in addition to imported Huruquilla wares. No lithic remains were found, with the exception of a single white quartz flake.

Taking into account the scarcity of Inka materials in the entire Oroncota region and vicinity, this evidence suggests that the residents of this Yoroma compound enjoyed high status as seen by the preferential, although limited, access to Inka imperial goods along with local prestige valuables. It is known that copper *tupu* pins were used by women of Inka origins, or given as gifts by the empire to cement vertical alliances.

Excavation of one of the enclosures in the residential complex (Structure 34) revealed the formation of an extensive midden. The fact that this enclosed patio was built on top of an earlier refuse mound left over from large-scale food consumption suggests that the range of earlier activities continued, although in a new architectural setting.

The midden in the patio contained a dense concentration of ceramics and bone fragments from camelids, fish, terrestrial mollusks (Hydrobidae and Bulimidae), ducks, small canids, and cavids (Capriles et al. 2008). In the pottery assemblage there was an emphasis on utilitarian storage vessels of different sizes, while the proportion of serving vessels was relatively high in comparison to other areas of the site (figure 4.6). The serving vessels were mostly decorated, belonging to a variety of styles including local Yampara (Classic Yampara, Simple Yampara, Oroncota White Ware) along with imported pottery (Huruquilla and Yura wares). In the trash, a relatively high concentration of quartz cores and flakes in different stages of reduction was found.

The enclosed patio had an attached structure used as a kitchen area judging by the dense concentration of ash remains. In this construction there was a moderate concentration of sherds, with a clear dominance of utilitarian cooking and storage vessels. The few serving vessels were mostly undecorated forms, while there was an absence of lithic production remains.

Judging by the dense concentration of trash in the enclosed patio of the residence, I argue that these remains were the product of large-scale food preparation and consumption beyond the domestic needs, and that they were related to feasting. The fact that the trash remains continued after the construction of the enclosed patios in the elite residential compound suggests that these activities persisted, although sponsored at a private level by emerging elites. The importance of this area as a space dedicated to public consumption and feasting in the previous Classic Yampara period might have attracted emerging local elites as a deliberate effort to appropriate a symbolic space while continuing to sponsor consumption feasts in their own patio residences. Interestingly, feasting was associated with a moderate production of lithic tools using quartz as raw material, suggesting that both production and consumption activities sponsored by local leaders were not compartmentalized, but rather complementary tasks.

The local residents of this elite residential compound maintained strong ties with the Inka Empire. These alliances were crystallized by preferential access to imperial prestige goods and, more indirectly, in the shift of the residential layout. Rather than being formed by a cluster of circular

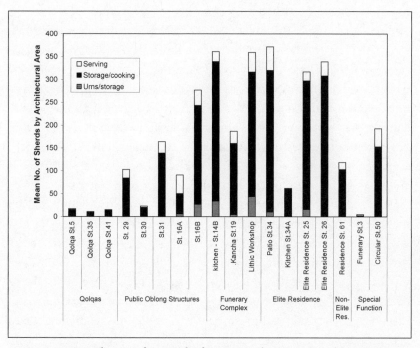

FIGURE 4.6. Distribution of pottery by function in the Yoroma settlement, Late Yampara-Inka period.

structures around an open patio, as other compounds, the elite residence was built in a terraced platform including an enclosed patio and a group of rectangular-oblong rooms of relatively large dimensions, perhaps emulating Inka residences. The fact that the elite residents of this compound sponsored consumption celebrations and lithic production also suggests the consolidation of their power by attracting followers and labor beyond the domestic household sphere.

Southern Area. To the south of the Yoroma settlement, concentration of the tightly clustered small circular stone structures increased. Although most of these structures have been destroyed by erosion, a few are still preserved. As can be seen in figure 4.5, most of these circular constructions had an average diameter of 3 meters. Two of these structures were excavated based on best preservation. Structure 41 was a *qollqa*, where excavation revealed a light cultural matrix formed by ash scatters, a few ceramic sherds, and a stone polisher in pink quartz. The few sherds all belonged to utilitarian storage vessels in different sizes, while there was an absence of decorated serving wares.

The second circular structure excavated was Structure 50. This structure, constructed in the earlier period, revealed a special use. A well-elaborated ritual cache was found in the cultural matrix, suggesting that at some point in the sequence, the structure shifted in function to an offering repository. The offering cache consisted of six sheet star copper bells carefully deposited in three pairs facing each other (figure 4.7). Inside each pair of bells a small ringer was found (either in the form of a cone, cylinder, or button), suggesting that when shaken, each pair of bells produced a specific set of sounds. Because of the clear association of pairs of bells and ringers, they were probably used as musical instruments (Gudemos 1998:111–146). A beautifully polished fine black stone (perhaps basalt) in the form of a corn kernel was also part of the ritual cache (figure 4.7).[1] It is widely documented that small stone statues (*conopas*) resembling cultigens such as corn or potatoes were used as household idols to promote production and agricultural fertility (Arriaga 1999). These objects were the subjects of periodic rituals in order to induce rain and good agricultural cycles. The ritual cache also included a stone polisher manufactured in black basalt,[2] a complete terrestrial shell (*churito*), a lithic bead with two holes, and a stone ax (figure 4.7). This offering was carefully deposited in a bed of gravel deliberately built for such purpose. Taking into account the scarcity of basalt stones in the region, their access might have been restricted and part of long-distance trade networks, indicating their value as prestige and esoteric objects. If we take into consideration the absence of Inka-related materials in the ritual cache, this offering served to channel a local religious ideology rather than being influenced by imperial principles.

Southeast of the cluster of circular constructions we excavated Structure 14B, built on top of the earlier cemetery (figure 4.5). This stone circular room evidenced the careful construction of an orange clay floor. In the cultural matrix, a relatively high concentration of large pieces of vegetal charcoal was found, along with a significant number of burned corncobs and kernels. A hearth pit filled with ash also held the remains of discarded pottery and corn kernels. In some parts of the structure, concentrations of large vessel remains for storage and food processing were found. Some of the bases were laid in situ on perfectly horizontal positions on the floor, suggesting that large storage containers were implanted into the floor.

FIGURE 4.7. Detail of an offering cache with six sheet star copper bells (Structure 50, Late Yampara-Inka period).

This structure was not part of a domestic complex, judging by the relative abundance of storage containers, ash, and corncobs. Taking into account the nature and intensity of the cultural remains, this kitchen room was used for large-scale cooking, preparing, and storing food. In addition, the well-prepared orange clay floor, also present in nearby public structures, suggests that this room was part of a broader architectural complex dedicated to the ancestors (see below) and that large-scale food preparation took place there.

To summarize, excavations in the southern cluster of circular structures suggests that some of them were part of residential compounds (more likely the ones around open patio space), while others had specialized functions as *qollqas*, nondomestic kitchen spaces, or special-purpose repositories. In either case, the inhabitants of this part of the settlement enjoyed access to structures involved with food processing and storage beyond the domestic needs.

Next to the group of circular structures, a large enclosed stone structure (Structure 19) was built to the east and was used as a funerary repository for the group of mortuary urns from earlier periods (figure 4.5). Excavations in the eastern portion of this enclosed space revealed that the group of elaborate funerary urns lay underneath a carefully built orange clay floor. In this sense, the construction of this large structure represents the architectural formalization of an early funerary area holding the remains of multiple individuals, most likely the founding ancestors of the community. Ethnohistorical accounts document that the remains of lineage ancestors (*mallquis*) were considered sacred, and therefore the subject of regular celebrations. *Mallquis* were often paraded in public events and given food and *chicha* (corn beer) as if they were alive. The fact that the orange clay floor was also found in the nearby circular structures suggests that all of these structures were not just contemporaneous in construction and use but also part of the ancestors complex involved with public rituals and large-scale food production and consumption.

To the southeast of this large enclosed structure, our excavations in the lithic workshop revealed continuity in the disposal of large amounts of broken pottery and quartz flakes, along with poorly preserved faunal remains from camelids, fish, ducks, canids, and cavids (Capriles et al. 2008). However, in comparison with the previous Classic Yampara period, the amount of broken pottery nearly doubled. Despite this dramatic increase, the proportion of serving vessels remained about the same (12 percent), still with a dominance of utilitarian storage jars (figure 4.6). About half of the serving vessels were decorated in a wide diversity of Yampara styles, along with imported Huruquilla pottery.

As in the earlier period, the evidence suggests that this open area was still used as a lithic workshop. Although the density of quartz cores and flakes increased significantly in this period (from a mean of 98.5 to 360 flakes by excavation unit), there were no major modifications in the lithic technology or raw materials used. Taking into account the increase of both lithic remains and pottery sherds, it might be argued that in this period there was an increase in the scale of production and a larger pool of participant producers. This evidence suggests that lithic production was sponsored and organized by local elites on a communal scale, who in reciprocity provided food to the laborers. It is documented that prior to the Inkas, local *kurakas* had access to communal *mit'a* labor in a network of reciprocal obligations, manifested in the celebration of hospitality feasts (Rostworowski 1988b; Rowe 1946). In the case of Yoroma, production and consumption took place in the same space, suggesting that both were complementary components of the productive cycle.

Farther east in the peripheries of the Yoroma settlement lay Structure 61, a residential compound formed by two circular stone structures (figure 4.5). Excavations of one room unveiled a light occupation as in the earlier period, with two intrusive primary burials. The first was an adult male in a lateral flexed position placed directly in the soil matrix, and with no associated artifacts. The second was an adult female lying in a frontal position and with the lower limbs crossed and flexed. On top and along this body, remains of a utilitarian vessel along with a perforated grinding stone were found as part of the funerary paraphernalia. Nearby was an ash pit with camelid bones. In comparison to the earlier occupation in the structure, the proportion of serving vessels declined (from about 39 to 18 percent). Taking into account that other primary burials were found in other residential structures, the vessels might have belonged to the residents.

Overall, this period is characterized by the intensification of earlier activities, including lithic manufacture and food consumption beyond the domestic sphere, along with the formalization of mortuary ritual activities in an enclosed structure. Important shifts are also evident in the construction of more facilities to accommodate specialized nondomestic activities. These included the construction of storage *qollqas* both in the northern and southern parts of the settlement; the construction of large oblong structures in the central part of the settlement in a cellular pattern designed to compartmentalize a range of public activities, including grain processing; and the construction of larger elite residences with enclosed patios and oblong structures, including preferential access to Inka and local status goods. Overall, these changes suggest important shifts in the domestic economy of Yoroma, with native elites concentrating more control of resources and power as they pooled more labor in a framework of reciprocal and redistributive relations with the locals.

All of the described changes are echoed in the distribution of the different kinds of artifact assemblages. In the following section, I focus on the distribution of decorated pottery styles and stone tools in order to understand shifts in the distribution of local and imported pottery and in the exchange networks before and after the Inkas.

Changes in the Scale of Feasting and Lithic Production

Comparison of the middens in the Yoroma settlement can provide important insight into the strategies of political domination of local elites in terms of feasting and production. While in the Classic Yampara period both midden areas were located in open spaces of the settlement to facilitate lithic production and food consumption, in the Late Yampara-Inka period both

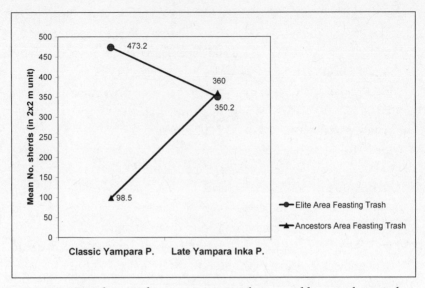

FIGURE 4.8. Distribution of pottery comparing the two midden areas by period, Yoroma settlement.

production areas shifted in nature. While the trash mound in the central part of the settlement was transformed into a terraced platform to accommodate an elite residential compound, the southern trash area was incorporated into the funerary complex devoted to the ancestors. In both cases, lithic production and food consumption continued as seen in the density of serving and storage vessels, but with different levels of intensity.

The changes in the intensity of lithic production and food consumption provide important information on the political strategies of emerging elites to enhance their power and status. As seen in figures 4.8 and 4.9, marked changes are observable in the distribution of lithic and pottery remains. Both figures are based on the mean distribution of lithic and pottery remains, by calculating the average density by excavation unit (2 by 2 meters), to account for the uneven excavation of units in each area. In figure 4.8, the average distribution of pottery sherds (all from storage and serving vessels) in both the Classic Yampara and Late Yampara-Inka periods distinguishes two different trajectories. While in the midden associated with the ancestors complex we see a relatively rapid increase in the density of ceramic remains (from 98.5 to 350.2 fragments), in the midden of the elite residential compound we see a decrease in the density of sherds (from 473.2 to 360.0 fragments). In other words, there is a reverse pattern

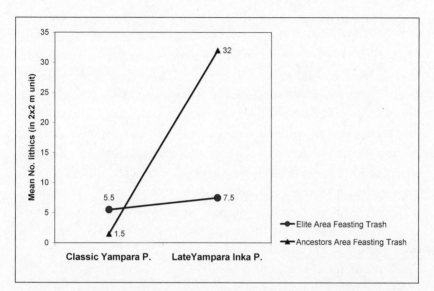

FIGURE 4.9. Distribution of lithics comparing the two midden areas by period, Yoroma settlement.

in the density of pottery remains, suggesting that the intensity levels of storage capabilities and food consumption were markedly different. More food consumption (liquids or solids) took place in the midden part of the ancestors complex during the last period, while there was a decrease in food consumption in the midden area involved with the elite residence.

The shift observed in the increase of food consumption in the ancestors complex is somewhat related to the changes in the distribution of lithic remains. As can be seen in figure 4.9, the steady increase of lithic remains in the midden of the ancestors complex (1.5 to 32.0 flakes and cores) echoes the increase in pottery sherds. A different pattern is observed in the distribution of lithic remains in the midden of the elite residence. A relatively steady increase is observed in the distribution of expedient lithics (5.5. to 7.5 flakes and cores), whereas the density of pottery sherds declined over time. This means that the intensification does not get reflected in the levels of food consumption, although in both trash middens we see a relative increase in lithic manufacture, whether sudden or relatively steady.

This might suggest either two different leadership strategies evolving in the Late Yampara-Inka period aimed at organizing lithic production or simply the compartmentalization of lithic production into elite, domestic, and public levels. In the first scenario, if these two forms of lithic flaking industry were part of different leadership strategies, I speculate that in the first strategy, an evolving cult to the ancestors provided the ideological basis for elites to pool increased labor for the large-scale production of lithics in the ancestors complex. This access to labor, perhaps in the form of taxes or some form of tribute, was also accompanied by substantial consumption activities as seen in the increased density of pottery sherds. In comparison, I speculate that the second strategy involved the appropriation by the elite of a public area originally used for the large-scale production of lithics. The appropriation of such space might have involved the disruption of existing production patterns. Although the lithic flaking industry remained about the same, there was a drastic decline of food consumption and feasting in the patio of the elite residence. I speculate that this shift involved access to a reduced labor pool, and that food consumption and feasting became supplementary activities in the production-consumption cycle sponsored in elite residences.

In the second scenario, we might have a case in which both forms of lithic production simply reflect the specialization and compartmentalization of two different forms of lithic industries. While one became more private and sponsored by emerging elites in their own residential compounds, the second remained public, although incorporated into an increasingly strong cult to the ancestors. In either case, it is clear that lithic manufacture and the sponsorship of feasting, along with a strong cult to the ancestors, were important aggrandizing strategies in the legitimization and consolidation of the power of Yampara elite in Yoroma.

A remaining question involves the effects of the Inka Empire on the Yoroma political economy and in the strategies used by local elites to extract surplus and labor. Taking into account that we do not see changes in the lithic technology or in the kinds of raw materials used, but rather an intensification of existing lithic production industries, we might conclude that the Inkas chose to expand existing forms of production. Even though we do not have direct evidence to measure the effects of imperial conquest on the local leadership strategies, the two evolving forms of organizing production — either in a public sphere under the sponsorship of the ancestors cult or in a private sphere controlled by the elite — might represent two evolving forms of manufacture, partly as a response to imperial intrusion. The lithic production in a private sphere sponsored and controlled by local elite might represent efforts of emerging leaders to maintain in-

dependent access to labor while controlling the production of a flaking industry in their own residential compounds. In comparison, the large-scale
production of lithic tools in a public context with the support of an emerging ancestors-based religious ideology might represent the intrusion of a
third party seeking to enlarge the scale of production for broader ends.
Taking into account the demands of the Inka Empire for projectile points
and lithic weapons, these might have been exported eastward to support
the Inka imperial expansion beyond the imperial borders.

Because the large-scale production of lithics in a public sphere supported by a cult to the ancestors expanded markedly while also being tied
to large levels of food consumption, I argue that this second strategy was
more successful in terms of attracting a large pool of laborers. In either
case, local elites were pivotal in the organization of lithic manufacture, as
such production took place in a local Yampara center rather than in the
Inka installations. In this context, the Inkas, instead of imposing an imperial religious ideology, enhanced the local religion for their own goals, and
thanks to the intermediation of strong native chiefs willing to benefit from
the alliances with the Inka Empire.

Conclusion

As one of the largest settlements of the Oroncota region primarily inhabited by local elites, Yoroma was the center of a range of specialized
activities. The long occupational history of the settlement suggests that
the site gained prestige over competing centers based on four dominant
features: the settlement enjoyed direct access to fertile land from the valley floor, it was an important center for feasting and large-scale consumption activities, it focused on the specialized production of lithic materials
to participate in the valley exchange networks linking different polities,
and it emphasized a cult to the ancestors, perhaps as a means of political
legitimization.

In regard to the questions that guided this research, the results can be
summarized as follows. Did the Inkas affect existing status and wealth
relations in the local Yampara communities? The results suggest that although the local elites enforced their status through ties with the Inkas,
they maintained a strong autonomy and political power. After the arrival
of the Inkas, elite residences maintained preferential access to locally

valuable prestige materials, including terrestrial white shells and sheet star copper bells, both widely used as markers of status in polities along the Chaco in the Bolivian and Argentinean regions. These prestige materials continued in significant use after the arrival of the Inkas and therefore maintained their value as markers of status. Although quite scarce, the few Inka materials in the settlement were found in elite residences, suggesting that they were used to enforce existing status rather than representing the incorporation of the elite group in the wider imperial political economy. Overall, the few prestige Inka materials found in the entire region were quite restricted in comparison to other parts of the empire, where they played a significant role in the reorganization of local political structures and economies, such as in the Mantaro Valley (Costin and Earle 1989; D'Altroy 1992).

What type of activities took place in the different architectural areas of the settlement, and did these activities differ across time? Rather than abrupt shifts, my investigations revealed continuity in the range of activities over time, with some of them changing in nature. A first type of activity involved feasting and public consumption, and although we see a continuum, there were also marked changes in their function. While in the Classic Yampara period two open areas in the settlement were dedicated to the celebration of public consumption activities, as seen by the extensive formation of middens, in the Yampara-Inka period this activity continued with two main shifts. On the one hand, the northern midden mound was remodeled to accommodate an elite residential complex as an elite strategy to sponsor public consumption feasts inside their own residence. On the other hand, in the southern area feasting and consumption activities were connected to the construction of a funerary building to keep the ancestral remains, along with a group of structures used as storage qollqas, as offering repositories or for the large-scale processing of food. In this sense, the Yampara-Inka period marks two distinct forms of feasting — one sponsored by emerging elites perhaps as reciprocity celebrations; the second, part of broader religious celebrations connected to the ancestors.

A second type of activity involved the processing of grains, as seen by the distribution of grinding stones. Evidence suggests that the processing of grains, including corn, was an important activity at domestic and suprahousehold levels during both periods. Judging by the concentration of grinding stones in some of the large oblong buildings during the Yampara-Inka period, we might conclude that these activities expanded beyond the domestic sphere and took place in public spaces at the end of the sequence.

A third type of activity involved the preparation of food. This activity was maintained throughout the sequence at a household level. However, during the Yampara-Inka period, the construction of kitchen structures for the large-scale cooking and processing of food associated with feasting and consumption activities is evident.

A fourth activity involved a flaking industry based on the use of local quartz. In both periods, we find evidence that this activity was conducted in the lithic workshop on a relatively large scale, while such production was more restricted in the rest of the domestic compounds. At the end of the sequence, Yoroma elite residences enjoyed significant access to lithic production in order to increase their resources.

A fifth activity involved funerary practices. In both periods we see two marked patterns, perhaps reflecting social status. On the one hand, we have primary burials with no funerary urns and ritual paraphernalia, and on the other, funerary urns holding the remains of secondary burials with ritual paraphernalia, including terrestrial shells and decorated pottery. In some cases, these funerary urns were either part of the residential complex or in special-purpose buildings as part of a broader cult to the ancestors. However, no clear evidence was found to indicate whether any of these funerary practices were dominant in either period.

Finally, did the Inkas promote shifts in craft production activities at communal and household levels? Excavations in the lithic workshop revealed that the production of lithic tools was a specialized activity beyond the household level and that the tools were destined for export. Judging by the distribution of unfinished projectile points on the surface, this production also involved their manufacture for export, perhaps to the eastern frontier fortifications. These activities took place during the Classic Yampara and Yampara-Inka periods with marked intensification in the latter period.

At a domestic level, local Yoroma elite also sponsored the production of lithic tools in their own residences along with feasting, perhaps to gain independent access to surplus and labor. However, remains of quartz flakes and cores in small settlements of the region, as revealed by my survey, suggest that lithic production also took place at a local level. Perhaps the simultaneous production of quartz lithic tools by local communities and households was a mechanism to maintain a certain level of autonomy and independent access to the wide exchange networks in the region. The increase in lithic production in the last period not only suggests an increase in the demands of lithic tools at the regional and supraregional levels but also that local elites were active agents in the sponsorship of such production. This strategy enabled them to secure privileged participation in the valley exchange networks while also enhancing their own status.

Despite this enlargement of lithic manufacture, I did not find evidence for the insertion of new craft production activities or the reorganization of the local economy to facilitate imperial economic extraction, as seen in other parts of Tawantinsuyu. Regardless of the proximity of the Inkarry Moqo building complex to the Yoroma site (about 4 kilometers), the Inka facility did not constitute a true center of Inkanization to local elites; neither was it the focus of population attraction or lithic production, as most of these activities took place in Yoroma.

Overall, my findings suggest that the arrival of the Inkas did not promote important changes in the local Yampara political economy. As seen through the Yoroma center, Inka conquest was a relatively indirect phenomenon affecting the lives of local populations. The local elites reinforced their power by benefiting from this interaction, rather than being lessened in status or subject to external control. If relations with the empire were diplomatic and through vertical alliances as stated in ethnohistorical accounts (AGI, Charcas 44ff. 151v, cited in Julien 1995:105; Barragán Romano 1994:58; Platt 1999:104), Yampara elites certainly benefited from this interaction as an additional mechanism to consolidate their local power. The Inka conquest of Oroncota did not involve significant shifts in the communal and local political economies. Rather, imperial conquest was selective and aimed at incorporating local leaders into the imperial sphere of influence.

In a comparative framework, the evolution of Yoroma illustrates the mechanics of imperial and native elite interaction, and the aggrandizing strategies that Yampara leaders used. As in Yoroma, in situations in which the administration of production was delegated to local chieftains, native lords played a crucial role in the mediation and materialization of the imperial agenda. Finally, Oroncota is another case study to illustrate that the

Inka Empire, just as any other ancient empire, tailored its incorporation strategies depending on existing levels of political complexity, on whether there was an existing local hierarchy of leaders, on the quality of valuable resources, and on the various reactions of local chieftains to imperial intrusion. For the Yampara elite in Oroncota, this involved cooperative relations in the face of Chiriguano encroachment, with the local leaders benefiting from this interaction as a means of enhancing their status while gaining support in defense of their eastern frontier.

Acknowledgments

I want to express my deepest gratitude to my colleagues and friends in Bolivia who generously helped in each phase of my 2003 research in the Oroncota region. Many thanks to Carla Jaimes, Soledad Fernandez, Edmundo Salinas, Orlando Tapia, José Capriles, and Juan José Mujica. The community members of Yoroma, particularly Cristobal Sarabia, were extremely helpful for sharing their knowledge, history, and experience. This project was funded by the Heinz Foundation in 2002 through the University of Pittsburgh.

Notes

1. According to local Quechua informants of the region, the Quechua term for lithic corncobs is *"sara,"* which can be translated as "corn."

2. The material of this stone polisher — known as *raya rumi* by local Quechua informants — is presently highly valued by local shamans as a potent medicine used against a variety of diseases.

Félix A. Acuto

Chapter Five

Living under the Imperial Thumb in the Northern Calchaquí Valley, Argentina

Editors' Introduction

The chapter provides the results of several years of intensive study of the Inka and pre-Inka occupation of the northern Calchaquí Valley of northwestern Argentina. In contrast to the previous chapter, this one provides a fine-grained study of the Inka presence at two specific sites: the local Inka centers of La Paya/Guitián and the four related areas of the site of Cortaderas. Using agency theory, Acuto's analysis identifies a new level in the political hierarchy that resulted from the Inka conquest. Architecture, ceramics, burial data, and settlement organization all support the view of a group who were local yet clearly displayed the material manifestations of Inka power. For Acuto, the evidence from the site of Guitián supports the chroniclers' accounts of the use of local leaders as *kurakas*, but he also indicates how these individuals were elevated in status from previous ephemeral political positions.

Given the significant amount of Inka material culture and the exceptional labor that went into building La Casa Morada, one might wonder if an actual Inka lord dwelled there, either a member of the nobility or an

Inka-by-Privilege. Local chiefs might then have occupied other positions of power at the site and at other sites where Inka-style houses are identified (such as AD 1 at Cortaderas).

At the site of Cortaderas, the archaeological evidence shows how the Inkas created an administrative area at Cortaderas Bajo and Izquierda and resettled a sizable community at Cortaderas Derecha. However, at the latter, through a careful study of the material remains from the site, Acuto shows how the local people resisted Inka domination and assimilation. This is seen in the presence of Inka pottery in trash areas, and their absence in burials and status-related contexts.

The evidence from this region reflects the problems discussed in the introduction regarding indirect/direct rule and territorial/hegemonic strategies. On the one hand, the evidence from La Paya/Guitián seems to show indirect rule, with a group of local leaders incorporated into the administrative hierarchy. Yet in this region there was no previous political hierarchy to use, only individuals who had ephemeral power during periods of political stress. In addition, without the detailed study provided, the archaeological evidence might be interpreted as support for a territorial strategy, as there appears to be a heavy investment on the Inkas' part in architecture, especially at the site of Cortaderas. For Acuto, the fact that Inka pottery is found in trash areas and not in status or domestic contexts at Cortaderas Derecha suggests the cultural resistance of the locals to imperial canons. An alternative way to understand this distribution may involve the use of imperial pottery in food redistribution tasks to state laborers, although this did not necessarily translate into the pottery's use as status markers.

Taken together, the information presented in this chapter shows how complex the Inka-local interaction could be, the multiple uses of imperial materials, and how Inka control was a combination of direct intervention in building infrastructure where it was needed, with indirect forms of rule. Moreover, it demonstrates how indirect rule could also be developed without an existing political organization to use. Finally, this study provides other information from Cortaderas Derecha concerning the resistance of local communities to Inka domination in ways that the ethnohistorical documents do not, and cannot, record.

Introduction

In general, archaeological studies about Inka occupation of "marginal" regions, such as the southern Andes, have rarely focused on how cultural encounters and colonization influenced and changed the social and cultural life of the colonized. There are a number of reasons that might explain this situation, some theoretical, others related to research topics, and still others associated with the nature of Tawantinsuyu development and geography. First, many investigations have applied a top-down approach to Inka colonization, focusing more on what the Inkas did than on how domination affected indigenous societies or how these societies dealt with Inka occupation (Bárcena 2001; D'Altroy et al. 2000; González 1980; Llagostera 1976; Raffino 1981, 1993; Stehberg 1995; Williams 1991). This is because scholars have learned to think that one of the principal goals of the Inka Empire was to extract labor from subordinate communities, avoiding impact on their social organization. Second, too much emphasis has been placed on constructing classificatory schemes of Inka sites and material culture (Calderari and Williams 1991; González 1980; Niemeyer and Rivera 1983; Raffino 1981, 1988; Rivera and Hyslop 1984; Stehberg 1995) or on studying the economic aspects of Inka domination (D'Altroy et al. 2000; Llagostera 1976; Raffino 1981; Williams 1991). Third, it has been believed that Tawantinsuyu only lasted a short time in many regions (sometimes less than a hundred years),[1] or that some provincial areas, such as the northern Calchaquí Valley, Argentina (figure 5.1), were too far from the empire's core and therefore did not receive much Inka influence (González 1980). These ideas have produced explanations about Inka rule in the southern Andes that neglected the cultural and ideological dimen-

FIGURE 5.1. (Facing page) Northern Calchaquí Valley. (A) Quebrada del Río Potrero and its connection with Quebrada del Toro, (B) mid-north Calchaquí Valley; (C) north extreme of the north Calchaquí Valley. Sites: (1) La Paya, (2) Guitián, (3) Tero, (4) Fuerte Alto, (5) Mariscal, (6) Borgatta, (7) Choque, (8) Las Pailas, (9) Loma del Oratorio, (10) Corral del Algarrobal, (11) Quipón 1, (12) Ruiz de los Llanos, (13) Valdez, (14) Buena Vista, (15) Tin Tin, (16) Agua de los Loros, (17) Tonco 2 and 3, (18) Pucará de Palermo, (19) Alto Palermo, (20) Cortaderas Alto, (21) Cortaderas Bajo, (22) Cortaderas Izquierda, (23) Cortaderas Derecha, (24) Belgrano, (25) Casa Quemada, (26) Potrero de Payogasta, (27) Ojo de Agua, (28) Corral Blanco, (29) Capillas, (30) Corralito, (31) Los Graneros, (32) Río Blanco, (33) La Encrucijada, (34) El Calvario/RP005, (35) RP002.

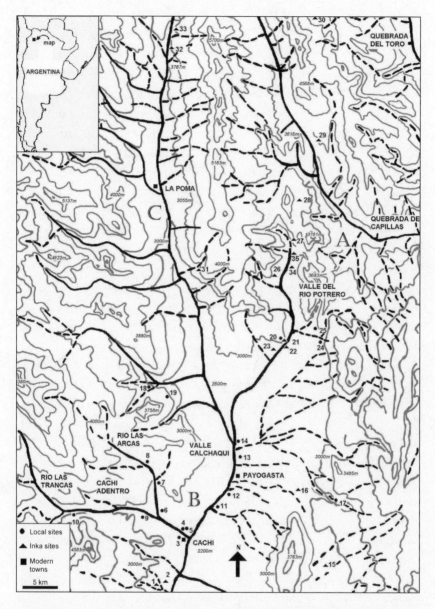

sions of Inka colonization. Only in a small number of cases have narratives about Inka domination considered the policies the Inkas developed to influence the cultural practices, social relations, or social categories of their subjects from the southern Andes, or paid attention to the unintended transformations that Inka rule produced in provincial communities' daily life and culture (e.g., Acuto 1999, 2004; Farrington 1999; Gifford 2003;

Gifford and Acuto 2002; Hyslop 1990; Leibowicz 2006; Meyers and Ul-
bert 1997; Nielsen and Walker 1999; Troncoso 2004; Uribe 2004).

In this chapter, I demonstrate that Inka colonization influenced and
transformed northern Calchaquí Valley's society. I claim that Inka domination affected, in specific ways, indigenous culture and social life. In
particular, I examine how Inka colonization, intentionally and uninten-
tionally, affected and changed the actions, cultural practices, and social
categories of their northern Calchaquí Valley subjects. In addition, I examine the way northern Calchaquí Valley communities and individuals
faced and engaged with Inka domination, demonstrating that whereas
some native people took advantage of this new situation, transforming
their material practices, expanding their agency, and improving their status, others stuck, more than ever, to their own cultural ways.

There is a long tradition of archaeological research in the northern Calchaquí Valley. These investigations have been especially oriented to the
analysis of Inka occupation in the region, as well as the study of the period
immediately before Inka arrival. These studies include, among other activities, extensive surveys (DeMarrais 1997; Díaz 1983, 1992; Tarragó and
Díaz 1972, 1977), architectural analysis (D'Altroy et al. 2000; De Lorenzi
and Díaz 1976; DeMarrais 1997; Gifford 2003), excavations of local and
Inka sites (D'Altroy et al. 2000; Díaz 1978–1980; Earle 1994; Gifford 2003;
Pollard 1983; Tarragó 1977), and the excavation of several burials (Ambrosetti 1907–1908; Díaz 1986). This chapter is based on the information
provided by this important body of research, as well as on my own studies
in the region. Since 1996, I have been conducting archaeological research
in the northern Calchaquí Valley, studying the nature of local social organization and the impact that Inka colonization had on the region. To
reach these goals, I have conducted intensive surveys, excavations, and architecture and surface analysis at Cortaderas (one of the two major imperial centers of the region) and Mariscal (a local pre-Inka site); systematic
surface and architectural analysis in several local settlements (such as La
Paya/Guitián, Las Pailas, Borgatta, Ruíz de los Llanos, La Hoyada, and
Epifanio Burgos, among others); and the study of nearly 200 pots from
museum collections.

This chapter begins with some theoretical considerations key to the interpretation of this archaeological case. In the first section, I explore cen-

tral aspects of practice and agency theories. Thereafter, I demonstrate that Inka intervention changed local communities' social organization as well as some people's statuses, promoting within native society the emergence of a previously absent elite group. As such, Inka domination transformed northern Calchaquí Valley agency and the way people perceived their own and other people's agency, or what subordinate communities thought an agent was able to achieve. During Inka rule in the northern Calchaquí Valley, some indigenous people benefited by their alliance with the Inkas and used this opportunity to set themselves apart from their community, acquiring more resources, power, new forms of knowledge, and a higher status. Thanks to their expanded agency, these people's room for action grew wider, involving more possibilities and a greater autonomy than what vernacular social structure and lifeworld allowed previously.

The last part of the chapter examines the way subjects' social lives unfolded in a case of direct Inka control. This section narrates the experiences lived by a group of people from the northern Calchaquí Valley when the Inkas forced them to settle in Cortaderas and work on Tawantinsuyu's projects. I address here how Inka domination affected those who were compelled to reside in this Inka center, how they coped with this situation, and what aspects of their social life changed and what others remained the same. Some key cultural practices are examined in this section, such as domestic consumption, ceramic production and style, building, and funerary rituals. In sum, I explore how communal life developed in a case of direct Inka control and how this situation differed from what other communities in the region experienced or did.

Agency, Lifeworld, and Colonial Encounters

Practice and agency theories play a central role in the interpretation of my case study. These theories, especially Bourdieu's (1977, 2000) and Giddens' (1979, 1984) versions, have been widely discussed and used in contemporary Anglo-American archaeology. However, there is not one single reading of these social theories, or a unique way to apply them to the interpretation of the past (Pauketat 2001). Agency, for instance, has many meanings, and it has been used in different ways in archaeology and to explain different social phenomena (see Dobres and Robb 2000; Dornan 2002). For this reason, before I proceed with my archaeological analysis, it is germane to briefly explain my understanding of these theoretical frameworks.

Practice and agency theories emerged in opposition to both objectivist perspectives (such as structuralism, functionalism, behaviorism, evolutionism, and so forth) and extreme subjectivist approaches (for example, rational choice theory, hermeneutics, or Sartreian existentialism) in philosophy and the social sciences. These theories focus on daily, routine, and minimal practices, since society constitutes and reproduces in this social realm. According to practice and agency theories, there exists a dialectical relationship between structure and people's social actions and practices: social structure shapes action (enabling and restricting it), but at the same time people's actions and practices produce and reproduce structural conditions. Through their actions, subjects not only reproduce social structure (especially structural conditions of which they are not aware) but can also transform it (especially through the unintended consequences of their actions).

In Bourdieu's and Giddens' perspectives, people are not tightly constrained by social structures, mechanically responding to social rules, laws, or norms beyond their comprehension, nor are they rational and strategic subjects capable of overcoming any structural condition. For practice and agency approaches, subjects typically act through a practical sense. Subjects are neither automats who follow a structurally predetermined course of action nor full-time strategists deploying intentional actions in order to reach their goals. On the contrary, most of the time people act in practical ways (in terms of their habitus, sensu Bourdieu). Therefore, the majority of actions people perform on a daily basis are not conscious or goal-oriented, but practical.

Subjects' potentials for action are not narrow (they do not follow just one predetermined course of action). Agents have a wide gamut of possible actions they are able to perform in any given situation. They have the capacity and knowledge (agency) to change their actions, not in a strategic but in a practical way. According to Giddens, any individual "could have acted otherwise" (1979:56). Agency implies a knowledgeable actor who "could have acted in a manner somehow different than she or he did" (Cohen 1987:284).

However, agents are not able to act in any way they like. First, in every society there are variations in agency according to people's power and cultural and economic capital. Second, there are always structural con-straints to social action, constraints that vary historically, culturally, and according to a subject's position within the social structure. In the daily course of their lives, there are types of actions that agents do not develop, either because they are not allowed to, they do not find the proper condi-tions to do so, they do not possess the knowledge to do so, or they do not know that this course of action is even possible.

In a nutshell, agency entails subjects' capacity for practical action — the potential and knowledge people have, as competent actors of their society, to reflect about situations (through a practical consciousness) and reorient their actions, acting in different ways. Agency, therefore, does not involve intentional and strategic actions, but rather subjects' abilities to shift their actions according to specific or changing circumstances, and in tune with their own goals.

Nonetheless, there are aspects of social life that are beyond both agency and intentional and strategic actions. These aspects belong to the sphere of lifeworld (Habermas 1987; Schutz and Luckmann 1973) or doxa (Bour-dieu 1977, 2000).[2] Lifeworld is the realm of reality where people participate daily in ways that are inevitable and patterned, and that they experience as uncontested and taken for granted (Schutz and Luckmann 1973). In daily life contexts, there are actions, practices, objects, and spatial layouts that no one discusses or tries to alter because they are perceived as natural, normal, necessary, and neutral. Practices, actions, and material aspects that belong to the realm of lifeworld, or are doxic, serve to simplify and facilitate communication and social relations (Habermas 1987) and to reduce the cognitive burden of individuals. Lifeworld is thus the famil-iar, unproblematic, and uncontested background of daily life (Bernbeck 1999:93–94). It is the normal and expected way in which daily activities, practices, spaces, and things are organized and structured for specific historical and cultural contexts. Lifeworld is beyond people's awareness; therefore, neither agency nor intentional and strategic actions can change it, at least where nothing contradicts or shows its arbitrariness. According to Bourdieu (2000), it is in contexts of economic/political crisis or cultural contact when people realize the arbitrariness of their lifeworld or doxa. In these situations, two strategies may take place. On the one hand, some people may use this opportunity to attempt to transform structural con-ditions, developing actions toward heterodoxy. On the other hand, those who do not want any social change may develop strategies, which Bourdieu (1977, 2000) describes as orthodoxy, to preserve the order of things.

Processes of cultural contact, colonization, and domination engender the transformation of the social life and lifeworld of the colonized. For different reasons, these processes impact on subjects' actions and agency because: the colonizers seek to change the cultural practices of the colonized (e.g., Comaroff and Comaroff 1997; Cooper and Stoler 1997; Rabinow 1989; Thomas 1997); the colonized, or some group within subject communities, find new opportunities (material and social) to change their situation (Thomas 1999); new courses of action that subjects did not know of or were not able to follow are now open (e.g., Comaroff and Comaroff 1997; Dirks 1992; Dobyns and Doughty 1976; Silverblatt 1987); and things that were taken for granted are now disputed (e.g., Comaroff 1997; Silverblatt 1987; Spalding 1984). This transformation (and perhaps extension) of action and agency may drive the colonized individual to attempt to change his or her position in his or her own society, or may urge him or her to retain the former social order via negotiation or resistance.

The Creation of New Agency

Archaeologists have described the Late period (A.D. 1000–1400/1470, the period right before Inka occupation of the region) in northwestern Argentina, the northern Calchaquí Valley included, as a time of sociopolitical complexity and institutionalized social inequality and economic stratification (Raffino 1988; Tarragó 2000). According to this interpretation, small-scale chiefdoms ruled over discrete territories. This perspective is the product of the rigid and uncritical application of social evolutionism's typology of societies and of models tested in the central Andes, and it does not stand up to a careful analysis of both ethnohistorical and archaeological data.

According to historical information, the situation in the northern Calchaquí Valley prior to the Inkas was one of political fragmentation. The region did not constitute a politically integrated territory or political-territorial confederation ruled from a paramount settlement. On the contrary, there were several polities in the region (Lorandi 1997; Lorandi and Boixadós 1987–1988; Raffino 1983), an idea also supported by archaeological studies (DeMarrais 1997; Gifford 2003). These indigenous chiefs acquired their position based on their skills in war and their political ability to organize their community and to make alliances with other groups. However, the chiefly office was temporary and quite weak, reinforced in times of war or conflict (as when the Inkas and the Spaniards invaded the region), to be dissolved later when the political situation changed (Lorandi and Boixadós 1987–1988). According to Lorandi (1988:255), when chronicles refer to a principal chief, they allude to native leaders who were capable of attracting followers, and not to chiefs who had real power, or who were capable of controlling the means of production and of extracting labor and goods from their people. Conflict management was thus a way for chiefs to acquire temporary power, but they were unable to keep and employ this power to reproduce and institutionalize their position.

The archaeological record does not offer clear-cut evidence of social inequality and economic stratification during the Late period. First, there is no evidence of resource mobilization, control, and administration, or the appropriation of surplus production that may have served to support ruling elites. There are no traces of centralized storage. Rather, this activity took place at the household level.

Second, we have not found in the main and larger settlements of the region public/administrative areas segregated from the residential parts of the site, or buildings whose dimensions, design, and architectural quality would indicate the existence of centralized political structures or a level of decision making above the household. There are no monumental structures that may indicate labor mobilization and control, or that would have served to aggrandize the figure of a leader and increase his or her power. There are, of course, some special structures at these sites, probably related to ceremonial and communal activities, but none of them constitute exceptional or monumental buildings whose construction may have involved a great investment of labor.[3]

Third, Late period sites have no central plazas or formal public spaces. In Andean stratified societies, plazas played a key role in the reproduction of social relations and power structures. These public spaces were stages for ritual and feasting hosted by elites seeking support and negotiating their social status. The lack of large and formal public spaces within northern Calchaquí sites suggests that chiefs did not co-opt, at least within their settlement, ritual practices. In contrast, archaeological evidence suggests that the domestic sphere was the focus of many ritual activities (DeMarrais 1997). In the majority of Late period sites, however, there is more than

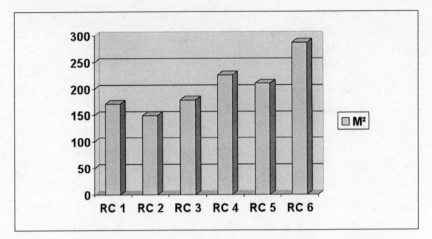

FIGURE 5.2. Northern Calchaquí residential compound sizes. Site: Mariscal.
RC 1: 171 square meters, RC 2: 149 square meters, RC 3: 179 square meters, RC 4:
226 square meters, RC 5: 210 square meters, RC 6: 287 square meters.

one open space (without formal layout) or large structure that could have
served as spaces for gathering and socialization. If these structures actually were public spaces, this would indicate lack of political centralization
and intense competition for leadership, prestige, and power among different groups within a single community.

Fourth, tombs are similar regarding location and architecture, both in
quality and style. No large funerary monument has been found that was
built to distinguish, immortalize, or create material memory of a particular individual, legitimating the status of his or her lineage. Burial goods
do not represent acts of conspicuous consumption. On the contrary, the
great majority of the artifacts deposited in Late period burials were objects of daily use. In general, funerary practices were linked to the domestic sphere, and they did not seem to have constituted political acts.

Fifth, the domestic sphere does not show evidence of social inequality and economic stratification during the Late period. Residential compounds do not differ in terms of their location within the settlement, size,
complexity, or architectural style and quality. In other words, there were
no houses placed in special locations or in favored parts of settlements.
In addition, all residential compounds have approximately the same size
and number of rooms and share their building techniques. Figure 5.2 is a
histogram of residential compound sizes from the local site of Mariscal

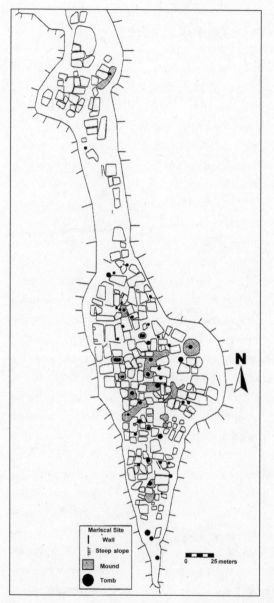

FIGURE 5.3. Mariscal,
Late period site from the
northern Calchaquí Valley.

(figure 5.3), showing that there were no significant differences between these residential compounds in terms of their surface area.

Sixth, according to surface studies and excavations I have conducted in several Late period settlements, and studies in other sites of the region (Díaz 1978–1980), artifacts are evenly distributed throughout Late period sites and among residential compounds. Archaeological evidence indicates that no household had a privileged access to resources and tools. For example, decorated ceramics were homogeneously distributed,[4] and the same is true for various tools of production: spindle whorls, grinding stones, molds, crucibles, ore, hoes, and obsidian (table 5.1). As seen in the 199 burials excavated in La Paya/Guitián,[5] a paramount local settlement, copper objects and tools were widely distributed as well.

Seventh, related to the previous point, there were no great variations with respect to the activities developed within residential compounds. Domestic, productive, or ritual activities were alike among different houses. This means that people shared skills and knowledge. There is no defined evidence of activities that would involve special or secret knowledge.

What was social life like during the Late period? What kind of experiences did people have in Late period settlements every day? What type of social relations did the spatial layout and architecture of these settlements articulate? Northern Calchaquí settlements were large and homogeneous clusters of stone structures arranged in cellular patterns, where wall sharing and wall abutments were typical (Gifford 2003:192) (figures 5.3 and 5.4, Cortaderas Alto). The residential compound was the basic unit of a northern Calchaquí community's spatial organization. It was the center of social organization and the main axis of spatial order. Northern Calchaquí sites actually grew by the accretion of one dwelling next to the other. It has been stated that a typical residential compound had an open patio, two or three large rooms, and a number of circular stone tombs (DeMarrais 1997; Díaz 1978–1980; Gifford 2003). In some cases, an earthen mound was integrated to a group of domestic compounds. Many of these mounds contained burials that have been related to ritual activities at the household level, perhaps ancestor worship (DeMarrais 1997). Nevertheless, my studies of surface architecture are showing that Late period domestic compounds were not closed and self-contained units. In contrast, the limits between dwellings are not always clear, which indicates permeability. Furthermore, these sites have several collective spaces. For instance, there are cases where a number of domestic compounds share one large patio.

In Late period settlements, architecture was semisubterranean, and buildings usually shared walls, halls, and passages. The majority of the structures were unroofed (Gifford 2003:242), and the low, 1-meter-wide walls, together with several artificially elevated passageways, created a

TABLE 5.1. Artifact Types Found in the Residential Compounds of Tero

	RESIDENTIAL COMPOUNDS TERO SITE								
FINDINGS	R1	R2	R3	R5	R6	R7-8	R9	R10	R12
Undecorated ceramics	x[a]	x	x	x	x	x	x	x	x
Santamariana ceramics		x	x	x	x	x	x	x	x
Metallurgy		x					x		
Ground stones	x	x	x	x	x	x	x	x	x
Textile production			x	x					
Clay				x			x		
Lithic artifacts	x	x	x	x	x	x	x	x	x
Worked bones or wood		x		x	x		x	x	x
Copper artifacts							x		
Red pigment		x	x	x	x	x			x
Shell		x	x						x
Beads									x
Animal bones		x	x	x	x	x	x	x	x
Storage		x		x	x	x	x		x
Burials		x		x		x	x	x	x
Fire hearths	x	x	x	x	x	x	x	x	x

[a] x = presence.

large network of paths that allowed movement among buildings. Circulation within these indigenous crowded centers entailed passing between, and above, the different enclosures. Although it is difficult to establish whether there were symbolic limits to circulation, there were certainly no physical restrictions.

In conclusion, living in Late period settlements implied experiencing on a daily basis: (1) A homogeneous material landscape where everybody resided in similar houses, used and consumed similar objects and resources, and carried out comparable activities. Beyond sharing a common identity, this situation created a sense of equality and sameness, where

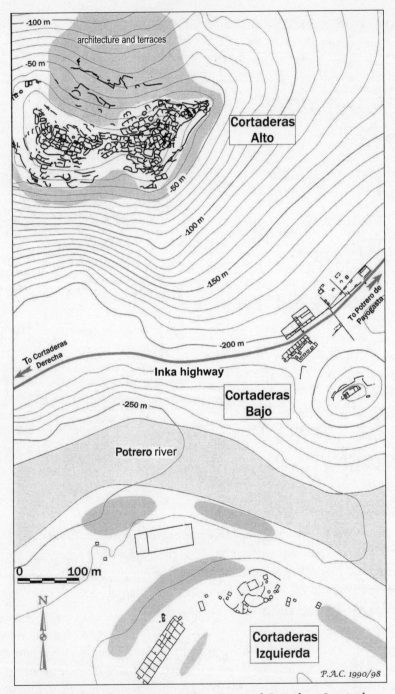

FIGURE 5.4. Cortaderas Alto, Cortaderas Bajo, and Cortaderas Izquierda.

every domestic unit reflected the other. (2) Openness and permeability. In these places, the organization of space facilitated knowledge of one's own community and promoted the constant interaction of people and households. The crowded spatial design of Late period settlements, as the way internal circulation was set up, made sounds, odors, and views permeable, enabling their inhabitants to be aware of what other households and individuals were doing. In addition, by walking around northern Calchaquí towns through the extensive network of elevated paths and wide walls, people were able to see into other residences (especially into the big, open patios), contact other inhabitants, witness the activities held and the rituals other households practiced, or acknowledge the goods they consumed. Northern Calchaquí settlements encouraged social interaction on a daily basis; privacy apparently was not a central concern. Many activities were thus open and exposed to the eyes of the community. This situation implied a high degree of communal control, with the accumulation of power and material benefits greatly noticeable and easy to restrain and regulate. In this way, the community controlled and limited social differences. (3) Communal integration. The spatial organization of Late period settlements avoided segregation. On the contrary, these places were a continuum of articulated architecture, constituting a unified whole. Settlements were an agglomerated web of buildings without fragmentation, one residential compound next to the other, one path connecting to others and reaching every corner of the site.

Inka intervention in the northern Calchaquí Valley disrupted native social life, albeit some communities seem to have been more affected than others. This was the case of the community that resided in the complex of sites known as La Paya/Guitián (figure 5.1). As they did in other regions, the Inkas established strategic alliances with some groups within northern Calchaquí Valley society. The La Paya/Guitián community had fluid and favored relationships with the representatives of Tawantinsuyu, relationships that deeply impacted native social structure and lifeworld.

La Paya/Guitián has two parts divided by a wide gully. La Paya is a typical Late period large agglomerated site of irregular residential architecture. Guitián, the smaller part of the site, lies to the north of La Paya, across the gully. First, it is important to note that La Paya/Guitián went from a modest secondary settlement during the Late period to a large paramount center during Inka times (Calderari 1992; González and Díaz 1992).

Under Inka influence, the site grew in size and infrastructure. Second, and following the Inka conquest, a small group of people began to be set apart from the rest of their community. Evidence obtained from the excavation of 199 burials shows that some people from La Paya/Guitián began to acquire a significant quantity of Inka artifacts and prestige goods during the Inka period, such as fine ceramics, *kero* wooden vessels, and metal objects (both utilitarian and sumptuary objects for personal adornment). Only 22 out of these 199 graves contained Inka paraphernalia alongside local-style artifacts, which suggests that those interred in these 22 burials were natives from the northern Calchaquí Valley and not *mitmaqkuna* brought from other regions.[6] Some of these burials also differ from the rest due to the great amount of goods they included.

Moreover, an outstanding Inka-style house (not seen anywhere else in the region), called La Casa Morada, was erected at this site (figure 5.5). La Casa Morada is a magnificent Inka-style building (13.55 meters east-west by 4.24 meters north-south) constructed of special reddish sandstone blocks obtained from a source more than 10 kilometers away. The house contained typical imperial architectural features, such as worked stone and double-faced walls, rectangular angles and shape, and rectangular niches in one of its walls — all foreign elements for local architecture. It was placed on the northwestern corner of this town, after the modification and rearrangement of older structures that formerly stood at that location. Connected with this special house were a series of native-style buildings, rooms, and patios, and four (perhaps six) storerooms, or *qollqas*, placed on an elevated platform and another two in front of La Casa Morada, with an average storage capacity of 3.3 cubic meters each. This elevated platform with four storerooms was a later addition, possibly contemporary with La Casa Morada, which altered adjacent rooms.

La Casa Morada has a single doorway oriented to the north. Facing this door, and a few meters from it, was the wall of an adjacent and higher structure. This special layout served to block an external gaze toward the interior of the building. Thus, the only way to look inside the house was by standing directly in front of the door. In addition, in order to avoid people freely entering into this peculiar building, a gate that connected the patio where La Casa Morada was built with a neighboring patio was closed and relocated a few meters to the south, on the same wall (figure 5.5). This new arrangement reoriented the circulation of traffic entering

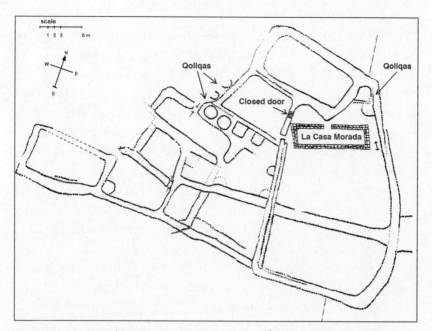

FIGURE 5.5. La Paya/Guitián. La Casa Morada area (modified from González and Díaz 1992).

La Casa Morada. The new location of this door prevented direct access to the interior of La Casa Morada, forcing a detour that compelled people to go around the house and use a narrow corridor to gain entrance. In this way, both gaze and circulation were controlled, and privacy was protected (González and Díaz 1992).

Besides using this particular building, one of a kind in the region, the residents of La Casa Morada obtained prestige goods. At the beginning of the twentieth century, an astonishing collection of objects — among them, Inka ceramic and wooden vessels and Inka-style personal adornments made of bone, bronze, copper, silver, and gold — was discovered buried underneath the floor of this building (Ambrosetti 1902; Boman 1908; González and Díaz 1992).[7]

Was La Casa Morada a house, a temple, or an administrative structure? Who used or resided in this particular building, Inka representatives or local persons? These questions are difficult to answer because the archaeological record of La Casa Morada has been deeply altered by treasure hunters. Nonetheless, there are some clues that may help us solve this issue. During the early 1980s, González and Díaz (1992) cleaned La Casa Morada from debris and carried out careful excavations in the large patio where La Casa Morada is placed. They found domestic utensils and traces of domestic activities, especially grinding and cooking. No evidence of other types of activity was found in these buildings, which shows that the La Casa Morada enclosure was a residential compound. In addition, the presence of local-style artifacts recovered from the La Casa Morada building and compound (González and Díaz 1992), as well as the architectural style of the buildings connected to La Casa Morada, suggests that local people inhabited this particular residential compound.

Inka intervention in the La Paya/Guitián community's social life not only impacted its social structure but influenced its cosmology as well. The section of the site known as Guitián presents a combination of indigenous and Inka buildings (figure 5.6). Among Inka buildings, there are four residential *kanchas* and a small-scale public/ceremonial enclosure. This Inka-style public/ceremonial complex had typical imperial ritual structures (such as plazas, *usnus*, *kallankas*, and associated *kanchas*), which can be found in other sites throughout the empire. Is this facility a local emulation of Inka public spaces (and activities) or did the Inkas promote their construction as a way to impose Inka ritual practices on native society? The great amount of Inka ceramics (especially *aríbalos* and plates) that we have found in recent excavation at Guitián suggests that the Inkas supported and promoted the activities carried out in this ceremonial precinct. Therefore, the Inkas allowed the La Paya/Guitián community, and not other communities, to build an Inka-style public/ceremonial complex and to perform Inka rituals at the local level, which stresses the importance gained by La Paya/Guitián under Inka influence. Indeed, if we consider that the Inkas had larger and better ritual complexes at their own settlements in other parts of the region, we can imagine that this small-scale ceremonial precinct within Guitián was oriented toward the reproduction of Inka rituals at the indigenous level.

The inhabitants of this transformed northern Calchaquí settlement also began to have a firsthand experience of Tawantinsuyu's cosmology. The Inkas introduced in this settlement a formal and large public/ceremonial space that centralized ritual activities. It is likely that the few privileged individuals of La Paya/Guitián (such as those who resided in La Casa Morada) conducted the activities developed in this public/ceremonial enclosure. If this were the case, it means that the Inkas empowered certain in-

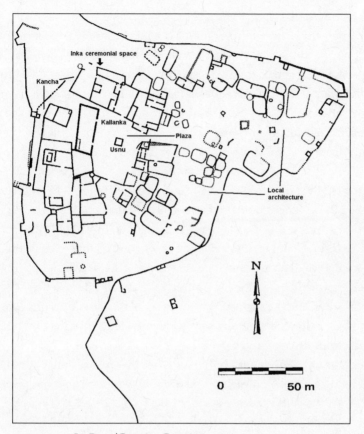

FIGURE 5.6. La Paya/Guitián. Guitián area.

dividuals of La Paya/Guitián, not only enabling them to control and reproduce Inka rituals but also bestowing upon them the agency and knowledge to do so.

Guitián also offers solid evidence of the dramatic fragmentation suffered by this local community during Inka colonization. Within this section of the settlement (figure 5.6), there was a clear demarcation between those who resided in Inka *kanchas*, who had direct access to the public space and the ritual/administrative buildings, and those who lived in local houses, either within the perimeter of the site or outside the west wall.

Social structure and daily life and experiences suffered a radical change in La Paya/Guitián during Inka times. By promoting the construction of imperial buildings, endorsing separation and privacy, encouraging the development of Inka ritual activities, and channeling important amounts of

Inka goods to this place, the Inkas promoted the transformation of social dynamics within this community. The people of La Paya/Guitián (or any local visitor to the site) did not reside in a homogeneous material landscape of similar and articulated residential compounds and evenly distributed artifacts anymore. Under Inka influence, La Paya/Guitián became a fragmented community, with some few residents distanced from the rest. The sense of equality and sameness previously lived was now fading away. Centralized political institutions and activities linked to the foreign rulers, distinction, and social polarization began to be experienced in this settlement with the onset of Tawantinsuyu colonization. The Inkas transformed the social structure of the northern Calchaquí Valley, promoting an elite social stratum and supporting distinction where it was absent. Whereas some people acquired more power and material privileges, others were relegated. The much deeper sense of solidarity and communal integration existing before Inka arrival changed into a sense of social stratification and inequality. A small group of people within this community (and within the region as well) were elevated above the rest in terms of status, knowledge, and power.

This group of privileged individuals became part of a new social stratum, and their role, power, and distinction were probably not just temporary, as the chief office was before Inka colonization. It is possible that these local elites, empowered by the Inkas, became a second layer (below the Inkas but above the local chief) in the new hierarchical social structure the Inkas imposed upon the region, with power to manage indigenous affairs beyond La Paya/Guitián.

Inka intervention favored the emergence of a new kind of agent and a new agency in the northern Calchaquí Valley. In this historical context of cultural contact and colonization, the local perception of agency shifted when some persons gained an expanded capacity for action according to indigenous standards.[8] These people acquired the capacity to develop actions (such as practices of distinction, control over the distribution of foreign prestige goods and knowledge, goods accumulation, privacy, ritual control, and probably institutionalized decision making) that were not previously known or that local social structure and the materiality of local settlements restrained. The Inkas influenced indigenous conception of agency by institutionalizing, legitimating, and reifying the idea of an agent placed above others within the social structure.

These new agents took the opportunity offered by the new political situation to overcome the structural constraints of the pre-Inka lifeworld. They employed Inka material culture as a way to develop a new set of capabilities and social actions, and to enact and justify their status and power before the rest of their community. In front of the other members of the La Paya/Guitián community (and of other people in the region), those who used imperial material culture became, in this context of domination, a new kind of competent, wealthy, and knowledgeable agent whose power resided in their association with the dominant Inka conquerors. Indeed, it is possible that this novel position of power was not totally desirable. Some people may have disliked it since it led to alienation from their own community. Perhaps some of these Inka-promoted agents may even have resented their new status.

Living with the Inkas

What happened in other parts of the northern Calchaquí Valley? How did other people and communities confront Inka domination? Cortaderas is a site divided into four parts (figures 5.1 and 5.4): (1) Cortaderas Alto, a pre-Inka defensive site, partially destroyed and abandoned once the region fell under imperial domination. (2) Cortaderas Bajo, an Inka sector placed below Cortaderas Alto. This part of the site has an impressive Inka fortress to the south, a residential area to the north-northeast, and two large and multiroom *kanchas* to the southwest. The complexity and design of these two buildings suggest that they were used in state activities, storage among them (see Acuto 1994). A large plaza separates both of these *kanchas* and the residential part of Cortaderas Bajo. (3) Cortaderas Izquierda, another Inka section of the site, has more than 50 buildings, most notably a large enclosure with 20 rooms arrayed in a double row (about 130 by 30 meters), a possible *usnu*, a possible *kallanka*, a number of big corrals, and a set of circular storehouses. Surface evidence suggests that craft production took place at Cortaderas Izquierda. (4) Cortaderas Derecha, a local village that lies on the right bank of the Potrero River, approximately 1 kilometer across the river from Cortaderas Bajo and Cortaderas Izquierda (figure 5.4).

Cortaderas Derecha is composed of indigenous domestic compounds encircling a central square structure of 23 by 23 meters, apparently some sort of public space. This is the only Inka-style construction within this village. There are also large midden mounds in Cortaderas Derecha, several tombs, and a great quantity of surface debris. Although Cortaderas Derecha could be linked to Cortaderas Alto, since both present indigenous ceramic and domestic architecture, evidence indicates that Cortaderas Derecha was not built during the Late period, but after Inka conquest. This is suggested by the presence of Inka ceramics throughout the stratigraphic sequence (even in the 2-meter-deep midden), the structuring of space around an Inka style central building (figure 5.7 AD 10), and the lack of evidence of a two-phase occupation throughout the site (such as an early level of occupation or the remains of older buildings). Based on this evidence, I claim that this village was occupied by resettled local people, forced to live next to (and work for) the Inkas. I also maintain that the inhabitants of Cortaderas Derecha were not temporary *mit'a* workers, but rather they comprised a community whose members were permanently attached to the empire. The solid character of the site and the fact that people interred their dead in this location suggest that they were not just provisionally settled in this place. Instead, it seems that these people comprised a single community that developed meaningful ties with this place and that resided at this location for more than one generation, or at least long enough to live and die in this small village. In addition, recent DNA analysis conducted on two skeletons recovered from a tomb excavated in Cortaderas Derecha showed that two of these individuals (a male 25 to 30 years old and a female 25 years old) were relatives on their mothers' side. This suggests that the Inkas resettled entire households in Cortaderas Derecha.

Between 1996 and 1999, I conducted investigations in Cortaderas Derecha that included surface collections, analysis of architecture, a 100 percent walk-over (in order to study the type and distribution of surface artifacts), the excavation of two burials (figure 5.7 AD 4 and one within AD 1), and the partial excavations of three domestic compounds (figure 5.7 AD 1, AD 2, and AD 6): middens, the central plaza (figure 5.7 AD 10), and one possible corral (figure 5.7 AD 5). By working in Cortaderas Derecha, I hoped to obtain a view of Inka conquest and rule from below, that is to say, from the perspective of the colonized.

Cortaderas's spatial organization and built environment stressed division and the subordinate position of those who resided in Cortaderas

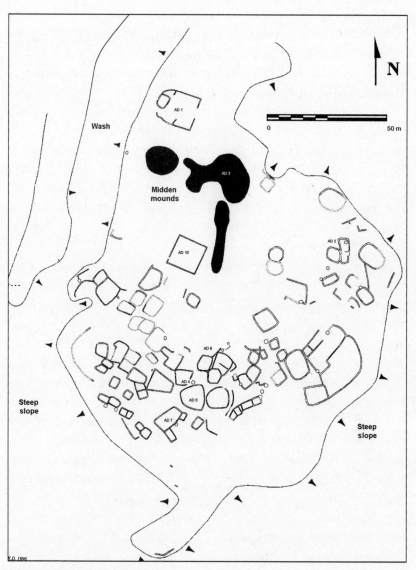

FIGURE 5.7. Cortaderas Derecha.

Derecha. As part of an Inka center, Cortaderas Derecha's native residents found themselves estranged from political authority (in the hands of Inka representatives who resided in Cortaderas Bajo), military power (represented by the destruction of the former local stronghold and the construction of an impressive Inka fortress), new ritual activities (that took place in Inka public places), and control over surplus production (deposited in Cortaderas Bajo's and Cortaderas Izquierda's storerooms). According to my studies in Cortaderas Derecha, vegetal resources processing and preparation and camelid husbandry and butchering were major and intensive activities in Cortaderas Derecha (Acuto 2004). Some metallurgy also took place in this part of Cortaderas, such as the production of copper ingots, which some have argued to be connected to the imperial economy (Earle 1994; Jacob 1999). The inhabitants of Cortaderas Derecha not only found themselves exploited and alienated from surplus production but also associated with mundane and low-prestige activities. Next, I examine some aspects of the life of those who resided in Cortaderas Derecha and their reactions while daily facing Inka domination.

ARCHITECTURE

As explained above, the newly formed elite of La Paya/Guitián dwelled in a fancy Inka-style house and in Inka *kanchas* beside Inka public space. Did something similar happen in Cortaderas Derecha? Was this community of local resettled people influenced by Inka architecture? Were other northern Calchaquí settlements influenced by the architectural tradition of the colonizers?

In Cortaderas Derecha, residential compounds were built using local techniques. Houses were smaller than the Inka dwellings at Cortaderas Bajo, and the amount of labor invested in their construction was not as great as that employed to erect Inka buildings or La Casa Morada. Nonetheless, one residential compound at Cortaderas Derecha (figure 5.7 AD 1) exhibits particular features that suggest its inhabitants may have emulated the Inkas. AD 1 was isolated from other residential compounds, and the door of its main room, as in La Casa Morada, was set in a position that avoided gazing inside. The way AD 1 was constructed is different from other buildings at Cortaderas Derecha. Instead of having the typical 1-meter-wide, core-filled walls and upright stones that characterize indigenous architecture, the walls of AD 1, like Inka architecture in the region, are thinner and composed of double-faced rocks cemented with clay-like mortar. In addition, instead of abutting in round angles, the walls of this residential compound form rectilinear angles, typical of Inka architecture.[9] However, AD 1 cannot be considered an Inka enclosure, but rather a mixture of local and Inka architectural features. This building testifies to a changed notion of agency (emulation of the Inkas) and a changed agency itself (the ability and possibility to produce such a new building, which was formerly outside of the northern Calchaquí lifeworld).

Beyond La Casa Morada and Cortaderas Derecha's AD 1, throughout the region there are a small number of indigenous buildings that emulated Inka architecture, or buildings that blended Inka and northern Calchaquí construction techniques and architectural features.[10] None of them, however, are comparable to La Casa Morada or any other Inka structure in terms of formality and investment of labor. This could mean two things. Either the great majority of indigenous communities, including those who resided in Cortaderas Derecha, were not interested in reproducing Inka building forms, ignoring or actively rejecting them, or the Inkas did not encourage the colonized to produce or fully copy Inka-style buildings because this was a privilege the Inkas only conferred to allied households. I believe both possibilities may have been likely to have occurred.

On the one hand, the small presence of imperial-style objects and architecture beyond Inka sites suggests that the Inkas controlled and restrained the distribution and consumption of Inka artifacts and buildings, such as La Casa Morada. This would mean that the Inkas used their material culture as an instrument to build up alliances and to lubricate political relations with subject leaders. On the other hand, Tawantinsuyu rule over the region was not strong enough to allow the Inkas to inspect every single building constructed in every single local settlement. Although imperial rulers seem to have been capable of restricting the construction of Inka-style buildings within indigenous settlements, domination was not tight enough to have closed off to local people the chance to emulate Inka architecture, at least in some degree. Nonetheless, Inka presence in the region did not influence local building tradition. Very few people in the northern Calchaquí Valley chose to copy some features of Inka architecture. In general, northern Calchaquíes, including the great majority of those who resided in Cortaderas Derecha, did not build their houses, patios, or corrals using Inka architectural techniques. Rather, they kept constructing their typical rounded structures with thick and core-filled walls.

DOMESTIC CONSUMPTION

The pattern of consumption of those who resided in Cortaderas Derecha is also informative about subjects' social life under Inka domination. The goods that people who resided in Cortaderas Derecha consumed did not

TABLE 5.2. Artifact Types Found in the Residential Compounds of the Cortaderas Derecha Site

	RESIDENTIAL COMPOUNDS CORTADERAS DERECHA SITE		
FINDINGS	AD 1	AD 2	AD 6
Red pigment (hematite)	x[a]	x	—
Shell	x	—	x
Beads	x	—	—
Spindle whorls	x (n = 4)	x (n = 2)	x (n = 1)
Clay	—	—	x
Mica	x	x	x
Grinding stones	x (n = 1)	x (n = 3)	x (n = 3)
Obsidian	x	x	x
Local rocks (silice, basalt, riolite, quartz)	x	x	x
Stone tools and lithic production debris	x	x	x
Tools for metallurgical production	—	x	—
Llama bones	x	x	x

[a] x = presence; n = number of findings.

significantly differ from what was consumed in other northern Calchaquí towns, such as Valdez (D'Altroy et al. 2000), Borgatta and Corral del Algarrobal (DeMarrais 1997, 2001; Pollard 1981, 1983), or Tero (Díaz 1978–1980). As in residential compounds located in other northern Calchaquí settlements, Cortaderas Derecha's inhabitants consumed llama meat and produced/acquired decorated and undecorated pottery, projectile points, and personal ornaments of mica and snail shell beads (table 5.2). These households also had the basic means and tools of production suitable for their daily activities: grinding stones, cooking pots, clay and pigments for pottery production, native and foreign lithic raw material, spindle whorls for textile manufacture, and tools for metallurgy. The surface studies and excavations I conducted in Cortaderas Derecha showed that no household possessed more artifacts or better goods than others (tables 5.2 and 5.3).

TABLE 5.3. Ceramic Types Found in the Residential Compounds of Cortaderas Derecha

	RESIDENTIAL COMPOUNDS CORTADERAS DERECHA SITE					
	AD 1		AD 2		AD 6	
CERAMIC TYPE	No.	%	No.	%	No.	%
Local Nondecorated	24	33	13	34	15	38.5
Local Polished Ordinary	13	18	7	18.5	5	13
Local Red Polished	5	7	3	8	2	5
Local Black Polished	4	5.5	3	8	2	5
Santamariana	14	19.5	5	13	10	25.5
Inka	11	15	6	16	5	10
Mixed-Inka/Inka Paya	—	—	—	—	1	2.5
Famabalasto	—	—	1	2.5	—	—
Yocavil Polícromo	1	1	—	—	—	—
TOTAL	72	100	38	100	39	100

The only difference between Cortaderas Derecha's inhabitants and those who resided in other indigenous towns was that every household in the former obtained Inka ceramic vessels. I found similar proportions of Inka ceramics in the three residential compounds excavated (table 5.3). Moreover, surface analysis showed that Inka ceramics were evenly distributed throughout Cortaderas Derecha.

In the northern Calchaquí Valley, Inka artifacts are scarce beyond imperial sites. Only a few Inka ceramic sherds have been found in a small number of local settlements.[11] Even in the area of Cachi Adentro, where the northern Calchaquí Valley population was particularly nucleated (figure 5.1), only a handful of imperial sherds have been recovered (DeMarrais 1997; Pollard 1981, 1983). This is also the case of the sites located in the north end of the northern Calchaquí Valley (Gifford 2003). As Gifford (2003:217) claims, "as evidenced by the sites that were only superficially affected by Inka activities . . . , in many cases Santamariano [local] life proceeded independently." There is actually only one native settlement where Inka ceramic and material culture conspicuously appears: La Paya/Guitián. However, Inka material culture is not homogenously distributed in this case.

Whereas in La Paya/Guitián Inka pottery constituted a prestige type of good and served the emergent indigenous elite to denote distinction and legitimate their status through their association with Tawantinsuyu, in Cortaderas Derecha this artifact did not seem to have been an elite object. Differently from the way La Paya/Guitián's new elite treated Inka objects, gently preserving and depositing them in ritualized contexts, Cortaderas Derecha's residents did not seem to have considered Inka vessels as a luxury or special good they needed to treat with care. On the contrary, large quantities of broken Inka pottery were found in the middens. Though they were able to obtain imperial ceramics, they consumed this item in mundane domestic contexts and did not employ them to heighten their social status.

CERAMIC PRODUCTION AND STYLE

Ceramic production and style provide fascinating information about the relationship between the Inkas and their subjects. There are two ceramic types associated with Inka expansion over the northern Calchaquí Valley: Inka ceramics proper, produced in the region or in neighboring regions and of lesser quality compared to the ceramics manufactured in the core of the empire; and ceramic vessels that combine Inka and local stylistic features. This latter type of pottery generally preserved Inka standard forms while incorporating non-Inka decoration and motifs.[12] Archaeologists have classified these ceramics as Mixed-Inka style that mingle Inka forms with non-Inka decoration (Calderari 1991; Calderari and Williams 1991; D'Altroy et al. 1994; Hyslop 1993; Menzel 1959).

There are different types of Mixed-Inka ceramics in the northern Calchaquí Valley. For example, the style archaeologists have defined as Inka Paya was the combination of Inka forms (arípalos; plates with a stylized bird head or with a round button as a handle; and short-necked, flat-bottomed bottles) and Chicha or Yavi decoration from southern Bolivia and northern Argentina (Krapovickas 1983). There are also some examples of Inka vessels (arípalos), with decoration from Quebrada de Humahuaca (Argentina), and Inka Pacajes style, or Inka pottery (simple plates or plates with a stylized bird head as a handle) with Pacajes motifs, originally from southern Titicaca.[13] Examples of Inka pottery with indigenous or Santamariana decoration are present as well, including arípalos and plates (forms that do not belong to Santamariana ceramic

FIGURE 5.8. Inka and local ceramics from the northern Calchaquí Valley:
(1) Santamariana bowls, (2) Santamariana urns, (3) Inka plates, and (4) Inka
aríbalos (modified from Ambrosetti 1907–1908).

repertoire) with Santamariana motifs or black-polished surfaces.[14] Figure
5.8 shows examples of Santamariana (figure 5.8, 1 and 2) and Inka pottery
(figure 5.8, 3 and 4). Some of the motifs painted on this Inka pottery are
typically Santamariana, such as circular and rectangular spirals, hands or
combs, and reticulations. The zoomorphic figure with an inner cross on
the *aríbalo* in the right bottom corner — probably a *suri* or Andean ostrich
— is also a distinctive northern Calchaquí design.

It is important to determine whether the Mixed-Inka style constituted
a local emulation of Inka pottery or a good whose production and distribution were controlled by the Inkas. There is some solid evidence to suggest
that the latter situation took place in the northern Calchaquí Valley. First,
both Mixed-Inka and provincial Inka pottery are not widely distributed
in the region and are only found, usually together, in Inka settlements
and in a handful of local sites, which suggests a restricted circulation of
this product. Second, Chicha/Yavi-Inka ceramics are associated with
Inka expansion in northwestern Argentina. Chicha/Yavi-Inka ceramics
have been found in almost every Inka site in northwestern Argentina. In
addition, there is no evidence for the presence of Chicha/Yavi-Inka or
Pacajes ceramics in the northern Calchaquí Valley before Inka times.[15]
All these facts suggest that the Inkas brought these styles into the region.

Third, macroscopic ceramic paste analysis of Chicha/Yavi-Inka sherds from the northern Calchaquí Valley indicates that this pottery was not manufactured in the region but brought from the altiplano (Williams 1999). Fourth, it is possible that at least some Chicha/Yavi-Inka vessels were produced in the northern Calchaquí Valley. It is worthwhile mentioning that historical accounts reveal the presence of Chicha *mitmaqkuna* in the region (Lorandi and Boixadós 1987–1988). As has been very well established, the *mitmaqkuna* worked exclusively for the Inkas, who not only controlled their labor but also the goods they produced.[16] Fifth, some evidence suggests that Santamariana-Inka pottery may also have belonged to imperial spheres of production. Santamariana-Inka vessels not only have Santamariana decoration but also generally present a combination of Santamariana, Inka, and Inka-related styles, such as Chicha/Yavi-Inka and/or Quebrada de Humahuaca style. Additionally, decoration of Santamariana-Inka vessels does not closely follow Santamariana stylistic standards, especially with respect to the organization and position of motifs on the vessel surface (figure 5.8, compare particularly the decoration of Santamariana bowls versus Inka plates), as if they were made by foreign pottery makers.

A clear proof that Mixed-Inka pottery was an Inka product comes from archaeological studies throughout the Andes. Hyslop (1993), who traveled extensively throughout Tawantinsuyu's territory, recognized the wide presence of Inka vessels decorated with the designs and motifs of subject societies, which suggests that the production of Mixed-Inka pottery could have been a common and accepted policy throughout the Inka Empire. Considering all these aspects, it is likely that the Inkas encouraged and controlled the production and circulation of Mixed-Inka pottery in the northern Calchaquí Valley and that they consented and promoted the inclusion of northern Calchaquí decoration in imperial-produced ceramics.

Nevertheless, while Inka conquerors included Santamariana decoration on the imperial vessels, this was not the case among subject communities. Santamariana ceramics were not affected by the Inka presence, remaining without major changes during the period the Inkas dominated the northern Calchaquí Valley. Indigenous pottery makers were not influenced by the Inka style and did not imitate Inka ceramics or the styles associated with the Inkas. Neither in the ceramic samples obtained during my excavations in Cortaderas Derecha nor in other collections from Late and Inka period sites[17] are there cases of Santamariana vessels with Inka, Yavi/Chicha-Inka, or Pacajes-Inka decoration.[18]

To sum up, there was not any major transformation in these objects after Inka conquest;[19] northern Calchaquíes kept making much the same ceramics as they did before. There are, however, some very few exceptions. Archaeologists have recovered a small number of local-style bowls with Inka and Chicha decorations from La Paya/Guitián, where the most influenced and Inkanized people of the northern Calchaquí Valley lived.[20]

Santamariana ceramic manufacture was not a specialized or centralized activity, but rather it constituted a household-level production. In addition, archaeological evidence shows that Santamariana pottery was homogeneously distributed among Late period people and households (Acuto 2004:60). In other words, the consumption and use of these ceramics were not restricted to a privileged social group or elite, but rather Santamariana ceramic vessels were enjoyed by everybody within indigenous communities. In this way, and although the recently formed elite of La Paya/Guitián began to employ Inka material culture to represent their status and legitimate their power, the great majority of the northern Calchaquíes continued producing and reproducing local styles and symbols. Even those who inhabited Cortaderas Derecha, and who subsequently might have been more affected by Inka culture, did not change their ceramic style or incorporate Inka motifs into their pottery. It seems that these individuals decided to keep their pots distinct from the symbols of their rulers and of their subjugation.

MORTUARY PRACTICES

Mortuary practices, like ceramic production, show a retention of indigenous practices under Inka domination. Although the goal of my research in Cortaderas did not include the excavation of tombs, I found two burials in Cortaderas Derecha. One of them was found underneath the floor of the principal room of the residential compound AD 1 (figure 5.7). It was a round pit 50 centimeters in diameter containing the remains of four unborn or newborn infants deposited inside a large fragment of a cooking pot. The fact that the bones were disturbed suggests that this burial was reopened several times to accommodate new individuals. As burial goods, an obsidian projectile point, a small bead, and a small piece of red pigment were left inside this tomb. The second burial was discovered within a circular stone structure 2.6 meters in diameter containing the articulated skeletons of three individuals and the isolated skull of a fourth person. The three complete individuals were a male 25 to 30 years old, and two females, one 20 to 23 years old and the other 25 years old. The skull belonged to a 12-year-old child (Aranda and Luna 1999). Items recovered within this grave included a group of broken decorated Santamariana vessels (both urns and bowls), undecorated ceramics, a big ovoid piece of red pigment (6 by 8 centimeters) and other pieces of red and white pigments, a small bronze chisel, an obsidian arrowhead, a beautifully decorated stone spindle whorl (typical of the indigenous Late period), a fragment of a grinding stone, and two pestles.

Despite the presence of Inka ceramics in the fill of these graves as well as in the residential compounds associated with them, we found no Inka ceramics or any Inka artifact as part of the grave goods. My studies in Cortaderas Derecha demonstrated the ubiquitous distribution of Inka ceramics throughout the site and in domestic contexts (Acuto 2004). Even though the inhabitants of this particular village obtained and used imperial pottery in different contexts and discarded it in the large middens, they did not incorporate Inka ceramics in their funerary rituals. It seems, therefore, that the inhabitants of Cortaderas Derecha did not want to contaminate this ritual context with the symbols of their domination. Although the sample is small, it is suggestive, indicating that the funerary practices of those who lived under direct imperial rule did not undergo dramatic transformation, but rather they maintained the general pattern of pre-Inka times (Aranda and Luna 1999; Aranda et al. 1999). This, of course, was not the case of those who resided in La Paya/Guitián, where a small group of people included Inka objects as grave goods.

Discussion

How can we explain the unimportance that Inka objects had for Cortaderas Derecha's inhabitants, clearly reflected in the careless use of imperial pottery? Why was there only one case of partial emulation of Inka architecture in Cortaderas Derecha and just a handful of cases in the northern Calchaquí Valley? Why did the inhabitants of this village avoid including imperial objects in their burials? Why was Inka decoration practically never incorporated into Santamariana pottery?

In my opinion, although the inhabitants of Cortaderas Derecha lived under direct Inka rule, intensively working for the Inkas in food production and especially food processing, and although they experienced the co-optation of their labor and the goods they produced, these people managed to carry out acts of resistance against imperial colonization, rejecting at least certain aspects of Inka culture (see also Aranda et al. 1999). It is unlikely that the Inkas prohibited the residents of Cortaderas Derecha from including imperial objects in their graves. In some sense, the presence of a significant amount of Inka pottery throughout the midden stratigraphy suggests that these people freely used and discarded Inka ceramics. On the contrary, I claim that Cortaderas Derecha's households intentionally did not place Inka items in their tombs. This indicates that they developed two parallel strategies: retaining their mortuary rituals immutable while assimilating foreign elements into their daily activities. A similar situation happened regarding Santamariana ceramic production, both in Cortaderas Derecha and in the whole region. There is yet no evidence that the Inkas directly controlled or influenced the household-level production of Santamariana pottery. This means that the inhabitants of Cortaderas Derecha, as well as the great majority of northern Calchaquí households, purposely ignored Inka designs and made sure not to include them in their ceramic vessels. In a similar way, the great majority of local people did not seem to have been interested in copying Inka architectural forms and techniques. Finally, despite the inhabitants of Cortaderas Derecha having access to Inka ceramic vessels, they did not consider them as a special kind of good worthy of being preserved or used in special social contexts. In other words, while a small group of people, especially from the La Paya/Guitián community, accepted and negotiated Inka domination (thus providing them advantages and a higher status), other inhabitants of the northern Calchaquí Valley engaged in acts of cultural resistance against Tawantinsuyu.

The three social fields (the production of domestic architecture and space, ceramic manufacture and consumption, and mortuary practices) where northern Calchaquíes chose to carry out these acts of cultural resistance and to avoid their contamination with the inclusion of the symbols of their subjugation were three of the most significant realms of vernacular social life, closely related to northern Calchaquí identity and worldview.

As explained above, residential compounds were the basic spatial and social unit of northern Calchaquí settlements. Late period society did not have any relevant, centralized, and formalized institutions above the house. Domestic spaces were of paramount significance for northern Calchaquí social life. Consumption, production, social and biological reproduction, family ties, and rituals were tightly entangled within Santamariana dwellings. Archaeological excavations in the region have shown that food processing and consumption, storage, ceramic and lithic production and use, metallurgy, and textile manufacture were all usually conducted inside domestic compounds (Acuto 2000; D'Altroy et al. 2000; DeMarrais 1997; Gifford 2003; Jacob 1999; Pollard 1981, 1983). In addition, the house was a key focus of ritual activities. The lack of big and formal public spaces in the majority of local Late period sites seems to confirm this. Within houses, local people buried their dead relatives in circular tombs or underneath room floors, or in mound platforms directly associated with domestic compounds. Another important ritual activity undertaken at the domestic level was the burial of infants, a practice that included Santamariana urns, one of the more ubiquitous material objects these communities produced (Pollard 1983). All in all, the importance of domestic spaces in northern Calchaquí communities was significant, since many social practices and activities took place within these spaces, and many social relations were articulated within and through houses.

Late period societies could be considered a House Society (Carsten and Hugh-Jones 1995). In this type of society, social life unfolds and reproduces within dwellings, and material practices are organized through the house. The house, as social unit and as built environment, has a dominant role in social organization and is a prime agent of socialization; "houses come to stand for social groups and represent the world around them" (Carsten and Hugh-Jones 1995:1). Since the world, social categories, and cosmology are experienced, learned, and embodied within dwellings, the house plays a central part in the constitution of people's subjectivities. In this sense, in House Societies the dwelling is a social unit that goes beyond practices of subsistence, kinship, or its inhabitants, but rather it entangles economy, social interaction, rituals, kinship, cosmology, metaphors, architecture, materiality, and people.

The material house and its inhabitants are tightly intertwined inasmuch as they form a dialectically constituted entity. The house and the body are intimately linked. The house is an extension of the person, and therefore of the self. Houses can be personified and people and groups objectified in buildings. Households' and houses' life cycles are linked; hence building, place, and identity are articulated.

As in House Societies, northern Calchaquí Valley residential compounds did not necessarily stand for private, feminine realm, domestic, or mundane. They overcame basic dualities by entangling within one place different social domains: inside/outside, public/private, masculine/feminine, domestic/political, life/death, and ritual/mundane. The meanings and activities of the compound changed according to the context. As in House Societies, northern Calchaquí Valley houses were a significant social and material realm, a key category, a focus of ritual elaboration, and a point of reference in people's understanding of the world (Carsten and Hugh-Jones 1995:21). The great significance that houses had in northern Calchaquí Valley society is probably the reason why they remained unchanged during Inka colonization.

The highly decorated Santamariana ceramic vessels were one of the most ubiquitous objects in the region. These vessels were widely and homogeneously distributed among the communities and households of the northern Calchaquí Valley (Acuto 2004:60–61) and participated in a number of social fields and activities: domestic, funerary, consumption, and storage, and probably in the construction of regional identity and the integration of local communities (Tarragó 2000; Tarragó et al. 1997). Ceramic vessels comprised a large portion of the material world of northern Calchaquí communities and were one of the paramount material objects on which indigenous communities portrayed their symbols and meanings. Indigenous iconography also appears on other portable objects (tablets and tubes used for inhaling hallucinogenic substances, dried and engraved calabashes, spindle whorls, wooden and ceramic figurines, and metal discs) and in rock art. However, and beyond issues of preservation, ceramic vessels were still a more common and ubiquitous material item than the other portable artifacts. In addition, while the majority of rock art was concentrated in specific places in the landscape, sometimes afar from settlements, and hence met in special occasions, ceramics had a daily occurrence.

Santamariana urns and bowls, as well as other types of vessel forms, were highly visible and ubiquitous canvases on which symbols and meanings were displayed, communicated, and shared (figure 5.8, 1 and 2). They operated as a medium that served to transmit social meanings and perhaps to narrate myths and stories. Ceramic vessels conveyed these symbols and narratives into many activities northern Calchaquíes developed, and gave these meanings a daily presence. The absence of Inka iconography in Santamariana pottery indicates that northern Calchaquíes chose to preserve vernacular meanings and symbolic narratives.

The funerary sphere constituted a central aspect of northern Calchaquí communal and domestic life, and social reproduction. The incorporation of the dead within domestic contexts (or in close proximity to habitation sites), which generated a constant interaction with ancestors, confirms the enmeshment of mortuary practices into daily life. This association is also represented by grave goods, which in their great majority were objects previously used in domestic contexts and daily activities. Therefore, funerary practices and domestic life and quotidian routines were two entangled social spheres.[21] Furthermore, the great number of adult and infant burials found in Late period sites, as well as the early age at which most people died, shows a high level of mortality. As such, funerary activities may have been a frequent practice in those times.

As this case shows, the colonized showed no passive acceptance and compliance to domination. Northern Calchaquí households, especially those who resided in Cortaderas Derecha under direct Inka power, were not submissive receptors of Inka cultural influence; quite the opposite, they had the agency to change their practical actions in order to develop strategic acts of resistance against Inka penetration in three meaningful realms of indigenous social life. It is likely that at least some aspects of these realms had been part of the northern Calchaquí lifeworld, mainly if we take into account that domestic architecture, ceramic style and use, and apparently funerary rituals were part of a 500-year-old tradition in the region. Consequently, those practices and artifacts that once were elements of the northern Calchaquí lifeworld went, under Inka dominance, beyond the sphere of practical (and semiconscious) actions that characterize agency, to become part of orthodoxy and, therefore, of conscious, deliberate, and strategic actions aimed to preserve native social order and culture. In this new context of domination, the production of domestic architecture, ceramic style, pottery manufacture and use, and funerary rituals were not taken for granted anymore, but became conscious and intentional practices. Then, certain indigenous artifacts became the focus of practices of resistance.

Conclusion

This chapter has explored the way Inka colonization affected the societies that inhabited the northern Calchaquí Valley in the southern Andes, particularly their social life, lifeworld, and cultural practices. My goal has been twofold. On the one hand, I have analyzed the transformations that the Inkas intentionally sought to impose on local societies. On the other hand, throughout this chapter I have examined how northern Calchaquí communities and individuals faced Inka domination. I have found two different reactions to Inka colonization, one opportunistic and of compliance, and another that resisted foreign intervention.

One of the principal effects Tawantinsuyu domination had on the social and cultural life of the northern Calchaquí Valley was the transformation of indigenous social structure and the idea and perception of agency, as well as the transformation of some people's agency itself. Before Inka conquest, power was loosely dispersed among several native leaders who acquired their position due to their skill in combat, their natural leadership, and their diplomatic talents (Lorandi and Boixadós 1987–1988). Nonetheless, power, social inequality, and economic and political stratification were far from being institutionalized, and these chiefs and their households did not monopolize decision making or obtain better access to resources, space, or probably labor. Daily life within northern Calchaquí settlements — supported by the spatiality and materiality of these places — avoided segregation, favoring communal integration and a close knowledge of one's own community. In these places, people experienced a homogeneous material landscape and a sense of place characterized by equality, sameness, and permeability.

At the onset of Inka colonization, some northern Calchaquíes began to stand out from the rest of their community. These local individuals took advantage of the new political situation in the valley to differentiate themselves from the rest of their community, improve their status, and increase their power. This was the case of a group of people from La Paya/Guitián who, through their alliance with the Inkas and the use of Inka material culture, became the institutionalized elite of this community, and whose hierarchy was above every single local chief. The newly formed elite of La Paya/Guitián not only monopolized the consumption of Inka goods and artifacts but also acquired knowledge and were empowered to conduct Inka rituals within indigenous contexts.

The Inkas promoted, improved, and legitimated the social status of a small group of people from La Paya/Guitián, thus affecting local political structures. The emergence of these native agents should have transformed local conception and perception of agency. In this new context of colonization, there were certain individuals who overcame the structural constraints of the pre-Inka lifeworld and acquired more power, new knowledge, and a greater capacity for action. Their position, however, could have had a negative aspect: it could have produced a fragmented community and alienated these elites from the rest of the people and the social and economic networks and solidarity that existed before the Inkas. Social rejection could have been one of the unintended consequences of these new forms of praxis pushed by the Inkas.

Contrary to this small group of natives who took advantage of this new social context to improve their own situation, those natives who resided in Cortaderas Derecha under direct Inka control developed acts of cultural resistance against Inka imperialism. First, in spite of obtaining Inka artifacts, it seems these objects were not highly esteemed goods among Cortaderas Derecha's inhabitants, who did not include them in meaningful social contexts. Although they were one of the few people in the region who received Inka pottery, the residents of this little village did not treat Inka ceramics with special care. Nor did they use them to improve their status. Second, there is only one case of emulation of Inka architecture at this site, and some other few examples throughout the region, but nothing as formal as La Casa Morada. However, in general terms Inka architecture did not affect northern Calchaquí building techniques. Third, even though there are Inka vessels that incorporated Santamariana painted designs, there is practically no local vessel with Inka decoration. Even the inhabitants of Cortaderas Derecha, who could have been more influenced by Inka culture, did not change their ceramic style. Finally, and in a similar vein, although the residents of Cortaderas Derecha had Inka ceramics, they did not include Inka material culture in their tombs.

Differently from the elite of La Paya/Guitián, the inhabitants of Cortaderas Derecha (as well as other local communities) rejected and ignored
Inka material culture and fought to preserve their lifeworld in some of
the more meaningful spheres of indigenous social life. Local decorated
vessels are the most visible and ubiquitous artifacts produced by northern
Calchaquí communities; they appear in domestic, ritual, and mortuary
contexts. They were also meaningful artifacts that served as canvases for
a variety of symbols. Santamariana ceramic style was the hallmark of local
culture. On the other hand, mortuary practices and ancestors cult were
highly significant practices in the northern Calchaquí Valley. These practices were tightly tied to both domestic and communal social life. Finally,
the domestic built environment was the most important locus of activities
and social reproduction in the region. The residents of Cortaderas Derecha actively defied Inka influence and resisted the "contamination" that
Inka artifacts could have produced in three of their more meaningful social fields.

The promotion of political centralization in regions that lacked clear-
cut social stratification was a common policy within Tawantinsuyu (Morris 1998; Pease 1982). In many cases, the Inkas pushed forward the creation
of a local elite to whom they would negotiate the conditions of colonization. There were, as well, other strategies of domination, some of which
the Inkas also applied in the northern Calchaquí Valley, that inflicted severe changes in the sociopolitical organization and daily affairs of subject
communities: displacement (Wachtel 1982), resettlement (Hyslop 1976),
the direct penetration into native settlements (Alconini this volume; Gallardo et al. 1995; Grosboll 1993; Hyslop 1990; Menzel 1959; Nielsen and
Walker 1999; Palma 1998; Schreiber 1993), or the transformation of local
religion or the destruction of local sacred objects, or wak'as (Besom 2000;
Silverblatt 1988; Spalding 1984; Troncoso 2004). This shows that the Inkas
intentionally sought to change some aspect of the social life of those whom
they ruled.

Although knowledge about Inka policies and strategies of domination
is solid, we still know little about subjects' reaction to imperial rule in the
southern Andes. As in the northern Calchaquí Valley, these reactions were
multiple, from acceptance (Gallardo et al. 1995; Leibowicz 2007; Sánchez
2004) to rejection (Williams 2000), and from compliance (Lorandi 1980;
Zanolli 2003) to resistance and rebellion (Alconini 2004; Lorandi 1988). In

this sense, this article sought to explore the way social life unfolded in the northern Calchaquí Valley when the region was under the imperial thumb.

Acknowledgments

I am grateful to Randy McGuire, Reinhard Bernbeck, Bill Isbell, and Juan B. Leoni for their stimulating and insightful comments on early drafts of this article. I would also like to thank Sonia Alconini and Michael Malpass for their kind invitation to participate in this volume.

Notes

1. Current investigations in the southern Andes are demonstrating that Inka domination lasted longer than what was usually thought (see Muñoz Ovalle and Chacama 1999; Palma 1998; Pärssinen and Siiriäinen 1997, among others).

2. Although there are some differences between these two concepts, overall they describe the same social phenomena.

3. DeMarrais (1997, 2001), who also studies northern Calchaquí Valley's Late period, argues that she has found in Borgatta, a large agglomerated site, evidence of the "materialization" of corporate labor and chief's power. According to DeMarrais, the existence at this site of a number of earthen mounds, with a few small retaining walls, is clear proof of the elite's mobilization and control of labor and display of power. Nonetheless, these mounds are far from being formal and monumental structures. They present a quite informal shape, they are not very tall (usually less than 5 meters high) or massive, and their construction did not involve a great deal of work because the volume of earth used is not very large. Moreover, these mounds are common in other Late period sites and are possibly related to the construction of residential compounds, which are usually semisubterranean. Thus, I think that the production of these shapeless mounds is more connected to mundane activities than to political strategies. They were created through the accumulation of soil removed during the construction of dwellings.

4. Here again DeMarrais (1997, 2001) has a different opinion. In her studies in Borgatta, she found that a small group of residential compounds had more ceramic bowls than the rest. She concludes that these were elite households attempting to gain control over certain social practices, especially feasting. According to the data she offers, however, the difference in bowl distribution among households is small and not statistically significant.

5. This total consists of the 177 burials excavated by Ambrosetti (1907–1908) at

the beginning of the twentieth century and the 22 excavated later by Díaz (1986). It is usually believed that Ambrosetti discovered 202 tombs in La Paya/Guitián; however, several of these 202 loci were not actually burials but concentrations of objects, especially ceramic vessels, or isolated pots.

6. It is highly likely that some of these 177 burials without Inka artifacts belonged to the Late period, while others were constructed during Inka occupation. Nevertheless, due to the way they were excavated and the lack of any type of dating, at the moment I am not able to establish this. Therefore, I have decided to use the entire sample, aware that some of the burials without Inka objects are pre-Inka, while some others belonged to people who did not obtain or did not deposit Inka goods in their graves.

7. Ambrosetti bought this collection from treasure hunters, and it is not clear whether they found it buried in a cache or in a burial.

8. The Inkas' presence itself may have also contributed to change natives' idea and perception of agency. The Inkas unified a politically fragmented region, centralizing power, institutionalizing social inequality, and becoming the upper social stratum, above the influence of every single local chief. The representatives of Tawantinsuyu had the capacity for controlling the economy and politics of the entire region, something that no local leader had achieved before.

9. Gifford, who has developed a detailed study of local and Inka architecture, explains that "rectified buildings with thinner walls (e.g., less than 75 cm) without upright stones are likely to be of Inka design, while rounded, or 'shaped' structures with thicker walls (e.g., greater than 75 cm) and upright stones are likely to be of indigenous design" (Gifford 2003:184). See Gifford (2003:chapter 5) for an excellent comparison of northern Calchaquí Valley and Inka architecture.

10. Other known examples are found in Loma del Oratorio in Cachi Adentro (Tarragó and Díaz 1972), SL005 and SL033 in the La Poma area, RP002 in the Potrero River area, and RC021 on the western bank of the Calchaquí River (Gifford 2003).

11. Preliminarily, only 42 out of 192 native sites contain Inka ceramics or some Inka architectural feature (DeMarrais 1997; Díaz 1983, 1992; Gifford 2003; Tarragó and Díaz 1972, 1977). However, Inka material culture is scarce at all these sites, with the exception of La Paya/Guitián, Tero, and Choque (figure 5.1).

12. See Bray 2003 for a description of the most frequent Inka pottery shapes found in the provinces.

13. I have found other foreign ceramic types associated with Inka expansion in the northern Calchaquí Valley — for example, Yocavil and Famabalasto Black on Red from Catamarca Province, Argentina. However, these sherds are too small, and I cannot say if they belonged to Inka-shaped vessels or to original Yocavil or Famabalasto Black on Red vessels.

14. Black-polished ceramics have a long tradition in the northern Calchaquí Valley. They were present in the region from the Formative to the Late period.

15. However, archaeologists have found in the northern Calchaquí Valley ceramics from Quebrada de Humahuaca in pre-Inka contexts (DeMarrais 1997; Gifford 2003:175–180, 199).

16. In a neighboring region, archaeologists have found clear evidence of the production of Mixed-Inka ceramics within Inka sites and produced by Inka *mitmaqkuna* (Lorandi 1991). This could have been also the case on the South Coast of Peru (Menzel 1959). This shows that the incorporation of native decoration on the surface of the imperial pottery was a regular Inka policy (see Hyslop 1993).

17. This interpretation is based on the analysis of Santamariana ceramic vessels published in Ambrosetti (1907–1908) and the study of 153 Santamariana pots from different sites (especially Tero, a local site occupied during the Inka period), deposited in the Museo Arqueológico P.P. Díaz, Cachi, Argentina.

18. I do not include Humahuaca-Inka, the other Mixed-Inka style found in the northern Calchaquí Valley, because there were contacts and exchange between the northern Calchaquí Valley and this region before Inka conquest. Moreover, there are designs that widely circulated throughout northwestern Argentina before the time of the Inkas, some of which Santamariana and Quebrada de Humahuaca styles share.

19. This is very different from what would happen later. The impact of the Spanish Conquest greatly transformed northern Calchaquí Valley ceramics, producing what some scholars have understood as the decadence of the Santamariana style (Tarragó 1984).

20. See Ambrosetti (1907–1908:figure 153); Boman (1908:vol. 1, plates XIII b and XIV h); and Calderari (1991).

21. This was not the case of other social spheres, such as practices associated with rock art sites, which were kept apart and far away from residential sites.

Claudia Rivera Casanovas

Chapter Six

Forms of Imperial Control and the Negotiation of Local Autonomy in the Cinti Valley of Bolivia

Editors' Introduction

This chapter presents novel information on the valley of Cinti, Chuqui-saca, part of the Qaraqara territory. Based on a regional-scale analysis, intrasite artifact assemblage, architectural analysis, and ethnohistorical information, Rivera discusses the kinds of changes that the Inkas intro-duced in the valley of Cinti to assess the nature of the Inka control. Using data from her regional survey, Rivera shows that prior to the Inkas, the region already had a three-tiered integrated socioeconomic system, with Jatun Huankarani as the regional center. This regional center and the subsidiary secondary settlements were not only located in the best agri-culturally productive areas but also had a significant number of corrals, suggesting the centers' participation in llama caravan exchange networks. In addition, these centers had large proportions of serving vessels, sug-gesting the involvement of local chiefs residing in these centers in feast-ing and redistributive tasks. By the time of the Inkas, important changes are observed. On the one hand, the absence of Inka facilities, imperial cultural materials, or sites with mixed Inka-local architecture suggests to

Rivera that the local elites did not choose to follow imperial canons and that the Inkas controlled the region in an indirect fashion. However, the author also suggests that despite this indirect control, the region was progressively incorporated into the Inka economy. Although the three-tiered settlement hierarchy with Jatun Huankarani at the top remained, important changes are observable. First, subsidiary sites along the road network witnessed an increase in the proportion of serving vessels in comparison to large centers; second, satellite settlements around the largest centers saw an increase in the number of corrals; and third, there was an agricultural intensification marked by the expansion of agricultural terraces and associated features. However, the distribution of prestige materials was not substantially different across sites. To Rivera, this indicates that in addition to enhancing the agrarian regional economy, the Inkas were strategically controlling and reorienting the nature of the exchange networks. The fact that proportionately more serving vessels were found in subsidiary settlements than in main centers suggests to the author that hospitality and redistribution activities shifted to support facilities along the road network.

Taking into account the absence of Inka facilities or circulation of prestige imperial materials, Rivera suggests an indirect form of imperial rule, although the region was progressively incorporated into the imperial economy. An aspect worth exploring further is the changing power relations of the regional elites at the time of the Inkas. An alternative way to assess the changes observed by Rivera may involve the possibility that these regional centers, despite their involvement in trade and exchange, were no longer the home of powerful chiefs having the capacity to engage in large-scale redistributive tasks. If such were the case, this would suggest that despite the indirect control that the Inkas exercised, the regional lords were increasingly lessened in status or changed residences, and that therefore their role in the emerging administrative structure was restricted to overseeing the proper functioning of the exchange networks. Clearly, future research by Rivera and colleagues in Cinti is crucial to assess the effects of the Inka conquest from household and communal levels. The value of this chapter is that it introduces this region to a broader debate relating the Inka influence in the southern Bolivian valleys from a regional perspective.

Introduction

Recent years have seen great emphasis in studies on the nature of Inka expansion and control in the southern Bolivian Andes (Alconini 2002, 2004; Angelo Zelada 1999; Cruz 2007; Lecoq and Céspedes 1997; Lima Tórrez 2000, 2008a, 2008b; Raffino 1993a; Rivera Casanovas 2002, 2004, 2008, 2008). Most of these studies point out the Inkas employed strategies of governance that included indirect or mixed control, especially in the valleys of this region. Indirect control seems to have been the response to the fact that most of societies in these areas were organized into regional federations; therefore levels of sociopolitical organization were complex enough for the Inkas to take advantage of them in order to implement imperial policies, extract resources, and assure security (D'Altroy 1987, 1992; D'Altroy and Earle 1985; Schreiber 1987). The processes of imperial annexation can be better understood by complementing the ethnohistorical sources with archaeological information that sheds light on local elite strategies of alliance and negotiation of local power within the imperial structure.

The Charkas Confederation and the Qaraqaras

Southern Bolivian polities were organized into multiethnic federations in the time previous to the Inka arrival into this region (figure 6.1). By the time of the Inkas, the Charkas confederation became one of the most prominent organizations, constituted by at least four regional federations known as the Charkas, Qaraqaras, Chuyes, and Chichas (Bouysse-Cassagne 1986; Del Río 1995b; Espinoza Soriano 1969). Although some scholars have suggested that the organization of this macroscale confederation could be the result of Inka policies of organization (Harris 1997), it is broadly accepted that it was constituted over an existing political structure (Platt 1982). Each one of the major groups within had a nested organization in which regional polities, probably with variable degrees of sociopolitical integration (Rivera Casanovas 2004), were macroregionally integrated. These polities had an *ayllu* type of organization with inclusive hierarchical levels and dual organization, and regional centers, or *markas* (Platt et al. 2006).

The Qaraqara was one of these federations. According to ethnohistori-

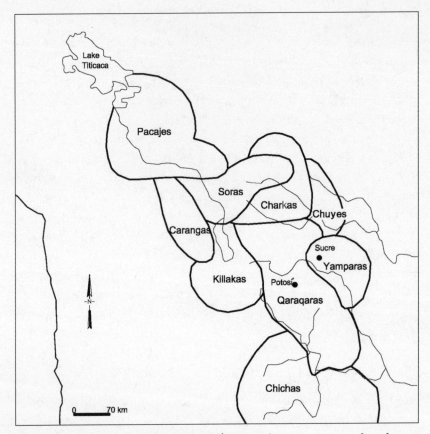

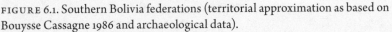

FIGURE 6.1. Southern Bolivia federations (territorial approximation as based on Bouysse Cassagne 1986 and archaeological data).

cal documents, its territory lay between the Charkas and the Chichas (Del Río 1995a). It encompassed a mountainous region composed of valleys intersected with highlands in what actually is the southern part of the Chayanta Province; the Frías, Saavedra, and Linares provinces; at least the eastern half of the Quijarro Province; and the northeastern part of the Nor Chichas Province in Potosí (Platt et al. 2006).

In Chuquisaca, the Qaraqara encompassed the western part of the Nor Cinti Province (Del Río 1995b), and probably part of the Sud Cinti Province, taking into account that Ayra Kanchi, lord of the Qaraqaras, built fortresses in Pilaya and Paspaya (Platt et al. 2006:72). The Qaraqara federation was composed of at least eight distinct ethnic groups that occupied different geographic areas (Del Río 1995a; Rasnake 1988). These groups were the Macha, Visijsa, Chaqui, Moro Moro, Colo-Caquina, Picachuri, Cara Cara, and Tacobamba. People from these groups had identifiable core areas but also were intermixed in some territories (Rasnake 1988).

The Qaraqara Federation from an Archaeological Perspective

Archaeological studies in the Qaraqara territory have been oriented to solve basic ceramic chronological sequences, establish cultural areas (Ibarra Grasso 1944, 1960, 1973; Vignale and Ibarra Grasso 1943), or explore the characteristics of human occupation through time (Lecoq and Céspedes 1997). None of these studies focused on understanding the dynamics of late polities in the region. There are just a few references to the Qaraqaras, and few suggestions about the relationship between late ceramic styles present in the area and their correspondence with the ethnohistorical groups (e.g., Raffino 1993a, 1993b). For instance, Lecoq (1999) suggests the Yura style might have been associated with the ethnohistorical Visijsas, which formed part of the Qaraqara federation. A recent regional study in the city of Potosí and neighboring regions has identified a dense occupation during the Late Intermediate period related to the Qaraqaras. This is seen in the concentration of big complex settlements in the valleys near Potosí, an intense modification of the landscape with the construction of agricultural terraces, mining, and interregional exchange through a system of roads and llama caravans (Cruz 2007).

Considering that ceramic styles convey information about ethnic identity (Wiessner 1990), and that style can be emblematic of group identity, it is possible that the ceramic styles denominated as Yura and Huruquilla by Ibarra Grasso (1973) correspond to component groups of the Qaraqara federation. In fact, the distribution of the Yura and Huruquilla ceramic styles roughly corresponds to the Qaraqara territory described in ethnohistorical accounts. Ibarra Grasso named the Huruquilla and Yura styles based on local names mentioned in the Matienzo itinerary (a document from the late sixteenth century) for the area where they are distributed. Obviously, in the early 1940s the ethnohistorical information about the Qaraqaras and Visijsas was not available to him, and thus he used those names for identifying such "archaeological cultures." Enforcing the relationship between the Yura and Huruquilla ceramic styles with the territory comprising the Qaraqara, the recent studies of Pablo Cruz (2007:33) show the distribution of the Qaraqara-Yura ceramic complex for the region of Potosí. The styles within the Qaraqara-Yura ceramic complex include the Yura-Potosí, Qaraqara, Chaqui-Condoriri, and Huruquilla styles (Cruz 2007).

The fact that both styles, the Yura and Huruquilla (figure 6.2), are related to the Qaraqaras can be seen in the distribution of these ceramics in what was the area corresponding to the federation. Based on Ibarra Grasso's observations and actual archaeological information about the dispersion of these styles, an approximation to the Qaraqara territory would include the following places in Potosí: the provinces of Linares, Quijarro, Frías, and Saavedra; the southern part of Chayanta Province; and the northeastern part of Nor Chichas Province. In Chuquisaca, it encompasses most of Nor Cinti Province and the western part of Sud Cinti Province (figure 6.3).

The ethnohistorical territory and the ceramic distribution correlate well; there is little doubt about their correspondence. Recent research carried out in the western part of the Nor Cinti and Sud Cinti provinces also found that these regions probably formed part of the Qaraqara federation during the Late Intermediate period and the Late Horizon, and were not part of the Chicha territory as was stated in some colonial accounts. These narratives name the settlements in this region as *pueblos de reducción* (e.g., Bouysse-Cassagne 1986). It is likely that these ethnohistorical descriptions emphasize the presence of Chicha colonies inserted by the Inkas.

The Inka Expansion into the Charkas Confederation Territory

According to Cieza de León (1880), the Charkas confederation, after resisting the Inka conquest for some time, was conquered by Thupa Inka Yupanki. However, it is likely that diplomatic relations were established earlier with Pachakuti (Platt et al. 2006). The *Memorial de Charcas* mentions that groups forming part of this polity were given a special status as the warriors of the Inkas because of their eminent services in participating in military campaigns and guarding some points of the frontier against the Chiriguanos (Espinoza Soriano 1969:125; Platt et al. 2006). The for-

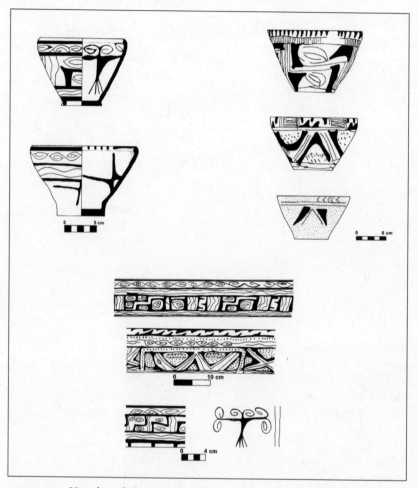

FIGURE 6.2. Vessels with Huruquilla-style motifs from the Cinti Valley, Late Regional Development period (A.D. 800–1430).

mer name of the Qaraqaras was "white Charka," given by the Inkas as an honorific title (Platt et al. 2006). Although it seems that Qaraqara groups as part of their privileges were exempt from paying tribute (Platt 1988), there were regional variations. For example, the Qaraqaras who settled in mining regions paid tribute in silver but were exempt from other services (Del Río 1995b; Espinoza Soriano 1969).

In this context, the Inkas, as a way to ensure the loyalty of the Qaraqaras and other ethnic lords, married regional chiefs with women of the royal *pa-*

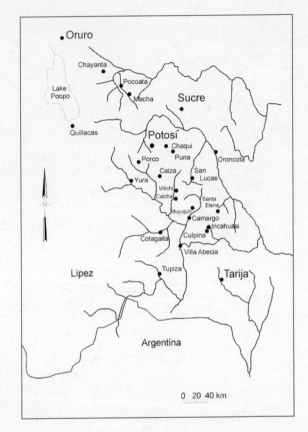

FIGURE 6.3.
Approximation of the
Qaraqara federation
territory (based on
Del Río 1995a and ar-
chaeological data).

naqas. In this way, domination was reinforced through kinship ties, and indirect control over these lords was established (Del Río 1995b; Platt 1988).

Therefore, the sociopolitical organization of the federation and the
capacity of negotiation of its leaders at the time of the conquest seem to
have been two important factors in the establishment of indirect control
in at least parts of its territory such as the valleys. In areas with mineral
resources, especially silver mines, the control might have been mixed — or
more direct — judging from the presence of imperial buildings and other
facilities associated with areas of mines such as in Porco (Lecoq and Céspedes 1997; see also Van Buren and Presta, this volume), Potosí (Cruz
2007), and San Lucas, Chuquisaca (Ibarra Grasso 1973; Rivera Casanovas
2008, 2008). In this context, the Qaraqaras enjoyed certain local autonomy, and their sociopolitical organization was maintained.

The Cinti Valley is an area where the Inkas established indirect control as is seen from archaeological information recently recorded (Rivera Casanovas 2002, 2004, 2005). Although this situation permitted the local leaders and population to maintain their sociopolitical structure, there were subtle changes over time that suggest the area was being progressively integrated into an imperial structure.

The Cinti Valley

The Cinti Valley is located in southwestern Chuquisaca in an area of steep mountains and dissected valleys (figure 6.4). It measures 80 kilometers long and constitutes a natural corridor linking the *puna* with eastern valleys and the piedmont slopes. The valley is topographically divided into the upper valley, which comprises a series of small subbasins with landscapes that range from *cabecera de valle* to high valley, and the canyon, with a dry, warm climate and an elongated topography.

A recent regional survey carried out in the valley covering an area of 253 square kilometers produced critical information for evaluating the processes of social complexity through time and assessing the nature of changes in local organization during the Inka domination of the region (Rivera Casanovas 2004). Regional organization and staple and wealth finance strategies were explored in order to understand continuity and change in local organization under the Inka rule. Even though the occupational sequence was long, I only focus on the Late Regional Development period before the Inka, and the Late period following the Inka conquest.

LATE REGIONAL DEVELOPMENT PERIOD

During the Late Regional Development period (A.D. 800–1430), which corresponds approximately to the Late Intermediate period in the Central Andean chronological scheme, there was regional population growth and nucleation, and a local polity developed in the Cinti Valley as part of a process initiated during the previous period (figure 6.5). This polity formed part of the Qaraqara federation judging by the widespread use of the Huruquilla style and architectural and mortuary patterns similar to those found elsewhere within the Qaraqara territory (Lecoq and Céspedes 1997; Vignale and Ibarra Grasso 1943).

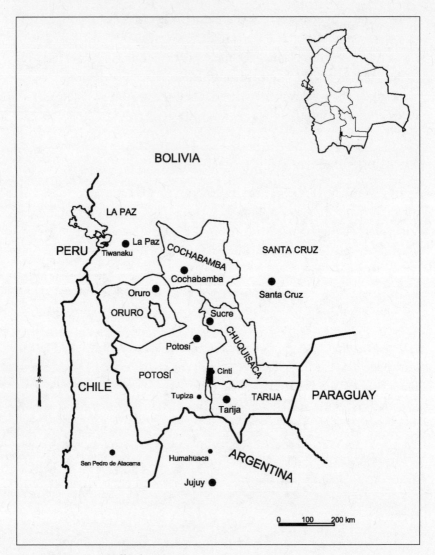

FIGURE 6.4. Cinti Valley location.

Regional Organization. In terms of regional organization, there was a continuation of hierarchy — as was witnessed in the previous period — in the upper valley. In this context, Jatun Huankarani (C-48), encompassing 17 hectares, emerged as a dominant center, and there was an expansion in the number of large villages that likely acted as subsidiary centers in the upper valley system. The settlement patterns suggest a regional hierarchy of three levels with one regional center on top, followed by several large

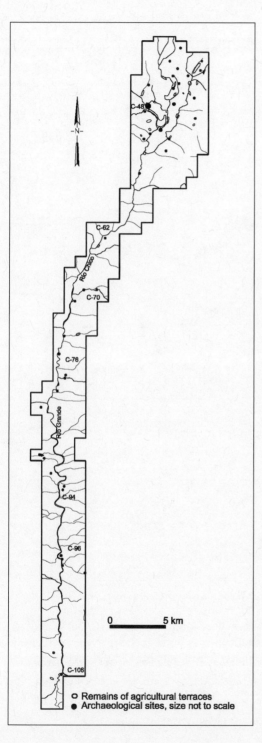

FIGURE 6.5. Late Regional Development period site distribution in the Cinti Valley. Jatun Huankarani is site C-48.

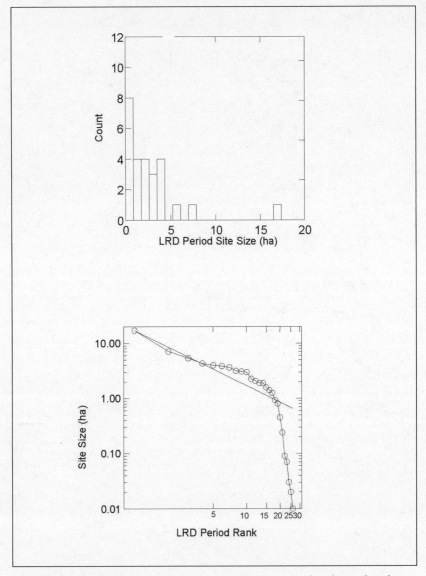

FIGURE 6.6. Late Regional Development period site sizes and rank size distributions for the Cinti Valley.

villages or local centers and small villages and hamlets (figure 6.6). A rank size analysis for the entire valley depicts a nearly perfect log-normal pattern in which the system is integrated under a large site, Jatun Huankarani, followed by the local centers. This log-normal distribution for the valley suggests a well-integrated settlement system.

However, while a three-tiered settlement hierarchy is present in the upper valley, suggesting an integrated system, in the canyon zone there are only two levels, formed by small and large villages. Rank size distribution of sites in the canyon area presents a convex pattern. This pattern could be interpreted as indicating that there was little horizontal integration among the lower sites, and that their articulation into an overarching system, if they were articulated at all, was through interaction with upper valley settlements. In addition, the regional center and some local centers present a more elaborated layout and architecture in some sectors along with spatial zonation, suggesting the presence of elite areas or barrios with differential status.

Economic Patterns. In the canyon zone, complex agroeconomic patterns developed, and the size of the settlements was increasingly governed by investment in agricultural intensification in the form of systems of terraces and irrigation, and/or by sociopolitical factors (possibly including political competition and tribute flow).

An intersite analysis of ceramic materials revealed no strong differences in proportions of serving vessels among sites. However, sites located in the upper valley and the northern part of the canyon had higher proportions of serving vessels than sites located farther south in the canyon, suggesting residents in the latter area were less engaged in activities using serving wares. Considering settlement patterns, site hierarchy, and the different clusters of sites identified, it appears that there was always more complexity toward the northern part of the valley than in the south. If feasting or serving activities were important for leadership strategies, this might suggest higher social status households may have been concentrated in the northern part of the valley. In terms of storage vessel proportions, centers, on average, have higher proportions than villages, suggesting differential involvement in storage/surplus accumulation.

Intrasite assemblage patterns parallel the other lines of evidence (architectural and spatial) for marked social differentiation at the regional center of Jatun Huankarani and some local centers in the upper valley. The variability among sectors within this site in serving vessels and fine ware corresponds to our ranking of the degree of investment in domestic architecture, with sector 3 standing out as a high-status residential zone. Residents of this sector were engaged in serving/feasting activities. Intrasite variability in proportions of storage vessels and grinding technology, together with the presence of specialized storage structures in some of the higher status zones of this site, suggests some form of staple finance strategy. Late Regional Development period elites may not have been accumulating vast amounts of staple surplus, but the Jatun Huankarani evidence suggests that they were more involved than other households in storing, processing, and serving staple goods.

In addition, there was no evidence of wealth strategies as manifested in the concentration of prestige goods at the centers, control of craft production, or differential association of llama corrals with the centers.

LATE PERIOD

The Late period (A.D. 1430–1535), which corresponds to the Late Horizon farther north, witnessed the expansion of the Inka Empire into the region. In the Cinti Valley, there was a continuation of previous settlement trends (figure 6.7): the continued growth of regional and local centers; population growth and expansion, with the spread of small settlements throughout the valley; and agricultural intensification, with the extension of terrace systems into the upper valley and the canyon. Jatun Huankarani remained the dominant center in the valley, expanding to 23 hectares. During this period, there was a strong use and extension of what had been a preexisting road system that connected most of the larger settlements and the terraced agricultural areas. It is also likely that the Inkas settled Chicha *mitmaqkuna* in the canyon where significant proportions of Chicha style ceramics, both decorated and domestic, were recorded associated with sites occupied during this period.

Regional Organization. In the Late period marking the Inka conquest, a three-tiered hierarchy was maintained in the upper valley (figure 6.8). In comparison, in the canyon zone, for the first time in the sequence there was the development of a three-tiered hierarchy, with the rise of large secondary centers. In the earlier Late Regional Development period, only two tiers were found in the canyon zone. This suggests the integration of the canyon zone into the entire settlement hierarchy with the development of supplementary centers in the Late period. Therefore, the rank size distribution for the entire study region takes a log-normal pattern nearly identical to that of the earlier Late Regional Development period, indicating the continuation of the settlement hierarchy with Jatun Huankarani at the apex.

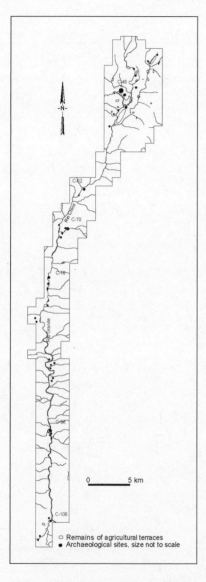

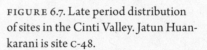

FIGURE 6.7. Late period distribution of sites in the Cinti Valley. Jatun Huankarani is site C-48.

Patterns of local architecture are similar to those of the previous period. Internal segmentation was maintained at the regional center and some local centers. In the regional center of Jatun Huankarani, a long delimiting wall that surrounds the southern part of the settlement for more than a kilometer might have been built during this period. Such a feature could have been an element of status; similar features have been described for other centers from the Late Horizon (Alconini 2002; Niles 1987). How-

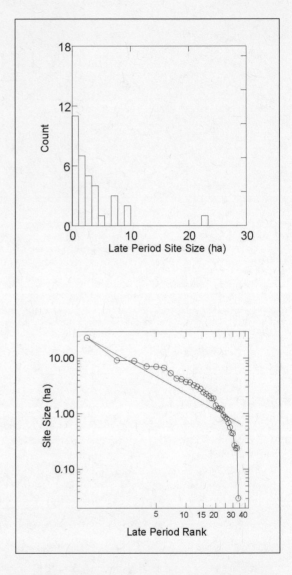

FIGURE 6.8. Late period site sizes and rank size distributions for the Cinti Valley.

ever, there is no evidence of Inka settlements or constructions following Inka architectural patterns in the valley. The fact that we have not identified buildings with Inka canons suggests an indirect imperial presence. Local elites were not copying or identifying with the Inkas through the adoption of this type of architecture.

Economic Patterns. An increased intensification in agriculture is observed in the extension of terrace systems in all areas of the valley. As the population grew, catchment zones of many centers were not enough for sustaining their population. Therefore, these centers depended on surplus produced at other sites for feeding their populations, which suggests some mechanisms to assure agricultural products or even tribute flow. During this period, sites with corrals appear associated with local centers and villages, which suggests an increase in goods and their distribution through the centers. It is likely that the Inkas had some type of control over these movements.

Intersite analysis of ceramic material corresponding to this period, or with a preponderant occupation dating from this time, shows a great deal of variation in serving vessel proportions in the Late Huruquilla and Inka-Huruquilla styles (figures 6.9 and 6.10). High proportions of serving vessels are not limited to centers. Smaller sites (such as c-16 and c-53) associated with expanses of agricultural fields also present higher proportions. It is possible that higher proportions of serving vessels at these sites are related to some specific activities carried out there. For instance, agricultural tasks and labor required in the *minka* form (labor organized to the group level for large projects) might have been sponsored by local elites, and some type of feasting, for feeding people engaged in such work, could have taken place in these locations.

The small village c-68 may also represent a "special" purpose site, as it is mainly an area of corrals associated with some structures and likely housed caravans of llamas that moved goods. It is possible that activities involving serving vessels were performed here, or even that serving vessels were moved as goods. A significant percentage of serving vessels at this site is imported pottery, suggesting that these products were being received at this place and then moved to El Patronato (c-70), a local center nearby, and distributed from there. A similar pattern has been documented for sites with corrals in the nearby region of Tupiza, at the Inka site of Chuquiago located along the Inka road network (Raffino 1993b).

In the case of storage vessels, there are marked differences in proportions in domestic storage among sites. In contrast to patterns in the previous period, villages during the Late period have more storage vessels than larger sites, perhaps suggesting a change in storage patterns.

To examine the differences among sites in imported pottery preferences, it was necessary to group the Late Regional Development and

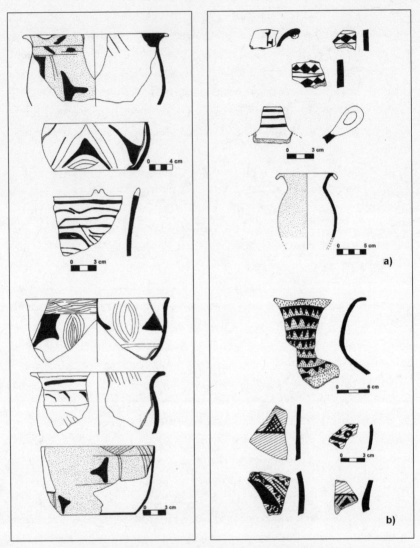

FIGURE 6.9. (Left) Late period, late Huruquilla-style vessels.

FIGURE 6.10. (Right) Late period vessels from Cinti: (a) Inka-Huruquilla style (gray paste), (b) provincial Inka styles.

Late periods together because we cannot yet separate imported styles by chronological period. The distribution of imported ceramics shows an interesting pattern, probably structured in part by the Inka presence in the region and in part by local incorporation into Inka-dominated ceramic exchange systems.

The most common imported pottery is in the Chicha style, coming from regions located to the southwest and south of the Cinti Valley. Although some of this material can be dated to the Late Regional Development period, it is most common in Late period occupations. This may in fact reflect the movement of Chicha populations into the valley as Inka *mitmaqkuna*. It is also possible that this style was the most common in Cinti because the "borders" of the Qaraqara and Chicha polities were located nearby, around the town of Las Carreras, 20 kilometers south of the research area. The closeness to the Chicha might have had an influence on the use and distribution of these ceramics in Cinti, including the influx of Chicha *mitmaqkuna*.

Surface samples yielded a small proportion of sherds coming from the Yampara area, and they were distributed through all the site hierarchy. The rest of the imported pottery, such as the altiplano styles, includes the Pacajes, Tarija, and Inka wares and materials from the highlands whose affiliation is not clear.

Centers did not exhibit proportionally more imported goods than sites at lower levels in the settlement hierarchy in surface collections. Intersite differences in imported ceramic preferences appear to be structured by population movements and proximity to exchange routes.

Late period intrasite patterns show one important change from the previous period. This shift was an increase in overall proportions of serving vessels — not only in the regional center but in other villages and smaller sites as well. This shift may relate to Inka policies that affected local sociopolitical organization as in other parts of the Andes (D'Altroy 1992; D'Altroy et al. 2000). For instance, the increase in serving vessels during this time could be linked to reciprocity, hospitality, and feasting practices that formed part of the Inka state ideology and political economy.

The very high proportion of serving vessels even at some small sites is puzzling. If serving activities are truly a measure of status or social position, these findings are intriguing. One possibility is that these sites were in some way "specialized"— for instance, serving as way stations along the road system. However, another possibility is that high-status individuals or elites were not all concentrated at Jatun Huankarani, but were instead "dispersed" through the system even down to the smallest settlement units. Clearly more research is needed to explore this pattern.

Continuity and Change during the Late Period

As can be observed from the data, the Inka domination of the Cinti Valley was indirect but possibly included the movement of foreign *mitmaqkuna* into the valley. Inka hegemony did not lead to any appreciable interruption of regional settlement trends; population growth, nucleation, and expansion all continued in the Late period. The entire valley was likely integrated into a single polity during this period, with subsystems of settlement interacting with the larger upper valley centers.

Staple finance strategies were important for Cinti leadership during the Late Regional Development and Late periods. This is seen in three main aspects: political centers were associated with the most productive agricultural lands and were disproportionately large in relation to local productivity; agricultural intensification (terraces, irrigation) was differentially associated with the centers; and the centers were the focus of the mobilization of agricultural surplus as evidenced in storage.

During the Late period, proportions of storage vessels declined at the centers and increased at smaller sites, which might suggest local elites were not controlling surplus as earlier. It is possible that some surplus would have been moved outside of the valley as part of the political economy of the Inka Empire or that there was a change in strategies at this time. In any case, this point requires more regional research in order to be addressed.

Wealth strategies seem not to have played an important role for Cinti leadership because a differential or exclusive association of centers with llama corrals during the Late Regional Development period was not identified. However, during the Late period it seems there was an increase in the number of corrals at sites close to the centers, suggesting goods were moved in and out of the centers through llama caravans. It is likely that the Inkas would have exercised more direct control of the caravans or reoriented the trade or movement of goods within their political economy. Such a pattern has been reported from other regions of the southern Andes (Costin and Earle 1989; Santoro 1995). Likewise, surface collections did not indicate a domination of craft production or circulation of high-valued goods by elites in both periods. There were no signs of differential concentration of such goods at the centers or within the centers. Valuable items such as shell beads, metal objects, alabaster, and foreign ceramics were found in small quantities at different sites in the settlement hierarchy, including small sites.

Conclusion

The Qaraqara federation was able to maintain its sociopolitical organization under the Inka rule thanks to its levels of internal organization, the capable negotiation of its leaders, and the preferential treatment of Qaraqaras as warriors of the Inkas.

However, the data also suggest the progressive integration of Qaraqaras into the Inka Empire and its administrative structure (Platt et al. 2006), as in other regions in the South-Central Andes (Stanish 1997). Forms of control varied according to the region, depending on the security and the resources available. Areas with mines, with important agricultural resources, or near the Chiriguano frontier suffered a more direct intervention, including the installation of important numbers of foreign populations as *mitmakquna*.

In the case of the Cinti Valley, the empire extracted resources and governed without direct intervention. In this sense, Inka control was indirect. Although the general trends of development were maintained, the Inka domination also produced a series of changes that probably affected control of agricultural surplus by the local elites and a reordering of the systems of regional exchange, as happened in other regions of the Andes (D'Altroy 1992). The probable presence of *mitmaqkuna* in the valley also might have had a certain impact on local organization.

The spread of serving activities in different settlements of the hierarchy might also indicate certain changes in the local organization. Either small settlements were more involved with serving activities as part of the circuits of reciprocity involving trade and *mit'a* labor, or the elites were not only residing in major centers. In addition, changes in vessel shapes and ceramic technology suggest that the local population was adopting Inka canons but not passively. They were reproducing local styles and mixing them with new elements (figures 6.9 and 6.10).

These are the first exploratory steps in approaching the Inka impact in the Cinti region by presenting a broad picture of the processes involved from a regional perspective. In the future, more research is needed for getting a finer understanding of the changes generated by the Inkas on the communal and household levels.

Mary Van Buren and Ana María Presta

Chapter Seven

The Organization of Inka Silver Production in Porco, Bolivia

Editors' Introduction

The most important contribution of this chapter is its assessment of the degree of imperial control in provinces that were distant and ecologically marginal and with low population levels, but that nevertheless held valuable resources for the Inkas. This was the case of Porco, the silver mines located near the city of Potosí, in what was the territory of Qaraqara. Although this chapter is part of an ongoing research project, the results are already suggestive. Based on a survey around Porco, including limited excavations, ethnohistorical research, and ethnoarchaeological data, the authors of this chapter highlight the economic importance of this region for the Inkas as a source of valuable metals, including silver. In a region of poor agricultural potential and low population densities, the Inkas intensified the extraction of metal by creating imperial mining facilities staffed with *mit'a* and *mitmaq* laborers. Whereas nonlocal *mit'a* workers, perhaps of Lupaca and Caranga origins, were in charge of nonspecialized labor, including the mining, collection, and extraction of ores on a temporal basis, the smelting in wind (*huayrachinas*) and refining furnaces was conducted by nonlocal specialists.

Altogether, these findings are important to understand the Inka imperial strategies of control in distant, although critical, pockets of metal extraction. Taking into account the Inka alliances with the Qaraqara lords, the different trajectories of two Qaraqara regions — Porco and Cinti — are striking. Whereas Cinti did not evidence direct imperial control, Porco was the focus of direct imperial intervention. This difference supports the assertion that despite privileged alliances with local lords, the Inka Empire sought to centralize control over the production of valuable ritual and sumptuary goods. In the case here, this held true even when ecological and demographic conditions were adverse. For Porco, this implied the construction of imperial facilities "de novo" near mining sources, including residential areas, a support agricultural base, and the installation of facilities dedicated to the processing of metals. Second, it highlights that despite such limitations, Inka control in areas with key resources was targeted and selectively intense (Williams and D'Altroy 1998).

Introduction

The search for mineral wealth was the primary motive for Inka expansion into the southern Andes, and Porco, in southern Bolivia, was one of the most important mines in the empire, supplying the silver that adorned the Coricancha in Cuzco (Cieza de León 1963:385) and the royal litter on which the Inka ruler was transported (Ocaña 1969). This chapter is based on an ongoing investigation of Porco, the overarching goal of which is to illuminate the organization of both prehispanic and Colonial period silver production in an attempt to better understand how different political regimes approached the extraction of a highly valued resource. The focus here is specifically on the nature of Inka control over the production of silver, an issue that will be examined in light of data derived from excavation, limited survey, historical sources, and observation of contemporary smelting practices. The research conducted thus far suggests that Inka exploitation of this zone was shaped by a convergence of different factors, including the skills demanded by the extractive process as well as imperial interests and local conditions. It also indicates that Inka control over mining and smelting was direct, and thus supports both Costin's (1996) predictions regarding the level of centralized control over the production of ritual and sumptuary items and Berthelot's (1986) document-based model of Inka mining.

Geographic and Historical Background

Porco is located in the Cordillera Oriental of southwestern Bolivia, 35 kilometers to the southwest of the mining center of Potosí (figure 7.1). The village and eponymous mines are situated in a large caldera (Cunningham et al. 1994) on the southern edge of the Los Frailes volcanic field at an elevation of 4,000 meters. The surrounding landscape is characterized by jagged ridges and aeolian dunes formed by the prevailing southwesterly winds. Annual precipitation is approximately 200 millimeters, and the area experiences only two frost-free months per year (Montes de Oca 1989:figure 4.4, table 4.5). As a result of the extremely arid, cold conditions, agricultural production today is limited to the occasional pasturing of sheep and llamas, although some households supplement their diets with *haba* beans and tubers produced in small fields along the San Juan River, 6 kilometers to the west of Porco. The closest agriculturally productive regions of any size are the lower, temperate valleys along the Yura and Caiza rivers, approximately 35 kilometers to the southwest and southeast, respectively.

Colonial documents indicate that after the Spanish Conquest, Porco was almost entirely provisioned by distant *encomienda* holdings or the markets in Potosí (Presta 2000). Food, charcoal, and other supplies required to support workers and the labor process were most likely imported by the Inkas as well, perhaps from the center they established at Visijsa — contemporary Yura — which was also the site of an important pre-Inka settlement. Thus, while Porco was rich in minerals, there were few other resources to attract a permanent population.

The nature of indigenous organization in the southern Andes prior to Inka times is still unclear (Barragán Romano 1994), although it appears to have been characterized by the division of successively more inclusive social groups into complementary halves. At the regional level, these were referred to as *urcosuyo* and *umasuyo*, the upper and lower halves of large populations such as those analyzed by Bouysse-Cassagne (1986:chapter 4) in the Titicaca Basin. Del Río (1995b) makes a convincing argument

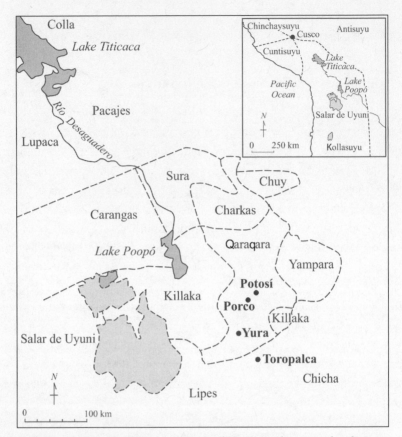

FIGURE 7.1. Location of Porco relative to the *señorios* that existed at the time of the Spanish Conquest. Redrawn from Platt et al. 2006:45.

that while this bipartite division was present in the Aymara *señorios* to the south of Lake Titicaca, the symbolic nature of dualism often obscures the actual politics of alliance building and conflict in which these groups engaged. The use of multiple systems for categorizing people (Aymara, Inka, Spanish) and conflicts of interest, both of which are reflected in the documentary record, also impede the reconstruction of pre-Inka social organization and dynamics, as does the general lack of colonial documents from this region (Julien 1993). Thus, the nature of prehispanic social identity and interaction in the southern altiplano is still quite murky, but historians have been able to identify the outlines of Aymara organization that, while presented in a schematic fashion here, can serve as a point of departure for understanding the pre-Inka situation.

At the time of the Spanish Conquest, much of northwestern Kollasuyu, the southern sector of the Inka empire, was occupied by the Charkas confederation, a political alliance that itself was divided into the Charkas, whose territory extended from Potosí north to the Cochabamba Valley, and the Qaraqara, who occupied roughly what is now southern Potosí as well as parts of Chuquisaca and Tarija (Alconini, this volume; Barnadas 1973; Bouysse-Cassagne 1986:figure 13; Rivera Casanovas, this volume). The Qaraqara *señorío*, in turn, was composed of an array of groups that Del Río believes were also organized along dual lines: the Macha, which included Puquta, Aymaya, and Macha; and the Chaqui, which included Chaqui, Visijsa, Colo, Caquina, Picachuri, Tacobamba, Moromoro, and Qaraqara. Porco was probably within the territorial orbit of Visijsa, although neither the historical nor archaeological records are clear on this point.

While Del Río refers to the named divisions composing the Charkas and Qaraqara *jefaturas* as ethnic groups, the nature of the internal relations or sense of identity that bound them together is unclear. As Barragán Romano (1994:150) notes in her analysis of the Yamparas to the northeast of Potosí, ethnic, language, and sociopolitical boundaries do not necessarily coincide. However, specific groups do appear to have been associated with core territories, although the existence of colonies, or archipelagos (sensu Murra 1972), resulted in many areas in which households from different groups were interspersed (Rasnake 1988:97). In addition, Rasnake (1988:98) argues that genealogies provided by the leaders of the larger divisions, such as the Macha, Charkas, and Qaraqara, indicate the existence of a hereditary elite at the time of European contact that could trace their ancestry into Inka and perhaps pre-Inka times as well. At a minimum, then, some degree of territorial circumscription and shared acknowledgment of an overarching authority provided the basis for group cohesion.

Recent historical research (Abercrombie 1998; Platt et al. 2006) suggests that, prior to the Inka conquest, Porco was the location of silver mines as well as an important ritual center that attracted pilgrims from throughout the southern Andes. The primary source analyzed by Platt and his colleagues is a proof and merit of service addressed by the priest Hernán González de la Casa to the viceroy in support of his request for a promotion. González had been assigned to Toropalca, 80 kilometers to the south of Porco, and at some point in the 1570s discovered and destroyed a clandestine native shrine in the nearby valley of Caltama. The shrine, or *wak'a*, consisted of five idols, all of which were named for mountains in which silver and lead mines were located. The most important of these was Tata Porco and consisted of a piece of *tacana*, a high-grade silver ore from that mine. This divinatory shrine attracted pilgrims from throughout the old Charkas federation who came to confess and be cleansed of sin (Abercrombie 1998:267-269). The *wak'a* also appears to have been regarded as a source of success in warfare, an activity closely associated with members of the Charkas federation whose primary obligation to the Inkas was to serve as soldiers. Platt et al. (2006) emphasize its role in unifying the disparate groups that inhabited the region prior to the Inkas and posit that it was concealed in Caltama soon after the Spanish Conquest, an interpretation that will be addressed below in the discussion of the archaeological evidence from Porco.

The historical sources thus suggest that the Inkas would have encountered an extant mining operation and shrine at Porco that was exploited by a hierarchically organized population that was segmentary in nature. The immediate area would have been sparsely occupied as a result of the poor agricultural conditions, but more populous areas to the south could have been tapped for resources and labor. However, while the archaeological data support some aspects of this reconstruction, others, particularly the presence of mines or a religious center at Porco prior to Inka rule, cannot be confirmed by the material record.

Archaeological Research at Porco

The research presented here is based on an ongoing project, Proyecto Arqueológico Porco-Potosí, which is shaped by a holistic approach to the study of technology (e.g., Dobres and Hoffman 1999; Knapp et al. 1998; Lechtman 1976, 1984; Schmidt 1996, 1997; Shimada 1994). This entails examining metallurgical processes from a multidisciplinary perspective as well as situating them in a broader social and cultural context. However, the paucity of previous research in the Porco area currently inhibits the examination of this nexus of sites in regional terms. While the regional context will be briefly examined on the basis of recently expanded survey coverage as well as reconnaissance conducted by Lecoq (Lecoq 2003; Lecoq and Céspedes 1996, 1997), this chapter focuses primarily on the sites adjacent to the Porco mines and their administration by imperial authorities.

In 1995, Lecoq (2003; Lecoq and Céspedes 1997) initiated a large-scale reconnaissance project in the southern part of the Department of Potosí to investigate Formative, Middle Horizon, and Late Intermediate period sites and the relation of the last of these to the development of the Charcas confederation. He specifically targeted areas that historical documents indicated were populated by various components of the confederation during early colonial times, including Porco and Yura. Lecoq's investigation revealed that the historical and archaeological records — particularly with regard to population density and ethnic boundaries — sometimes fail to correspond (for a similar difficulty in the Yamparas area near Sucre, see Barragán Romano 1994). Lecoq found only two sites with Late Intermediate period ceramics near Porco: a tomb and an isolated residential structure. No Late Intermediate period settlements or sites related to mining were found in the immediate vicinity, although Inka installations were identified near the mines (see below). A number of Late Intermediate period settlements, however, were located to the northeast of Porco in the area around Condoriri where a series of springs, or *bofedales*, currently allow the pasturing of llamas as well as some agriculture. Both Late Intermediate and Inka sites were found near Yura, confirming that the area sustained modest agricultural populations in late prehispanic as well as colonial times.

In 2003, a pedestrian survey was initiated in the Condoriri area by Proyecto Arqueológico Porco-Potosí in order to gain more information about pre-Inka populations as well as some insight into Inka treatment of areas outside the immediate vicinity of Porco. The survey employed 30-meter intervals and covered approximately 15 square kilometers during the first season. The results to date confirm Lecoq's findings in that 15 Late Intermediate period settlements were identified, all of which are dominated by Condoriri-Chaqui ceramics (originally termed "Chaqui" by Ibarra Grasso in 1965 but renamed by Lecoq as this style does not occur in Chaqui itself). However, a variety of styles, including Hedionda and Chilpe as well as yet unidentified wares, are present at the larger sites, suggesting contacts with other altiplano groups. Porco appears to be located at some sort of cultural boundary as indicated by the distribution of ceramic styles; Lecoq has found that Late Intermediate period sites to the southeast and southwest of Porco are dominated by Yura ceramics, while those to the northeast contain primarily Condoriri-Chaqui wares.

Most Late Intermediate period sites near Condoriri are located in defensive positions on mesa and ridgetops, and as Lecoq notes regarding the majority of Late Intermediate period sites in the region, they are relatively close to water, are associated with abandoned agricultural fields, and command excellent views of transportation routes that were used by llama caravans. Based on both total area and the number of structures, populations were at their highest in the Condoriri area during Late Intermediate period times, but the settlements themselves appear to have been internally undifferentiated.

The reconnaissance and survey data available to date thus suggest that the area immediately surrounding Porco was only sparsely populated, if at all, during the Late Intermediate period, and that denser populations resided near Yura and, to a lesser extent, in the oases created by water sources on the altiplano, such as Condoriri. In contrast, the Inkas targeted critical resources — mineral deposits, in the case of Porco, and the caravan routes and relatively productive agricultural lands found in the warmer valleys such as Yura — that were used, perhaps, to provision the workforce in mining zones like Porco.

The sites at Porco itself were identified by project members during a brief visit in 1995, and limited survey and excavations were conducted during six subsequent seasons of varying lengths. Intensive but limited pedestrian survey, mapping, excavation, and the observation of traditional smelting practices that are still employed provide the basis for the following discussion of the Inka occupation of Porco. A pilot survey conducted in a 2.5-kilometer-square block surrounding the current village and using 5-meter intervals between transects revealed 78 sites. On the basis of surface ceramics, over half can be dated to the Late Horizon period, the Early Colonial period, or, most frequently, both periods, and almost all were related to the extraction and processing of minerals or the support of workers and administrators engaged in these activities. Sites include mines, ore-grinding and smelting facilities, and storage complexes as well as modest administrative and living quarters. Survey of an additional 12 square kilometers in the area surrounding the initial survey block using a 2-meter interval between transects resulted in the identification of only 72 sites. None were clearly Inka or colonial in date, but eight Late Intermediate period sites were found. These consist of ceramic and lithic scatters that were sometimes associated with stone foundations that were probably the remains of single-family dwellings. No evidence of mining or metallurgical activities was found at these sites, all of which are located 2 kilometers or more to the north of the Cerro Huayna Porco mines. This pattern suggests that prior to the Inka conquest, human occupation in the vicinity of Porco consisted of isolated agro-pastoral households and did not focus on mineral exploitation or associated ritual activities.

The absence of evidence for pre-Inka mining, shrines, or other indications of ritual activity at Porco may be due to the destruction of the archaeological record as a result of subsequent mining activities. However, it is also possible that the description of the pilgrimage center found in the source analyzed by Platt and colleagues (2006) does not accurately reflect the organization or intensity of pre-Inka ritual. In particular, the document does not indicate the original disposition of the idols; it is likely that prior to the Inka conquest, they were located in their mines of origin, perhaps under the control of different ethnic groups. The Inkas may have gathered them in Porco in conjunction with their development of the mining center there. Alternatively, imperial authorities may have allowed them to remain in mines that continued to be worked by local authorities while elevating the importance of Tata Porco. Abercrombie (1998:267) notes that the centripetal movement of pilgrims to Caltama echoes that of *mitayos* during colonial, and presumably Inka, times, and research by Bauer and Stanish (2001) has demonstrated that the Inka practice of elaborating local cults was part of a broader strategy of ideological manipulation. The ritual significance of the shrine at Porco under the Qaraqaras may thus be exaggerated as a result of its importance to the Inka regime and because González was motivated to emphasize the significance of his own role in the *wak'a*'s destruction in order to bolster his petition. However, additional survey in outlying areas is necessary in order to further evaluate the possibility that an important shrine or mining operations existed there prior to Inka rule.

In any case, the Inka occupation of Porco was constructed entirely de novo by the empire, rather than embedded in a previously established settlement, as Lecoq's reconnaissance data from the region suggests was common (Lecoq 2003; Lecoq and Céspedes 1996). Of the seven sites with

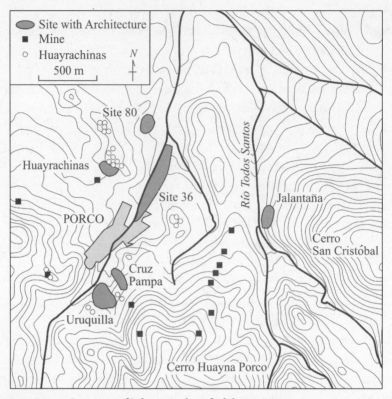

FIGURE 7.2. Location of Inka sites identified during survey.

substantial architecture (more than five buildings or connected rooms) identified during the survey (figure 7.2), five were constructed during the Inka regime; a sixth (Site 36) may also have been Late Horizon in origin, but it was destroyed before it could be tested. These five sites are functionally as well as spatially distinct.

Jalantaña is located on the east side of the Todos Santos River directly downstream from the mines currently being operated by the Compañía Minera del Sur (COMSUR), and is unusual in that it includes buildings that were constructed entirely of stone; at all other sites, except Site 80, adobe walls were built on top of stone foundations. The best-preserved building at Jalantaña, and indeed in all of Porco, is a gabled structure with interior trapezoidal niches that is clearly of Inka origin. This building is located in the central portion of the site and appears to be part of a *kancha*, an architectural unit employed by the Inkas that consisted of single-room rectangular buildings arranged around a courtyard. Occasional segments of straight, stone walls are visible elsewhere at the site, but the overall pattern is difficult to discern because of the disturbance caused by recent agricultural activities. Provincial Inka and European ceramics occur on the surface, and three Spanish furnaces are situated at the east edge of the site, which is delimited by a large stone wall to the west and south. Test excavations conducted in the *kancha* described above yielded few artifacts; while analysis is not complete, most decorated sherds appear to be from provincial Inka vessels. Jalantaña appears to have been a modest administrative complex or, perhaps as Lecoq (2003) suggests, a small *tampu*.

The site of Huayrachinas consists of the stone foundations of 30 circular and 15 rectangular structures, which are dispersed around the head of a dry *quebrada* approximately 500 meters to the north of the current plaza (figure 7.3). The area is named for the remains of at least 20 *huayrachinas*, indigenous wind furnaces used to smelt lead and silver, that are situated on the ridgetop to the east of these buildings. The architectural remains at Huayrachinas are similar to those found at other Inka storage centers in the southern Andes (e.g., Raffino 1993b:201) where circular and rectangular storage buildings (*qollqas*) are interspersed. The nature of the architecture at Huayrachinas strongly suggests that the site was constructed by the Inkas to store provisions for mining personnel. This would have included fuel for the *huayrachinas* as well as food and supplies for workers and administrators, almost all of whom would have been imported from lower elevations. However, all excavated structures contained early colonial components that reflect reuse for housing and refining activities.

The two sites closest to the mines, Uruquilla and Cruz Pampa, are residential complexes that may have housed workers. Both are located on the flanks of Cerro Huayna Porco, to the south of the modern village. Uruquilla, also known locally as Porco Viejo, consists of agglutinated rectangular structures arranged in irregular rows that are separated from a plaza to the south by two large rock outcrops. The entire settlement is enclosed by a stone wall to the east, south, and west; to the north the site is delimited by a steep *quebrada* with a perennial stream. The architectural layout of Uruquilla and its association with provincial Inka ceramics suggest that it had been constructed under the Inkas, perhaps to house mining personnel. However, as is the case with Huayrachinas and Jalantaña, the site

FIGURE 7.3. Plan of the site of Huayrachinas showing foundations of Inka storage structures.

continued to be used into the Colonial period. A smaller complex, called Cruz Pampa, is located on the other side of the ridge to the northeast of Uruquilla and may have served a similar purpose.

Finally, Site 80 is situated approximately 1 kilometer downstream and to the north of the village of Porco, on the west side of the Yana Machi River. It was constructed in an unusual location, on a steep, southeastern-facing slope covered by a large sand dune approximately 100 meters below and to the northeast of a large concentration of wind furnaces. Crucibles and Late Horizon ceramics are scattered across the surface. Three rectangular buildings have been excavated, and one of these contained a burned clay feature measuring 95 by 55 centimeters and 23 centimeters high, slightly larger and deeper than a traditional cooking hearth, or *concha*. The presence of crucible fragments and the paucity of domestic debris recovered from this structure suggest that the feature was used to refine small quantities of metal.

The simplicity of the architecture present at the Inka sites in Porco, the absence of elaborate ceremonial features such as an *usnu* or a large plaza, and the relatively thin cultural deposits all evoke a rather brief, or perhaps seasonal, occupation with silver production being the one overriding goal. This impression is supported by the evidence recovered during excavation that reflects an extremely limited repertoire of activities. While artifacts and features associated with mineral extraction are nearly ubiquitous, as are ceramics associated with the preparation and consumption of food, few other activities appear to have occurred at these sites on a regular basis. Evidence of lithic production was recovered only from Site 80, spinning and weaving tools occurred in very limited numbers and were restricted to Cruz Pampa, and no hoe blades or other agricultural implements were recovered.

The range of activities associated with metallurgical production is also limited. There is abundant evidence for mineral extraction and the crushing and separation of ore, as well as smelting and refining. However, the manufacture of finished products appears to have been accomplished elsewhere; no molds, scrap metal, or stone tools used in the final production stages of metal objects have been recovered. The spatial segregation of production stages was also found by Epstein (1993) in his examination of Late Horizon copper production at Cerro Huaringa on the North Coast of Peru, as well as by Howe and Petersen (1994) in the Mantaro Valley of Peru, by D'Altroy and his colleagues (2000) in the Calchaquí Valley, and by Scattolin and Williams (1992) at Ingenio del Arenal in northwest Argentina. At Cerro Huaringa, the Inkas reorganized a Chimú metal production complex so that smelting and slag-grinding facilities were separated, and the workshop for forging was relocated approximately 1 kilometer away. In the Mantaro and Calchaquí valleys, as well as at Ingenio del Arenal, the manufacture of metal objects occurred at some distance from mines and smelters.

The Organization of Labor at Porco

Berthelot's (1986) investigation of colonial texts containing information about Inka gold mining is the most holistic study yet published on pre-hispanic mineral extraction in the Andes. He argues that, in many ways, agriculture and mining were organized in a similar fashion, and that just as agricultural land was controlled by either the state or the community, there were also distinct state and community mines. Berthelot focused on the Carabaya and Chuquiabo regions to the east of Lake Titicaca, and found that imperial mines were centralized in the zones with the most productive deposits, employed relatively sophisticated technology such as subterranean galleries, and were closely supervised by state personnel. Workers included both local populations complying with the *mit'a*; a rotating, state-imposed labor draft; and *mitmaqkuna*, colonists who were permanently relocated in order to supply a self-sufficient labor force. Native informants interviewed in Huánuco in 1559 (Berthelot 1986:74) also explicitly stated that the Inkas recruited couples, rather than individual adult men, to work in mining centers. In contrast, community mines in the Carabaya and Chuquiabo regions were small, dispersed, located in alluvial deposits, and worked with simple technology by local populations under the control of their *kurakas*, or local leaders. A final distinctive feature of state mines, according to Berthelot, is that because they tended to be located in mountains, rather than alluvial deposits — and here he is referring specifically to gold deposits — they were highly sacralized. As he expresses the relationship between the mines, the mountains that contained them, and particularly notable pieces of ore, "On the one hand they are a symbolic link between the world on high (*hanaqpacha*), the special domain of the sungod; on the other, the world within (*ukhupacha*), revealed in the gallery mines but also in the domain of seeds, the ancestors, and — according to ancient Andean cosmogony — the primordial beings as well" (Berthelot 1986:84).

In the case of Porco, a colonial source cited by Berthelot (1986:72) specifically states that in Charkas, there were the *cerro* mines of Porco, from which the Indians extracted silver for the Inkas, and other mines that were in each village. While the systematic investigation of outlying areas for the purpose of locating community mines has not yet been conducted, the Late Horizon remains present at Porco are clearly the result of imperial activity, and the evidence collected thus far confirms and augments many aspects of Berthelot's analysis. The Inkas dominated this highly productive deposit and developed a centralized infrastructure for the extraction, comminuting, smelting, and refining of ores as well as for the support of laborers; no evidence exists for independent Qaraqara mining within or adjacent to state facilities.

Archaeological evidence does not provide insight into the specific ethnic origins of the people who worked at Porco under Inka auspices since both the buildings and ceramics — two types of material culture that often reflect ethnic affiliation and which are well preserved in the record — were provided by the state. The majority of decorated ceramics recovered during excavations at Porco as well as at other Late Horizon sites identified in the region by Lecoq and Céspedes (1996) are provincial Inka and share stylistic similarities with Lupaca and Pacajes wares from the west shore of Lake Titicaca. However, while this similarity is suggestive, it does not necessarily demonstrate that Lupaca and Pacajes populations were physically present at Porco, since the Inkas could simply have supplied workers with ceramics produced in workshops by Lupaca potters (Murra 1978; Spurling 1992; Van Buren 1996).

Fortunately, colonial documents do contain definitive information about the ethnic affiliation of some workers at Porco. At least two distant ethnic groups provided *mit'a* labor under the Inkas — the Lupacas and the Carangas (Presta 2000), the latter a population who were concentrated to the west of Lake Poopó, just to the south of Pacajes territory. In the case of the Lupacas, witnesses interviewed during the 1567 census stated that the Inkas had occasionally required them to go to Porco in order to extract silver (Diez de San Miguel 1964:39), a demand that was continued into the seventeenth century by the Spaniards (Bakewell 1984:94). All of these people appear to have been serving their *mit'a* obligation, and thus would have resided at Porco only temporarily, perhaps during the winter months when there was a lull in the agricultural cycle.

A preliminary reconstruction of the way in which silver production was organized at Porco suggests that most, but not all, of the tasks could have been accomplished by *mit'a* laborers with relatively little training. Today, the silver minerals present in the deposits at Porco are sulfide and mixed ores that include pyragyrite, acanthite, and stephanite, but in the past, oxide ores and native silver, now exhausted (Cunningham et al. 1994),

FIGURE 7.4. Hand-dug
mine identified during
survey.

and perhaps argentiferous galena were the most important sources. These
minerals are associated with a series of narrow veins radiating from the
Huayna Porco stock, many of which crop out at the surface (Cunningham
et al. 1994). Both open-cast and subterranean mines have been identified
in these areas but are difficult to date because of the lack of diagnostic
artifacts (figure 7.4). The ore would then have been crushed in order to
remove the metallic mineral from the rocky matrix, or gangue. A number
of small (approximately 12 by 12 centimeters) blocks of igneous rock that
are dimpled on three or four surfaces have been recovered near mines
and were probably used for this purpose. *Huayrachinas* — small conical
furnaces made of rocks and clay that are perforated with holes so that the
wind can oxygenate the burning charge — were then used to smelt the silver ore. Palimpsests of *huayrachina* remains mixed with slag, small chunks
of charcoal, and Late Horizon and colonial ceramics have been found on
the ridgetops surrounding Porco where the afternoon and evening winds
are strongest (figure 7.5). Silver produced by this process would then be re-

FIGURE 7.5. Huayrachina remains identified during survey. The large rocks were used as platforms on which the furnaces were constructed. Fragments of *huayrachinas* can be seen in the lower left.

fined in small cupellation hearths in more protected locations, most likely within structures at lower elevations.

The relatively unskilled tasks of mineral extraction, crushing, and sorting were probably accomplished primarily by *mit'a* laborers. However, observations of traditional smelting and refining practices suggest that while these activities do not require full-time specialization, they do demand a high level of skill that would not have been available among the general tributary population.

Don Carlos Cuiza, a retired miner who resides near Porco, allowed us to observe his use of a *huayrachina* and cupellation (refining) furnace to smelt high-grade silver ore on three separate occasions. Cuiza produced silver using a two-stage process that entailed first smelting lead ore in a *huayrachina* on a ridge above his house. The lead was then used in a small cupellation furnace to produce a lead bath in which finely ground silver ore was refined (for a detailed account of this procedure, see Van Buren 2003; Van Buren and Mills 2005).

During two of the instances when Cuiza was observed producing silver, he was assisted by his adolescent son as well as his compadre, a retired cooperative miner with a great deal of experience extracting tin and zinc. Cuiza himself was taught to smelt as a young adult by his in-laws, and continues to do so approximately three or four times a year. He smelts small quantities of very high grade ore acquired — usually illicitly — by miners who give him half the smelted metal as payment for his services. Despite the fact that he has 40 to 50 years of experience, Cuiza frequently encounters problems during smelts. For instance, one of the two newly constructed *huayrachinas* extant when we conducted our observations did not function properly, and after a few failed smelts, he simply restricted his activities to the other. A similar problem was encountered with the cupellation furnaces. The original furnace was constructed by his in-laws, but due to a family conflict, Cuiza decided to build a second one based on measured plans of the first. The latter never worked efficiently, and as a result he continues to refine silver only in the original.

Observations of Cuiza interacting with his two assistants also suggested that a great deal of skill is required to smelt and refine. Neither his son nor his compadre was allowed to assume responsibility for the operations, and they were continuously chided for allowing the charge to cool and not adding inputs at the appropriate times. Thus, both the design and use of these facilities require a level of specialized knowledge and skill that simply is not current in most populations. This suggests that either seasonally employed *yanakuna* (individuals who worked for the state rather than living in their native villages) who specialized in smelting or *mit'a* workers with previous experience in mining and smelting, perhaps within their own territories, were required to work at Porco for the Inkas. The former interpretation gains support from the presence of *yanakuna* working Spanish-owned mines at Porco in the mid-sixteenth century (Bakewell 1984:35, 51), although whether these were the same individuals who were employed under the Inkas is unknown.

Discussion and Conclusion

The overall organization of production at Porco is explicable in terms of the range of geopolitical strategies (D'Altroy 1992; Schreiber 1992) employed by the Inkas for exploiting resources in conquered territories, as well as the specific requirements of the technological processes they employed to extract silver. In this case, state officials were confronted by a highly valued resource in a lightly populated area with low agricultural potential, and they decided to construct a new facility at some distance from local populations, one that was staffed primarily by *mit'a* and perhaps seasonally employed *yanakuna* rather than permanent colonists. In addition to mineral extraction, smelting and refining were carried out in order to eliminate the cost of transporting raw materials to production centers. The manufacture of finished objects occurred elsewhere, perhaps at local settlements under Inka control, where items could be produced for introduction into the regional political economy, or in Cuzco, where artisans well versed in the imperial style created ritual and sumptuary objects for use in the capital. The spatial arrangement within the Porco complex was determined in part by technological demands, such as the location of high-grade ores and access to windy or sheltered locations, but perhaps also by the way in which labor was organized, with distinct types of workers or ethnic groups responsible for different aspects of the process.

The data from Porco thus support Costin's (1996) argument that goods that were highly valued, required skill to manufacture, and circulated among a restricted number of individuals — such as metal ritual and sumptuary objects — would be produced in centralized workshops directly controlled by the Inka state, perhaps with parallel production by local elites. They also concur with Berthelot's (1986) documentary study of Inka gold mining. His investigation suggests that state mines were centralized, tightly controlled, and worked with sophisticated technology, while local elites oversaw production at community mines that employed simpler procedures and were dispersed in the surrounding area. While the latter have not yet been located, clearly the record at Porco does not reflect an integration of activities conducted by Inka and local elites and represents instead a centrally controlled state enclave.

The organization of production at Porco under the Inkas thus represents a fine-tuned strategy that was shaped not only by local socioeconomic conditions and imperial needs but also by the specific requirements of the technology the state deployed for the extraction of mineral wealth. Thus, Inka control over the mines of Porco is not a reflection of a general strategy for incorporating a marginal province but represents, instead, a very specific approach to social and environmental conditions as well as task-specific requirements generated by the labor process.

Acknowledgments

Special thanks go to Veronica Arias, Ludwing Cayo, Holly Stinchfield, Barbara Mills, Delfor Ulloa, and Edwin Quispe for their work on survey, excavation, and the collection of ethnographic data. Don Carlos Cuiza and his children, Abram and Elsa, as well as his compadre Don Dionicio Ecos, kindly allowed us to document their activities during three smelts. We are also very grateful to the many crew members from Porco who have served on excavation and survey crews and to Arq. Javier Escalante, director of the Unidad Nacional de Arqueología de Bolivia, for his support of Proyecto Arqueológico Porco-Potosí over the years.

Research at Porco was funded by the National Endowment for the Humanities, the National Science Foundation, the National Geographic Society, the H. John Heinz III Charitable Trust, the Curtiss T. & Mary G. Brennan Foundation, the Robert Kiln Foundation, Trinity University, and Colorado State University.

Susan J. Haun and
Guillermo A. Cock Carrasco

Chapter Eight

A Bioarchaeological Approach
to the Search for *Mitmaqkuna*

Editors' Introduction

This study marks a milestone in Inka studies by the authors' analysis of a skeletal population to evaluate imperial practices concerning a local population of weavers. The study uses Rostworowski de Diez Canseco's (1972, 1975, 1977, 1978, 1988a, 1990) ethnohistorical research to indicate that the local Ychma ethnic group of the region was one of several groups whose member *ayllus* might have been economically specialized. Due to this existing situation, the Inkas had to do little resettlement after their conquest. In addition, the documents also remark that colonial *mitmaqkuna* groups were present from nearby regions. The goal of this chapter is to identify who is buried in the cemetery of Puruchuco-Huaquerones through a combination of bioarchaeology, analysis of funerary paraphernalia, and burial location.

The study by Haun and Cock Carrasco shows that the cemetery, consisting of nearly 1,300 mummies, was occupied during several cultural periods, but mostly the Late Horizon. For this chapter, only burials from the Late Horizon were selected. The results indicate that grave goods did show an emphasis on local Ychma pottery, along with Inka Cuzco, Inka regional, and foreign ceramics from the Chimú and Ica regions. Nearly all burials, male and female, were associated with textile tools — none with agriculture, ceramic production, or metallurgy. A small sample of both males and females shows characteristic muscle attachments of weavers, but the authors say the sample is too small to generalize. However, other cemeteries in the region show few weaving tools and more abundant ones of other trades, supporting the idea of specialization.

Using various biodistance measurements, the authors found that two-thirds of the males were homogeneous and from the coastal region, whereas roughly half of the females were not only from the highlands but also biologically more diverse. However, the authors also emphasize that when compared with coastal populations, the residents of Puruchuco-Huaquerones showed more biological affinity with central Andean groups. On the one hand, these results suggest a patrilocal residence, with highland women from distinct regions marrying local coastal men. On the other hand, they show that coastal populations from the Late Intermediate period with central Andean origins had a preference for marrying women from the highlands.

This contradicts the accepted practice of local *ayllu* endogamy and indicates that intergroup marriage was important in the establishment of political and economic relations across the ecological spectrum. In addition, it reveals that despite the acculturation of highland groups residing in the coastal region since the Late Intermediate period, as suggested by the use of Ychma cultural materials, men did prefer to marry women from their original regions. Perhaps this strategy ensured access to diversified resources while minimizing intergroup conflict or simply represents a marrying preference of diaspora populations. In either case, the role of women was crucial in such processes.

In addition, despite the craft specialization of the residents of Huaquerones-Puruchuco as weavers, the authors find that there is not a clear correlation between biological affinity, burial location, and mortuary preparation in the cemetery. Nevertheless, the abrupt appearance of weavers in the Huaquerones-Puruchuco cemetery could indicate the relocalization of specialists by the Inkas in order to optimize land use and craft production. The authors agree, however, that it cannot be ascertained whether this was due to imperial command or a local lord seeking to improve production.

At any rate, this chapter shows how biological studies can inform our knowledge about the actual people who comprised the empire. While such studies are in their infancy, they show much promise in providing new results about the varying Inka policies in the provinces.

Introduction

In less than a century, the Inkas created an empire that spanned the western area of South America from southern Colombia to central Chile. How this small regional polity was able to establish and control an empire composed of over 10 million people from extremely diverse cultural and socioeconomic systems has been a focus of inquiry since the sixteenth century.[1] Current ethnohistorical and archaeological evidence suggests that political authority was exercised through a variety of direct and indirect means, including direct control of the labor force. Frequently, large numbers of people were forcibly resettled to ensure continuous imperial access to goods and services as well as to reduce the threat of revolt. The way in which the average person experienced Tawantinsuyu's presence may well have been predicated on preexisting levels of local or regional social, political, and economic organization. Nonetheless, D'Altroy (1992, 2005) argues that no other imperial policy changed the Andean social fabric more thoroughly than did resettlement.

The extent to which relocated individuals or groups, referred to as *mitmaqkuna*, altered the preexisting social landscape is not well understood. Nor do we know how people, colonists, and native inhabitants positioned themselves within newly created or altered sociopolitical environments. Available ethnohistorical sources including chronicles, early colonial administrative reports, and indigenous legal petitions suggest that relocation was a widespread phenomenon (Cobo 1993; Espinoza Soriano 1970, 1973, 1987; Murra 1980; Wachtel 1982), yet its impact may have varied greatly from province to province (Rowe 1963, 1982). Our knowledge of who was moved where and for what purpose is greatly limited because documentary evidence is lacking for many provinces. The existing documentation often provides conflicting information as well. To further complicate matters, Late Horizon (ca. A.D. 1470–1532) archaeological research has rarely been able to substantiate documentary evidence of Inka relocation policies. Research designs aimed at identifying imperial rather than *mitmaqkuna* presence in provincial contexts may explain much of the inconsistency. Alternatively, archaeological signatures of state colonies may simply be difficult to define or recognize (D'Altroy 2002, 2005). Studies that have attempted to locate Late Horizon ethnic boundaries (Grosboll 1993) or *mitmaq* settlements (Makowski 2002; Ogburn 2001; Schreiber 1993; Spurling 1992) underscore the difficulty in doing so archaeologically.

In this chapter, we argue that the biological remains of people who were directly or indirectly affected by Late Horizon social changes offer an additional yet complementary means of understanding the extent to which imperial policies altered local and regional ethnic composition. With rare exception, information derived from human skeletal remains has not been used to identify the presence of *mitmaqkuna* in the archaeological record (but see Verano 2003). This omission has occurred despite the fact that the human body is frequently encoded with social identity and values (Bentley 1987; Bourdieu 1977; Strathern 1994), not only in the more mutable forms of clothing, hairstyle, and ornamentation but also in practices of cranial and dental modification, scarification, and tattooing, which create distinct and permanent physical markers (Blom 1999).

Social values may also extend to cultural practices regarding mate selection such that "within the reproduction of social forms, biological and cultural transmission [may be] jointly expressed" (Chapman 1993:21). To the extent that relatively endogamous groups existed in the Late Intermediate period (ca. A.D. 1100–1470) and Late Horizon, skeletal characteristics with a genetic basis can provide information related to group membership. When combined with other lines of evidence (ethnohistorical, archaeological, ethnographic), a more robust understanding of Late Horizon social and biological relations may be possible. Recent Andean studies detailing the presence of altiplano colonists and their descendants in Middle Horizon and Late Intermediate period coastal contexts clearly demonstrate the explanatory advantages that such integrative research designs provide (e.g., Blom 1999; Sutter 1997, 2000).

Cock Carrasco's excavation of a large Late Horizon cemetery at the Central Coast site of Puruchuco-Huaquerones offers an opportunity to explore the impact that state relocation policies had in this particular locale. Material culture recovered from funerary contexts strongly suggests that members of the burial population belonged to a community specializing in textile production. Ethnohistorical sources note that the state established multiethnic "productive enclaves" (*mitmaq*) of weavers and potters throughout the empire (Julien 1987). Did the Inkas establish such an enclave at Puruchuco-Huaquerones, or did they simply incorporate the preexisting local economic structure into their political economy? If an imperial socioeconomic system was imposed, then additional questions arise. Were the members of the burial population drawn from extant local populations or created from a mixture of culturally and biologically diverse populations?

Our research uses ethnohistorical and archaeological information regarding general aspects of social organization and ethnic composition in the lower and middle Rimac and Lurin river valleys during the Late Intermediate period and subsequent Late Horizon as a starting point.[2] Skeletal correlates of biological affinity in the form of craniofacial phenotypic (metric) traits are analyzed and then compared with potential material cultural correlates of ethnic identity such as ceramics, head ornamentation, and mummy bundle construction to examine the ethnic composition of the cemetery.

Ethnohistorical Evidence

Ethnohistorical research conducted by Rostworowski de Diez Canseco (1972, 1975, 1977, 1978, 1988a, 1990) provides the basis for our understanding of Late Intermediate period social, economic, and political organization in the lower and middle Rimac and Lurin river valleys. Populations residing in these areas appear to have been loosely articulated into the *señorio* of Ychma through a complex series of hierarchically ranked lords. The most important or powerful of these lords controlled populations in an area of the lower Lurin Valley that also included the religious center of Pachacamac. *Señorios* essentially consisted of numerous smaller polities (minor *señorios*),[3] each comprised of several endogamous corporate kin groups, or *ayllus*. Rostworowski de Diez Canseco (1975) argues that economic specialization, practiced at the level of the *ayllu*, and exchange of commodities or resources characterized these complex coastal polities. Although sociocultural differences at the level of the *ayllu* and/or minor *señorio* likely existed, individuals appear to have identified with a mythical common origin, spoke a common language or local dialect, and shared a common style of dress (Rostworowski de Diez Canseco 1990).[4]

Documentary sources indicate considerable, and possibly hostile, interaction between highland (Huarochiri/Yauyos) and coastal (Ychma) ethnic groups during the Late Intermediate period. This seems particularly true in the *chaupiyunga*, or middle valley ecozone, where highland and coastal populations may have established contemporaneous settlements (Rostworowski de Diez Canseco 1988b; Salomón and Urioste 1991). Unlike the adjacent Chillon River valley, archaeological evidence of fortifications or defensive structures is lacking in the Rimac and Lurin river valleys during this period, which suggests that if any form of highland domination was exercised over coastal inhabitants, it occurred through upstream control of lower valley irrigation canals (Rostworowski de Diez Canseco 1988a:55).

Ychma incorporation into the Inka state occurred during the reign of Thupa Inka (ca. A.D. 1471) and appears to have been accomplished through diplomatic coercion rather than warfare (Cobo 1979:139). The level of social organization present in the *señorio*, along with the *señorio's* relatively peaceful political transition, suggests that Inka control operated within and expanded upon local socioeconomic structures rather than dramatically altering them. If Rostworowski de Diez Canseco (1975) is correct with regard to preexisting economic specialization, then the majority of inhabitants in the lower and middle Rimac Valley likely experienced little change in socioeconomic organization. The presence of a North Coast *mitmaqkuna* of camelid herders in the minor *señorio* of Maranga (Rostworowski de Diez Canseco 1978:93) nevertheless indicates that the ethnic composition of the lower valley changed under Inka rule.[5] More important, a 1617 lawsuit involving disputed land ownership in the Rimac Valley suggests that people from the North Coast may have been relocated to the minor *señorio* of Lati (Ate) (see figure 8.1), an area that encompasses the archaeological site of Puruchuco-Huaquerones (figure 8.2). Witnesses testified that the father-in-law of one of the claimants could rightfully assert two birthplaces — Trujillo and Lati (Charney 2001:15). Charney (2001:15) interprets this testimony as evidence that the man's ancestors may have been relocated from the North Coast as *mitmaqkuna*. In addition, a more recent lawsuit suggests Yauyos *mitmaqkuna* may also have been placed in the middle Rimac Valley: in 1973, members of the modern community

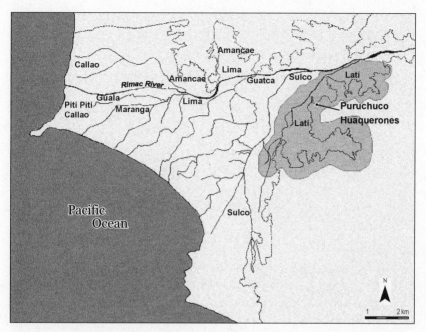

FIGURE 8.1. Map of Late Intermediate period minor *señoríos* of the Rimac River valley. Adapted from Rostworowski de Diaz Canseco 1978:49.

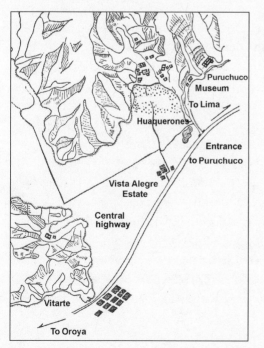

FIGURE 8.2. Map of the archaeological site of Puruchuco Huaquerones, Peru. From Tabio 1965:91–106.

of Jicamarca (highland Chillon Valley) filed legal claim to approximately 100,000 hectares of land in the Chillon and Rimac valleys on the basis of colonial legal acknowledgment of Yauyos's occupation of the land during the Late Horizon (Rostworowski de Diez Canseco 1988a:56).

Archaeological Evidence

Despite a long history of archaeological investigation, our ability to assess ethnohistorical reconstructions of Late Intermediate period social and political organization is greatly limited. Conlee and colleagues (2004:220) attribute much of this problem to research designs focused at the local rather than regional scale, making systematic comparison of information obtained from individual sites difficult at best. The absence of well-defined local or regional ceramic sequences, for example, has made it difficult to recognize Late Horizon sites or site components where clear cultural indicators of Cuzco influence are lacking. This inability to separate Late Intermediate and Late Horizon occupations has created confusion regarding Late Intermediate local and regional social organization and the extent to which Late Horizon imperial policies altered the status quo. As Guerrero (1998) states, new research is needed to identify the settlement patterns, urban characteristics, and ceramic styles that characterize local Late Intermediate populations.

A recent comparative study of a specific type of Late Intermediate public monumental building, "pyramids with ramps," conducted by Conlee and colleagues (2004:220–222), seeks to overcome some of these problems. A minimum of 40 such structures, including 15 at the site of Pachacamac (Shimada 1991:xl), were evaluated on four criteria: structural design, location within the Rimac and Lurin river valleys, location within the site, and orientation within the site. Preliminary analysis suggests that each structure was built by a different semiautonomous group and signified territorial position in relation to specific canals flowing from the Rimac and Lurin rivers. In addition, within-site location and orientation argue for a dual system of organization. These findings provide tentative support for Rostworowski de Diez Canseco's hypotheses discussed above, and suggest that imperial domination may have had a relatively minor impact on the social landscape.

Puruchuco-Huaquerones:
Site History and Archaeology

The archaeological site of Puruchuco-Huaquerones is located in the Rimac Valley in the district of Ate-Vitarte, Province and Department of Lima.[6] The site occupies land once controlled by the minor *señorio* of Lati (Ate) during the Late Intermediate period (figure 8.1). Currently, Puruchuco-Huaquerones lies in the eastern extent of metropolitan Lima in an area that transitions between the relatively flat coastal plains and the western margins of the Andes. The site encompasses two hills, or *cerros*, Puruchuco and Huaquerones, as well as the intervening *quebrada* (dry ravine) of Huaquerones (figure 8.2) (Cock Carrasco 1999, 2001; Farfán Lobatón 2000). The palace of Puruchuco, restored between 1953 and 1956 by Jiménez Borja, sits on the western flanks of Puruchuco. Previous research indicates that this building was constructed during the Late Intermediate period, possibly as the residence of a local lord. The structure was subsequently remodeled in a style that is clearly affiliated with the Late Horizon (Jiménez Borja 1988; Tabio 1965). The remains of terraces outlined by retaining walls of stone or adobe stand on the hillsides. A series of Late Intermediate period monumental structures ("pyramids with ramps") are located in the northeastern portion of the *quebrada*, while the cemetery of Huaquerones, which is the focus of this study, occupies the majority of the *quebrada* floor.

The cemetery, like many pre-Columbian remains in Peru, has experienced a long history of looting. Noting the presence of hundreds of desecrated tombs, Tabio (1965:93) compared the cemetery to a World War I battlefield. In 1989, the cemetery suffered additional abuses when it was illegally occupied by hundreds of highland families fleeing terrorist activities. Subsequent construction of residences and other structures in the community of Tupac Amaru covered or disturbed much of the cemetery. Because the community lacked public utilities, water was transported into the settlement and later dumped into the surrounding streets or excreted as human waste. An estimated 50,000 gallons of liquid waste was poured daily into the previously arid cemetery soils, promoting decomposition of both human and material cultural remains.

Relatively little has been published about the excavations conducted at the site complex. Although Iriate Brenner (1960) and Tabio (1965) both refer to excavations in the cemetery of Huaquerones, neither offers details concerning the location of excavated units or a description of recovered materials. Tabio (1965:96–97) does, however, describe the excavation of a tomb discovered near the site's museum (see figure 8.2). To date, Farfán Lobatón's (2000) preliminary report of 1985 excavations conducted in various sectors of the Puruchuco-Huaquerones complex is the only other published account of archaeological investigations undertaken there.

Our current investigation of the site complex began in 1999. A team of Peruvian archaeologists, under the direction of Cock Carrasco, conducted excavations in areas of the cemetery of Huaquerones that were not covered with modern structures. Based on results of testing, the cemetery was arbitrarily divided into 16 sectors. Observations made in the field later suggested the existence of three burial "zones" (A, B, C) that appeared to be physically separated from each other on the floor of the quebrada. Zone A includes Sectors 7, 8, 9, and 12; Zone B is comprised of Sectors 3, 4, 5, 11, and 16; while Zone C consists of Sector 15. Material remains dating to the Initial period, Early Intermediate period, Late Horizon, and Early Colonial period were recovered, including 1,286 mummy bundles. All but approximately 20 of these bundles date to the Late Horizon. Preservation of both human and cultural remains ranges from poor to excellent. A multidisciplinary team that includes five physical anthropologists is currently studying these materials.

Cultural Material

Elements of material culture (specifically ceramics, funerary bundles, and head ornamentation) found in association with the burials exhibit a wide range of variation. Preliminary analysis indicates that the majority of the ceramics are probably of local origin (that is, Ychma), but display a mixture of local and Cuzco stylistic elements. Several vessel forms and decorative techniques are similar to those found in Late Horizon contexts outside the walls of the site of Pachacamac in the Lurin Valley (Uhle 1991:63–66). Large Cuzco-style polychrome *aríbaloid* jars and smaller undecorated *aríbaloid* jars are present in small numbers in all three zones. Further, several Ica Tardío–style vessels, including those of the Ica-Inka and Ica-Chimú (Menzel 1976) and Chimú-Inka styles (C. Donnan, personal communication), are also present. These foreign ceramics are associated with a few mummy bundles recovered from Zones A and B.

Considerable variability is evident in mummy bundle preparation as well. Preliminary analysis by Cock Carrasco and Elena Goycochea found two major types of funerary bundles — those employing cane litters or stretchers (*camillas*) and those that do not (*fardos*). With the exception of two probably Early Colonial period burials, *camillas* are associated exclusively with young children and will not be further discussed in this chapter.[7] *Fardos* are associated with both adults and children and range in complexity from simple cotton shrouds containing a single person to larger, more complex bundles that may contain multiple individuals. The major differences between the larger bundles include the type of material used to make the layers of textiles (cotton versus other plant materials) that encircle the deceased and the type of material (cotton fiber, cotton-seeds, or leaves and grasses) that was placed as padding between textile layers.

Cock Carrasco and Goycochea have tentatively identified six types of *fardos* associated with adult remains. These include: simple cotton textile shrouds (FT); woven (botanical) mats layered with leaves and/or grasses (FVV); a series of cotton textiles alternately layered with leaves and/or grasses (FTV); a series of cotton textiles alternately layered with unprocessed cotton fibers lacking seeds (FTA); a series of cotton textiles alternately layered with cottonseeds (FTP); and a series of cotton textiles alternately layered with unprocessed cotton fibers and cottonseeds (FTM).

Approximately 6 percent of the recovered *fardos* included a false head (*falsa cabeza*). False heads were attached exclusively to bundles that were packed with cotton fibers (FTA), cottonseeds (FTP), or a mixture of fibers and seeds (FTM). In addition, no false heads were recovered from funerary contexts in Zone A. Bundles with *falsas cabezas* were generally larger in size, contained more than one individual, and were associated with a greater number and higher quality of internal and external offerings than were other bundles. With few exceptions, such bundles were found in pairs or groups that included bundles lacking false heads. Unlike the false heads that adorn some mummy bundles recovered from Middle Horizon and possibly Late Intermediate period contexts at the Central Coast site of Ancon (Reiss and Stübel 1880–1887), almost all of those recovered from Huaquerones lack facial features. The only exceptions consisted of three bundles on which a copper mask had been attached to the anterior aspect, or "face," of the false head. Furthermore, long black wigs made of plant fiber (maguey?) were attached to the false heads of bundles containing an adult female (see Reiss and Stübel 1880–1887:lámina 21a).

Variation is also evident in head ornamentation. Forms of ornamentation include cotton bandanas, slings (*hondas*) made of different types of material or displaying different colors, combinations of bandana and sling headdresses comprised of slings with colorful tropical feathers or tapestry bands with brown and cream-colored feathers attached, and flat braided bands wrapped around the head like a turban. One individual wore a plain brown cap of knitted cotton that was tied beneath his chin. Such diversity of head ornamentation is perhaps the most intriguing aspect of this study, due to ethnohistorical evidence that the Inkas mandated retention of existing ethnic practices, including the wearing of traditional clothing, hairstyle, and headdress (Cobo 1979:196–197; Jiménez de la Espada 1885, cited in Julien, 1983:45; Rowe 1963). Differences in traditional clothing imply that relocated individuals or groups would have been visibly distinct from local residents.

Unfortunately, ethnohistorical descriptions of differences in ethnic headwear style are limited to a few regions of the empire. Cobo (1979:196–197) provides some information concerning this practice, although it is of a general nature and insufficient for specific ethnic identification. Julien (1983:42–44) describes differences in headwear worn in some of the highland provinces in the Titicaca region (Qolla, Lupaca, Pacajes, Canas, Cabanas, and Paria). Of these, only the description of the small woolen bonnet worn by men in the province of Paria seems similar to any of the headwear found in burial contexts within the cemetery. Headwear comprised of slings (with or without feathers), tapestry bands, and slings combined with bandanas are reminiscent of headwear illustrated by Guamán Poma de Ayala (1993) for coastal populations. However, a more specific analysis is difficult because of the relative lack of detail and color available in the illustrations.

In contrast to the variability discussed above, the vast majority of tools recovered from the cemetery are related to textile production. Implements related to agriculture, ceramic production, and metallurgy are noticeably absent. Males and females were both found in association with weaving implements and/or spun fibers of cotton and wool. Although it is tempting to suggest that the cemetery contains the remains of an economically specialized community, a detailed study of skeletal muscle attachments must be conducted. Data collected by Haun from a sample (n = 20) of males and females are consistent with those recorded for weavers (Nelson et al. 2000), but the sample is too small and insufficiently representative of the population to draw definitive conclusions.

Additional support for the possibility of craft specialization can be found, however, at the nearby site of Rinconda Alta. Artifacts associated almost exclusively with metal smelting and weaving were recovered from Late Horizon contexts at the site (Frame et al. 2004:818). Further, Cock Carrasco's most recent excavation of a small Late Horizon cemetery located on the western side of Cerro Puruchuco recovered far fewer weaving implements than were found in the Huaquerones cemetery. Agricultural tools, flutes (*quenas*), and panpipes (*antaras*) appear to dominate the assemblage instead.

The Huaquerones cemetery population offers an excellent arena in which to compare indicators of cultural and biological affinity and to investigate the impact of abrupt Late Horizon political changes on ethnic composition in the lower Rimac Valley. The sample is large and tightly circumscribed in time (ca. A.D. 1480–1560).[8] Whether Huaquerones represents a long-standing native community or an ethnically homogenous *mitmaq*, there should be little or no correlation between biological kinship, cultural material variability, or burial location within the cemetery. If the cemetery population is composed of more than a single ethnic group, then we should expect to see a one-to-one relationship between biological affinity and material cultural markers of socially ascribed group membership. Ethnohistorical accounts of Andean mortuary practices further suggest that each ethnic group would have established discrete areas of burial within the larger cemetery complex (Doyle 1988:118, 267–268).

Sample Selection

To investigate the range of biological and cultural diversity present in the Huaquerones cemetery, a sample of 165 adults was selected for analysis. Individuals were considered to be adults if the cranial basilar suture was completely fused. Each of the selected remains dates to the Late Horizon. Sample selection was based on completeness of skeletal remains, sex, burial location within the cemetery, and type of funerary preparation. An attempt was made to select a sample representative of the adult cemetery population with regard to demographic profile and material cultural variability. However, access to individual biological remains was limited to mummy bundles that were found in varying degrees of deterioration.[9]

Centuries of grave looting and decades of construction activity frequently produced funerary contexts that contained incomplete human remains or individuals who could not be clearly associated with specific types of mummy bundle preparation, headwear, or ceramics. Individuals who were represented by skeletal remains that were less than 75 percent complete were not included in this study.[10] The only exception to this rule involved disturbed contexts in which the individual was missing a large number of postcranial elements, but where a complete cranium was present. Human remains that could not be securely associated with Late Horizon contexts were also omitted. These factors created a sample that did not adequately reflect the composition of the cemetery population. Females were slightly underrepresented, while individuals associated with Chimú-Inka- and Ica Tardío–style ceramics were minimally represented. In addition, the percentage of individuals associated with three categories of mummy bundle construction (FT, FTV, FVV) was not representative of the actual percentage of these bundle types in the cemetery. Bundles containing cotton fibers and/or cottonseeds (FTA, FTP, FTM) comprised approximately 70 percent of the recovered bundles.

Four additional pre-Columbian Andean cranial samples — three coastal and one highland — were chosen for comparative purposes. Previous research (Newman 1943; Verano and DeNiro 1993) suggests that cranial samples derived from coastal populations are more similar to each other than they are to samples from highland populations. These samples were used solely to provide a general framework within which to assess a coastal versus highland biological affinity for individuals recovered from the Huaquerones cemetery. Despite several ethnohistorical indications that people indigenous to the North Coast or central highlands were present in the lower Rimac Valley during the Late Horizon, there is no a priori evidence that individuals recovered from Huaquerones are directly related to the specific populations represented by the comparative samples used here.

The southernmost sample comes from the archaeological site of Jahuay in the Cañete Valley (n = 54). The cemetery dates to the Middle Horizon II (ca. A.D. 800–1000). The Late Intermediate period component (ca. A.D. 1100–1470) from the site of Pacatnamu in the Jequetepeque Valley (n = 87) and the Late Intermediate period site of Malabrigo in the Chicama Valley (n = 52) comprise the North Coast samples. Although each of these samples consists of crania recovered from looted contexts, all were obtained from single cemeteries of known provenience and cultural association (Verano 1987:79–81). The highland sample (n = 150) contains crania recovered from a series of undated sites in the central highlands provinces of Huarochiri and Yauyos (Tello Collection, Peabody Museum of Archaeology and Ethnology, Harvard University).

Methods

Haun collected skeletal data in the form of metric and nonmetric cranial traits (including dental nonmetric traits) from each individual in the Huaquerones and central highlands samples, while Verano generously provided us with raw data from the coastal comparative samples. Only craniofacial metric characteristics have been analyzed and will be discussed here. Numerous studies (Buikstra et al. 1990; Byrd and Jantz 1994; Hanihara 1996; Howells 1973; Pietrusewsky 1996; Verano 1987, 2003) have established the usefulness of multivariate analysis of craniometrics in estimating biological distance both within and between populations.

To estimate interobserver error, a sample of data recorded from individual crania (n = 15) in the Tello Collection was compared with that recorded by Howells (1973) from the same specimens. All measurements were within 1 millimeter of each other. Since Verano (1987) followed Howells's description of landmarks used to obtain each of the craniofacial measurements, the data from the Pacatnamu, Malabrigo, and Jahuay samples should be consistent with those obtained from the Huaquerones sample and the Tello Collection.

Intentional artificial cranial modification, a custom frequently practiced by pre-Columbian Andean people, can affect many traditional craniometric traits to the extent that these measurements may be useless in calculating biological distance (Anton 1989; Bjork and Bjork 1964; Cheverud et al. 1992). Kohn and Cheverud (1991) argue that cradleboarding, a cultural practice that results in unintentional modification of the skull, also has quantifiable effects on the cranial base and face. This study contradicts results obtained by Verano (1987) for skeletal samples from the sites of Pac-atnamu, Malabrigo, and Jahuay. Verano (1987:109–112) found that although intentional anterior-posterior modification did alter various dimensions of the cranial vault,[11] the practice did not produce significant differences be-tween modified and unmodified crania in certain craniofacial dimensions. Further, multivariate analysis of facial dimensions was useful in estimat-ing biodistance at the population and subpopulation levels. These results suggest that the degree to which anterior-posterior modification impacts craniofacial morphometry may be population specific. Thus, the use of craniofacial metric analysis in biological distance studies involving modi-fied and nonmodified crania should not be dismissed without testing the effect of modification on craniofacial dimensions.

Approximately 85 percent of the Huaquerones sample exhibited some degree of posterior flattening or anterior-posterior modification, resulting in crania that were shorter and wider than would be observed in the ab-sence of modification. In the majority of individuals observed, pad place-ment was obvious only on the posterior aspect of the skull, while changes to the frontal bone were frequently subtle in nature. To determine the extent of shape differences between unmodified and modified crania, all crania were scored for the presence and degree of artificial modification. Following Konigsberg and colleagues (1993), modification was scored on an ordinal scale as "nonmodified," "slightly modified," "modified," and "greatly modified." Univariate tests (independent t-test and ANOVA) were conducted to determine if significant differences existed between group means with respect to each of the selected craniofacial dimensions. These dimensions included basion-nasion length, basion-prosthion length, nasion-prosthion height, nasal height, nasal breadth, orbit height, orbit breadth, biorbital breadth, interorbital breadth, bimaxillary breadth, palatal breadth, maximum malar length, minimum cheek height, and nasion-bregma chord.[12] Separate analyses were conducted for males and females to elimi-nate potential bias due to sexual dimorphism. The central highlands sample did not undergo similar testing because all crania selected for the sample exhibited no evidence of modification.

Prior to multivariate analysis, the univariate and multivariate outliers in each sample were identified through SPSS 11.0 DESCRIPTIVES and RE-GRESSION, respectively, and then removed (see table 8.1 for corrected sizes of comparative samples). Again, separate analyses were run for males and

TABLE 8.1. Results of Canonical Discriminant Function Analysis for Reference Samples and Unknowns (*Huaquerones*)

MALES

Actual Group[a]	Central Highlands	Jahuay	Malabrigo	Pacatnamu	Total
Central Highlands	69 (90.8%)	0	1 (1.3%)	6 (7.9%)	76
Jahuay	2 (6.9%)	21 (72.4%)	2 (6.9%)	4 (13.8%)	29
Malabrigo	2 (7.4%)	5 (18.5%)	13 (48.1%)	7 (25.9%)	27
Pacatnamu	2 (5.3%)	5 (13.2%)	7 (18.4%)	24 (63.2%)	38
Huaquerones	23 (25.6%)	4 (4.4%)	35 (38.9%)	28 (31.1%)	90

FEMALES

Actual Group[b]	Central Highlands	Jahuay	Malabrigo	Pacatnamu	Total
Central Highlands	60 (81.1%)	3 (8.1%)	4 (5.4%)	4 (5.4%)	74
Jahuay	1 (4.3%)	17 (73.9%)	3 (13.0%)	2 (8.7%)	23
Malabrigo	1 (4.8%)	3 (14.3%)	11 (52.4%)	6 (28.6%)	21
Pacatnamu	2 (4.3%)	6 (12.8%)	8 (17.0%)	31 (66.0%)	47
Huaquerones	31 (43.1%)	3 (4.2%)	11 (15.3%)	27 (37.5%)	72

[a] Overall percentage of correct classification (excluding Huaquerones) is 74.7%.
[b] Overall percentage of correct classification (excluding Huaquerones) is 72.1%.

females. Homogeneity of variance-covariance matrices was established using Box's meters test as well as visual inspection of scatterplots for the first two discriminant functions generated for each group (Tabachnick and Fidell 2001:463). Stepwise canonical discriminant function analysis was conducted to evaluate the ability of the independent variables (that is, craniofacial measurements) to correctly classify members of the four comparative samples into their respective groups. The data from 90 male and 72 female crania from the Huaquerones sample were then entered individually as unknowns to be categorized into one of the four comparative samples by canonical variates. In an effort to determine if individuals from the Huaquerones sample were more similar to each other than to one of the four comparative samples, data from the male and female components of the cemetery were entered into the analysis as known groups (that is, not as individuals of unknown origin).

Male and female samples from Huaquerones were then divided into three subpopulations based on the location of the mummy bundles within three previously noted burial zones. Classification results (that is, coastal versus highland biological affinity) derived from the initial stage of canonical discriminant function analysis were entered for each individual in the Huaquerones sample and compared via chi-square analysis to individual funerary preparation (FT, FTA, FTP, and so forth), as well as location within the cemetery (Zones A, B, C). This information was also plotted by zone to visually examine the possible clustering of individuals with regard to highland versus coastal biological affinity and/or type of funerary preparation.

Finally, hierarchical cluster (complete linkage) analysis was conducted on the male and female samples from Huaquerones to determine if any of the generated metric clusters approximated artifactual or spatial clusters. Cluster analysis provides a visual means of assessing biodistance between individuals in the population. A cluster membership solution of three was selected for analysis due to evidence suggesting three spatially discrete areas of burial within the cemetery.

Results

Univariate testing of cranial modification effects indicated that individual crania scored as "greatly modified" were significantly different ($p < 0.05$, two-tailed) from all other crania in the Huaquerones sample, leading us to remove them (two males and one female) from further analysis. Among the remaining females, no significant difference was documented between modified versus nonmodified crania for any of the 14 dimensions. However, "nonmodified" males exhibited significant differences in three measurements (nasion-prosthion height, nasal height, and orbit height) when compared with "slightly modified" or "modified" males. Consequently, these three variables were eliminated from multivariate analysis involving the male component of each sample.

CANONICAL DISCRIMINANT FUNCTION ANALYSIS

Results obtained from canonical discriminant function analysis indicate the effectiveness of the variables in differentiating between the comparative samples: 74.7 percent of males and 72.1 percent of females were correctly classified into their original groups. This is an acceptable rate of classification considering prior probability (0.250) of assignment to a particular group by chance alone. The majority of misclassifications occurred within coastal samples, rather than between highland and coastal groups (see table 8.1), as would be expected on the basis of research noted above. In addition, eigenvalues indicate that at least 94 percent of the total between-group variance (male = 94.0 percent; female = 95.6 percent) is explained by the first two functions.

When the Huaquerones sample was entered into analysis as individuals of unknown origin, important classification differences between the sexes were noted. Among males, the majority of individuals (74.4 percent) were most metrically similar to (that is, were classified as) the coastal samples of Malabrigo (38.9 percent), Pacatnamu (31.1 percent), and Jahuay (4.4 percent); 25.6 percent were classified as central highlanders. Although the majority of females (56.9 percent) were classified as coastal — 37.5 percent as Pacatnamu, 15.3 percent as Malabrigo, and 4.2 percent as Jahuay — 43.1 percent were more similar to the sample from the central highlands.

Finally, the results of analysis in which the male and female Huaquerones samples were entered as a known group indicate each of these to be distinct from all of the comparative samples. Graphic representations of group means (biodistance) for males and females are shown in figures 8.3 and 8.4, respectively. As anticipated, the three coastal comparative samples cluster together and are obviously distinct from the highland sample. In addition, the North Coast samples from Pacatnamu and Malabrigo demonstrate greater affinity to each other than to the central coast sample from Jahuay. Among males, Function 1 separates the Huaquerones sample from the four comparative samples. Although Function 1 distinguishes the female sample from the coastal comparative samples, the addition of Function 2 is needed to clearly separate it from the highland sample. Classification results (table 8.2) also indicate that few crania from the comparative samples were misclassified as members of the Huaquerones population: 84.4 percent of Huaquerones' males were correctly assigned to their established group; females were correctly classified at a somewhat lower rate of 77.8 percent.

Among the Huaquerones sample, 77 percent of individuals were misclassified as members of one of the three coastal populations. A total of 30 individuals (14 males and 16 females), or 18.5 percent of the sample, were incorrectly assigned to one of the comparative samples. Of these,

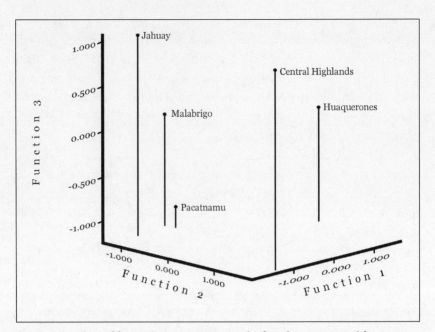

FIGURE 8.3. Plots of five male group means on the first three canonical functions.

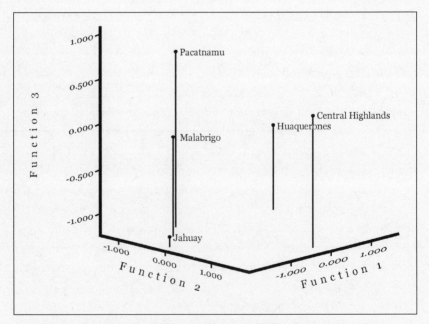

FIGURE 8.4. Plots of five female group means on the first three canonical functions.

TABLE 8.2. Results of Canonical Discriminant Function Analysis for All Samples

MALES

Actual Group[a]	Central Highlands	Jahuay	Malabrigo	Pacatnamu	Hua- querones	Total
C. Highlands	67 (88.2%)	0	0	4 (5.3%)	5 (6.6%)	76
Jahuay	2 (6.9%)	20 (69.0%)	3 (10.3%)	3 (10.3%)	1 (3.4%)	29
Malabrigo	2 (7.4%)	5 (18.5%)	13 (48.1%)	5 (18.5%)	2 (7.4%)	27
Pacatnamu	1 (2.6%)	6 (15.8%)	5 (13.2%)	23 (60.5%)	3 (7.9%)	38
Huaquerones	3 (3.3%)	1 (1.1%)	5 (5.6%)	5 (5.6%)	76 (84.4%)	90

FEMALES

Actual Group[b]	Central Highlands	Jahuay	Malabrigo	Pacatnamu	Hua- querones	Total
C. Highlands	58 (78.4%)	6 (8.1%)	3 (4.1%)	3 (4.1%)	4 (5.4%)	74
Jahuay	0	16 (69.6%)	4 (17.4%)	2 (8.7%)	1 (4.3%)	23
Malabrigo	0	2 (9.5%)	11 (52.4%)	8 (38.1%)	0	21
Pacatnamu	2 (4.3%)	6 (12.8%)	9 (19.1%)	27 (57.4%)	3 (6.4%)	47
Huaquerones	4 (5.6%)	2 (2.8%)	5 (6.9%)	5 (6.9%)	56 (77.8%)	72

[a] Overall percentage of correct classification is 76.5%.
[b] Overall percentage of correct classification is 70.9%.

all but three were assigned to the same comparative sample in each of the two analyses (that is, when entered as individuals of unknown origin as well as members of a known group). Seven of the 30 — three males and four females — were classified as highlanders in both analyses. All of the misclassified males were located in Zones B and C, while only two of the misclassified females were recovered from Zone A.

CHI-SQUARE ANALYSIS

Chi-square analysis and visual inspection of differences in funerary preparation and burial location within the Huaquerones cemetery indicated little, if any, patterning that would suggest segregation on the basis of a coastal versus highland phenotypic similarity. Individuals who were misclassified into one of the comparative samples during discriminant function analysis provide an interesting exception. When the location of each mummy bundle was manually plotted on a map of the excavated sectors, those who had been misclassified were generally found to occur in loosely defined clusters within Zone B. An additional cluster of three was observed in Zone C. The two misclassified females in Zone A were recovered from adjacent excavation units. All of these individuals were associated with bundles packed with cotton fibers and/or cottonseeds (FTA, FTP, FTM). Two of these bundles in Zone C included a false head. Differences in the degree of postmortem disturbance associated with each of these mummy bundles makes a comparison of the relative time, energy, and resources spent in each of their burials difficult. Several, however, were buried with numerous *Spondylus* shells, ceramic vessels, and/or small rectangular sheets (*láminas*) of metal, suggesting an elevated social status. Nevertheless, such indicators of status were not restricted to these few individuals, but were found in association with other burials, especially those recovered in Zones B and C.

A comparison of headdress styles and biological affinity (as derived from the initial discriminant function analysis) reveals that 78 percent of the individuals wearing slings (*hondas*) were assigned to one of the three coastal comparative samples, as were individuals wearing either a bandana or braided turban. Two individuals — one wearing a knitted cap, the other an elaborate headdress consisting of a cotton bandana topped with *hondas* comprised of thin strips of animal pelt — were classified as members of the highland sample.[13] Similar results were obtained when ceramic style was compared to the coastal/highland "signature." No one initially assigned to the highland sample was interred with Chimú-Inka- and/or Ica Tardío–style ceramics. Of the 30 individuals who were ultimately misclassified, only 4 were found in association with stylistically foreign ceramics. All were recovered in Zone B. Three, a male and two females, were part of a larger group burial that included a cache of three large Inka-style polychrome *aríbalos*. The fourth individual was an older female, uniquely distinguished from the remainder of the (recovered) cemetery population by strawberry blonde hair. Included among her mortuary offerings was an Ica Tardío–style vessel.

HIERARCHICAL CLUSTER ANALYSIS

Hierarchical cluster analysis indicated a difference between males and females at the ultimate level of agglomeration, Clusters One, Two, and Three.

The major separation among females occurs at the level generating these final three clusters. Among males, Clusters One and Two are more closely related to each other than they are to Cluster Three. Despite these differences, visual inspection of each dendrogram suggests that the results are similar to those obtained in chi-square analyses. Burial location is a poor indicator of interzonal biodistance; each of the final three clusters contains individuals from all three burial zones. There are, however, smaller clusters consisting of two to four individuals who were buried in the same zone. Small groups of individuals who were initially categorized as highlanders occur in all three clusters, although these groupings are larger and far more numerous in Clusters One and Two than they are in Cluster Three. For example, the first intermediate cluster (one of six clusters in Cluster One) generated for females consists of nine individuals, eight of whom were initially classified as members of the central highlands sample. Three of these women were also misclassified as highlanders when the sample from Huaquerones was entered as a known group.

Overall, misclassified males and females are scattered throughout the initial level of the dendrogram, yet grouping does occur in lower intermediate level clusters in three instances. One such grouping was described in the preceding paragraph. A second example occurs in female Cluster Three, where three in a cluster of seven were misclassified into one of the coastal comparative samples. Finally, male Cluster Two includes a cluster of six in which four were misclassified, one into the highland sample and three into the North Coast samples.

Discussion and Conclusion

On the basis of ethnohistorical information, we proposed two competing models to explain the degree of cultural material variability observed in the Late Horizon cemetery of Huaquerones. The results obtained from hierarchical cluster and chi-square analyses indicate an overall lack of correlation between biological kinship (as measured by metrically based biodistances), burial location, and mortuary preparation. Although headdress and foreign ceramic style do seem to have some association with a coastal versus highland biosignature, the number of instances in which these items can be securely assigned to a specific individual is insufficient to obtain statistically significant results. In addition, there is little correspondence between individual burial location and these items of material culture. In sum, these results strongly suggest that the people buried in the Huaquerones cemetery do not represent an artificially constructed community comprised of biologically and culturally diverse groups.

Ascertaining the origin and ethnic identity of the cemetery population is highly problematic at this point in our research. As figures 8.3 and 8.4 demonstrate, the male and female components of the Huaquerones sample are clearly separated from each of the comparative samples on the basis of canonical discriminant function analysis. However, the distance is obviously greater between Huaquerones and the coastal comparative samples than it is between Huaquerones and the highland sample. These results tentatively suggest a central Andean origin for the people buried in Huaquerones despite an absence of close biological affinity with the Jahuay sample.

Even if the cemetery is comprised exclusively of individuals who would have identified themselves as members of the Ychma polity, the coastal-highland biological signature present in the sample argues for a more extensive sphere of interaction between central coastal and highland populations during the Late Intermediate period than previously thought. Because almost twice as many females (43.1 percent) as males (25.0 percent) exhibit greater morphological similarity to the highland sample than the coastal comparative samples, women may have been used to establish or strengthen sociopolitical ties between Late Intermediate period highland and coastal ethnic groups. Ethnohistorical evidence indicates interaction between coastal and highland groups in the Rimac middle valley ecozone during the Late Intermediate period (Rostworowski de Diez Canseco 1988b; Salomón and Urioste 1991). As the easternmost minor *señorio* in the Rimac Valley, the Lati polity occupied the primary highland-coastal corridor and thus may have been involved in socioeconomic relationships with highland ethnic groups. Any highland control over the lower valley's water supply (Rostworowski de Diez Canseco 1988a:55) may also have promoted marriage alliances between coastal and highland groups.

Results obtained from hierarchical cluster analysis also indicate greater morphological variability among females than males, although not primarily along the lines of a coastal versus highland affinity. Two-thirds (Clusters One and Two) of the males are much more closely related to each other than they are to those in Cluster Three. Female Clusters One,

Two, and Three demonstrate equivalent distances from each other and exhibit greater internal variability than do the male clusters. Contrary to ethnohistorical evidence (Rostworowski de Diez Canseco 1975), these results tentatively suggest an exogamous patrilocal community in which females are the more mobile sex (Stojanowski and Schillaci 2006:64–68), thereby providing additional support for an extended kinship network.

The presence of a local ceramic tradition throughout the cemetery also implies that these people were ethnically Ychma, although ceramics alone may be a misleading indicator of ethnic identity (Makowski 2002, 2003; Stanish 2005; but see Sutter 2005). Spurling (1992), for example, notes that a *mitmaq* of potters relocated to the highland site of Milliraya supplied ceramic vessels to other groups in the immediate area. The notable absence in the Huaquerones cemetery of tools related to ceramic production suggests that these people may have obtained their vessels in a similar fashion. In addition, foreign (Inka, Chimú-Inka, Ica Tardío) ceramics may have been acquired through trade or as gifts, their presence in grave lots indicative of status rather than ethnic differences (Makowski 2002, 2003). Differences in headwear are more difficult to explain. Slight variation in headdress style, such as differences in color, materials, or even combinations of similar styles, may reflect *ayllu*, moiety, gender, or status differences rather than ethnic ones (Costin 1998). Alternatively, burial garments, including headdresses, may have been selected to reaffirm specific coastal or highland kinship ties.

Although Late Intermediate period use of the Huaquerones cemetery cannot be completely dismissed, the abrupt appearance of a cemetery in the *quebrada* during the Late Horizon suggests a change in local settlement planning and/or land use. As documented for the provinces of Umasuyu (Toledo 1975:57, cited in Julien 1983:75; Spurling 1992) and Huánuco (Helmer 1955–1956:40–41), the Late Horizon component of Puruchuco-Huaquerones may be the result of attempts to increase economic output by concentrating labor in key locales. This could explain the observed biological heterogeneity and instances of variation in associated material culture. Small hamlets and relatively isolated households, each with their own kinship networks, would nonetheless share in a larger regional identity as ethnic Ychma. Although having a significant effect on individual households and communities, these changes could easily be accomplished without direct imperial intervention. Local lords, seeking to meet increasing production demands and maintain (or improve upon) their status within the provincial hierarchy, could have instigated such changes.

In conclusion, preliminary results indicate that the Huaquerones cemetery population does not represent a multiethnic community. While these results are also suggestive of a population native to the region, the biodistance methods employed here are insufficient to corroborate this impression. Determining the origin and ethnic identity of this community will require additional biodistance and phenotypic variance methods as well as data from Late Intermediate period populations indigenous to the Rimac Valley, southern coastal valleys, and other highland regions. Intracemetery biological kinship analyses using metric and nonmetric traits are currently being conducted to investigate community social organization. The addition of sample data from the smaller Late Horizon cemetery at Puruchuco-Huaquerones more recently excavated by Cock Carrasco should also allow us to examine cultural and biological similarities and differences between groups seemingly involved in different occupations. Despite the need for much additional research, our work highlights the potential skeletal biology offers as a complementary source of information in understanding the extent to which Late Horizon imperial policies altered Andean social organization and identity.

Acknowledgments

Site excavation and artifact conservation were partially supported by grants from the National Geographic Society. Fieldwork conducted by Haun was made possible by a dissertation research grant from the Department of Anthropology, University of Pennsylvania. We are indebted to the tireless commitment of project field and laboratory supervisor Elena Goycochea; project archaeologists Violeta Chamorro, Antonio Gamonal, and Berta Herrera; and physical anthropologists Trisha Biers, Cathy Gaither, Melissa Murphy, and Jocelyn Williams. Thanks also go to the community of Tupac Amaru, several of whose members joined the hardworking field crew that helped with site excavation and the recovery of material remains. We are grateful to Clark Erickson, Tad Schurr, Andrew Nelson, and an anonymous reviewer for their insightful comments and criticisms on earlier drafts of this chapter. Haun also wants to thank the following individuals: John Verano for generously making his skeletal data available,

Steve Ousley for his time and suggestions regarding statistical methodology, and Michele Morgan and Patricia Kervick for their assistance in obtaining access to the Tello Collection and corresponding archives.

Notes

1. D'Altroy (2002:48) estimates that by A.D. 1400, the Inka population around Cuzco included approximately 100,000 individuals.

2. The term "lower valley" denotes one of three major ecological zones present in coastal valleys (Tosi 1960). The subtropical desert coastal zone of the lower valley contrasts with the subtropical desert transitional zone of the middle valley and the lower sierra zone of the upper valley.

3. Minor *señorios* in the Rimac River valley, including Lati (Ate), Sulco, Guatca, Amancaes, Lima, Maranga, Guala, and Callao, seem to have occupied land along the principal irrigation canals that flowed from the river (Rostworowski de Diez Canseco 1978) (see figure 8.1).

4. Any given individual's social identity was largely context specific. As Spanish documents indicate, most people identified themselves as members of a particular *ayllu* or community. For *mitmaqkuna*, however, ethnic identity assumed greater significance (D'Altroy 2005:265).

5. Rostworowski de Diez Canseco (1978:93) identifies the members of this *mitmaq* as Mochica, subjects of the Chimú state. "Mochica" is likely a reference to the language spoken by these people and suggests that they were originally residents of the Jequetepeque or Lambayeque river valleys (Rowe 1963:191).

6. We use the name Puruchuco-Huaquerones to refer to the entire site complex, but follow Iriate Brenner (1960) in dividing the site into two sections, Puruchuco and Huaquerones. In the context of this chapter, the name Huaquerones refers to that portion of the site located on the *quebrada* floor (figure 8.2).

7. With the exception of dental nonmetric traits, children are omitted from studies of biological affinity based on metric and nonmetric skeletal traits because these characteristics are age related.

8. Cock Carrasco has tentatively established cemetery dates based on the existence of Chimú- and Ica-Inka-style vessels and two Early Colonial period burials in the cemetery. The presence of nonlocal ceramic styles resulting from population relocation, trade, or diffusion would require a hiatus of several years following Inka conquest of the Chimú and Ica polities, suggesting establishment of the cemetery in approximately A.D. 1480. An end date of A.D. 1560 is suggested by the presence of Early Colonial period burials that contain adults in extended positions. Following the Spanish Conquest, indigenous people continued traditional mortuary customs by burying individuals in a seated position. Catholic edicts established in 1551–1552 made it difficult for these practices to continue, es-

pecially in areas surrounding Lima where parish priests were ubiquitous (Doyle 1988:34, 204–205, 246).

9. In only one case (Sector 3, Burial 64, Bundle A) were remains obtained through the systematic unwrapping of an intact bundle by archaeologists and museum personnel.

10. In each of these cases, the remains included a cranium sufficiently complete to collect all craniofacial metric and nonmetric data.

11. Anterior-posterior modification results in crania that are shorter and wider than would be expected in the absence of cultural modification.

12. Measurements follow definitions in Howells (1973) and Verano (1987) and were taken with a digital sliding caliper and rounded off to the nearest millimeter.

13. Highland classification of the individual wearing the knitted cap is interesting in light of the previously noted ethnohistorical description (Julien 1983:44) of small woolen bonnets worn by the men from the highland province of Paria.

Carol Mackey

Chapter Nine

The Socioeconomic and Ideological Transformation of Farfán under Inka Rule

Editors' Introduction

The kingdom of Chimor was the most complex society that fell to the Inkas. This chapter provides the most detailed information to date about how the Inkas manifested control over this state-level polity. As a well-developed society, theory suggests that the Inkas should have exercised hegemonic control, with little need to construct facilities for their imperial uses. Yet it is evident that the Inkas significantly transformed the local Chimú architecture for their own administrative purposes. In contrast to other regions, the Inkas did not impose their own administrative architecture at the site, but incorporated elements of the local building traditions. Mackey makes the case that this was a deliberate synthesis of styles, possibly showing deference for the local elites, rather than a practical decision based on materials available. On the other hand, the presence of an *usnu* reflects Inka ideology imposed on the local community.

The evidence from Farfán, the Chimú regional capital for the Jequetepeque Valley, indicates that the Chimú had taken over the earlier Lambayeque polity's center and put it to their own uses. Mackey's research indicates there were at least three levels of administrators present after the Inka conquest, and that some at least represent local elites. Some of these administrators may have been actual Inkas from outside, though the evidence is uncertain. It is also clear the Inkas developed new uses for the center, including craft production and expanded storage, supporting ethnohistorical references to what this valley provided to the empire.

In addition, artifactual and mortuary evidence indicate the incorporation of not only local Chimú elites but also earlier Lambayeque ethnic elites into the local administration, or at least honored them by burials in the Inka regional center. Skeletal evidence, at a preliminary stage, indicates most individuals were from coastal populations, not highland ones. This in turn supports the notion that they are Chimú and Lambayeque elites, incorporated into the local administration. Artifactual data backs this up. Evidence from the most impressive mortuary facility suggests that *aqlla* were present, although most appear indigenous. If this is true, then it might indicate that local women were used in this capacity, not brought in from elsewhere. Another possibility is that these women were simply local elites who were sacrificed for state purposes.

This chapter indicates how significantly the Inkas modified existing infrastructure for their own purposes. It also gives tantalizing clues into the origins of the bureaucrats who served in this center. Artifacts and skeletal analyses point to a significant presence of local individuals, especially the male buried in the Huaca Burial Platform.[1] This evidence argues for hegemonic control; still, the possible presence of Inka nobility in the Type A residence could indicate direct supervision of the settlement.

Introduction

Scholars have traditionally assumed that the Inka Empire had little impact on Peru's North Coast. Nevertheless, recent field investigations (e.g., Hayashida 1995; Heyerdahl et al. 1995; Mackey 2003) are revealing that Inka influence was, in fact, more pervasive than previously assumed. The traditional concept of weak Inka authority reflects, in part, insufficient archaeological investigation of Late period North Coast sites, coupled with a scant knowledge of the hallmarks of North Coast Inka architecture. Earlier investigations of Inka occupations in the upper reaches of the Virú Valley (Collier 1955) or at Chiquitoy Viejo in the Chicama Valley

(Conrad 1977) were largely ignored since the architectural and artifactual remains appeared so similar to earlier Chimú traditions. In addition, the archaeological model assumed — based on what is known of the Inka occupation of the South Coast — that the Inkas built a state infrastructure and established direct control in areas that had previously lacked this type of political organization (e.g., Menzel 1959). Following this line of reasoning, it was assumed that since the highly centralized Chimú state controlled the North Coast prior to the Inka conquest and had established an infrastructure, it seemed unlikely that the Inkas would impose direct rule. Finally, there is little ethnohistorical data on the impact of Inka rule on the North Coast. Although the sources touch on the conquest of the Chimú capital and the ensuing resistance to the Inka advance (Hayashida 1995; Netherly 1977; Ramirez 1996; Rowe 1948), little was said about Inka administration or political strategy.

This chapter presents the conclusions of our research on the Inka occupation of Farfán in the Jequetepeque Valley (figures 9.1A and B). The data were collected during six seasons of fieldwork from 1999 to 2004. At the onset, the project focused on the governing strategy of the Chimú rather than on that of the Inkas, since Farfán was believed to have functioned solely as a Chimú regional capital. The results of our investigations contradicted the long-held notion of a single occupation at Farfán by the Chimú, and also established that they arrived in the Jequetepeque Valley 100 years later than the traditional date of A.D. 1200. In addition, our excavations revealed that the Lambayeque occupied the site prior to the Chimú. In sum, Farfán was occupied by the Lambayeque (A.D. 1100–1300), the Chimú (A.D. 1300–1460), and the Inkas (A.D. 1460–1535) (figure 9.2).

Our excavations demonstrate that the Inkas not only built new structures but also remodeled the interiors of the Chimú compounds in all parts of the site. The resulting architectural style is unique to the North Coast and reflects neither known Inka architectural canons nor North Coast traditions. Rather, a new style emerged, which for the purposes of this study is called "conciliatory or diplomatic architecture" (Mackey 2003), suggesting that the Inkas were attempting to negotiate with two ethnic groups — the Lambayeque, who continued to reside in the valley after the Chimú conquest in A.D. 1300 (Sapp 2002), and the Chimú, who had been in the valley for approximately 150 years prior to the Inka occupation. The Inkas consciously chose not to use their iconic architectural

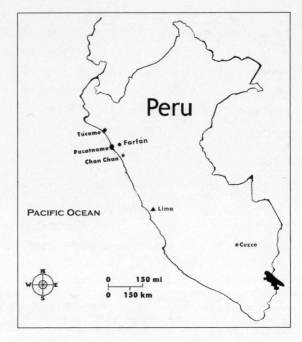

FIGURE 9.1A. Location of sites mentioned in this chapter.

FIGURE 9.1B. The Jequetepeque Valley showing the location of Farfán, the other sites, and the roads mentioned in the text.

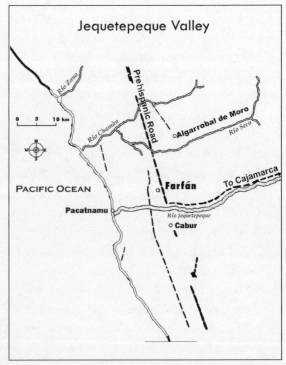

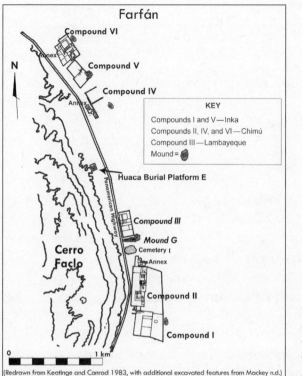

FIGURE 9.2. Map of Farfán showing the cultural affiliation of the six extant compounds.

style, perhaps to appease the Chimú and the local Lambayeque lords as a means of preventing discontent or future rebellion.

The Administrative Center of Farfán

When the Inkas conquered the Jequetepeque Valley in the 1460s, they occupied Farfán, a center that had previously been under Chimú rule. Currently, the site includes six large compounds, some with adobe perimeter walls reaching 6 to 7 meters in height. The compounds are aligned north-south for 4 kilometers along the base of Cerro Faclo. The compounds' interiors contain rooms, patios, and large plazas. The compounds were built during different occupations of the site. The earliest compound, III, was constructed by the Lambayeque, while the Chimú built Compounds II, IV, and VI. The Inkas remodeled or modified the three Chimú-built compounds and in addition added Compounds I and V (figure 9.2). The size of the Jequetepeque Valley, the third largest on the Peruvian coast, prompted Cieza de Leon (1959:321) to call it one of "the most fertile and thickly settled" of all the coastal valleys he visited. In addition, Farfán served as a "gateway" center, straddling the north-south coastal road and one of the main routes leading to the highlands and the large Inka administrative center at Cajamarca (figure 9.1B).

Farfán was first excavated in 1978 by Keatinge and Conrad (1983). Their investigation, which focused on Compound II, demonstrated that its architecture mimicked that of the Chimú capital, Chan Chan (figure 9.3). They also recognized that Compound II had all the characteristics of an "empty or artificially created" administrative structure (Morris 1972) given the limited space devoted to housing state functionaries (Keatinge and Conrad 1983:259). The empty nature of the administrative center under Chimú rule stands in stark contrast to Farfán under Inka control (figure 9.4). Our recent investigations demonstrate that the Inkas completely transformed the site's social organization by increasing the number of resident bureaucrats and converting the site into a center for craft production. Some of the major constructions and changes also revolved around ideological activities, both political and religious. The transformation of Farfán influenced all realms of the social structure.

Changes to the Political System

Inka rule included marked changes in the political system, demonstrated by the number of new elite residences constructed at the site. Based on data gathered from the residences, it was possible to distinguish three types, designated as Types A, B, and C. The residence types are set apart by size, location, and construction materials. The results of the analysis also made it possible to speculate about the activities of the administrators who occupied these residences and to order the types in a hierarchical fashion.

The first factor, residence size, is composed of several interrelated components, such as the overall size of the residence, the number of rooms and their spatial relationships, and the architectural details within the rooms such as benches and sleeping platforms. The second factor includes the residences' locations and their proximity to other features. The residences' locations took into account whether they were located inside or outside the high-walled compounds. This is significant for security, protection

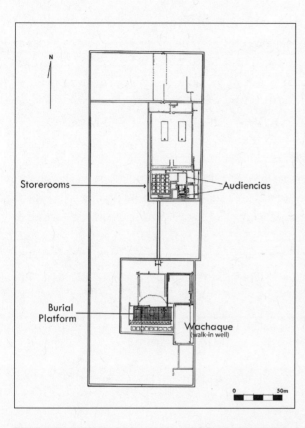

FIGURE 9.3. (Left) Plan of Farfán's Compound II illustrating the architectural features and layout that are similar to the Chimú capital, Chan Chan. Redrawn from Keatinge and Conrad (1983), with additional excavated features from Mackey (n.d.).

Storerooms

Audiencias

Burial Platform

Wachaque (walk-in well)

0   50m

FIGURE 9.4. (Below) Plan of Farfán's Compound VI showing the original Chimú architecture in dark color while the light-colored architectural features are those added by the Inkas. To the west is the annex built by the Inkas.

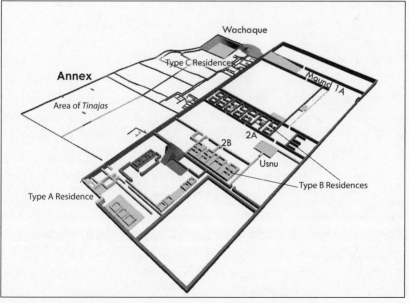

Wachaque

Type C Residences

Annex

Mound 1A

Area of *Tinajas*

2A

2B

Usnu

Type B Residences

Type A Residence

from the natural elements, and privacy. Higher-ranking individuals who lived in Type A or B residences, for example, lived within the confines of the compound, while those housed in Type C residences resided in annexes attached to the exteriors of the large compounds. These annexes lacked perimeter walls. Proximity to other architectural features such as storerooms or production facilities is also significant in assessing occupants' activities.

The final factors considered are construction techniques and materials. The construction materials varied among the residences: Type C housing is built of *tapia* or *tapia* and adobe brick, while Type A and Type B residences are constructed only of adobe brick. The height and width of the walls and presence or absence of plaster were also noted. Brick size, the amount of mortar between brick courses, the width of the walls, and the presence of walls with rubble fill were also important aspects of construction that not only defined the Inka occupation but also the type of housing.

Types of Elite Residences

TYPE A RESIDENCE

There is only one Type A residence identified at Farfán. The Inkas built this multiroom residence in the southwest corner of Compound VI (figure 9.5). This residence is the largest and most complex, and its associated features suggest that a high-ranking Inka official lived there.

The total area of the residence measured 9 by 10 meters and included five rooms and an adjoining kitchen. It was the most secluded of all the residences and was reached through a series of tortuous passageways. It was built during a single episode as evidenced by the similarity of the construction techniques and the wall abutments. Four separate doorways led to distinct activity areas (figure 9.5). Room 1 was approached through a pilastered entry on its north wall. The passageway leading to this entrance had a series of subfloor offerings on its eastern and western sides. The holes that contained the offerings had been plastered over and were approximately 18 to 20 centimeters in diameter and from 10 to 12 centimeters in depth. The two illustrated offerings show the contents of the hole,

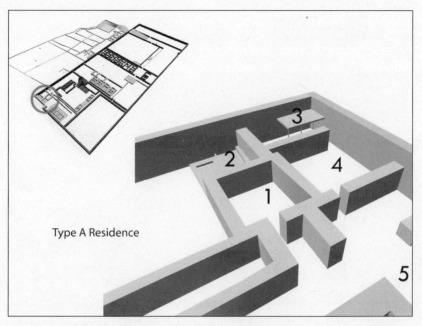

Type A Residence

FIGURE 9.5. Detail of the rooms of the Type A residence located in the southwest corner of Compound VI.

which included shell, animal bone, plant remains, and pottery (figure 9.6). Inside of Room 1 and along its southern wall we excavated more offerings, including the remains of a guinea pig (*cuy*) and both valves of a *Spondylus princeps* shell. Room 1's maintenance and construction were of the highest quality. Its plastered floor, for example, was 6 centimeters thick and made of fine silt.

Directly to the south is Room 2, whose open, eastern side could only be reached from the adjacent storeroom patio (figure 9.5). This room included a low, narrow bench and a rectangular fire pit, which, based on excavation, was not used for food preparation. Room 2 may have served as a sitting room either for the occupants of the residence or for the storeroom's guard since this room faces three storerooms. Room 3, in the southwest corner, contained remains of roofing materials and postholes and may have been used as a sleeping and/or working area. This room opens onto Room 4 — an enclosed patio. The kitchen area (Room 5) is to the north of the patio and contains several hearths, cooking vessels, and food remains (figure 9.5).

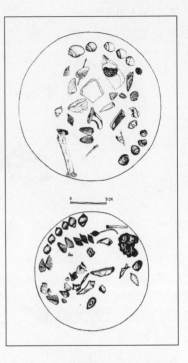

FIGURE 9.6. Examples of subfloor offerings found in the passageway leading to Room 1, Type A residence, located in Compound VI.

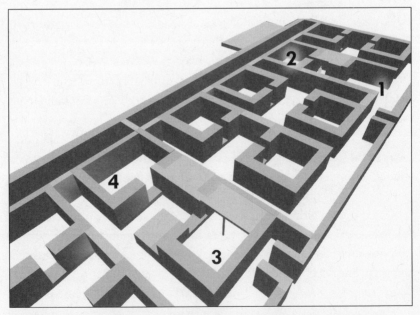

FIGURE 9.7. Isometric reconstruction of the location of the Type B residences, Rooms 1–2 and Rooms 3–4, showing their close proximity to the storerooms.

TYPE B RESIDENCES

Type B residences were also located inside Compound VI. These residences were not as large as Type A, and they contained fewer rooms, although they did have certain architectural details such as roofing and benches, and all contained subfloor offerings. These residences were located within the storage area of Compound VI and were probably associated with long-term storage (figure 9.4).

The Type B residences are found in Unit 2 of Compound VI and are divided into Units 2A and 2B (figure 9.4). The residences in Unit 2A once functioned as Chimú storerooms that were remodeled in Inka times into two connecting rooms (figure 9.7). However, on the opposite side of the patio, the residences located in Unit 2B consist of only one room and were constructed in a section of Inka-built storerooms (figure 9.4) (Mackey 2006).

Unit 2A, Type B Residences, Rooms 1 and 2. Under Chimú rule Storerooms 1 and 2 were two distinct rooms, with their entries facing each other. Under the Inka occupation, these two facing rooms, which are the most intriguing of the Type B residences, were joined to form a single residential unit. One of the notable features of this set of rooms is that the south wall of Room 1 was removed, thus providing an unobstructed view for the resident official to monitor goods and people entering into this eastern section of storerooms (figure 9.8). Subfloor offerings, similar to those found in the Type A residence, were found within Room 1. These offerings included various species of shell, such as *Prisogaster niger* and *Polinices uber.* They were placed in prepared holes aligned in an X shape within the room, along a north-south and east-west axis. The eastern portion of the existing corridor between Rooms 1 and 2 was widened, blocked off at its eastern end, and roofed, thus creating a long, narrow room that probably served as the sleeping area (figure 9.8).

In the Andean region, bureaucratic infrastructure often provided tools for record keeping (Schreiber 1992). In Room 2, we found a unique feature that closely resembles an Inka *yupana,* an aid used in counting large numbers of items (Mackey et al. 1990). The *yupana* consists of small squares incised into the plaster floor on the east side of the room. These squares were arranged in a pattern of 17 rows and 23 columns for a total of 391 squares (figure 9.8). In the center of each square was a round depression

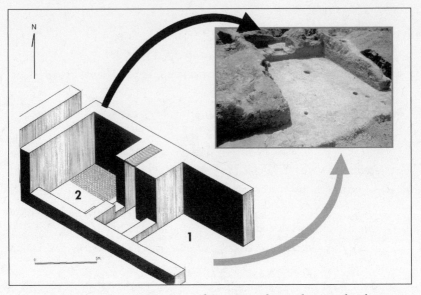

FIGURE 9.8. Isometric reconstruction of Type B residence, showing the placement of the subfloor offerings in Room 1 and the *yupana* in Room 2.

that could have held a small object such as a stone or a kernel of maize, which was used to tally the total number of items. The total obtained from a *yupana* was generally knotted onto a *khipu* string to record the total number of a given object (Locke 1923; Mackey 1970). The association of a *yupana* within the storeroom complex may indicate that a *khipukamayuq*, an Inka official in charge of record keeping, resided here. The *khipukama-yuq* is illustrated by the chronicler Guamán Poma de Ayala (1956:251, 271) holding a *khipu* and flanked by storerooms; another drawing shows the *khipukamayuq* holding a *khipu* with a *yupana* sketched into the left corner of the drawing. The presence of the *yupana* and possibly a *khipukamayuq*, along with the site's large storage capacity, reinforces the idea that this was an administrative center under close Inka control.

Unit 2A, Rooms 3 and 4. Like Rooms 1 and 2, Rooms 3 and 4 are con-verted Chimú storerooms joined to form one residential unit (figure 9.9). Because one wall had not been removed, this residence had a different configuration than Rooms 1 and 2. Room 3 was totally enclosed and prob-ably served as the sleeping area, as it had a roofed section along its east side. The roof was supported by the east wall of Room 3 and on the west side by a substantial wooden pole. Room 4, to the north, did not contain

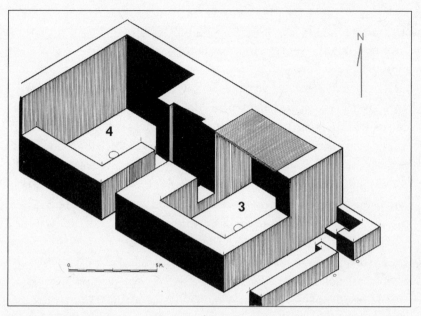

FIGURE 9.9. Isometric reconstruction of Type B residence illustrating the roofed sleeping area in Room 3.

a counting device, but it did have subfloor offerings. We excavated two offering pits in the northwestern corner of the room. These contained guinea pig (*Cavia porcellus*) bones and a shell offering near the door. The administrator occupying these rooms did not control as many storerooms as the administrator in Rooms 1 and 2, perhaps indicating different rank or different products being stored (Mackey 2006).

Unit 2B, Rooms 5 and 6. Although Rooms 5 and 6 share many of the characteristics of the other types of elite residences, such as subfloor offerings and roofing, they are smaller since they consist of only one room. Each room contains subfloor offerings and a sleeping/working area in one space — activities that are separated in the other residences. Both of these rooms have evidence of being partially roofed (figure 9.4).

TYPE C RESIDENCES

Type C residences are located in annexes attached to the perimeter walls of several compounds. The annex to Compound II is located on its northern perimeter wall, while the annex to Compound VI is attached to its western perimeter wall. Compound IV also has an annex on its west side (figure

9.2). I would argue that this annex also contained Type C residences, but because of poor preservation only the storage bins remain.

Several features of Type C residences suggest that the individuals they housed were of lower rank: they were located outside of the compounds and therefore unprotected by the high perimeter walls; their interior walls were low (less than the height of an adult), were not very wide, and were constructed of *tapia* or *tapia* and adobe brick; the sleeping areas were unroofed; the residential quarters were communal rather than single residences; and the activities of the residents differed from those living in the compound's interior. The bins associated with the Type C residences contained the implements necessary for the manufacture of ceramics and textiles, suggesting that these administrators supervised craft production.

The Annex of Compound VI. The northernmost annex, constructed mainly of *tapia*, is found on the west side of Compound VI and is the largest in area of all the annexes. However, only a small portion of it was devoted to residential space (figure 9.4). The residential area was divided into two separate functional spaces: the northern group consisted of unroofed rooms with sleeping platforms, while the southern group was composed of a communal kitchen that contained storage facilities, hearths, and a grinding stone, or *batán* (figure 9.10). This large kitchen served the communal residences and probably the elite Type B residences in the interior of the compound (figure 9.4). The large expanses to the west of the residences may have served as areas to collect goods or tribute, as evidenced by the remains of hundreds of large *tinajas*, or storage vessels, found there (figure 9.4). The occupants of this annex may have assisted the higher-ranking administrators who lived within the compound in the transport, sorting, or counting of goods that were brought to the annex.

The Annex of Compound II. Another example of a Type C residence is found in the annex attached to the north end of Compound II (figure 9.11). This annex had multiple functions, and the living area is only one part of the activities that took place there. The residential area is constructed of *tapia* and brick, and the residence consisted of several sleeping rooms. Originally, the eastern portion of this residence may have been larger, but a modern road has bisected and destroyed much of it. Associated with the sleeping rooms are a series, generally three in a row, of small bins that measure less than 1 meter square. These bins are enclosed by a low wall the width of two adobe bricks in height (24 centimeters). The bins con-

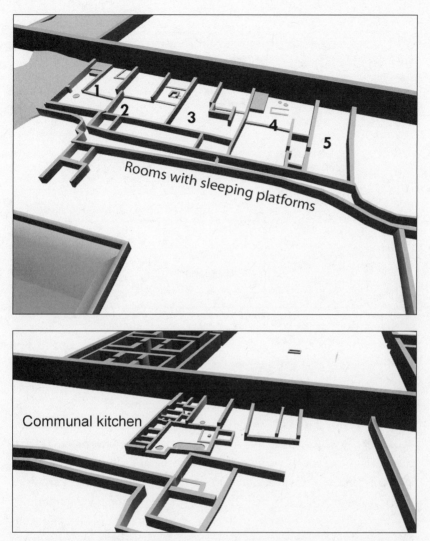

FIGURE 9.10. Isometric reconstruction of the Type C residence in the annex on the west side of Compound VI. At top, Rooms 1–5 were sleeping rooms, while the bottom illustration is the communal kitchen located to the east of the sleeping rooms.

tained tools used in ceramic production such as polishing and anvil stones of different sizes, indicating that the individuals who lived there were engaged in production activities located within the annex of Compound II. Ethnohistorical sources noting that Inka administrators provided the implements required for various production tasks (Netherly 1977) support our evidence.

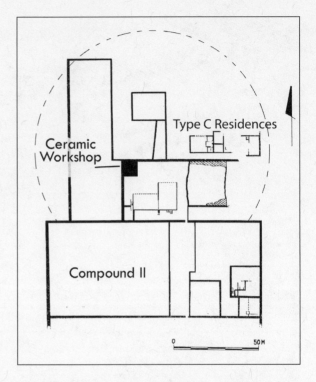

FIGURE 9.11. Plan of the annex to Compound II. The Type C residences, sleeping rooms, and bins appear to be in two parts because of the modern road that has bisected and destroyed much of the structure.

Summary. The architecture, construction techniques, and social complexity of Inka Farfán's residences contrast with those of the prior Chimú occupation. Type A and B Inka residences housed the site's highest-status administrators. These residences' high perimeter walls and roofing protected inhabitants from the elements. All of the rooms included subfloor offerings. By comparison, residents in Type C housing lived in communal quarters consisting only of sleeping rooms and, in one example, an adjoining communal kitchen. Unlike lower-class domestic structures, however, these rooms were well maintained and had plastered walls and floors swept clean of debris.

All of the elite residences are associated with the collection or storage of staples or tools. The elites residing in the compound's interiors were associated with long-term storage. Some of the individuals in Type B residences may have been in charge of counting the goods warehoused in the interior storerooms, as evidenced by the *yupana*-like device found in Room 1. The people who resided in the annexes, on the other hand, controlled short-term storage of tools used in craft production and possibly the collection of goods.

As Schreiber (1992:32) notes, conquering groups often introduced structures built in a foreign style that contrasted with local architectural canons. The architecture and spatial organization of Farfán's elite rooms do not follow this observation, however, because the Inkas opted to use a "conciliatory or diplomatic architectural" style. This style was unique and did not reflect either Inka or North Coast architectural canons. Farfán's residential architecture and artifacts point to increased political complexity as demonstrated by the diversity of residents' ranks and occupational specialties. Similar characteristics have been documented at other Inka installations at Huánuco Pampa and in the upper Mantaro Valley (Earle et al. 1987; Morris and Thompson 1985). At Farfán, these changes were planned and maintained by Inka officials — perhaps not Inkas by birth, but midlevel Inka administrators.

Ceramics Associated with the Three Types of Residences

We found two types of ceramics associated with the residences. These are the hybrid Chimú-Inka and the provincial Inka styles. Two general statements can be made about Chimú-Inka wares. First, certain Chimú vessels and their associated rim forms, such as plates and ollas, continued into the Late Horizon and the Inka occupation of Farfán. For example, a major marker of the Late Horizon is that plate rims change from round to square, and olla rims are curved on the interior wall of the rim (figure 9.12A and C), while jar rims curve outward (figure 9.12B). On the other hand, *tinaja* rims show continuity and do not change from their Chimú forms (figure 9.12D). Second, reduced wares continue to predominate, although there is also an increase in oxidized wares. This acceptance of some Chimú stylistic and technological traits may reflect Inka diplomatic strategy, or, as Hayashida (1998) suggests, the Inkas may have found it cost effective to continue using Chimú ceramic forms and technology since to do so required little retraining of potters.

The blending of some Cuzco Inka stylistic elements with Chimú ceramic features is best seen in certain forms. Analysis of more than 450

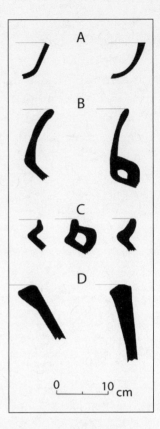

FIGURE 9.12. Chimú-Inka
rim profiles. A: plates; B: jars;
C: *ollas*; and D: *tinajas*.

whole vessels from Farfán's Late Horizon tombs indicates that most of
the modifications occurred on interchangeable parts of the vessels. A
spout with an Inka flaring rim, for instance, replaces a Chimú spout or
the decorative element of a lug, or a bird replaces the well-known Chimú
monkey at the spout's base (figure 9.13A). Wide strap handles, so typical
of Inka pottery (Julien 1987-89), are added to a variety of Chimú forms
(figure 9.13B). Highly polished blackware plates have decorated bases (figure 9.13C). Face neck vessels are common, either in a bird (figure 9.13B) or
human form (figure 9.13D). One interesting innovation combines an Inka
face neck jar over an inverted Chimú plate that is used as a pedestal. This
vessel is decorated with black paint on red slip (figure 9.13D).

   As noted, the second most common ceramic type is the provincial Inka
style. Only two Cuzco forms were excavated at Farfán — dishes with bird
handles and Cuzco bottles (*aríbalo* jars) (Julien 1987-89) (figure 9.13).

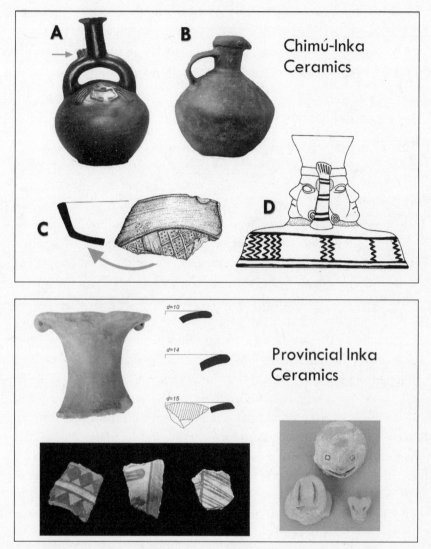

FIGURE 9.13. Examples of Chimú-Inka and provincial Inka ceramics.

These forms are decorated with painted geometric designs that imitate Cuzco polychrome wares. According to a recent petrographic study, only one *aríbalo* sherd was of highland manufacture, while the rest were locally made (Sidoroff, personal communication, 2004).

Changes in the Economy

The Inkas instituted major changes in Farfán's economy by increasing the areas devoted to storage and introducing textile and ceramic production.

STORAGE

An important aspect of Inka provincial policy was building storage facilities, and Farfán was no exception. The Inkas built new storage facilities in Compounds II and VI, doubling the number of storerooms built by the Chimú. Even though Farfán's storage facilities do not equal the storage capacity of some of the highland Inka centers, the Jequetepeque Valley, as Cieza remarked, contained "great storehouses" (1959:322). Farfán may have served as the largest Inka storage depot in the Jequetepeque Valley and on the northern North Coast. Much of the surplus may have been shipped to the closest highland regional center, Cajamarca (Hayashida 1999; Ramirez 1996), linked to Farfán by road. Cieza (1959:322) also noted that the Inkas gathered tribute in the Jequetepeque Valley (referred to in the chronicles as the Pacasmayo Valley) and from there dispatched it to the provincial capital (most probably located in Cajamarca). Not only did the Inkas boost Farfán's storage facilities, but they also increased security around the warehoused goods by changing access patterns leading to the storage areas and by placing Type B residences within the storehouse areas (Mackey 2006).

CRAFT PRODUCTION

The Inkas introduced two important changes to the economic system. The first was full-scale textile production. The evidence for textile production is underscored by the discovery of bins that held some of the implements used in textile production. These bins, located in the poorly preserved annex on the west side of Compound IV, measure 1 by 1.5 meters with a short rim around the top. On the plastered floor of these bins we encountered spinning and weaving implements such as spindles, whorls,

FIGURE 9.14. Examples of the small bins found in the annexes to Compounds IV and II that contained the implements for various production tasks related to weaving and *tinaja* manufacture.

and copper needles (figure 9.14). The bins could also have served as receptacles for completed textiles. The second line of evidence for textile production is found buried with the women in the Huaca Burial Platform on the west side of the site (figure 9.2). The women were accompanied by bolts of finished textiles, raw cotton, spindles, sewing baskets, and weaving swords. Traveling through Peru 15 years after the fall of the Inka Empire, Cieza noted that the Jequetepeque Valley still produced "cotton clothing in great quantity" (1959:322).

The Inkas also introduced ceramic production. We excavated a ceramic workshop in the annex connected to the northern perimeter wall of Compound II (figure 9.11). This workshop produced only one type of pottery vessel — large *tinajas*, some with openings of 50 centimeters or more — used mainly as vessels for *chicha* (corn beer) or for storing dry goods. The workers were clearly skilled, as these large vessels are constructed of coils and finished by the paddle and anvil technique (Bankes 1989). The annex also contained Type C residences whose inhabitants most likely supervised the production of these vessels.

Several features underscore this area's function. We found a meter-high pile of wasters of broken *tinaja* vessels near the production site. The open

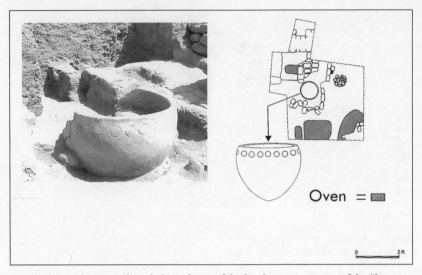

FIGURE 9.15. Photograph and plan of part of the kitchen area in one of the "hospitality mounds"— Mound C — that was most likely attached to the eastern perimeter wall of Compound IV.

firing area occupied a corner of the workshop and measured some 8 by 6 meters (figure 9.11). Excavations revealed a 25-centimeter-deep deposit of charcoal, ash, and burned earth. Within the firing area we excavated the remains of 10 partial circles formed by pieces of adobe brick, which were probably used to support the rounded bases of the *tinajas* and to permit air circulation. The Type C residences, located nearby, housed bins that held implements such as the large flat stones that were used as anvils for forming and smoothing the vessels. The *tinajas* manufactured at Farfán display a distinct incised circle on their rims. Excavations throughout the site have shown that *tinajas* with this design were distributed and used in areas dedicated to feasting (figure 9.15).

Summary. One of the major differences between Chimú and Inka provincial rule is that the Chimú allotted only limited storage space away from their capital, whereas the Inkas distributed goods more widely by building a large number of storehouses at their principal regional centers (e.g., Morris 1967). Even though the storage facilities at Farfán are not as extensive as those in some highland Inka centers, Farfán appears to be the largest Inka storage depot on the northern North Coast. In addition, the Inkas also introduced textile and ceramic production, key elements in their redistribution system. Textiles were offered as gifts to local lords

(Murra 1962), and feasting played a major role in the incorporation of new territories (Morris and Thompson 1985).

Changes in the Ideological System

Inka ideology was closely tied to politics and religion. All spheres worked together to ensure the functioning of the state, integrating the local lords and the conquered populace into the empire. Under Inka rule at Farfán, areas associated with feasting and ritual increased. The principal plazas of the compounds, built by the Chimú, continued to be used by the Inkas, but the Inkas also constructed additional areas that focused on ideological activities. These included an *usnu* for smaller ritual gatherings, "hospitality mounds" outside the compounds to serve large crowds of people, and five mortuary areas for funerary activities, rituals, and feasting.

Usnu

The Inkas constructed one of their iconic architectural features, an *usnu*, at Farfán (figure 9.16). The *usnu* figured prominently in Inka civil and religious ceremonies and is generally found at most important Inka provincial centers as well as in Cuzco (Hyslop 1990; MacCormak 1998; Protzen 1993).

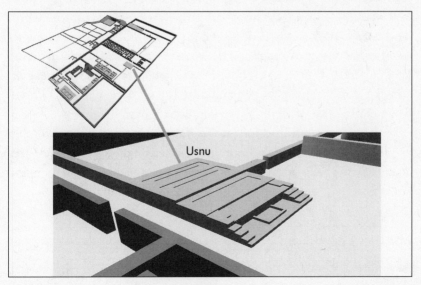

FIGURE 9.16. Isometric reconstruction of the Inka *usnu* and an inset of its location showing its close proximity to the Type B residences in Compound VI.

Farfán's *usnu* is a 2-meter-high, low adobe platform measuring 17 by 15 meters that faces west toward Cerro Faclo. Its closest analogy in form and construction is the *usnu* at Tambo Colorado on the South Coast (Hyslop 1990:85). *Usnus* are generally associated with liquid offerings. Depressions or small canals in the rear portion of Farfán's platform could have been used to receive water or *chicha*. The *usnu*'s location, in the patio close to the Type B residences, is revealing because the Inkas intentionally did not place it in the main plaza, but opted instead to locate it close to the residences of the elite administrators in a more restricted area. Excavations within the *usnu*, at its center point, revealed an undisturbed cache of broken Provincial Inka and Chimú-Inka ceramics.

Mounds Associated with Feasting

An Inka innovation at Farfán was the construction of "hospitality mounds" for the expressed purpose of preparing and serving food and drink to large numbers of people. Excavation showed that these mounds did not serve as burial facilities, but instead may have had civil and ritual functions. Four of the compounds — I, IV, V, and VI — had brick mounds attached to their eastern exterior perimeter walls, facing the intervalley north-south road located approximately a kilometer to the east (figure 9.2). The long, oval mounds vary in length from 50 to 60 meters and stood 2 to 3 meters in height. *Tinajas* with a circle design on the rim, similar to those manufactured in the annex of Compound II, were excavated in Mound C flanking Compound IV (figure 9.2). These vessels were associated with hearths, guinea pig pens, broken bowls, and ollas (figure 9.15). The areas immediately to the east of all of these mounds are covered either by modern cultivation or houses; therefore, it was impossible to determine whether plazas were associated with the mounds. Based on the excavated features and artifacts, the mounds appear to have functioned as preparation and serving areas for public ceremonies outside the compounds.

Mortuary Practices

The mortuary practices identified at Inka Farfán reflect the site's social, ethnic, and occupational diversity. We excavated five mortuary facilities, both within and outside of the compounds (Mackey 2003; Mackey and

Jaúregui 2001–2003) (figure 9.2). The total number of burials within all of these facilities is 98 and included three types of interments: 58 primary or undisturbed burials and their associated grave goods; 33 secondary burials that consisted of intentionally selected skeletal remains and their associated artifacts; and the remains of seven individuals from a looted burial chamber. The five mortuary facilities differ in their location. Two of the mortuary facilities are located within adobe Compounds II and VI, and two are located in cemeteries outside the compounds. These four facilities share similar burial patterns: seated individuals wrapped in burial shrouds, generally in single interments and placed in unprepared tombs. The fifth mortuary facility stands apart physically from the other four since it is located on the site's west side at the base of Cerro Faclo. It is an artificially constructed tiered platform that functioned as a *wak'a*, constructed of adobe bricks that contained interments in both constructed chambers and unlined tombs. All of these burials, however, whether primary or secondary, were composed of two or more individuals.

MORTUARY FACILITIES LOCATED
INSIDE THE COMPOUND

Though both Compounds II and VI contained cemeteries within their walls, the form and construction of the mortuary facilities differ. Both facilities were located near areas that once had ritual significance — north of the Chimú burial platform in Compound II and north of the main plaza in Compound VI. In Compound II, the burials were placed below the floor of a former Chimú patio, while the interments in Compound VI were found in an unfaced earthen mound that reached some 2 meters in height. Both mortuary facilities contain three planned stratigraphic layers of burials.

Compound II, Cemetery J and Tomb JO. Cemetery J consists of at least three strata lying below a former Chimú patio that the Inkas converted into a cemetery (figure 9.17). In total, we excavated 15 primary and five secondary burials. Most of the individuals were buried alone in unlined pits. All of the adult primary interments were in a seated position with the legs crossed, while the children were buried in an extended position. The bodies were not oriented in any apparent pattern. These burials represent a middle-class population, perhaps those associated with Inka administration, since the offerings associated with the tombs contained the highest

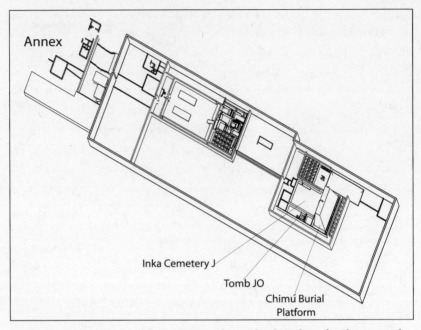

FIGURE 9.17. Illustration of the location and reuse by the Inkas of a Chimú ritual area within Compound II. The Inkas converted a former Chimú patio that faced the Chimú burial platform into a cemetery and blocked the access to the Chimú platform with an aboveground tomb, JO.

percentage of Cuzco bottles (*aríbalo* jars) and Provincial Inka ceramics of any of the burial facilities.

Immediately west of Cemetery J was a small, aboveground tomb (JO) that measured 4 meters in length by 3 meters in width and 1 meter in height. It was constructed of adobes, plastered on the exterior, and composed of three small compartments. Only the western two compartments held remains, while the narrow compartment to the east was empty. Compartment 1 was very small, only 80 centimeters long and 1.2 meters wide. It contained the complete disarticulated remains of an elderly female, over 40 years of age, accompanied by some 30 ceramic vessels and several metal artifacts, including a silver spoon. In the adjacent space lay the complete articulated skeleton of an adult camelid, 12 to 14 years of age, that is the oldest llama identified at Farfán (Richter, personal communication, 2006).

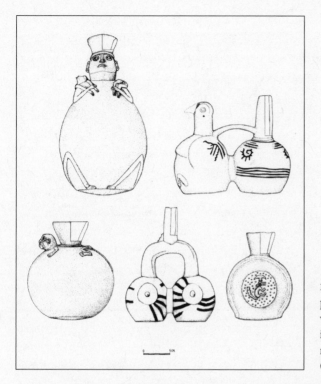

FIGURE 9.18. Examples of Chimú-Inka vessels excavated in Mound 1A in the northern portion of Compound VI.

Compound VI, Mound 1A. This cemetery consisted of an unfaced earthen mound, 2 meters above the surface, that held three stratigraphic levels containing 11 primary burials. No secondary burials were excavated in this mound. The 11 bodies were single interments, placed in unlined, unprepared pits. The burials faced east and had been placed in a seated position with the legs crossed. On average, each tomb contained four Chimú-Inka-style vessels, including ollas, many with soot on their exteriors, as well as fine ware vessels such as stirrup spouts (figure 9.18). The tombs of the adults also contained llama bones and copper objects.

MORTUARY FACILITIES LOCATED
OUTSIDE THE COMPOUND

Three mortuary facilities were excavated outside of the compounds. Mound G and Cemetery I are located close together on the east side of the site, while the Huaca Burial Platform (E) is on the west side at the base of Cerro Faclo (figure 9.2).

Mound G. Mound G, a 180-meter-long, irregular, unfaced mound, is located to the south of Compound III (figure 9.2). During the Lambayeque occupation of Farfán ca. A.D. 1100, this mound served as the principal burial facility, and we excavated over 50 Lambayeque period tombs. The bodies were placed in either seated or extended positions, although higher status individuals were more often extended (Mackey and Jaúregui 2001–2003). Substantial evidence suggests that Lambayeque ethnic enclaves continued to live in the Jequetepeque Valley during the Chimú and Inka occupations (Mackey 2003; Sapp 2002). During the Inka period, an empty area in the western portion of Mound G was used to bury individuals whose fronto-occipital head modification and/or ceramics identified them as ethnic Lambayeque. A ramp with a plastered floor was constructed on the western portion of the mound, and seven individuals, both adults and children, were interred along the ramp and at its summit.

At the mound's summit, an area was flattened and partially enclosed with adobe bricks. Within the area enclosed by the bricks we excavated two females, apparently the principal burials. The faces of both women had been painted with cinnabar (mercuric sulfide), a practice with a long history on the North Coast (Donnan and Mackey 1978). One, an adult woman who did not have the Lambayeque head modification, was buried in an extended position with copper discs in each hand. An infant was placed in a niche near her head. Her extensive burial goods included weaving implements as well as decorated gourds and ceramic plates containing food remains. Several of the jar forms had rim profiles similar to those identified by Tschauner (2001) as Lambayeque-Inka. Next to her was a seated female with the typical Lambayeque cranial modification, who was surrounded by ceramics that were Chimú-Inka in style. In addition, next to the seated female were the skeletons of two articulated llamas, one adolescent and the other neonatal. The seated woman had also been placed over the partial remains of two adult llamas (Richter, personal communication, 2006) (figure 9.19). The interment of the seven individuals in the former Lambayeque funerary mound and the elaborate burials of the principal females may indicate the persistence of cultural memory as well as indicating the Inka recognition of the women's rank and ethnic affiliation.

Cemetery I. Cemetery I, located in a sandy area to the north of Compound II, has the greatest area of the cemeteries at Farfán and dates to the

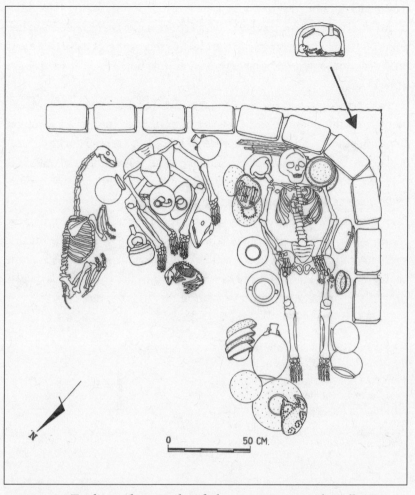

FIGURE 9.19. Tombs 4 and 11 were identified as containing two ethnically Lambayeque females, buried on the summit of Mound G. The seated female was associated with two fully articulated camelids and sitting on top of the bones of two partial llamas. The shaded artifacts are gourds.

Inka occupation (figure 9.2). Currently it is divided into two sectors, north and south, a division most likely caused by runoff from nearby Cerro Faclo during an El Niño event. The northern sector measures some 80 meters in length and 55 meters in width, while the southern sector is 55 meters long by 50 meters wide. Since this cemetery is not enclosed and is next to the Pan American Highway, it is in a poor state of preservation. The cemetery mound was elevated 1.5 meters above the surrounding surface and had once contained four stratigraphic levels. Prior to placing the bodies in the lowest strata, the intended cemetery area had been leveled and had a 20–25-centimeter layer of fine sand scattered over it. The bodies were placed on top of the sand layer. No such preparation was made for the other strata.

This cemetery yielded five primary and eight secondary interments. The single interments had been placed in unlined, unprepared tombs. Both adults and children were represented. Adults were seated with the legs crossed, with no apparent orientation of the bodies (figure 9.20); all of the children were in an extended position. Offerings included Lambayeque-style bowls as well as Chimú-Inka-style ceramics with Inka traits such as flaring lip jars and the pointed bases of Cuzco bottles. This portion of the cemetery is clearly divided into northern and southern sectors. The Inka associated burials are to the north while those individuals with Lambayeque characteristics are buried in the southern sector. These individuals display the typical Lambayeque cranial modifications and ceramics.

FIGURE 9.20. Example of one of the burials in Cemetery I. The adult male was facing west; however, the torso and head had been disturbed and were separated from the lower body. The shaded artifacts are gourds.

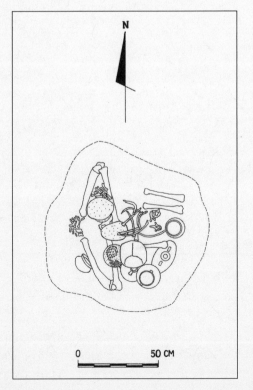

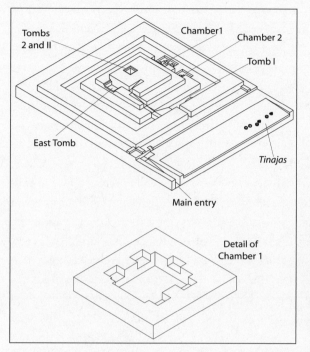

Tombs 2 and II

Chamber 1

Chamber 2

Tomb I

East Tomb

Tinajas

Main entry

Detail of Chamber 1

FIGURE 9.21.
Isometric of the
Huaca Burial
Platform viewed
from the northern
main entry and the
location of the ex-
cavated tombs and
chambers.

The Huaca Burial Platform. The Huaca Burial Platform, situated at the base of Cerro Faclo (figure 9.2), was placed at almost the exact center of the site and is the largest known platform from this time period on the North Coast. It is comprised of four tiers and at its base measured 52 meters north-south by 40 meters east-west (figure 9.21). Although the upper tier of the platform was damaged, its original height was more than 7 meters. A ramp on the northeast side provided access to a corridor that led to the entrance of the three remaining tiers and a ramp system that led to the summit. The exterior walls are covered with a fine plaster that is a different color from the adobes, indicating two different sources for these materials.

Although the osteological remains and tomb contents are still under analysis, clear trends are emerging. There are 20 primary burials, 19 secondary burials, and 7 individuals from a looted context, Burial Chamber 1. These burials represent several separate funerary events and were placed in the Huaca Burial Platform at different times during the Inka occupation (figure 9.21). The majority of the identifiable interments are female (Nelson, personal communication), and all interments, even the secondary burials, were composed of multiple individuals (Mackey 2003; Mackey and Jaúregui 2001–2003).

PRIMARY BURIALS

The primary burials were excavated in four undisturbed, multiple tombs that contained from three to seven women per tomb. Several of the tombs were specially constructed roofed chambers. Analysis of the this material is still underway, but preliminary results for two of the four tombs will be described below.

The East Tomb contained seven individuals, all probably female, ranging in age from 7 to 40-plus years (figure 9.22). They were all interred simultaneously. The tomb was created by removing the bricks from a portion of the east side of the Huaca to create a box, 3 meters long by 2 meters high and 1.5 meters deep, where the seven bodies were placed on three levels. The individuals on the bottom level all face inward toward a communal offering of 40 vessels that rested on finished bolts of cloth, some of which measure a meter in length. Two more individuals were placed in the tomb above these five: a female on the second level who faces east and another woman at the top of the tomb with her head oriented northwest and her face resting on a pillow filled with raw cotton. Burial positions varied. Among the three females seated on the bottom level facing northwest, T-5 was seated with knees bent, while T-6 and T-10 were seated with their legs crossed. The south-facing woman, T-7, and the juvenile, T-9, were both seated with knees bent. In the upper levels, T-4 and T-1, both females had their legs crossed.

In addition to the textiles and ceramics in the center of the tomb, there were also individual offerings. The two females with the largest number of grave goods were T-4, an adolescent female, and T-7, who was over 40 years of age. They had offerings of Chimú-Inka-style pottery, as well as weaving swords, raw cotton, and dishes filled with plant and animal remains. On the top tier of the Huaca Burial Platform, immediately above this tomb, as well as one other, were two round basins, each 50 centimeters in diameter, filled with small stones from the adjacent mountain that marked the burials (figure 9.22). The Spanish chronicler Juan de Betanzos (1996:168) noted a similar occurrence. He speaks of basins of stones being prepared to receive *chicha* and sacrifices on the top of a platform for the visit of an Inka. Although Betanzos may have been referring to an *usnu*,

FIGURE 9.22. A schematic view of the East Tomb in the Huaca Burial Platform, showing the relative position of the seven females within the tomb.

it is noteworthy that this same concept was used by the Inkas on Farfán's burial platform and not on their *usnu* in Compound VI.

Tomb 1. Another example of a complete, multiple burial was excavated in the northern portion of the platform at bedrock level. This burial included three individuals: a seated juvenile female, with body and head oriented west, and a seated female, more than 40 years of age, facing north and holding a neonate. The three individuals were placed on a woven mat that rested on bedrock, and a fine textile had been wrapped around the three and their grave goods (figure 9.23D). On and around the bundle we recorded three complete articulated llamas: one adult, one juvenile, and one neonate (Richter, personal communication, 2006). The llamas and quality of grave goods suggest that the women interred in Tomb 1 were of high status. In addition, both women had metal offerings. Both women had silver objects that measured some 30 centimeters in height, with a triangular top and a solid handle. A human face made of textile had been pasted to the triangular top (figure 9.23A). The jewelry of the older woman

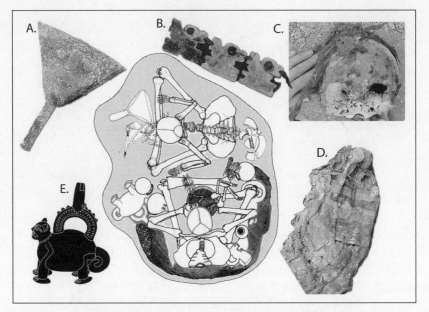

FIGURE 9.23. The burial positions of the females within Tomb 1 in the Huaca Burial Platform, and examples of some of the artifacts.

included several shell necklaces composed of beads carved in the form of pelicans (figure 9.23B). The face of the older female had been painted with cinnabar (mercuric sulfide) (figure 9.23C). Offerings placed next to her body included a silver bowl and several small gold beads. A communal offering of 33 ceramic vessels had been placed around the bodies.

SECONDARY BURIALS

Nineteen of the individuals appear to be intentional, secondary burials. This signifies that these individuals had been buried or curated elsewhere, and then parts of the skeletons were selected to be used as offerings (Nelson 1998). Originally, we thought that these were looted burials, but when they were found below several undisturbed floors or within ramps we realized that these had served as intentional offerings. Some of these burials included a scattering of bones, while others were almost complete and missing only some extremities. Secondary burials have a long history in the Andean region (e.g., Millaire 2004; Nelson 1998; Verano 2001); however, there was substantial variation in the processes that created these partial burials. Nelson's (personal communication, 2004) osteological

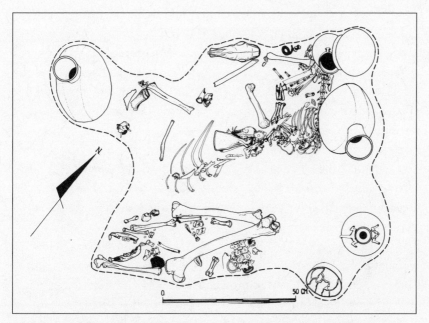

FIGURE 9.24. Example of a secondary burial within the Huaca Burial Platform that contained the remains of at least three individuals and two llamas.

analysis noted the absence of cut marks and that many of the bodies were disarticulated. These findings may signal the curation of the bodies for some time prior to burial (Nelson 1998). Although there is little evidence for their depositional history before burial, once the bodies were placed in the burial platform at Farfán, the tombs were not reopened. This supports Isbell's (1997:144) hypothesis that North Coast *wak'a* burials were not intended to be reopened.

In the Huaca Burial Platform, the secondary burials also consisted of several individuals. Tomb 1 (described above) was flanked by two partial interments — one to the west and one to the east — consisting of parts of the skeletal remains of multiple individuals. Although these burials are under analysis, figure 9.24 shows that the western secondary burial consists of portions of three individuals and two llamas as well as the associated ceramics.

LOOTED BURIALS FROM BURIAL CHAMBER 1

Looted burials are not generally described. However, Burial Chamber 1, located on the western side of the platform, was clearly an important tomb, so we decided to include it here. The analysis revealed some surprising results because this chamber contained evidence for the only male buried in the platform. Burial Chamber 1 was a niched, plastered, and roofed room where we excavated the partial remains of seven individuals. This is the largest of the three burial chambers in the platform and contained five niches and an interior that measures 3.4 meters in length by 2.6 meters in width (figure 9.21). Fallen wooden beams lying across the chamber indicate that it had once been roofed.

Analysis of the remains in this chamber revealed the partial skeletons of four subadults, probably all female. We also recorded the remains of two adult females and one male (Adickes, personal communication, 2000; Nelson, personal communication, 2001). The one adult male is particularly intriguing, since he is estimated to have been unusually tall for this population — at least 166 centimeters in height — approximately 7 centimeters taller than the mean for the rest of the males from the site. The screening of the chamber debris exposed fragments of gold, copper, and animal bone (llama, guinea pig, dog, and bird) and complete polished Chimú-Inka blackware ceramics. This was just one of the high-status burials in the platform, but it contained the only male thus far identified.

Osteological Analysis

Andrew Nelson, the physical anthropologist who is analyzing all the skeletal remains from Farfán, makes several interesting observations regarding the total sample (Nelson, personal communication, 2004, 2008). The first is that there is a wide age range, including many older individuals who are often underrepresented in other archaeological populations used as demographic exemplars (such as the Libben site, data in Ubelaker 1984), the large Peruvian samples (e.g., the Nazca Valley) (Drusini et al. 2001), and the Moche occupation of Pacatnamu in the Jequetepeque Valley (Verano 1997). The second is that there are many more females represented than males. In the Huaca Burial Platform, the majority of sexable primary tomb burials are female (the others are probably also female given their associated artifacts). Outside of the Huaca Burial Platform, the other burial facilities contain approximately one and a half times as many females as males. In the Moche cemeteries at Pacatnamu, the numbers of males and females are approximately equal (Verano 1997). The third observation is that based on physical characteristics and oxygen isotopic analysis, the population appears to be largely derived from local North Coast anteced-ents, with a few individuals who were from or spent time in the highlands. Finally, the Farfán sample does not demonstrate high frequencies of infec-tious disease or trauma, but it does reveal high rates of dental pathology (caries, abscesses, and so forth) and spinal pathology (especially vertebral collapse). These conditions would have caused considerable amounts of pain and high levels of stress, and would have severely compromised the overall health status of many individuals at Farfán.

Summary. The Inkas at Farfán emphasized ideological activities, both political and religious. As elsewhere in the Inka Empire, the Inkas high-lighted large-scale feasting that in Farfán took the form of "hospitality mounds," and they built an *usnu*. A diverse sample of Inka period burials was found in five mortuary facilities. While the Huaca Burial Platform stands apart because of its monumental size, high-status burials, and em-phasis on female gender, the four other mortuary facilities (Mound 1A in Compound VI, Mound G, Cemetery I, and Cemetery J in Compound II) shared other characteristics, including single interments placed in un-lined tombs that appeared to be middle class in rank; burial ceramics that were mainly Chimú-Inka, with some vessels of Provincial Inka style; and cemeteries that consisted of three or four stratigraphic levels.

The Huaca Burial Platform, a structure containing multiple interments, was unique for this time period on the North Coast. The Huaca Burial Platform contained six major tombs, three of which were described above. These tombs represent separate funerary events during the Inka occupa-tion. The females, who made up the majority of primary interments within this platform, were high-status individuals. They recall the groups of sac-rificed females from Inka period burials found at the sites of Túcume in the Leche Valley (Heyerdahl et al. 1995) and Pachacamac near Lima (Uhle 1991). The archaeological context suggests that the women buried in Far-fán's Huaca Platform may have been sacrificed. The abundance of textile paraphernalia and the similar burial contexts suggest that the women buried at Túcume, Pachacamac, and Farfán were *aqlla* (so-called chosen women whose duties included weaving as well as making *chicha*) who served the Inka administration. Chamber 1's unusually tall male was also of interest.

The predominance of Chimú ceramics found in Chamber 1 suggests several interpretations. The most likely explanation is that the occupants of the chamber were members of the local Chimú elite who were given an elaborate burial by the Inkas to recognize their ethnic affiliation and status and thereby further their integration into the Inka imperial system.

Conclusion

Archaeological and ethnohistorical evidence indicates direct political control by the Inkas of this administrative center. The results of our research have been crucial in identifying new archaeological markers of the Inka occupation and how the Inkas wielded control. The Inkas transformed the site physically, socially, economically, and ideologically. Almost all of the transformations initiated by the Inkas at Farfán appeared to have been geared toward two objectives: supplying the highlands with coastal products and produce, and integrating Farfán and the Jequetepeque Valley into the Inka Empire.

Acknowledgments

The fieldwork at Farfán would have not been possible without the collaboration of many people. My thanks to our workforce who commuted every day from the pueblo of San José de Moro. Thanks also to our crew of students from Universidad Nacional de Trujillo and from Pontificia Universidad Católica del Perú as well as the many universities in the United States such as Stanford, Michigan, and UCLA. I would also like to express my thanks to the project's two codirectors, Lic. Enrique Zavaleta (2000) and Lic. César Jaúregui (2001–2004), and to the physical anthropologist, Andrew Nelson. The project would not have been possible without financial support, and I would like to thank the individuals, especially Baerbel Struthers and William and Marcia Herrman, and the institutions that supported us. I also want to thank the Brennan Foundation, the John B. Heinz Charitable Trust, National Geographic Society, and California State University Northridge. A number of colleagues have made valuable comments and suggestions, and I am grateful for the time they took to read the many versions of this manuscript. Thanks to Christopher Donnan, María Jesús Jiménez, William Sapp, Melissa Vogel, and Adriana von Hagen. A special thanks to Lic. César Jaúregui for many of the drawings that appear in this chapter and to Dean Abernathy and his staff at the UCLA Experimental Technology Center for the Auto Cad drawings.

Note

1. The editors chose to use the spelling "Huaca" rather than *"wak'a"* for this structure due to the hispanicized form used in the literature.

Ronald D. Lippi and
Alejandra M. Gudiño

Chapter Ten

Inkas and Yumbos at Palmitopamba in Northwestern Ecuador

Editors' Introduction

The research by Lippi and Gudiño provides an important window into the poorly understood issue of the Inka conquest of northern Ecuador. We know from the chroniclers that the local groups provided fierce resistance, and their conquest took many years. Yet the exact nature of the relationship between the Inkas and these groups after conquest has yet to be firmly established.

This chapter indicates that the Yumbos, who occupied the transitional zone between the highlands and tropical forest to the west of the Quito Basin, were unusual in that they were not annexed as a typical province. Salomón (1997) notes a lack of significant change in Yumbo settlement patterns and other aspects. The authors point out that this region was important in trade between the Quito groups and tropical forest groups prior to the Inkas, and suggest that the Inkas simply maintained this special relationship to continue access to valued exchange goods. In fact, they make the point that the Inkas may never have actually settled in the region until after the Spanish Conquest, at which point Inka nobility fleeing the Spaniards established a presence at the site of Palmitopamba.

This chapter examines possible ways through which the Inkas interacted with groups at the margins of their empire. The authors make a convincing argument for why Palmitopamba was the most important Yumbo fort in the territory, hence the reason the Inkas selected it for their own uses. Yet they show how the Inka presence at the site reflects a respect for the Yumbos, considering the lack of Inka material culture at the summit, the most sacred part of the site.

The evidence taken together shows how the Inkas could use respect and deference for a local group as a means to obtain valued resources in the absence of military might. The information stands in contrast to that discussed in chapter 2, where the Inkas built a fort and introduced plants and *mitmaq* to manifest symbolic and political control over the region in an area where trade relations were not of great importance. As with the other chapters in this book, the information provided gives a broader view of how the Inkas interacted with indigenous groups at the far reaches of the empire.

Landscape Archaeology

Palmitopamba in the western Ecuadorian rain forest was apparently the center of a Yumbo chiefdom and later was also occupied by Inka troops and possibly Inka nobility during the short resistance period after the Spanish Conquest. The aim of this chapter is to understand the role, function, and nature of the relation between Yumbos and Inkas. To do so we shall apply principles based on landscape archaeology as a mechanism to perceive and interpret the environment of past human activities. Joyce (1997) introduces us succinctly to a landscape perspective: "What makes a place distinctive — different from anywhere else? Landscape, language, occupations, customs, food, buildings, and spaces between buildings are some of them. Combined, they determine the identity of a place, the characteristics that become familiar and give people a sense of belonging."

Landscapes can be used in many ways in archaeology — including as tools of analysis, for hypothesis building, and as the focus of culture historical reconstructions. The burgeoning domain of landscape research, as pointed out by Fisher and Thurston (2004), involves many scholarly disciplines, among which is archaeology. Landscape archaeology represents something of a spin-off of regional archaeology projects that are interested in the human use of a physical environment and the human conception of that environment. Furthermore, the approach posits that people do not just live somewhere but build a social landscape with symbolic value in addition to meeting their economic needs. This approach is delineated by Criado Boado in several publications (e.g., Criado Boado 1991; Criado Boado and Villoch Vazquez 2000) regarding symbolic spaces. Several other scholars have recently tried a landscape approach in Andean archaeology, especially with regard to the southern periphery of Tawantinsuyu and in an attempt to identify ethnic boundaries and the impact of imperialism. Some notable examples regarding the Inkas include articles by Vitry (n.d.), Aldunate et al. (2003), Sánchez Romero (2004), and Herrera Wassilowsky (2005).

The landscape is not simply the physical environment but also the "anthropogenic ecosystem" and "the manner in which these landscapes are conceptualized, experienced and symbolized" (Fisher and Thurston 2004). Archaeological sites are no longer isolated remnants but become focal points in a network involving a people's relationship with the environment they occupy and conceptualize.

Looking at archaeological sites in a regional context of physical landmarks that might have had special meaning to past occupants is one strategy of landscape archaeology. This involves trying to perceive the land in the same way that ancient peoples did. While this involves some speculation, it has the potential of producing valuable hypotheses to be tested in future fieldwork and analyses. In this study, we attempt to do this in particular with the natural landmarks as well as with landmarks that were constructed for culturally momentous reasons. Principal among these cultural landmarks are rectangular earthen platform mounds, known in Ecuador as *tolas*, though the hillside terracing at Palmitopamba is also a culturally significant landmark that we consider.

This approach looks at the monuments and their scenic effects. We look for regularities and try to construct a model based on these effects. We look for an attempt to create an artificial environment and what motivated that work. Among these basic elements are the visual perception of the monuments themselves, the lines of movement and lines of sight across the region, and the relationship to other elements in the natural environment.

As Earle (1997:155) comments, "One factor common to all monuments . . . is their ability to be experienced simultaneously by large numbers of

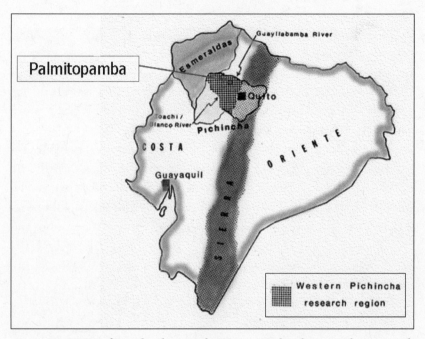

FIGURE 10.1. Map of Ecuador showing the Western Pichincha research region and the site of Palmitopamba.

individuals." This common experiencing strengthens social and political bonds, and the monuments become identity markers. Those outsiders who are excluded see the monuments as signals of forbidden land or as symbols of the greatness and strength of their neighbors.

The research presented here is held together by three unifying premises. The first is the recognition of a humanly constructed environment. The second is the conception of this landscape as evocative in a specific historical and cultural context that we try to understand in some tenuous way. The third is the belief that there is ongoing feedback between humans and their landscapes. With this perspective in mind, let us turn to a consideration of Yumbos and Inkas at the constructed landscape of Palmitopamba.

Introduction to Palmitopamba

Lippi has been directing a long-term archaeological exploration of the western slope of the Andes in northern Ecuador's Pichincha Province since the mid 1980s (figure 10.1). Several years of regional surveying in this rugged tropical forest region have shed much light on the indigenous peoples of the region from the Formative period onward and especially on the Yumbos, a mostly extinct ethnic group of Barbacoan (partly Macro-Chibchan) ancestry who occupied the cloud forest region from about A.D. 700 until their virtual disappearance as a recognizable ethnic group by the early 1800s (Lippi 1998, 2004).

In 2002, this project shifted its focus to excavations at the Palmito-pamba site, first cataloged in 1984, when the terraced hillside caught the eye of Lippi. This is a Yumbo site on a high hill that was taken over by the Inkas around 1500 and may have served as a refuge for Inka nobility who fled from the Spanish circa 1534. The interaction between the Yumbos and the Inkas at this important site is a main topic of this chapter, since the Yumbos appear to have occupied an atypical situation within Tawantin-suyu in the final years of that empire.

The Western Pichincha research region lies on the western slope of the Andes and is neither highland nor coastal but a vast transitional zone of very rugged terrain that was, until recently, covered by tropical rain forest. This ecological zone is known locally as *montaña*. Palmitopamba is a mere 45 kilometers (as the condor flies) northwest of Quito in the highlands but is between 1,300 and 1,400 meters above sea level, contrasting with Quito, which lies above 2,900 meters and between the two parallel ranges of the Andes.

Inkas in the Northern Andes

Inka expansion into what is today Ecuador began with Thupa Inka Yupanki around 1470 and was continued northward by Wayna Qhapaq. Fierce resistance from several allied chiefdoms — known collectively as the Caranquis — in the northern Ecuadorian highlands stalled the advance, though the Inka army, according to Cieza de León (Von Hagen 1959:49–50), finally defeated the Caranqui armies and massacred large numbers of their troops around 1490–1500. This effectively consolidated Inka rule over the entire Ecuadorian highlands only two generations before the Spanish Conquest (Salomón 1980:219).

Inka incursions into the Ecuadorian coastal lowlands were short-lived and not altogether successful. The natives annihilated Inka troops while ferrying them from Puná Island in the Gulf of Guayaquil during Wayna Qhapaq's expedition northward from Tumbes, probably in the early 1490s (Cieza de León, in von Hagen 1959:293–299). Once Wayna Qhapaq exacted revenge for the treachery, he pulled out of the region and left no lasting imprint except a road from the Cañari highlands near Cuenca in southern Ecuador to Guayaquil on the South Coast.

We also know, mostly from the work of Salomón (1997:21), that there was some Inka presence in the western *montaña* of Pichincha, including an *ingañán* (Inka road). Salomón (1997:23–26) cites Cabello Balboa regarding an expedition by General Guanca Auqui (half-brother of Wáskar and Atawalpa) into Yumbo territory. It is said that he quickly defeated and subdued the Yumbos but was so unimpressed by their nakedness and poverty that he quickly returned to Quito. At best, this suggests only a nominal conquest. At worst, one might conclude that the Inkas found the Yumbos a feisty foe and turned tail and ran, as sometimes happened when the Inka army ventured into rugged tropical rain forest habitats where they were ineffective against guerrilla tactics. Salomón (1997) found that Yumbo territory in Western Pichincha was not incorporated administratively into Tawantinsuyu in the manner that other provinces were. Neither the *hanan/hurin* moiety distinction was made there nor the quadripartite division into *suyus*. Nor could Salomón find any mention of tribute paid by the Yumbos to the Inkas. All in all, he concluded that the Yumbos maintained an anomalous position within the empire, which leaves the question of the nature or degree of Inka hegemony over the Yumbos unanswered. What we know is that the Yumbos played a very important role in tropical forest–highland exchange with the *circumquiteño* highland chiefdoms prior to the arrival of the Inkas, and we think it reasonable to suppose that the Inkas maintained this special economic relationship with the Yumbos.

Archaeological remains of Inka presence in Western Pichincha are rare, as are place names suggesting Inka presence (*ingachaca, ingahuaicu,* and so forth). The subterranean pool complex at Tulipe is of Yumbo and/or Inka construction — excavations at the site by Ecuadorian restoration specialists never satisfactorily resolved that fundamental question (figure 10.2). At least one small anomalous structure there appears to be provincial Inka or an imitation thereof, while the other larger *piscinas* are of uncertain affiliation. Jara Velástegui (n.d.) did not find any Inka pottery during

Semi-circular   **Circular**

Double stall   **Polygonal**

FIGURE 10.2. Four pool types at the site of Tulipe, approximately 12 kilometers southwest of Palmitopamba.

his excavations and reconstructions there; a single sherd of an Inka *aríbalo* was found a couple of kilometers away by Lippi. Tulipe was undoubtedly an important and perhaps sacred site in Yumbo territory, but Inka presence there is uncertain.

Finally, it is also known from early documents that some Inka leaders sought refuge from Benalcázar and his Spanish army in the highlands (Salomón 1997) by fleeing to Yumbo country and building one or more forts there. Viteri (2003:31, 38, 40, 42) cites Fernández de Oviedo and others regarding Rumiñahui (captain of Atawalpa's personal guard) taking Atawalpa's corpse, his heirs, and a fortune to northern Yumbo country, where they built a *pukara*, or fort. Details on the royal family and Rumiñahui while in Yumbo country are very sparse, but suffice it to say that a royal Inka contingent was there and built one or more forts after the Spanish Conquest and before returning to the highlands. Part of our research at Palmitopamba is focused on the possibility that it was precisely that fort where Rumiñahui and some Inka royalty sought refuge and tried to build up some armed resistance.

Inka Forts in Northern Ecuador

"*Pukara*" is the Quechua word for the fortified hilltop sites that are found scattered throughout the Andean highlands. References to *pukaras* are fairly common in the ethnohistorical materials from the region, and certain archaeological ruins can be identified with specific forts mentioned by chroniclers. Scholars such as Plaza Schuller (1976, 1977), Oberem (1969, 1986), Gondard y López (1983), Antonio Fresco (personal communication, 1986), and Gifford et al. (2002) have performed surveys and some excavations of *fortalezas* in the northern Ecuadorian sierra.

Given the very late annexation of the Quito and Caranqui regions to Tawantinsuyu and the prolonged military resistance encountered by the Inkas, it is not surprising that the only well-known Inka architecture in the northern Ecuadorian highlands today corresponds to these many *pukaras*. There is little doubt that these sites were intended primarily as garrisoned strongholds, though some scholars have argued that they served other functions in addition to the obvious military one. The distribution of *pukara* sites suggests a concern with control of access and internal movement as well as affording an unobstructed view of the population centers below. The distribution of these forts and the ethnohistorical record led scholars to assume that they correspond chronologically to the period of Caranqui-Inka conflict (Plaza Schuller 1976).

While there is little doubt that these sites date to the late prehispanic period, there is still considerable debate as to whether they were local or Inka in origin. Neither the archaeological data nor the ethnohistorical materials offer conclusive proof on this matter. In his discussions about the northern sierra, Cieza remarks that the locals, "in order to resist those who came looking for them, made fortresses and shelters and many weapons" (Cieza de León 1962:180). But in the same section he notes that the Inka king "ordered his shelters and strongholds, which they called *pukaras*, be built and sent his people and servants there" (Cieza de León 1962:179). In a lawsuit filed by the cacique Puento, one of the witnesses states: "they showed me many *pukaras*, which are hills fortified by the Inka in the aforementioned war; the local people were ordered by the Inka to build moats and fortresses, I was told, because the Inka had become worried during this War of the Caciques because they were unable to subject the local population; the war lasted eight or nine years" (Puento 1579–1583, cited in Espinoza Soriano 1980).

It seems likely that both the Inkas and the local population built and utilized these fortress sites during the period of the Inka-Caranqui wars (Espinoza Soriano 1983:387; Plaza Schuller 1976:117). In a recent presentation, Schauer (2007) noted differences in construction materials and location between Inka and Caranqui (or Cayambe) forts. In general, the majority of the pottery (around 94 percent, according to Antonio Fresco [personal communication, 1986]) recovered at these fortress sites is local, and 6 percent appears to be Inka, judging by observable attributes of the sherds.

Yumbo Landscaping at Palmitopamba

We believe that the Inkas constructed at least four and possibly more *pu-karas* in the Yumbo region (Lippi 1998:162–169), but Palmitopamba appears to be unique and of paramount importance among these in a few ways, as will be explained below. There appears to be only one other Yumbo site that rivals — in fact, probably surpasses — Palmitopamba in importance and grandeur, and that is the enigmatic monumental site of Tulipe with its several subterranean stone pools and aqueducts surrounded by many *tolas* in the nearby hills (figure 10.3). Both Tulipe and Palmitopamba represent very special landscapes, and, at least in the case of Palmitopamba, we are certain that the landscape modification was done primarily by the Yumbos; we suspect that is also the case for Tulipe. While we are not yet able to write with any confidence about the symbolism of the landscaping at Palmitopamba, we shall form some hypotheses in this chapter, with the ultimate goal of trying to understand why the Inkas subsequently chose this site for occupation.

The first surprise at Palmitopamba during our excavations in 2002 was the discovery that even though this hill rises high above the surrounding countryside and offers a spectacular panorama of 360 degrees, the Yumbos were not satisfied with the overall height and conformation of the summit. On the summit, we excavated downward through nearly 3 meters of fill without reaching the natural summit. It was obvious from this that

FIGURE 10.3. Photograph of the Palmitopamba site as seen from the village of the same name. The terraces are barely visible in the high pasture.

the Yumbos had taken great pains to create a level, elevated platform on the hilltop. Even though there had been some erosion and slumping that disturbed the usual symmetry, it was apparent that they had constructed a platform mound, or *tola*, at the summit.

It is puzzling why they did not consider the hill sufficiently high as they found it, but the *tola* is a very important structure for the Yumbos. Lippi (1998) and Isaacson (1982) each cataloged a few dozen of these earthen platform mounds in the region, and similar but much more famous structures are diagnostic of the Caranqui chiefdoms in the highlands north and east of Yumbo territory. As is true of the rectangular platforms of the Mississippian complex of North America, these Ecuadorian *tolas* are considered to have been the platforms for political and religious activities and perhaps even for the homes of chiefs, though this interpretation is not yet verified for Ecuador. From a landscape perspective, at least three leads emerge that may in some way help to explain what seems to have been a symbolic effort of monumental proportions.

First, chiefdoms among the Yumbos may have engaged in some competition to see who could build the most imposing *tola*, as was reportedly the case among competing chiefdoms in the highland Caranqui region (Espinoza Soriano 1983). *Tolas* on the plateau at the base of Palmitopamba lie far below, suggesting lesser importance in the locality.

The *tola* of Palmitopamba dominates much of the northern Yumbo region. This may have been nothing more than competition, though it is also possible that the imposing height was a sign of cooperation wherein neighboring *caciques* could easily communicate with each other by lighting beacons on their *tolas*, by using obsidian or metallic mirrors or flags, or by other means. The *tolas*, at least the largest ones, were normally placed on ridgetops or hilltops, and of those the one at Palmitopamba is the highest of all in this region.

Northeast of the *tolas*, across the Guayllabamba River gorge, lay the lands of the highland Caranquis. Lippi (2003) has argued elsewhere that the northern Yumbos were descended from Caranquis who migrated southwestward into the cloud forest and took with them their language, the practice of building *tolas*, and pottery styles. Nonetheless, in the protohistorical period, the Yumbos were considered wholly distinct from the Caranquis. The fact that Palmitopamba is a very conspicuous landmark from Caranqui territory may have stimulated the Yumbos to punctuate their autonomy and their power by building a monument that the Caranquis who journeyed in that direction could not help but see. In this case, the Palmitopamba monument may have served as a boundary marker of great importance.

A third clue to the importance of the *tola* comes to us from the mythology of the Tsáchilas, who Salomón (1997:95–96) and Lippi (2003) have argued are in one way or another descended wholly or in part from the Yumbos. Tsáchila myths of an ancient flood speak of the ancestors taking refuge on a mound (Calazacón et al. 1985), which is called *tola* in the Tsafiki language. "*Dula*" and "*tola*" are two Tsafiki words that literally mean hill or mound, but "*dula*" is used to refer to natural elevations, while "*tola*" refers to artificial mounds or other elevations of special significance (Robert L. Mix, personal communication, 2005). We are proposing here that the Yumbo practice of constructing flat-topped artificial mounds recreates the sacred landscape of mythology, and the mound itself becomes an icon of danger, salvation, and sanctity.

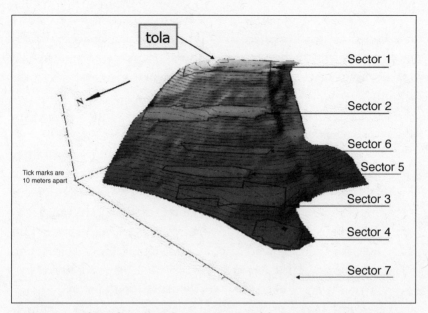

FIGURE 10.4. Three-dimensional representation of the upper part of the Palmi-topamba site showing the location of the hilltop *tola* and the various artificial ter-races or platforms (labeled "sectors" in this diagram). The area of the portion of the site shown here is approximately 2 hectares, and the vertical drop is 43 meters.

The second characteristic of the hill site, the one that first drew Lippi's attention when he discovered the site more than two decades ago, is the presence of a few horizontal terraces at irregular intervals down the north side of the hill (figure 10.4). A total of seven terraces have been investigated so far through subsurface surveying (magnetometry, ground-penetrating radar, and electrical resistivity), shovel testing, and excavation test units. Sector 2 is the largest terrace and was created by removing a huge quantity of soil, which is most likely the source of the fill used 17 meters higher to create the *tola* at the summit.

Agricultural terraces are practically nonexistent in northern Ecuador, and the only recorded defensive terraces are associated with Inka *pukaras* in the northern highlands. Despite decades of study by a few archaeolo-gists, as previously mentioned, it has only recently been determined with some confidence in one area of the highlands whether these *pukaras* were built by the Inkas or were pre-Inka sites that were taken over by the Inkas (Schauer 2007). This question was answered early on at Palmitopamba, where our excavations revealed a horizontal volcanic ash layer on a sloping hillside. The ash has been traced to an eruption that took place approximately 800 B.P. (Mothes 2003), providing convincing evidence that the terraces were constructed some six centuries before there were any Inkas in northern Ecuador. Just as the construction of the *tola* at the top of the site implied Yumbo construction, so do these several terraces.

One is left wondering, however, how the terraces functioned. While Inka terracing at *pukaras* was certainly defensive in nature, we have no evidence one way or another about the possibility of Yumbo warfare or Yumbo defensive sites. Of a couple hundred Yumbo sites cataloged by Lippi (1998) during years of surveying, Palmitopamba is one of only two with obvious terracing. More than 100 excavation units (1 meter by 1 meter) on these terraces reveal domestic debris, especially cooking pots and evidence of maize and other foods in the residue burned on the pots (Thompson 2003). If the terraces were not originally for defensive purposes, perhaps they resulted from symbolic landscaping for mythological purposes. It is known that the Tsáchila cosmos (Mix 2004) was three-tiered. There are three major and four minor terraces at the site, but it seems like quite a stretch to have the site conform to the cosmology. Perhaps the terracing simply served the practical purpose of providing horizontal living space on an otherwise quite steep hillside, though countless other sites in the region show that the Yumbos had no problem living on steep hillsides without terracing. A more symbolic explanation of some kind may be warranted.

We have already referred to the lines of sight from Palmitopamba to Caranqui territory and to various other platform mounds in the area. Part of the importance of Palmitopamba may very well have been as a central observation point among northern Yumbo chiefdoms as well as from the western Caranqui frontier. Just as "all roads lead to Rome," it seems that all lines of sight from other important Yumbo sites in the region lead to Palmitopamba.

A third line of sight is to Pichincha Volcano, which sits immediately west of the Valley of Quito. Again, if visual communication was a consideration, then beacons or large metallic or obsidian mirrors could have allowed instantaneous communication from deep within Yumbo territory to an outpost immediately above the densely populated Quito area. The Yumbos were known in the early Spanish period as traders par excellence with the many highland communities in and around the Valley of Quito.

Also visible from Palmitopamba is the highest peak of the western cordillera in Caranqui country, Cotacachi. Palmitopamba is probably unique in affording, on a clear day, a view of these two high volcanoes. Both peaks mark lands from which the probable ancestors of the Yumbos migrated, and both show the way to important highland communities in the trade network. By the same token, both peaks also mark the western margin of effective Inka hegemony in the early 1500s.

Even if the idea of beacons or mirrors seems far-fetched, the lines of sight could not have been ignored and must have been significant in the "worldview" (in the usual anthropological sense and also in a more literal sense) of the inhabitants. Palmitopamba was certainly strategically located, whether or not the inhabitants took advantage of their geographical prominence for direct communication over long distances.

It seems obvious from these circumstances that the site we know today as Palmitopamba was a unique site for the Yumbos in terms of location, and that it was of considerable importance, probably one of the most important of all Yumbo sites over a territory of some 4,200 square kilometers (Lippi 1998:figure 8.13, 2001:3). We also believe that the Inkas chose to settle here precisely for that reason. One way the Inkas could consolidate their authority in Yumbo country was by occupying the most important Yumbo monuments.

Inka Presence at Palmitopamba

We have not yet been able to date precisely the arrival of the Inkas in Western Pichincha, but it may be safely assumed that it was no earlier than about 1490, based on historical evidence previously discussed. It may very well have been after 1500 and possibly even (see below) as late as 1534 or 1535.

In archaeological terms, Inka pottery at the site is limited to the upper 50 centimeters of deposition, where it is mixed together with Yumbo pottery. Neutron activation analysis (NAA) of both Yumbo and Inka pottery from the site indicates that the two distinctive styles were made from the same compositional group, or clay source, which we are tentatively concluding was local until a positive NAA match can be made (Descantes et al. 2004; Speakman and Glascock 2003). The presence of domestic pottery of Inka and Yumbo types intermingled in the deposits and apparently all made locally suggests a period of détente if not actual peaceful coexistence. Given the very high value the highland native communities placed on Yumbo trade prior to the Inka conquest, we have no reason to believe the Inkas would not have encouraged and maintained a similar exchange relationship after consolidating their hegemony in the highlands. Principal Yumbo products greatly valued in the highlands included cotton, tropical maize varieties, various tropical fruits, salt (from Yumbo salt springs known as Cachillacta), and possibly coca (Salomón 1997:17–19).

A special trading relationship may explain why the Inkas did not incorporate Yumbo territory into the imperial administrative structure with normal Inka districting and tribute. The "conquest" of Yumbo territory attributed to Guanca Inkas by Cieza de León may have amounted to nothing more than the Inkas formally taking control of the widespread highland-*montaña* trade that had been established centuries earlier.

As mentioned earlier, Inka presence at the very important Tulipe site is not yet verified, and a smattering of Inka pottery and place names throughout the region plus reports of an Inka road from Quito through northern Yumbo territory all suggest some limited Inka familiarity with the region but more interest in peaceful trade than conquest and assimilation.

In the absence of very precise dating at Palmitopamba that can tell us to within a few years when the Inkas arrived there, we can only infer that their presence at Palmitopamba was fairly short-lived, given the general absence of Inka masonry, except for modest walkway borders, retaining walls, and associated anomalous stone features (figure 10.5). Inka *pukaras* in the highlands show much more substantial masonry structures and modification of the sites. At Palmitopamba, we see an Inka occupation mixed with the local Yumbo occupation and a minimal amount of landscaping and building at the site by the Inkas. Either they lacked time to undertake their own building projects of any substance there or they were satisfied with the landscaping and building (with perishable materials) previously done by the Yumbos.

Moreover, the Inkas apparently respected the sanctity or political importance of the *tola* at the summit. That highest platform is the only part of the site that so far has not produced any Inka ceramics. The only Inka presence at the summit was by way of an interesting series of features on the front edge of the *tola* platform, where we found a line of six or more sling stone caches (see figure 10.5). This was intended as the last defensive

FIGURE 10.5. Photographs of four Inka stone features at Palmitopamba. A: sling stone cache; B: walkway border; C: stone circle 2 meters in diameter; and D: short retaining wall.

position of the Inkas at the site in case of attack and was apparently the only way in which the Inkas compromised the special status of the *tola* at the summit.

Throughout our three seasons of excavations at the site, we have been alert for the presence of any sign that the Inka presence may have come after the Spanish invasion of Ecuador's northern highlands, which occurred in 1534 under Sebastián de Benalcázar. We have fragments of one unusual vessel that is clearly exotic, though its provenience and age are as yet undetermined. It could show Spanish influence, but we just do not know for sure. A couple of Inka *aríbalo* fragments have what might be an imitation whitish glaze, which may or may not suggest an Inka vessel form with Spanish decorative influence.

Another reason to suspect that at least part of the Inka occupation of Palmitopamba was post–Spanish Conquest is the report of Inka nobility fleeing to Yumbo territory and building a *pukara* to try to establish resistance to Spanish dominion. Viteri (2003) has researched this matter in some depth. As already mentioned, reports have Rumiñahui taking refuge in northern Yumbo territory with Atawalpa's heirs, wives, and part of his fortune, and even perhaps with Atawalpa's mortal remains. The purported presence of an Inka *pukara* in this region and the paramount importance of Palmitopamba among the four *pukaras* identified by Lippi (1998) point to Palmitopamba as the most likely place for Inka royalty to take refuge and regroup.

Yumbo-Inka Interaction on the Northwestern Periphery of Tawantinsuyu

What exactly do we have at Palmitopamba? There can be no doubt that Palmitopamba was a site of great importance to the Yumbos and undoubtedly was well known throughout northern Yumbo territory. The Yumbos, who otherwise are very poorly known archaeologically except for their many *tola* sites and the unique pool site of Tulipe, undertook landscaping of monumental proportions to transform a natural hill of some prominence into a cultural locale that later drew the Inkas like a magnet. The Inkas themselves seem to have taken relatively little interest, as was their custom, in this tropical forest habitat except to maintain the important trade with the highlands that the Yumbos had established centuries earlier. Only in a desperate situation did they possibly seek refuge in the Yumbo *montaña* region to escape the conquering Spaniards.

Whether the Inkas settled at Palmitopamba a generation or more before the Spanish arrival or only temporarily after the Spanish arrival has yet to be determined. It is even possible that there was an early Inka settlement there, a hiatus, and then a return of Inka nobility to Palmitopamba under the military leadership of Rumiñahui. Whatever the actual chronology, it appears that peaceful trade and coexistence were the rule, and evidence for warfare is absent. The Inkas moved in alongside the native Yumbos for some undetermined period of no more than two generations and perhaps only a few years. The prior importance of the site helped to legitimize Inka hegemony in the region.

Rumiñahui soon marched back into the highlands, where he ultimately met his death. We ardently hope that he took Atawalpa's treasure with him since the last thing we need at Palmitopamba is gold fever among the local inhabitants, some of whom are still suspicious about our motives in working there. There was no significant armed resistance by the Inkas to the Spaniards in northern Ecuador as there was in southern Peru. Despite Rumiñahui's efforts, Palmitopamba did not become the Vilcabamba of the north. Some Inkas may have stayed behind and blended with the Yumbos. The Yumbos themselves suffered from Old World epidemics, Catholic missionaries, Spanish *encomiendas*, workshops, and road building, and eventually all but disappeared through death, emigration, and assimilation. What is left at Palmitopamba are some tantalizing clues to the unique nature of the site, the imposing work done for uncertain reasons by the mostly unknown Yumbos, and a brief glance at Inka relations in the final days of empire with a tropical forest people best known as consummate traders. The line of movement, an important consideration in landscape archaeology, focuses on this trade as well as on Yumbo chiefdoms interacting with each other and making bold landscape statements to outsiders.

More work is planned for Palmitopamba, so these various hypotheses will be put to the test, and additional data should shed more light on this fascinating site in the coming years. That work must continue to focus on Palmitopamba as a highly modified, symbolic as well as physical landscape in a key position of a regional network of chiefdom centers. The more we understand about the Yumbos' use of the site, the more we will also come to understand the need felt by the Inkas to establish their presence there without upsetting local traditions.

Acknowledgments

All fieldwork and subsequent analyses at Palmitopamba have been generously funded by the Butler Foundation of Concord, New Hampshire. The Maquipucuna Foundation of Ecuador has provided valuable logistical support. Tamara L. Bray, Wayne State University, was assistant director of fieldwork for the 2002 and 2003 field seasons. Robert G. Thompson, University of Minnesota, participated in the 2003 field season (and very briefly in 2004) and continues to do ethnobotanical studies for our analyses. David O. Brown, University of Texas, participated in the 2004 field season and is a consultant to the project on the Inkas. Vulcanologists

Patricia Mothes and Minard "Pete" Hall, Escuela Politécnica Nacional del Ecuador, continue to do vulcanological analyses of sediments from the site. Michael Glascock, Robert Speakman, and Christophe Descantes at the Missouri University Research Reactor continue to provide important neutron activation analyses for our study, and geophysicist Donald Johnson has collaborated with subsurface testing at the site. The National Institute of Cultural Heritage (INPC) of Ecuador has been supportive in granting excavation and exportation permits. Thanks also go to several students from the United States and Quito who have participated in the fieldwork and to the excellent workers from the village of Palmitopamba who have provided their services at the site as well as to the residents of Palmitopamba for their hospitality.

Sonia Alconini and
Michael A. Malpass

Chapter Eleven

Toward a Better Understanding of Inka Provincialism

Introduction

The many chapters in this book have deepened our understanding of the different forms of Inka control and Inka provincialism. Because of the geographical scope of the chapters, the contributions provide the foundation for a comparative work on the strategies used by the Inka elite in the control of the provinces, the distinct organizational layouts of the imperial provinces, and the different effects of the imperial administration on the local populations. More important, they provide a wealth of novel information on regions so far not clearly understood, as is the case in Ecuador, the western Peruvian coast, and Chile.

This volume has extensively documented how the Inka Empire incorporated a diversity of environments and ethnicities with varying levels of political complexity. Therefore, it is not surprising to find that the use of a range of power strategies was tailored to specific local conditions, which has also been reported by other scholars (D'Altroy 2002; Malpass 1993; Schreiber 1992; Stanish 2001b). As illustrated in the various contributions, these different forms of provincial control were the product of a series of competing factors. These included the kinds of resources available in the

provinces that were valued by the empire, the degree of cooperation or resistance manifested by local leaders, the existing levels of political organization convenient to the imperial administration, how recently the Inkas
conquered a region, and the variation in distance to the imperial core.

The initial goals of the book were to explore five basic themes: the Inka
relations to groups external to the imperial borders; the nature of the interaction between archaeological and ethnohistorical research seeking to
understand the various manifestations of Inka imperialism; the various
forms of Inka provincialism; the local reactions to imperial control, including resistance, colonization, and negotiation of power as seen through
archaeology and ethnohistory; and the various scales of analysis and archaeological correlates used to understand Inka provincialism and imperial control.

Each one of these topics was addressed at different levels of detail by
the authors. While in all contributions there was a clear concern for evaluating the nature of imperial control in the various provinces, the lines
of evidence and scales of analysis were refreshingly different. In some
cases, the point of departure was the use of ethnohistorical information
as a complementary avenue of archaeological research (Rivera Casanovas, Mackey, and Acuto). In other cases, both sources provided somewhat
contradictory views, particularly when dealing with pre-Inka populations
(Van Buren and Presta, Santoro et al.).

Differences in the chosen scales of analysis ranged from a regional perspective (Rivera Casanovas, Acuto, Santoro et al.) to communal and site
levels (Rossen et al., Lippi and Gudiño, Van Buren and Presta, Mackey,
Alconini). This also included an array of approaches to the study of cultural and biological materials, such as bioarchaeology (Haun and Cock
Carrasco) and archaeobotany (Rossen et al.).

These different ways of addressing Inka provincialism and imperial
control provided a rich tapestry that builds on the different ways in which
both the conqueror and the conquered perceived the Inka conquest phenomena, the correlation of archaeological and ethnohistorical data, and
the shifts promoted by the empire at different scales, ranging from a regional perspective to one of local households.

Overall, the chapters provide a rich assortment of novel issues to the
study of Inka provincialism, which can be divided into five main areas:
different strategies of Inka imperial domination; imperial control along

the Inka frontiers; the role of midlevel administrators in the Inka provinces; the challenge of finding Inka *mitmaqkuna* enclaves in the provinces;
and issues of resistance and acculturation in the provinces. A summary of
each topic follows as a comparative framework for parsing out the similarities and differences posited in the chapters.

Inka Imperial Strategies of Domination

Two forms of control often describe the ways in which the Inka Empire
established domination. These are direct and indirect strategies of imperial administration, depending on whether the empire established a
direct government in the provinces through imperial administrators or
governed indirectly through local leaders. These two types of administration correlate to the territorial/hegemonic forms of control widely used
to describe both forms of government in other ancient empires in Mesoamerica (Hassig 1992) and in the Old World (Luttwak 1976). In this context, it is assumed that a territorial administration was a high investment–
high extraction strategy because it involved the large-scale investment
of imperial facilities and personnel to ensure large economic revenues.
These investments include intense forms of agricultural production and
the construction of administrative facilities and road networks tied to the
direct administration of the provinces by the imperial elites.

This strategy was markedly different from an indirect-hegemonic
form of control, in which the empire invested less in the construction of
imperial facilities while delegating the imperial administration to local
leaders. In this sense, hegemonic control was a low investment–low extraction strategy that allowed ancient empires to expand over broad territories with a minimum effort. Such was the case of the Aztec Empire, for
example, which was based on hegemonic control of the provinces through
native leaders and a tributary system (Hassig 1992).

For the Inkas, a combination of both strategies often has been assumed
to be a response to distance factors, existing levels of sociopolitical complexity of the conquered groups, and the level of imperial interest in the
extraction of wealth resources (D'Altroy 1992, 2002; Menzel 1959; Stanish
2001b; Williams and D'Altroy 1998). Territorial control was more common in core regions incorporated early into the empire, where the Inkas
targeted the investment of imperial facilities, such as storage *qollqas*, road

systems and *tampus*, agricultural terraces, and administrative centers that were in turn accompanied by the direct rule of these regions by Inkas of noble origins (*orejones*). This direct form of administration had significant effects on the local political economies, as it often reshaped the existing forms of agricultural and craft production to fulfill imperial needs while also promoting increased social stratification and the flow of surplus to the imperial core.

By contrast, hegemonic-indirect strategies of domination are assumed to be more common in distant regions outside the imperial center core of later incorporation, where the Inkas delegated the administration of the provinces to local elites while investing the minimum in imperial infrastructure. This form of administration did not have significant effects on the indigenous economies, as it relied on existing forms of economic production and social relations (D'Altroy 1992, 2002).

Despite this loose correlation of the forms of control to distance, important exceptions remind us about the flexibility of Inka administration. First, along the Peruvian coast, the prevailing view has been that the Inkas exercised indirect control of the region through the mediation of local elites, which means that the empire benefited from existing sociopolitical hierarchies and administrative facilities. As with the Chimú, a state-level formation subdued by the empire, early interpretations contended that the Inkas minimized labor investment, infrastructure, and organizational efforts by co-opting the Chimú bureaucratic structure and leadership system into the imperial realm. Hence, it was assumed that in situations of significant political centralization and the availability of infrastructure, the Inkas would choose to govern indirectly through the mediation of local lords in order to minimize investment. Alternatively, in areas with lesser forms of political development and marked political fragmentation, the Inkas preferred to exercise direct forms of control tied to marked construction levels of imperial infrastructure (Menzel 1959; Schreiber 1992).

Second, even in marginal regions within the confines of the empire where an indirect government was expected, there is growing evidence of selective Inka control in targeted territories, despite conditions of heightened political fragmentation, low levels of political hierarchy, and poor agricultural productivity. In regions such as northwestern Argentina, which occupied the southern margins of the empire, there is documentation of pockets falling under the direct control and supervision of the empire as cases of selectively intense forms of domination (Williams and D'Altroy 1998).

Recent studies have also challenged the notion that both hegemonic and territorial strategies were mutually exclusive in the makeup of ancient empires (Stanish 2001b). In fact, most authors in this book have provided evidence for the combination of both imperial strategies. Even though most contributors agree that the Inka Empire often opted for the delegation of the provincial administration to local lords — a fundamental feature of hegemonic indirect control — marked differences were also evident in the varying levels of investment in imperial facilities and in the effects of conquest on the local economies. These diverse levels of investment and effects on the native finances reflect somehow the mixed forms of imperial administration used by ancient states. D'Altroy (1992) suggests that rather than being fixed forms, the territorial-hegemonic approach should be understood as extremes at either end of a continuum, with varying levels of control in between.

Therefore, regardless of the levels of imperial investment in the provinces, the fact that the Inkas often delegated the administration to local leaders is an issue that deserves an explanation. In our view, this might contribute to greater elucidation of the political ideology of the Inka Empire regarding conquest and incorporation. The underlying issue is that, all factors being equal, ancient empires sought (as do modern ones) to maximize their revenues with as little investment as possible. In this context, the optimum strategy should be in fact a combination of both forms of domination, in which low investment levels of imperial infrastructure (hegemonic strategy) are combined with significant changes in the local economies geared to ensuring large revenues for the empire (territorial strategy). Obviously, this ideal might have been limited by the constraints inherent to the provinces, varying in the availability and quality of resources, the total supply of people available for service, distance, and the different reactions of the native elite to imperial conquest.

In order to reach this ideal, there is evidence that the Inka Empire promoted the circulation of a wealth economy with prestige Inka materials aimed at strengthening the alliances with native lords, promoting kinship ties with those privileged groups through the exchange of women, and expanding a redistributive economy in the form of state-sponsored hospitality feasts geared to the symbolic repayment of the *mit'a* labor tax to the commoners (Covey 2003, 2006; D'Altroy and Earle 1985; Morris 1982, 1998; Murra 1982, 1958, 1960).

Of course, in the perspective of the local lords, the arrival of the Inkas was multistranded. On the one hand, it represented a threat to their own sovereignty, with the consequent response ranging from open resistance to calculated alliances. On the other hand, it also opened unique opportunities for the native chieftains to advance their own political agendas of empowerment. In other words, the incorporation into the empire at least in the earlier phases might have provided the local leaders the opportunity for the reorganization and expansion of the local economies to accommodate the production of targeted imperial products, while also maintaining their own independent access to surplus. In exchange for the surplus flowing into the imperial core, local leaders benefited from the circulation of Inka wealth products while also enhancing their own status both in the eyes of the locals and the empire.

There is no doubt that these adjustments implied the reorganization of not only the economy but also the existing forms of social interaction established between native lords and commoners. While the commoners were compelled to intensify their own production and payment of tribute in *mit'a* labor, the local *kurakas*, with the help of the empire, had to create alternative ways to legitimate the new situation by intensifying hospitality celebrations and feasts, the circulation of imperial gifts, and the insertion of a new religious ideology. How many of these changes were absorbed by the typical resident is still very much in debate.

Addressing these issues, the contributions to the book help us expose the mechanics of imperial control in the various provinces, which involved a combination of territorial and hegemonic strategies and the consequent adjustments of the elites to the new system.

In her contribution, Mackey (chapter 9) provides a new perspective on Inka control by challenging earlier assumptions of an indirect imperial administration in the Chimú region. Based on extensive excavations in Farfán, she finds a more direct than expected Inka occupation, manifested in the marked changes in the local economy that favored the production of Inka status materials such as textiles, the construction of imperial infrastructure emphasizing the storage capabilities of the settlement, and the presence of midlevel imperial administrators. The evidence also highlights the importance of local elite in the administration of the settlement. While Lambayeque leaders are found to be associated with the supervision of ceramic production, Chimú elite segments are associated with textile production, as seen in the concentration of Chimú-Inka pottery in the Huaca Burial Platform. In this platform, along with a large number of female burials (possibly *aqllas*), the remains of a high-status and unusually tall Chimú male were found during the Inka period.

Similarly, the administration of polities along the Bolivian valleys and in northern Argentina, including the Qaraqara in Camargo, Yampara in Oroncota, and the Calchaquí Valley in Argentina, illustrates that the local elites were key agents in the provincial administration on behalf of the empire. In Camargo, occupied by the Qaraqaras, the arrival of the Inkas marked the reorganization of the local economy through local leaders by the expansion of agricultural terrace production and control of exchange routes. However, the progressive incorporation of the region into more direct forms of control is also evident (Rivera Casanovas, chapter 6). The increased presence of corrals in large villages rather than the local center, along with the wider distribution of serving and storage vessels across sites, suggests somehow that serving and storage activities were no longer limited to local centers. Rivera Casanovas explains these shifts as the possible dispersal of elites along the settlement system, or simply the reorganization of serving and storing activities assumed by smaller villages. Whatever the nature of these shifts and taking into account the near absence of Inka facilities or imperial presence, local elites in Camargo played a key role in the administration of productive activities on behalf of the empire.

Similar forms of indirect control through the mediation of local lords were also evident in Oroncota, Yoroma, with the intensification of lithic production for export (Alconini, chapter 4). In Cortaderas Derecha, Calchaquí, there was evidence of the insertion of textile, lithic, and food production through attached specialists (Acuto, chapter 5).

Likewise, in the coastal valleys and Arica highlands of Chile, local rulers played an important role in the reorganization of the economy, including the expansion of agriculture and the textile *mit'a* as seen in the increased use of spindle whorls (Santoro et al., chapter 3). In all of these cases, the authors document targeted pockets of imperial investment. While in Camargo and Arica imperial architecture was nearly absent, in other areas the construction of facilities was limited to restricted areas, either in the form of elite residences, ceremonial centers, or productive features. Such was the case of La Paya/Guitián, where La Casa Morada was used as the residence of a local leader (Acuto, chapter 5). By comparison, in Oroncota, the construction of fine architecture was reserved for specific buildings (Alconini, chapter 4). In all of these cases and irrespective of the existing level of political complexity, we see a clear imperial effort either to minimize or strategically target the investment of infrastructure while maximizing the *mit'a* labor tribute, thanks to the mediation of native elites. Also, in most of these situations the local leaders were rewarded by the imperial administration through preferential access to prestige Inka goods.

Therefore, we can assume that the Inkanization of native elites might have been a top imperial priority for ensuring the successful delegation of administrative duties with the least effort possible. Taking into account the expensive nature of a direct-territorial strategy, along with the unprecedented expansion of the Inka Empire, the Inkas might not have been able to afford investing equally everywhere. Some strategies used to account for this limitation might have included the use of mobile military troops within and across the borders, periodic visits by the Inka ruler to the subject provinces to symbolize the imperial power while also reinstating previously existing alliances, and the strategic construction of outposts, shrines, and temples in selected areas.

In this perspective, one inexpensive strategy — although efficient — was the Inkanization of local lords. Ethnohistorically, extensive descriptions exist of the various mechanisms used by the Inka Empire to ensure the successful Inkanization of native lords, including preferential distribution of imperial wealth and status objects along with the establishment of kinship ties with provincial lords based on the exchange of women. This entailed the imperial distribution of elite Inka and *aqlla* women to local lords, and the acquisition of secondary wives by the Inka king across the provinces. Most important, the education of elite youth from the subjugated provinces in the Cuzco capital to learn the proper Inka norms, beliefs, and moral codes might have facilitated their indoctrination. Of course, this incorporation strategy was backed up by the threat of military intervention in the provinces and even death (Cobo 1979; Rostworowski de Diez Canseco 1999; Rowe 1946).

As a result, the Inkas, like rulers of other ancient empires, sought to minimize their investment while also maximizing revenues by expanding their control through the mediation of local elites. In the case of the Inkas, this optimization strategy was reflected in a targeted policy designed for the provincial lords to expand the production of targeted goods through the *mit'a* system with a minimal investment effort. Because of the volatile nature of such a situation, this strategy was tied to an imperial redistributive economy involving hospitality feasts for the producers that featured the regular redistribution of *chicha* (corn beer) and a gift-giving economy aimed at distinguishing vertical relations. In this scenario, the role of the local lords was crucial as they applied and transmitted the imperial agenda to the commoners based on their own claims of legitimacy and privilege, while also taking advantage of existing solidarity ties with the locals based on common ancestry and ethnicity.

As such, the native lords might have been the catalysts of important social changes in the imperial political structure, involving the gradual but irreversible disarticulation of ethnic solidarity in favor of a marked class structure. Of course, we should not underestimate the internal dynamics in some provinces where aggrandizers, overachievers, and competing elite lineage factions might have been important factors in the continuous cycles of internal rebellion and conflict.

Hence, refining the territorial-hegemonic spectrum, an optimization strategy that was located at the midpoint of both, implied the successful combination of these two forms of imperial administration. This combined strategy was manifest in the governing of the imperial provinces through local lords incorporated into the bureaucratic system through a gift-giving economy, privileged and enhanced positions in the new system, and an acculturative program, all aimed at maximizing the imperial revenues with the least investment and effort possible.

Imperial Control along the Inka Frontiers

A second group of chapters provides case studies for understanding the different forms of imperial interaction established with the locals in frontier territories. Lippi and Gudiño (chapter 10) focus on the northern Inka frontier in Ecuador, while Rossen et al. (chapter 2) address the nature of the southern frontier in Chile and Argentina. Lippi and Gudiño argue that the Western Pichincha frontier, located in the Ecuadorian tropical *montaña*, was inhabited by the Yumbo tropical chiefdom, who maintained extensive trade networks with highland polities for the provision of exotic materials from the forest. When the Inkas arrived, the Yumbos, rather than being incorporated into the imperial administration, were maintained in their status as traders, while the empire controlled the important exchange networks for their own benefit. In fact, Lippi and Gudiño suggest that Palmitopamba, one of the largest Yumbo mound sites, was inhabited both by the Yumbos and Inkas and that the site might have been the home of the last Inka refugees after the Spanish Conquest.

In comparison, the highlands occupied by the rebellious Caranqui, among other polities, was the setting of continuous processes of alliances and conflict with the empire, expressed in the construction of strings of fortresses. It is possible that these sites were Inka fortresses or that the empire used local labor to build the defensive outposts manifested in a mixed architecture. Alternatively, it is also possible that they were used at different times by Inka and Caranqui troops. Whatever was the situation, the presence of these cordons of forts testifies to the marked cycles of conflict along the northern imperial frontier (Plaza Schuller 1976; Salomón 1980, 1986).

Rossen et al. stress the importance of archaeobotanical studies for understanding processes of imperial expansion, interaction, and conquest across the borders. Based on their detailed examination of botanical and architectural remains of the Cerro del Inga fort in the Cachapoal Valley, one of the most far-flung Inka installations, the authors advance our understanding of the ways in which the southern frontier was established. Not only did the Inkas reoccupy an existing local settlement, but they also incorporated Cerro del Inga into their military network intended to strengthen the defense of the borders while facilitating the economic and political annexation of outer polities. Moreover, detailed botanical studies from the site demonstrate that the Inka presence also involved the systematic adoption of local cultigens, fruits, and medicinal plants to supply the needs of the imperial troops while introducing other crops to the local economy, such as quinoa. These results suggest broader processes of imperial and native interaction.

Both contributions reflect the multidimensional nature of defensive *pukara* forts along the imperial borders, often placed in ecological transitional areas and inhabited by populations with lesser forms of political organization and population density. In this sense, a degree of variability can be found across the imperial frontiers. Some segments of the southern and southeastern Inka frontier facing the tropical forest were designed to defend against external invasions, such as from the belligerent Chiriguano-Guaraní and Lule tribes (Alconini 2005; Julien 1997; Lorandi 1980; Raffino 1981, 1993b). However, such incursions took the form of intermittent attacks rather than permanent threats to imperial security. In other areas of the northern frontier, such as in Ecuador, similar populations posed a more challenging threat, as the situation described for the Caranqui (Bray 1992; Gifford et al. 2002, Plaza Schuller 1976; Salomón 1986). Furthermore, in frontier areas such as central Bolivia and even Ecuador, the tropical populations, including the Chuncho and Yumbo, were used as nexuses to facilitate trade in the exchange networks across the forest for the imperial provision of exotic resources (Lippi and Bray 2003a, 2003b; Meyers 2002). In contrast, in the frontier areas located in the central eastern piedmonts near Mantaro, the Inkas simply did not seek to promote social interaction or to establish marked political boundaries (D'Altroy 1992; Hastings 1985). Finally, in the far southern frontiers facing Araucanian and Diaguita groups, the limits of Inka political expansion were surpassed by a broader economic zone of imperial influence (Dillehay and Netherly 1988; Hyslop 1990).

It is fundamental that future studies of Inka frontiers address this noted variability and develop explanatory frameworks to account for such situations. Therefore, future research should strive to define the multiple functions that outposts played along the frontier, the frontier dynamics, and the frontier functions in the processes of imperial expansion, retraction, and political consolidation.

The Role of Midlevel Imperial Administrators in the Inka Provinces

A third topic discussed in a number of articles is the role of midlevel administrators and intermediate elites in the supervision of some Inka provinces. In her investigation of Farfán in the Jequetepeque Valley, Mackey (chapter 9) discusses the various effects of the empire on the settlement's economy manifested in the targeted craft production of textiles and pottery, and she sheds new light on the important function that midlevel imperial administrators played in structuring such changes. Excavations and analysis of architecture in the residential areas revealed the presence of at least two kinds of bureaucrats. The first, high-status bureaucrats (Elite A and B), perhaps *khipukamayuqs*, were found associated with the monitoring of long-term storage strategies, as seen by the concentration of storage facilities near their residences as well as the presence of counting devices such as *yupanas*. These individuals also enjoyed privileged access to Inka-sponsored rituals, manifested in the location of an Inka *usnu* platform close to their residences, rather than being in the open plaza. The second kind, a lower rank of bureaucrats (Elite C), was found associated with the collection and short-term storage of goods, along with the supervision of craft production tasks. Even though these officials might not have been Inka by birth, they were Inkanized and practiced the imperial official religion, and so constituted the representatives of the imperial administration in the settlement.

The case of Farfán illustrates the strategy of the Inka Empire regarding administration. Taking into consideration the complex political structure of the Lambayeque, rather than establishing an enclave of Inka *orejones* in the site for direct control, the Inkas opted for delegating control to local lords while also inserting into the provincial administrative structure a new layer of bureaucrats and midlevel imperial administrators. This inexpensive strategy might have allowed the empire to maintain the area under supervision while also minimizing internal revolts by keeping the levels of political interference to a minimum. It also provided the opportunity for local lords to continue to advance within the political power structure. Because of the potential chances of rebellion by local elites seeking to regain their absolute power, the role of these midlevel administrators might have been crucial in keeping the area under surveillance while also segmenting authority and enforcing acculturative programs. Of course, in any situation in which the new bureaucratic positions were filled by local elites, the distinction between administrators and local lords might have been blurry.

A similar role played by bureaucrats is observed in the northernmost Inka provinces in Chile, where low-status administrative positions were filled by nonlocals. Santoro and his colleagues challenge earlier assumptions that Inka control in the highlands of Arica and nearby valleys was indirect and through the mediation of altiplanic populations from the Circum-Titicaca region such as the Inka Pacajes (known locally as Saxamar). In part, this interpretation was based on ethnohistorical data and the influential work of Murra. Employing a vertical model, Murra (1980) suggested altiplanic polities had already established colonies in the southern regions in order to have direct access to complementary resources. The implication of this view is that the later Inka alliances with the Pacajes paved the way for the imperial expansion into distant territories such as Arica.

Challenging this assumption, Santoro and his colleagues document a strong Inka presence in these regions, suggesting that the imperial administration was more direct and was manifested in two stages. The first stage was hegemonic and based on the direct imperial alliances with native lords rather than with the foreign altiplanic populations. These direct alliances with local leaders were evident in the coastal valleys of northernmost Chile, including Lluta, Azapa, and Camarones. In these regions, Inka control was expressed in the privileged access of Inka status materials and the insertion of new economic activities through the *mit'a* system directly benefiting the empire. These new activities involved intensification of textile production, as revealed by the wide distribution of spindle whorls and related tools, and population concentrations in larger villages perhaps to facilitate the control of labor. A restricted distribution of imperial infrastructure accompanied these shifts. In the second phase, these valleys were increasingly incorporated into direct-territorial control as seen in the substantial construction of imperial architecture including *kallankas*, *usnus*, the large number of storage *qollqas*, and the recovery of *khipus* in the region, indicating their insertion into the decimal system of administration. By comparison, in the altiplano of Arica and Tacna the evidence suggests a territorial control all along the sequence, as seen in the significant distribution of Inka provincial architecture, *tambos*, *qollqas*, an imperial road network, and funerary *chullpa* towers (Santoro et al., chapter 3).

The evidence presented by Santoro and his colleagues supports the presence of the Inka Empire as directly involved in local affairs, including the substantial investment of facilities to channel surplus flow through alliances with local elites. In this context, imperial alliances with local lords and *not* with altiplanic colonies facilitated the annexation of the provinces. Nevertheless, and as a cautionary note, we should not underestimate the role of trustworthy altiplanic colonies as important vehicles of consolidation and surveillance of distant southern provinces. In this line,

Santoro et al. also note the correlation of Pacajes pottery in Inka facilities, along with the construction of Pacajes funerary towers in the Inka style. A similar role of Pacajes as midlevel and low-level administrators is also reported for other regions, such as Oroncota inhabited by the Yamparas, where foreign Pacajes residences were also found in association with Inka installations (Alconini 2002).

Acuto notes that the Inka conquest led to a new agent in the bureaucracy, a midlevel administrator who was probably local and actively used the Inka association to increase his or her status vis-à-vis his or her peers. These individuals occupied Inka-style architecture but used local artifacts. Their intermediate status, above their indigenous peers but below the Inka *orejones*, reflects an increased complexity in the control apparatus. The Inkas clearly manipulated willing locals to fill these posts for imperial purposes. It is obvious from Acuto's research at Cortaderas Derecha that other locals rejected Inka attempts at assimilation.

In our view, these essays open new avenues of research for understanding the important role that administrators and trustworthy ethnicities played in the imperial expansionist program. Midlevel administrators and allied colonies did not just facilitate the surveillance of imperial provinces that either were too far from the core or that constituted a potential focus of rebellion; they also alleviated the expenses of direct-territorial forms of administration. Therefore, in situations in which the empire sought the consistent channel of surplus from imperial provinces without direct intervention or with the minimum investment of imperial infrastructure, midlevel administrators might have represented the most viable alternative to supervise the governance of local lords. These agents might also have been effective in the dissemination of the Inka way of life, religion, and customs to the locals.

As a result, the empire might have chosen to compartmentalize administrative tasks in such a way as to minimize chances for revolt and the over-concentration of power in the hands of a few individuals. In this context, while local lords were directly involved in dealing with local populations based on allegiances of common ancestry and ethnic ties, surveillance and espionage tasks might have been delegated to nonlocal populations and entrusted ethnicities. This strategy might also have facilitated the supervision of the provinces with minimal imperial interference.

Taking into account these findings, we should expect that future studies will further address the varying roles of midlevel administrators and intermediate elites, whether these were local or not, in the range of administrative and surveillance tasks throughout the empire. This information might provide a more textured understanding of the mechanisms of imperialism, colonialism, and Inka imperial annexation of distant provinces.

Finding Inka *Mitmaqkuna* Enclaves in the Imperial Provinces

A fourth issue addressed by the authors is the archaeological manifestation of *mitmaqkuna* colonies in the Inka provinces. There is abundant ethnohistorical data describing the relocation of large numbers of people from their original homeland to distant regions as colonies, either to expand the production of selected materials into new territories, to fragment competing polities by reducing chances for internal revolts, for military and defensive reasons, or simply to populate new territories. However, few archaeological studies focus on this important topic.

In this book, various chapters discuss this fascinating issue. Van Buren and Presta (chapter 7) provide important information from the Porco region in Potosí, where the Inkas established an enclave of *mitmaqkunas* to facilitate the direct extraction of silver. Contrary to ethnohistorical accounts suggesting a consistent pre-Inka population in the region, they suggest that there were scarce local settlements, perhaps as a response to the near absence of fertile agricultural soil. In this sense, they stress the importance of the region in the extraction of silver for imperial ends, where the Inkas had to accommodate to severe environmental and social conditions. In contrast to other marginal regions with indirect forms of administration, Van Buren and Presta argue, Inka expansion into the Porco region was direct and targeted, in the sense that the imperial administration moved temporary *mitmaqkuna* colonies near the mines to provide a more stable labor force. This direct control also included the supervision of exchange caravan routes, the construction of selected Inka architecture to facilitate extraction, and agricultural production in selected areas to supply internal needs. As in other regions with valuable minerals, the Inka administration intended to directly control the extraction of silver, while the subsequent stages of refinement were conducted somewhere else. Rather than being a typical Inka province, Porco represents a case where, despite the distance and ecological and labor restrictions, the empire established a direct enclave of control in a marginal region to facilitate the access of valuable minerals through *mitmaqkuna* miners.

Haun and Cock Carrasco (chapter 8) provide a wealth of novel information to reconstruct the ethnic affiliation of ancient Andean populations through biological and cultural indicators, as well as methodological considerations to test the presence of *mitmaqkuna* populations. More specifically, they analyze the mortuary remains in the Huaquerones cemetery located in the Rimac Valley, used during both the Late Intermediate period and the Late Horizon. This region was the home of the Ychma coastal *señorío*, where presumably the Inka established a colony of *mitmaqkuna* weavers.

Seeking to explore the dimensions of the *mitmaqkuna* policy and its effects on the local social dynamics, Haun and Cock Carrasco provide a detailed account of their mortuary analysis. This analysis was based on a range of metric and nonmetric cranial data combined with the analysis of material culture, patterns of cranial modification, stylistic variability in the funerary bundles, and spatial locations of the burials in the cemetery. Contrary to their initial expectations, they found no conclusive evidence to suggest a colony of foreign *mitmaqkuna* markedly different from the rest of the population. There was no clear correlation between biological affinity and patterns of funerary preparation, association of artifacts, or spatial segregation. Rather, they conclude that the inhabitants of the cemetery were part of a biologically heterogeneous community already settled in the Central Coast prior to the Inka conquest. This indicates an extensive sphere of interaction between coastal and highland populations even prior to the Inka conquest. According to Haun and Cock Carrasco, the presence of this heterogeneous cemetery might have been the product of the Ychma lords' policies aimed at concentrating labor in selected locations. Another interesting finding involves nearly twice the frequency of women of highland origins as coastal women, suggesting to Haun and Cock Carrasco the possibility that women played an important role in strengthening sociopolitical ties between both coastal and highland populations through marriage exchange.

Rossen and his colleagues identified possible *mitmaqkuna* by the appearance of quinoa, a plant little known in southern Chile prior to the intrusion of the Inkas. They mention the intriguing possibility that this crop was introduced by *mitmaqkuna* brought to this region. The fact that quinoa is still grown by isolated groups near Cerro del Inga lends ethnographic support to the idea.

One important implication of these studies is that although *mitmaq* populations were quite important in the Inka imperial policies, we do not yet know the interactive nature of such populations with native people. Did this interaction lead to an effective maintenance of ethnic boundaries as dictated by Inka imperial policies (Cobo 1979) or to a process of ethnogenesis, including the formation of new social identities combining different cultural traditions? In the case of the Haun and Cock Carrasco chapter, we have a group combining both highland and coastal features.

In fact, similar results are also available for other regions, such as the Oroncota part of the Yampara territory in the southern Bolivian valleys, which according to ethnohistorical accounts was not only multiethnic but also was placed in the midst of two local polities. Despite the great variability of ceramic styles in Oroncota, analysis of the spatial distribution of cultural materials failed to identify clearly defined boundaries that would suggest ethnic colonies in the typical archipelago model (Alconini 2002, 2008b). Rather, the cultural materials, which included a conspicuous variation of ceramic styles and decorations, suggest fluid processes of social interaction manifested in the formation of a multiethnic mosaic with less well defined boundaries. Further analyses in the coast and valley regions where ethnohistorical accounts report a range of ethnicities having simultaneous access to land should reveal whether multiethnic coexistence in the Andean past took the form of ethnic islands or if multiethnicity was expressed in the formation of mosaics with less defined ethnic and political boundaries. In addition, these studies will hopefully clarify whether *mitmaqkuna* colonies were absorbed into the indigenous cultures, or, alternatively, under which conditions such colonies maintained well-defined ethnic and cultural boundaries.

Issues of Resistance and Acculturation in the Imperial Provinces

A final topic addressed in some of the chapters is related to issues of local resistance, acculturation, collusion, and imperial emulation. In the spectrum of interactions ranging from violent to nonviolent, resistance and emulation were two forms of local reaction to imperial conquest so far not clearly documented archaeologically. As such, it is important to understand the different responses to imperial conquest by the different social segments in the provinces as well as the varying strategies used by the empire to incorporate such social disparity. For example, although it is assumed that elite groups were the focus of forced Inkanization, and therefore more likely to emulate imperial behavior and materials, we should also consider that the local emulation of imperial stylistic canons might have been a strategy used by local factions to compete for status and resources as well. In a reverse pattern, we still do not know the archaeological manifestations of local reactions to colonialism and resistance to cultural imposition, and the most likely groups involved with such responses.

In this respect, the chapter by Acuto provides a fascinating account of how local Calchaquí and Pular-Santamariana populations in the Calchaquí Valley reacted differently to imperial conquest. Seeking to provide a perspective of Inka rule from the point of view of the colonized, Acuto compared two Inka centers to evaluate the different ways in which the Inkas affected the lives of local populations, and the different strategies employed by the Inkas in their domination. The first settlement, known as La Paya/Guitián, acquired particular importance under imperial rule, as it was a dominant center with clear evidence of Inka architecture and significant access to prestige imperial materials. La Casa Morada stands out as a residence built in the fine Inka-style architecture and as the home of an important leader who had conspicuous access to Inka imperial materials, including personal adornments in valuable metals. According to the author, La Casa Morada was the residence of a local lord who either received the residence as a gift from the empire, was the home of a high-status *mitmaq* imperial administrator, or simply was an imperial emulation aimed at enhancing the status of the resident. In the vicinity, there was a significant construction of imperial facilities, including a plaza, *usnu*, and *kallankas*, suggesting that Inka rituals were performed at the site. Using this evidence, Acuto argues that La Paya/Guitián represents the emergence of a new social actor with a dominant position in the society, whose power resided in his or her association with the Inka conquerors and who was delegated the role of performing imperial rituals on behalf of the empire. In a preexisting social landscape of undifferentiated social differences in terms of status or wealth, the insertion of this new actor might have reshaped the ethnic and social landscape significantly with more defined social inequalities.

Comparatively, the residents of the site of Cortaderas, one of the major imperial centers in the northern Calchaquí Valley, displayed considerably different interaction with local groups. The area of Cortaderas Derecha was occupied by an indigenous village whose inhabitants were attached producers who specialized in the large-scale preparation of food, textiles, and lithics for imperial needs. However, the lifestyles of the domestic residents were not significantly affected by the empire, nor did the local population seek to emulate or copy the imperial architecture or Inka pottery. Neither access to existing long-distance trade materials nor indigenous funerary practices were significantly affected by the empire, as imperial materials were deliberately excluded from mortuary rituals. Rather, Inka materials were quickly discarded in midden areas, suggesting their use was in a range of administrative tasks delegated by the empire but not accepted into the cultural core of the community.

While Cortaderas Derecha represents a case of local resistance against imperial oppression as the locals deliberately rejected and ignored Inka material culture despite their insertion into the imperial economy as attached producers, La Paya/Guitián provides an example of successful incorporation and acculturation of the elite into the imperial political economy and ideology.

Farfán provides another interesting example for understanding the local reactions to imperial control and the strategies of the empire. The conquest of Lambayeque by the Chimú lords in the thirteenth century was related to the establishment of Farfán as a Chimú administrative center and the subsequent replacement of Lambayeque lords in the governance structure. With the arrival of the Inkas, the rivalry and internal competition between both elite segments had become evident. The Inkas, rather than polarizing the situation as they did in other regions, used a unifying strategy. In other words, the Inkas opted for incorporating both elite segments into the imperial administration in Farfán while maintaining their status and privileges. Perhaps because of the volatile nature of the region, or the competing population segments in the settlement, the Inkas chose to use a unifying policy to maintain the stability of the region rather than risking an internal revolt.

This strategy contrasts markedly with other provincial regions, in which

the Inka Empire deliberately accentuated local ethnic competition by favoring selected ethnicities or leaders in the delegation of administration
while positioning themselves on top of the social ladder. Such was, for example, the case with southern Argentina (Acuto, chapter 5) and Oroncota
(Alconini, chapter 4).

In the Oroncota case, ethnohistorical information and archaeological
data illustrate the multiethnic composition of the region, manifested in
the conspicuous variation of ceramic styles (Alconini, chapter 4). In addition, this region was also positioned at the boundary of two local polities
and was an important enclave to support the range of activities on the
frontier outposts in the eastern Chaco region. Based on extensive excavations in Yoroma, a regional Yampara center, Alconini explored the effects
of the imperial centers in the dynamics of the region from communal and
household perspectives. Specifically, Alconini evaluated whether local
Yampara elites sought to advance their privileged position in their own
communities through alliances with the empire, or if this situation involved their status being lessened in the local sociopolitical arena. In the
Classic Yampara period prior to the Inkas, no marked differences in the access of wealth or prestige materials were evident across households, which
were mostly formed by a group of circular structures around open patios.
However, the settlement was involved in specialized lithic production
using white quartzite for export. This lithic production was accompanied
by food consumption activities, as seen in the significant concentration of
serving and storage vessels beyond the domestic scale. Nevertheless, there
is no evidence of marked social inequality, as the power of the emerging
leaders was not manifested in the monopoly of wealth materials but rather
in their ability to mobilize labor for lithic production and in their redistributive capabilities.

In the following period during the Inka conquest, Yoroma grew in size
and complexity. Rather than dramatic shifts in the domestic and communal economies, there is continuity in the range of productive activities. At
a public scale, the intensification of lithic production and food consumption in the lithic workshop is evident, associated with a growing cult to
the ancestors as a mechanism of political legitimization to facilitate the
extraction of labor. The evidence also suggests the increased power of the
local leaders in their differential access to regional wealth networks, including star copper sheets and shells, along with their privileged access to

imperial materials, including copper *tupu* pins and imperial pottery. The residences of these leaders were also relatively larger, with clear changes in their configuration, perhaps emulating imperial architecture. In one of the patios, evidence of large-scale lithic production and food consumption was found, suggesting that the Yampara elite sought to have independent access to surplus and labor. At a communal scale, the insertion of new productive activities for imperial purposes is also manifested in the construction of a modest number of storage *qollqas* and grain-processing oblong structures in the central part of the settlement.

To summarize these findings, Alconini suggests that the arrival of the Inkas into the region did not promote significant changes in the domestic Yampara economy. Instead, the empire adapted to existing productive trends, including the increased manufacture of lithic tools on a communal scale. Rather than being lessened in status after imperial conquest, local elites reinforced their power and wealth as local administrators. Despite the proximity of the Inka center of Inkarry Moqo, the lithic workshop remained in the Yoroma center under the control of local leaders. Taking into account the multiethnic composition of Oroncota before the arrival of the Inkas, along with the relocation of Inka *mitmaqkuna* in the region, the Yampara elite benefited from the Inka conquest, as it provided them with the mechanisms to enhance their own power in a multiethnic landscape.

To conclude, all the contributions in the book provide a wealth of novel information to advance our understanding of the Inka strategies of domination and the diverse manifestations of Inka provincialism. Hopefully, the book also opened new avenues of future research. Some issues that deserve further exploration include the various roles of midlevel administrations in the supervision of inner and distant provinces, the diverse reactions and perceptions of the colonized to Inka imperial conquest, the archaeological manifestations of *mitmaqkuna*, and the different kinds of interaction that the empire established with local populations across its borders. Andean and Inka scholars will benefit from the various approaches posed by the authors in the volume, as we the participants of the symposium did.

Contributors

FÉLIX A. ACUTO received his Ph.D. from the State University of New York, Binghamton. He is currently a full-time researcher at the Instituto Multidisciplinario de Historia y Ciencias Humanas (CONICET), Argentina. His research focuses on Inka ritual activities and landscapes in the southern Andes and on the way Inka colonization affected the experiences, cultural practices, and social relations of indigenous societies. He is author of "Lugar, Arquitectura y Narrativas de Poder: Relaciones Sociales y Experiencias en los Centros Inkas del Valle Calchaquí Norte," *Arqueología Suramericana*, World Archaeological Conference, with Chad Gifford, and "Experiencing Inka Domination in Northwest Argentina and the Southern Andes" (2008) in *Handbook of South American Archaeology*, edited by Helaine Silverman and William H. Isbell.

SONIA ALCONINI is assistant professor in the Department of Anthropology, University of Texas at San Antonio. She focuses on the study of the Inka Empire, the ancient imperial frontier in cross-cultural perspective, and the kinds of imperial and provincial interactions established with the Inkas. Among her latest publications are: "The Southeastern Inka Frontier Against the Chiriguanos: Structure and Dynamics of the Inka Imperial Borderlands," in *Latin American Antiquity* (2004); "Military and Cultural Imperial Frontiers: Dynamics and Settlement Patterns of the Southeastern Inka Frontier," in *Untaming the Frontier in Anthropology, Archaeology, and History* (2005); and "New Perspectives on Territorial and Hegemonic Strategies of Domination," in the *Journal of Anthropological Archaeology* (2008).

GUILLERMO A. COCK CARRASCO received his B.A. and M.A. degrees in ethnohistory from the Pontificia Universidad Católica del Perú and pursued doctoral studies in archaeology at the University of California, Los Angeles. He currently owns an archaeological firm in Lima, Peru. Much of his most recently publicized work has occurred at the site complex of Puruchuco, including the first documented evidence of Spanish use of firearms against Andean indigenous populations. Among his many publications are *La Edad del Cobre en el Perú* (1990) and *El Cielo de los Antiguos Peruanos: El Libro de Oro de las Líneas y de las Figuras de Nasca* (1989).

ALEJANDRA M. GUDIÑO of the University of Missouri in Columbia has archaeology, anthropology, museum, and business degrees from Colombia, Mexico, and the United States as well as coursework on Caribbean archeology in Cuba. Her archaeology thesis at the Escuela Nacional de Antropología e Historia in

Mexico City was on Caribbean lithics industries, and she has also studied South American chiefdoms and hunter-gatherers in southwest Colombia. She has co-directed the Palmitopamba Project in Ecuador with Ronald D. Lippi for the past several years and has coauthored various papers, articles, and reports with him.

SUSAN J. HAUN received her M.A. in anthropology from the University of Memphis and is currently a doctoral candidate in physical anthropology at the University of Pennsylvania. As a member of Project El Purgatorio, she is researching the burial practices of the Middle Horizon–Late Intermediate period Casma polity at the Casma Valley site of El Purgatorio. Previous publications include: "A Brief Commentary: A Study of the Predictive Accuracy of Mandibular Ramus Flexure as a Single Morphologic Indicator of Sex in an Archaeological Population," in the *American Journal of Physical Anthropology*, and (coauthored with Hugh E. Berryman) "Application of Forensic Techniques to Interpret Cranial Fracture Patterns in an Archaeological Specimen," in the *International Journal of Osteoarchaeology*.

RONALD D. LIPPI, professor of anthropology at the University of Wisconsin–Marathon County, has worked in Ecuadorian archaeology for about three decades. He has been principal investigator of a major regional exploration of the western flank of the Andes in northern Ecuador, the Western Pichincha Project, which has resulted in two books and many articles on the subject. The Palmitopamba excavations are a spin-off of the Western Pichincha Project, and work at that important Yumbo-Inka site with Alejandra Gudiño continues moving forward.

CAROL MACKEY is professor emerita, Department of Anthropology, at California State University, Northridge. She has conducted extensive archaeological fieldwork and research in the Peruvian highlands and in the Casma, Moche, and Jequetepeque valleys on the North Coast of Peru. Some articles from these investigations include "The Middle Horizon as Viewed from the Moche Valley" (1982), "The Southern Frontier of the Chimú Empire" (1990), "Transformación Socio-Económica de Farfán durante la Conquista Inka" (2003), "Elite Residences at Farfán" (2006), and "Chimú Statecraft in the Provinces" (2009).

MICHAEL A. MALPASS is a professor of anthropology and Charles A. Dana Professor in the Social Sciences at Ithaca College, where he has been teaching since 1989. His chief publications include *Provincial Inca: Archaeological and Ethnohistorical Assessment of the Impact of the Inka State* (1993) and *Daily Life in the Inka Empire* (1996). He has conducted research and published on the Middle Horizon Wari state, on the evolution of agricultural systems during the late prehispanic period in the Colca Valley, Peru, and on the archaic adaptations along the Pacific Coast during the Preceramic period.

MARÍA TERESA PLANELLA is a Chilean scholar specializing in the prehistory of this region. She is a member of the Chilean Society of Archaeology. Her latest publications include "Consolidación Agroalferara: Zona Central," in *Culturas de Chile Prehistoria: Desde sus Orígenes hasta los Albores de la Conquista* (1989, coauthored with Eliana Durán); "El Complejo Defensivo Indígena del Cerro Grande de La Compañía (Valle del Cachapoal)," in *Clava* (1992); "La Fortaleza Indígena del Cerro Grande de La Compañía (Valle del Cachapoal) y su Relación con el Proceso Expansivo Meridional Incaico," in *Actas del XII Congreso Nacional de Arqueología Chilena* (1993); and "Complejidad Arquitectónica de las Ruinas Prehispanas de Chada en la Antigua Ruta entre los Ríos Maipo y Cachapoal," in *Xama* (1997) (coauthored with other Chilean scholars).

ANA MARÍA PRESTA is a professor of pre-Columbian Latin American history at the University of Buenos Aires and a researcher in the Latin American History Program (PROHAL). She has extensive experience in both the Potosí and Sucre archives, where she has conducted research on the indigenous and Spanish populations of the southern Andes since the early 1980s. Most of her recent research and publications have focused on the social and economic networks established by Spaniards, including a number of prominent families who had holdings in Porco during the Early Colonial period.

CLAUDIA RIVERA CASANOVAS is professor in the Anthropology-Archaeology Program at the Universidad Mayor de San Andrés, La Paz, Bolivia. She has worked in different regions of Bolivia, such as the Titicaca Basin and the inter-Andean valleys of Bolivia, carrying out investigations on the development of complex societies, organization of ceramic production, forms of sociopolitical organization, settlement patterns, and rock art. Among her latest publications are: "Complejidad Social y Esferas de Interacción durante el Horizonte Medio y el Período Intermedio Tardío en los Valles Interandinos del Suroeste de Chuquisaca" (2006), "Sociedades Prehispánicas Tardías en los Valles Interandinos del Suroeste de Chuquisaca, Bolivia" (2005), and "Ch'iji Jawira: A Case of Ceramic Specialization in the Tiwanaku Urban Periphery"(2003).

ÁLVARO ROMERO, archaeologist, is currently a student in the master's program of anthropology at the Universidad de Tarapacá/Universidad Católica del Norte (Arica and San Pedro de Atacama, Chile). His research focuses on pottery and architectural analysis of prehistoric farming societies and the Inka. He has published various papers in national and international journals.

JACK ROSSEN is associate professor and chair of the Department of Anthropology, Ithaca College. He specializes in archaeobotany and Andean studies. Among his latest publications are: "Arqueobotánica de Cerro Grande de la Compañía," in *Arqueología de Chile Central, Segundo Taller* (2005); "Preceramic Irrigation Canals in the Peruvian Andes," in *Proceedings of the National Academy of Sciences* (2005) (coauthored with Tom Dillehay and Herbert Eling); and "Plant Use Schedules, Decreased Mobility, and Social Differentiation: Hunter-Gatherers in Forested Chile," in *Hunters and Gatherers in Theory and Archaeology* (2004) (coauthored with Tom Dillehay).

CALÓGERO M. SANTORO is professor of archaeology at the Instituto de Alta Investigación, Departamento de Antropología. He is also the executive director of the Centro de Investigaciones del Hombre en el Desierto, Universidad de Tarapacá, Arica, Chile, and editor of *Chungará Revista de Antropología Chilena*. His research focuses on late prehistoric farming societies, the Inka state, and Pleistocene-Holocene hunter-gatherers in the Atacama Desert. He has published several papers in national and international journals and book chapters in edited volumes.

VIVIEN G. STANDEN, is professor of bioarchaeology in the Departamento de Antropología, Universidad de Tarapacá, Arica, Chile, and researcher in the Centro de Investigaciones del Hombre en el Desierto in that institution. She is also editor of the journal *Chungará-Revista de Antropología Chilena*. Her research focuses on understanding the cultural and environmental factors that shaped the prehistoric populations in the Atacama Desert including hunter-gatherers and farmers. She has published several papers in national and international journals and book chapters in edited volumes.

RUBÉN STEHBERG is senior archaeologist at the National Museum of Natural History in Santiago, Chile. His research focuses on the history and evolution of cultures in the region of Chile. His latest publications include *La Fortaleza de Chena y su Relación con la Ocupación Incaica de Chile Central* (1976), and "Instalaciones Incaicas en el Norte y Centro Semiárido de Chile," in *Colección de Antropología, Dirección de Bibliotecas, Archivos y Museo* (1995). He has also coauthored a number of articles such as "Los Inicios del Desarrollo Agrícola y Alfarero: Zona Central," in *Culturas de Chile Prehistoria: Desde sus Origenes hasta los Albores de la Conquista* (1989) (coauthored with Fernanda Falabella), and "Complejidad Arquitectónica de las Ruinas Prehispanas de Chada en la Antigua Ruta entre los Ríos Maipo y Cachapoal," in *Xama* (1997) (coauthored with other Chilean scholars).

DANIELA VALENZUELA is an archaeologist and a Ph.D. candidate in the Doctorado de Antropología, Universidad Católica del Norte/Universidad de Tarapacá, Chile, under a CONICYT fellowship. Her research focuses on rock art. She has published various papers in national and international journals and book chapters in edited volumes.

MARY VAN BUREN is an associate professor of anthropology at Colorado State University. She has over a decade of experience and publications investigating the consequences of Inka and Spanish expansion on populations incorporated into these empires. For the last six years she has been investigating indigenous and European participation in the mining economy of colonial Potosí.

VERÓNICA I. WILLIAMS is researcher of CONICET (Argentina) in the Instituto de Arqueología, Facultad Filosofía y Letras, Universidad de Buenos Aires, Argentina. She has written and published in national and international journals and edited volumes on the archaeology of northwestern Argentina. Among her edited books are *Género y Etnicidad en la Arqueología Sudamericana* (2005) and *Sociedades Precolombinas Surandinas* (2007).

Bibliography

Abercrombie, Thomas A.
1998   *Pathways of Memory and Power: Ethnography and History among an Andean People.* Madison: University of Wisconsin Press.

Acuto, Félix
1994   La Organización del Almacenaje Estatal: La Ocupación Inka en el Sector Norte del Valle Calchaquí y sus Alrededores. Unpublished Licenciatura Thesis, Facultad de Filosofía y Letras, Universidad de Buenos Aires, Buenos Aires.

1999   Paisaje y Dominación: La Constitución del Espacio Social en el Imperio Inka. In *Sed non Satiata: Teoría Social en la Arqueología Latinoamericana Contemporánea,* edited by Andrés Zarankin and Félix Acuto, 33–75. Buenos Aires: Ediciones Del Tridente.

2000   Investigaciones sobre la Dominación Inka en el Valle Calchaquí Norte (Provincia de Salta): Un Análisis de la Ocupación Imperial en el Sitio de Cortaderas. Informe Final. Buenos Aires.

2004   Landscapes of Ideology and Inequality: Experiencing Inka Domination. Ph.D. diss., State University of New York, Binghamton.

Albarracín-Jordán, Juan
1991   Petroglifos en el Valle Bajo de Tiwanaku, Bolivia. *Boletín SIARB* 5:35–56.

Albarracín-Jordán, Juan, and James Mathews
1990   *Asentamientos Prehispánicos del Valle de Tiwanaku.* Vol. 1. La Paz, Bolivia: Producciones Cima.

Alcaya[ga], Diego Felipe
1961 [1605]   Relación cierta que el Padre Diego Felipe de Alcaya, Cura de Mataca, envió a su Excelencia el Señor Marqués de Montes Claro, Visorrey de estos Reynos, sacada de la que el Capitán Martín Sánchez de Alcayaga, su padre, dejó hecha. In *Cronistas Cruceños del Alto Perú Virreynal,* edited by Conmemorativa del IV Centenario de la Fundación de Santa Cruz de la Sierra, 47–86. Santa Cruz de la Sierra, Bolivia: Publicaciones de la Universidad Gabriel René Moreno.

Alcina Franch, José, and Segundo Moreno Yáñez
1986   *Arqueología y Etnohistoria del Sur de Colombia y Norte del Ecuador.* Guayaquil, Ecuador: Ediciones Abya-Yala.

Alcock, Susan E., Terence N. D'Altroy, Kathleen D. Morrison, and Carla M.
        Sinopoli, eds.
2001   *Empires: Perspectives from Archaeology and History.* Cambridge:
        Cambridge University Press.

Alconini, Sonia
1996   Structure and Dynamic of the Inka Frontier: New Archaeologi-
        cal Evidence of Inka Borderlands in the Southeastern Bolivian
        Chaco. Paper presented at the 15th Northeast Conference of
        Ethnohistory and Archaeology, Philadelphia.
2002   Prehistoric Inka Frontier Structure and Dynamics in the Bolivian
        Chaco. Ph.D. diss., University of Pittsburgh.
2004   The Southeastern Inka Frontier against the Chiriguanos: Struc-
        ture and Dynamics of the Inka Imperial Borderlands. *Latin
        American Antiquity* 15:389–418.
2005   Military and Cultural Imperial Frontiers: Dynamics and Settle-
        ment Patterns of the Southeastern Inka Frontier. In *Untaming
        the Frontier in Anthropology, Archaeology and History,* edited by
        Bradley Parker and Lars Rodseth, 115–146. Tucson: University of
        Arizona Press.
2008a   Dis-embedded Centers and the Architecture of Power in the
        Fringes of the Inka Empire: New Perspectives on Territorial and
        Hegemonic Strategies of Domination. *Journal of Anthropological
        Archaeology* 27:63–81.
2008b   *El Inkario en los Valles del Sur Andino Boliviano: Los Yamparas
        entre la Arqueología y Etnohistoria.* Oxford: BAR International
        Series No. 1868.

Aldunate, Carlos
2001   The Inka in Tarapacá and Atacama. In *In the Footsteps of the Inka
        in Chile,* edited by Carlos Aldunate and Luis E. Cornejo, 18–33.
        Santiago: Museo Chileno de Arte Precolombino.

Aldunate, Carlos, Victoria Castro, and Varinia Varela
2003   Antes del Inka y después del Inka: Paisajes y Sacralidad en la
        Puna de Atacama. *Boletín de Arqueología, PUCP* 7:9–26.

Aldunate, Carlos, and Luis Cornejo
2001   *In the Footsteps of the Inka in Chile.* Santiago: Museo Chileno de
        Arte Precolombino.

Ambrosetti, Juan Bautista
1902   El Sepulcro de La Paya Últimamente Descubierto en los Valles
        Calchaquíes, Provincia de Salta. *Anales del Museo Nacional*
        8:119–148.

1907–1908   *Exploraciones Arqueológicas en la Ciudad Prehistórica de La Paya (Valle Calchaquí, Pcia. de Salta).* Revista de la Universidad de Buenos Aires. Sección Antropología 3, Vol. 8. Buenos Aires: M. Biedmaé.

Ampuero, Gonzalo

1989   La Cultura Diaguita Chilena. In *Culturas de Chile Prehistoria: Desde sus Orígenes hasta los Albores de la Conquista,* edited by Jorge Hidalgo, Virgilio Schiappacasse, Hans Niemeyer, Carlos Aldunate, and Iván Solimano, 277–287. Santiago: Editorial Andrés Bello.

Angelo Zelada, Dante

1999   Tráfico de Bienes, Minería y Aprovechamiento de Recursos en la Región de los Valles del Sur Boliviano. (Una Aproximación Arqueológica a la Región de los Chichas, Provincia Sur Chichas — Potosí). B.A. diss., Universidad Mayor de San Andrés, La Paz, Bolivia.

Anton, Susan

1989   Intentional Cranial Vault Deformation and Induced Changes of the Cranial Base and Face. *American Journal of Physical Anthropology* 79:253–268.

Aranda, Claudia, Cristian Jacob, Leandro Luna, and Marina Sprovieri

1999   Dominación y Resistencia. El Impacto Inka en el Valle Calchaquí Norte. Paper presented in the Congreso Nacional de Arqueología Argentina, Córdoba, Argentina.

Arkush, Elizabeth N.

2006   Collapse, Conflict, Conquest: The Transformation of Warfare in the Late Prehispanic Andean Highlands. In *The Archaeology of Warfare,* edited by Elizabeth N. Arkush and Mark W. Allen, 286–332. Gainesville: University Press of Florida.

Arriaga, Pablo José de

1999 [1621]   *La Extirpación de la Idolatría en el Pirú.* Cuzco: Centro de Estudios Regionales Andinos Bartolomé de las Casas.

Bakewell, Peter

1984   *Miners of the Red Mountain: Indian Labor in Potosí, 1545–1650.* Albuquerque: University of New Mexico Press.

Bankes, George

1989   *Peruvian Pottery.* Aylesbury, England: Shire Publications.

Barfield, Thomas J.

2001   The Shadow Empires: Imperial State Formation along the Chinese-Nomad Frontier. In *Empires,* edited by Susan E. Alcock, Terence N. D'Altroy, Kathleen D. Morrison, and Carla M. Sinopoli, 10–41. Cambridge: Cambridge University Press.

Barnadas, Josep M.

1973   *Charcas 1535–1565, Orígenes Históricos de una Sociedad Colonial.* La Paz,
Bolivia: Centro de Investigación y Promoción del Campesinado.

Barragán Romano, Rossana

1994   *¿Indios de Arco y Flecha?: Entre la Historia y la Arqueología de las Poblaciones del Norte de Chuquisaca (Siglos XV–XVI).* Sucre, Bolivia: ASUR
3. Antropólogos del Surandino (ASUR), Inter-American Foundation
(IAF).

Barraza, José

1995   Los Depósitos de Alimentos en los Valles de Azapa y Lluta en el
Período Prehispánico Tardío. Paper presented at Seminario para
Optar al Título de Profesor de Educación Media en Historia y
Geografía, Universidad de Tarapacá, Arica.

Bauer, Brian

1996   Legitimization of the State in Inca Myth and Ritual. *American Anthropologist* 98:327–337.

2002   *The Development of the Inca State.* Austin: University of Texas Press.

Bauer, Brian, and Charles Stanish

2001   *Ritual and Pilgrimage in the Ancient Andes: The Islands of the Sun and
the Moon.* Austin: University of Texas Press.

Bentley, G. Carter

1987   Ethnicity and Practice. *Comparative Studies in Society and History*
29:24–55.

Berenguer, José

1995   Impacto del Caravaneo Prehispánico Tardío en Santa Bárbara, Alto
Loa. *Revista Hombre y Desierto* 9:185–202.

Bernbeck, Reinhard

1999   Structure Strikes Back: Intuitive Meanings of Ceramics from Qale
Rostam, Iran. In *Material Symbols: Culture and Economy in Prehistory*, edited by John E. Robb, 90–111. Occasional Paper No. 26, Center
for Archaeological Investigations. Carbondale: Southern Illinois
University.

Berthelot, Jean

1986   The Extraction of Precious Metals at the Time of the Inka. In *Anthro-
pological History of Andean Polities*, edited by John V. Murra, Nathan
Wachtel, and Jacques Revel, 69–88. Cambridge: Cambridge University
Press.

Besom, J. Thomas

2000   Mummies, Mountains, and Immolations: Strategies for Unifying the
Inka Empire's Southern Quarters. Ph.D. diss., State University of New
York, Binghamton.

Betanzos, Juan de
1996 [1551]   *Narrative of the Incas.* Edited by Roland Hamilton and Dana Bu-
              chanan. Austin: University of Texas Press.
Bibar, Gerónimo
1966 [1558]   *Crónica y Relación Copiosa y Verdadera de los Reynos de Chile.*
              Santiago: Edición Facsimilar del Fondo Histórico y Bibliográfico
              J. T. Medina.
1979 [1558]   *Crónica y Relación Copiosa y Verdadera de los Reynos de Chile.* Ber-
              lin: Edición Sáez-Godoy.
Bjork, Ame, and Lise Bjork
1964   Artificial Deformation and Cranio-facial Asymmetry in Ancient
              Peruvians. *Journal of Dental Research* 43:353–362.
Blom, Deborah E.
1999   Tiwanaku Regional Interaction and Social Identity: A Bioarchae-
              ological Approach. Ph.D. diss., University of Chicago.
Boman, Eric
1908   *Antiquités de la Región Andine de la République Argentine et du
              Désert d'Atacama.* Vol. 2. Paris: Imprimerie Nationale.
Bourdieu, Pierre
1977   *Outline of a Theory of Practice.* Cambridge: Cambridge University
              Press.
2000   *Pascalian Meditations.* Stanford, Calif.: Stanford University Press.
Bouysse-Cassagne, Thérèse
1986   *La Identidad Aymara. Aproximación Histórica (Siglo XV, Siglo
              XVI).* La Paz, Bolivia: Hisbol.
Bray, Tamara L.
1992   Archaelogical Survey in Northern Highland Ecuador: Inca
              Imperialism and the País Caranqui. *World Archaeology* 24(2):
              218–233.
2003a   Inka Pottery as Culinary Equipment: Food, Feasting and Gender
              in Imperial State Design. *Latin American Antiquity* 14:3–28.
2003b   *Los Efectos del Imperialismo Incaico en la Frontera Norte.* Quito:
              Ediciones Abya-Yala.
Bray, Tamara L., Leah D. Minc, María Constanza Ceruti, José Antonio
              Chávez, Ruddy Perea, and Johan Reinhard
2005   A Compositional Analysis of Pottery Vessels Associated with the
              Inca Ritual of Capacocha. *Journal of Anthropological Archaeology*
              24(1): 82–100.
Briones, Luis, Persis Clarkson, Alberto Díaz, and Carlos Mondaca
1999   Huasquiña, las Chacras y los Geoglifos del Desierto: Una Aproxi-
              mación al Arte Rupestre Andino. *Diálogo Andino* 18:39–61.

Buikstra, Jane E., Susan R. Frankenberg, and Lyle W. Konigsberg
1990 Skeletal Biological Distance Studies in American Physical Anthropology: Recent Trends. *American Journal of Physical Anthropology* 82:1–7.

Burger, Richard L., and Lucy C. Salazar, eds.
2004 *Machu Picchu: Unveiling the Mystery of the Incas.* New Haven, Conn.: Yale University Press.

Bush, Leslie L.
2004 *Boundary Conditions: Macrobotanical Remains and the Oliver Phase of Central Indiana, A.D. 1200–1450.* Tuscaloosa: University of Alabama Press.

Byrd, John E., and Richard L. Jantz
1994 Osteological Evidence for Distinct Social Groups at the Leavenworth Site. In *Skeletal Biology in the Great Plains: Migration, Warfare, Health and Subsistence,* edited by Douglas W. Owsley and Richard L. Jantz, 203–208. Washington, D.C.: Smithsonian Institution Press.

Calazacón, Catalina, Ignacio Calazacón, Maruja Calazacón, Samuel Calazacón, Dolores Calazacón, and Domingo Zaracay
1985 *Ilushun: Kuwenta Layakajun Pila (Una Recopilación de Cuentos).* Guayaquil, Ecuador: Miscelánea Antropológica Ecuatoriana, Museos del Banco Central del Ecuador.

Calderari, Milena
1991 Estilos Cerámicos Incaicos en La Paya. *Actas del XI Congreso Nacional de Arqueología Chilena* 2:151–164.
1992 *Asentamiento y Dinámica Cultural en La Paya, Valle Calchaquí Medio.* Buenos Aires: Informe del CONICET.

Calderari, Milena, and Verónica I. Williams
1991 Re-evaluación de los Estilos Cerámicos Incaicos en el Noroeste Argentino. In *El Imperio Inka: Actualización y Perspectivas por Registros Arqueológicos y Etnohistóricos II,* 73–95. Córdoba, Argentina: Comechingonia.

Capparelli, Aylen, Verónica Lema, Marco Giovannetti, and Rodolfo Raffino
2005 The Introduction of Old World Crops (Wheat, Barley, and Peach) in Andean Argentina during the 16th Century A.D.: Archaeobotanical and Ethnohistorical Evidence. *Vegetation History and Archaeobotany* (online: ISSN 1617-6278). Berlin: Springer-Verlag.

Capriles, José M., Alejandra I. Domic, and Sonia Alconini
2008 Zooarqueología Yampara: Aprovechamiento de Recursos Faunísticos en Oroncota, Bolivia. In *El Inkario en los Valles del Sur Andino Boliviano: Los Yamparas entre la Arqueología y Etnohistoria,* edited by Sonia Alconini, 105–111. Oxford: BAR International Series No. 1868.

Cárdenas, Martín

1969   *Manual de Plantas Económicas de Bolivia*. Cochabamba, Bolivia:
            Imprenta Icthus.

Cardona, Augusto

2002   *Arqueología de Arequipa: De sus Albores a los Incas*. Arequipa, Peru:
            Centro de Investigaciones Arqueológicas de Arequipa.

Carneiro, Robert L.

1970   A Theory of the Origin of the State. *Science* 169:733–738.

Carsten, Janet, and Stephen Hugh-Jones

1995   Introduction. In *About the House*, edited by Janet Carsten and
            Stephen Hugh-Jones, 1–46. Cambridge: Cambridge University
            Press.

Castro, Victoria, Fernando Maldonado, and Mario Vázquez

1993   Arquitectura del Pukara de Turi. *Boletín Museo Regional de la
            Araucanía* 4:79–106.

Catalán, Dánisa

2007   Una Reflexión sobre las Reacciones Locales frente al Tawantin-
            suyu a partir del Estudio de Contextos Funerarios. El Período
            Tardío en los Valles Occidentales. Master's thesis, Tarapacá Uni-
            versidad Católica del Norte (in preparation).

Chacón, Sergio, and Mario Orellana

1982   El Tambo Chungará. *Actas del VIII Congreso de Arqueología Chi-
            lena*, 247–255.

Chapman, Malcolm

1993   Social and Biological Aspects of Ethnicity. In *Social and Biological
            Aspects of Ethnicity*, edited by Malcolm Chapman, 1–46. Oxford:
            Oxford University Press.

Charney, Paul

2001   *Indian Society in the Valley of Lima, Perú, 1532–1824*. New York:
            University Press of America.

Checura, Jorge

1977   Funebria Incaica en el Cerro Esmeralda (Iquique I Región). *Estu-
            dios Atacameños* 5:12–141.

Cheverud, James M., Luci A. P. Kohn, Lyle L. Konigsberg, and Steven R. Leigh

1992   Effects of Fronto-Occipital Artificial Cranial Vault Modification
            on the Cranial Base and Face. *American Journal of Physical Anthro-
            pology* 88:323–345.

Cieza de León, Pedro

1880 [1553] *Segunda Parte de la Crónica del Perú que trata del Señorío de los
            Incas Yupankis y sus Grandes Hechos y Gobernación*. Madrid: Bi-
            blioteca Hispano-Ultramarina.

1962 [1553]   *La Crónica del Perú. Primera Parte.* Madrid: Editorial Espasa-
                   Caspe.

1963 [1532–1550]   *Travels of Pedro de Cieza de León, A.D 1532–50.* Translated
                   and edited by Clements R. Markham. Reprint of the 1864
                   edition. New York: Burt Franklin.

Cobo, Bernabé

1979 [1653]   *History of the Inca Empire: An Account of the Indians' Customs
                   and Their Origin Together with a Treatise on Inca Legends,
                   History, and Social Institutions.* Translated and edited by
                   Roland Hamilton. Austin: University of Texas Press.

Cock Carrasco, Guillermo A.

1999   Estudio de Evaluación Arqueológica del Área Ocupada por
                   el Asentamiento Humano Túpac Amaru, en el Sitio Arque-
                   ológico de Huaquerones-Puruchuco, Distrito de Ate-Vitarte,
                   Prov. y Dpto. de Lima. Report to the Instituto Nacional de
                   Cultura, Lima.

2001   Recuperación de Contextos Funerarios del Período Inca
                   y Ampliación de Investigaciones en el Cementerio de
                   Huaquerones-Puruchuco, Dentro de la Zona Arqueológica
                   de Puruchuco-Huaquerones. Distrito de Ate-Vitarte, Prov.
                   y Dpto. de Lima. Report to the Instituto Nacional de Cul-
                   tura, Lima.

Cohen, Ira

1987   Structuration Theory and Social Praxis. In *Social Theory
                   Today,* edited by Anthony Giddens and Jonathan H. Turner,
                   273–308. Oxford: Polity Press.

Collier, Donald

1955   *Cultural Chronology and Change as Reflected in the Ceramics
                   of the Virú Valley, Perú.* Chicago: Chicago Natural History
                   Museum.

Comaroff, John L.

1997   Images of Empire, Contests of Conscience. Models of Co-
                   lonial Domination in South Africa. In *Tensions of Empire.
                   Colonial Cultures in a Bourgeois World,* edited by Frederik
                   Cooper and Ann L. Stoler, 163–197. Berkeley: University of
                   California Press.

Comaroff, John L., and Jean Comaroff

1997   *Of Revelation and Revolution: The Dialectics of Modernity on
                   a South African Frontier.* Vol. 2. Chicago: University of Chi-
                   cago Press.

Conlee, Christina A., Jahl Dulanto, Carol J. Mackey, and Charles Stanish
2004   Late Prehispanic Sociopolitical Complexity. In *Andean Archaeology*, edited by Helaine Silverman, 209–236. Malden, Mass.: Blackwell.

Conrad, Geoffrey W.
1977   Chiquitoy Viejo: An Inca Administrative Center in the Chicama Valley, Perú. *Journal of Field Archaeology* 4(1): 1–18.

Conrad, Geoffrey W., and Arthur A. Demarest
1984   *Religion and Empire: The Dynamics of Aztec and Inca Expansionism.* Cambridge: Cambridge University Press.

Cornejo, Luis
1995   El Inka en la Región del Río Loa: Lo Local y lo Foráneo. *Actas del XIII Congreso Nacional de Arqueología Chilena* 1:203–212.

Correa, Jacqueline, and Liliana Ulloa
2000   Bolsas de la Costa Sur de Arica, Período Tardío. *Boletín de la Sociedad Chilena de Arqueología* 29:9–19.

Costin, Cathy L.
1996   Craft Production and Mobilization Strategies in the Inka Empire. In *Craft Specialization and Social Evolution: In Memory of V. Gordon Childe*, edited by Bernard Wailes, 211–225. Philadelphia: University of Pennsylvania Museum of Archaeology and Anthropology.
1998   Housewives, Chosen Women, Skilled Men: Cloth Production and Social Identity in the Late Prehispanic Andes. In *Craft and Social Identity*, edited by Cathy L. Costin and Rita P. Wright, 123–141. Archaeological Papers No. 8. Washington, D.C.: American Anthropological Association.
2001   Production and Exchange of Ceramics. In *Empire and Domestic Economy*, edited by Christine A. Hastorf, 203–242. New York: Kluwer Academic/Plenum.

Costin, Cathy L., and Timothy Earle
1989   Status Distinction and Legitimation of Power as Reflected in Changing Patterns of Consumption in Late Prehispanic Peru. *American Antiquity* 54:691–714.

Covey, Alan R.
2000   Inka Administration of the Far South Coast of Peru. *Latin American Antiquity* 11:119–138.
2003   A Processual Study of Inka State Formation. *Journal of Anthropological Archaeology* 22:333–357.
2006   Intermediate Elites in the Inka Heartland, A.D. 1000–1500. In *Intermediate Elites in Pre-Columbian States and Empires*, edited by Christina M. Elson and Alan R. Covey, 112–135. Tucson: University of Arizona Press.

Criado Boado, Felipe

1991   Límites y Posibilidades de la Arqueología del Paisaje. *Spal* 2:9–55.

Criado Boado, Felipe, and Victoria Villoch Vazquez

2000   Monumentalizing Landscape: A Formal Study of Galician Mega-
        lithism. *European Journal of Archaeology* 3(2): 188–216.

Cruz, Pablo

2007   Qaraqara e Inkas: El Rostro Indígena de Potosí. Estrategias de Poder y
        Supervivencia Durante los Siglos XV–XVI. *Chachapuma* 2:29–40.

Cunningham, Charles G., Hugo N. Aparicio, Fernando S. Murillo, Néstor C.
        Jiménez, José Luis B. Lizeca, Edwin H. McKee, George E. Ericksen,
        and Frank V. Tavera

1994   Relationship between the Porco, Bolivia, Ag-Zn-Pb-Sn Deposit and
        the Porco Caldera. *Economic Geology* 89:1833–1841.

D'Altroy, Terence N.

1987   Introduction. *Ethnohistory* 34(1): 1–13.

1992   *Provincial Power in the Inca Empire.* Washington, D.C.: Smithsonian
        Institution Press.

2002   *The Incas.* Malden, Mass.: Blackwell.

2003   *Los Incas.* Barcelona: Ariel.

2005   Remaking the Social Landscape: Colonization and the Inka
Empire. In *The Archaeology of Colonial Encounters*, edited by Gil J. Stein, 263–
        295. Santa Fe, N.M.: School of American Research Press.

D'Altroy, Terence N., and Ronald Bishop

1990   The Provincial Organization of Inka Ceramic Production. *American
        Antiquity* 55:120–138.

D'Altroy, Terence N., and Timothy Earle

1985   Staple Finance, Wealth Finance and Storage in the Inca Political Econ-
        omy. *Current Anthropology* 26:187–197.

D'Altroy, Terence N., and Christine A. Hastorf

1992   The Architecture and Contents of Inka State Storehouses in the Xauxa
        Region of Perú. In *Inka Storage Systems*, edited by Terry Y. LeVine,
        259–286. Norman: University of Oklahoma Press.

2001   *Empire and Domestic Economy.* New York: Kluwer Academic/Plenum.

D'Altroy, Terence N., Ana María Lorandi, and Verónica I. Williams

1994   Producción y Uso de la Cerámica en la Economía Política Inca. *Arque-
        ología* 4:73–172.

1998   Ceramic Production and Use in the Inka Political Economy. In *Andean
        Ceramics: Technology, Organization and Approaches*, edited by Izumi
        Shimada, 284–312. Philadelphia: University of Pennsylvania Museum
        of Archaeology and Anthropology.

D'Altroy, Terence N., Ana María Lorandi, Verónica I. Williams, Milena Calderari, Christine A. Hastorf, Elizabeth DeMarrais, and Melissa B. Hagstrum

2000   Inka Rule in the Northern Calchaquí Valley, Argentina. *Journal of Field Archaeology* 27(1): 1–26.

D'Altroy, Terence N., Verónica I. Williams, and Brian S. Bauer

1997   Inka Expansionism: A Comparison of Radiocarbon and Historical Dates. Manuscript in authors' possession.

D'Altroy, Terence N., Verónica I. Williams, and Ana María Lorandi

2007   The Inkas in the Southlands. In *Variations in the Expression of Inka Power*, edited by Richard L. Burger, Craig Morris, and Ramiro Matos Mendieta, 85–134. Washington, D.C.: Dumbarton Oaks Research Library and Collection.

Dauelsberg, Percy

1983   Investigaciones Arqueológicas en la Sierra de Arica, Sector Belén. *Chungará Revista de Antropología Chilena* 11:63–83.

De Lorenzi, Mónica, and Pío Pablo Díaz

1976   La Ocupación Incaica en el Sector Septentrional del Valle Calchaquí. *Revista del Museo de Historia Natural de San Rafael (Mendoza)* 2(1–4): 75–88.

Del Río, Mercedes

1995a   Estrategias Andinas de Supervivencia: El Control de Recursos en Chaqui. In *Espacio, Étnias, Frontera: Atenuaciones Políticas en el Sur del Tawantinsuyu Siglos XV–XVIII*, edited by Ana María Presta, 49–78. Sucre, Bolivia: Ediciones ASUR 4.

1995b   Estructuración Étnica Qharaqhara y su Desarticulación. In *Espacio, Étnias, Frontera: Atenuaciones Políticas en el Sur del Tawantinsuyu Siglos XV–XVIII*, edited by Ana María Presta, 3–47. Sucre, Bolivia: Ediciones ASUR 4.

DeMarrais, Elizabeth

1997   Materialization, Ideology and Power: The Development of Centralized Authority among the Pre-Hispanic Polities of the Valle Calchaquí, Argentina. Ph.D. diss., University of California, Los Angeles. Ann Arbor, Mich.: University Microfilms.

2001   La Arqueología del Norte del Valle Calchaquí. In *Historia Prehispánica Argentina, Tomo I*, edited by Eduardo Berberián and Axel E. Nielsen, 289–346. Córdoba, Argentina: Editorial Brujas.

DeMarrais, Elizabeth, Luis Jaime Castillo, and Timothy K. Earle

1996   Ideology, Materialization and Power Strategies. *Current Anthropology* 37(1): 15–31.

Descantes, Christopher, Robert J. Speakman, and Michael D. Glascock
2004   Instrumental Neutron Activation Analysis of Palmitopamba
              Archaeology Project Ceramics. Report prepared for Ronald D.
              Lippi and Alejandra M. Gudiño at the Archaeometry Laboratory
              of the Missouri University Research Reactor, Columbia.

Díaz, Pío Pablo
1978–1980   Diario de la Excavación Realizada en el Sitio Tero SSalCac 14.
              Cachi, Argentina: Museo Arqueológico de Cachi.
1986   Diario de la Excavación Realizada en el Sitio La Paya SSalCac 1.
              Informe depositado en el Museo Arqueológico P. P. Díaz,
              Cachi.

Diez de San Miguel, Garci
1964 [1567]   *Visita Hecha a la Provincia de Chucuito por Garci de San Miguel en
              el año 1567.* Lima: Casa de la Cultura Peruana.

Dillehay, Tom D.
1987   Estrategias Políticas y Económicas de las Étnias Locales del Valle
              de Chillón durante el Período Prehispánico. *Revista Andina*
              5:407–456.

Dillehay, Tom D., and Américo Gordon
1988   La Actividad Prehispánica de los Incas y su Influencia en la Arau-
              canía. In *La Frontera del Estado Inca*, edited by Tom D. Dillehay
              and Patricia J. Netherly, 215–234. Oxford: BAR International Se-
              ries 442.

Dillehay, Tom D., and Patricia J. Netherly
1988   *La Frontera del Estado Inca: Proceedings of the 45th International
              Congress of the Americanists, Bogotá, Colombia, 1985.* Oxford: BAR
              International Series 442.

Dillehay, Tom D., Verónica I. Williams, and Calógero M. Santoro
2006   Áreas Periféricas y Nucleares. Contextos de Interacciones So-
              ciales Complejas y Multidireccionales. *Chungará Revista de An-
              tropología Chilena* 38:249–256.

Dirks, Nicholas
1992   *Colonialism and Culture.* Ann Arbor: University of Michigan
              Press.

Dobres, Marcia Anne, and Christopher R. Hoffman
1999   *The Social Dynamics of Technology: Practice, Politics and World
              Views.* Washington, D.C.: Smithsonian Institution Press.

Dobres, Marcia Anne, and John E. Robb
2000   Agency in Archaeology: Paradigm or Platitude? In *Agency in Ar-
              chaeology*, edited by Marcia Anne Dobres and John E. Robb, 3–17.
              London: Routledge.

Dobyns, Henry F., and Paul L. Doughty
1976   *Peru: A Cultural History*. New York: Oxford University Press.
Donnan, Christopher, and Carol J. Mackey
1978   *Ancient Burial Patterns of the Moche Valley*. Austin: University of Texas Press.
Dornan, Jennifer L.
2002   Agency and Archaeology: Past, Present and Future Directions. *Journal of Archaeological Method and Theory* 9:303–329.
Doyle, Mary Eileen
1988   The Ancestor Cult and Burial Ritual in Seventeenth and Eighteenth Century Central Peru. Ph.D. diss., University of California, Los Angeles.
Doyle, Michael W.
1986   *Empires*. Ithaca, N.Y.: Cornell University Press.
Drusini, Andrea G., Nicola Carrara, Giuseppe Orefici, and Maurizio Rippa-Bonati
2001   Paleodemography of the Nazca Valley: Reconstruction of the Human Ecology in the Southern Peruvian Coast. *Homo* 52(2): 157–172.
Durán, Eliana, and María Teresa Planella
1989   Consolidación Agroalfarera: Zona Central (900 a 1470 d.c.). In *Culturas de Chile Prehistoria: Desde sus Orígenes hasta los Albores de la Conquista*, edited by Jorge Hidalgo, Virgilio Schiappacasse, Hans Niemeyer, Carlos Aldunate, and Iván Solimano, 313–327. Santiago: Editorial Andrés Bello.
Durston, Alan, and Jorge Hidalgo
1997   La Presencia Andina en los Valles de Arica, Siglos XVI–XVIII: Casos de Regeneración Colonial de Estructuras Archipielágicas. *Chungará Revista de Antropología Chilena* 29:249–273.
Earle, Timothy K.
1990   Style and Iconography as Legitimation in Complex Chiefdom. In *The Use of Style in Archaeology*, edited by Margaret W. Conkey and Christine A. Hastorf, 73–81. Cambridge: Cambridge University Press.
1994   Wealth Finance in the Inka Empire: Evidence from the Calchaquí Valley, Argentina. *American Antiquity* 59:443–460.
1997   *How Chiefs Come to Power*. Stanford, Calif.: Stanford University Press.
Earle, Timothy K., Terence N. D'Altroy, Christine A. Hastorf, Catherine J. Scott, Cathy L. Costin, Glenn S. Russell, and Elsie Sandefur
1987   *Archaeological Field Research in the Upper Mantaro, Peru, 1982–1983: Investigations of Inka Expansion and Exchange*. Los Angeles: Institute of Archaeology, University of California.

Echeverría José A., and María V. Uribe

1995   *Área Septentrional Andina Norte: Arqueología y Etnohistoria,*
            Colección Pendoneros (8). Otavalo, Ecuador: Instituto Otavaleño
            de Antropología, Ediciones del Banco Central del Ecuador.

Eeckhout, Peter

2004   Reyes del Sol y Señores de la Luna: Inkas e Ychmas en Pachaca-
            mac. *Chungará Revista de Antropología Chilena* 36:495-503.

Elson, Christina M., and Alan R. Covey

2006   *Intermediate Elites in Pre-Columbian States and Empires.* Tucson:
            University of Arizona Press.

Epstein, Stephen Matheson

1993   Cultural Choice and Technological Consequences: Constraint of
            Innovation in the Late Prehistoric Copper Smelting Industry of
            Cerro Huaringa, Peru. Ph.D. diss., University of Pennsylvania.

Erickson, Clark L.

1988   An Agricultural Investigation of Raised-Field Agriculture in the
            Lake Titicaca Basin of Peru. Ph.D. diss., University of Illinois at
            Urbana-Champaign.

Espinoza Soriano, Waldemar

1969 [1582] El Memorial de Charcas. "Crónica" Inédita de 1582. In *Cantuta*
            No. 4, 117–152. Huancayo: Peru: Revista de la Universidad Nacio-
            nal de Educación.

1970   Los Mitmas Yungas de Collique en Cajamarca, Siglos XV, XVI y
            XVII. *Revista del Museo Nacional* 36:9–57.

1973   Las Colonias de Mitmas Multiples en Abancay, Siglos XV y XVI.
            Revista del Museo Nacional 39:225–299.

1980   El Curaca de los Cayambes y su Sometimiento al Imperio Es-
            pañol, Siglos XV y XVI. *Bulletin de L´Institut Francais d´Etudes*
            Andines 9(1–2): 89–119.

1983   *Los Cayambes y Carangues, Siglos XV–XVI: El Testimonio de la*
            Etnohistoria, Colección Pendoneros Nos. 61–62. Otavalo, Ecuador:
            Instituto Otavaleño de Antropología.

1987   Migraciones Internas en el Reino Colla: Tejedores, Plumeros
            y Alfareros del Estado Imperial Inca. *Chungará Revista de An-*
            tropología Chilena 19:243–289.

Estupiñán Viteri, Tamara

2003   *Tras las Huellas de Rumiñahui.* Quito: Publicado por la Autora en
            Quito con el Auspicio del Banco General Rumiñahui.

Farfán Lobatón, Carlos

2000   Informe Sobre Entierros Prehispánicos en Huaquerones, Valle
            del Rímac. *Arqueológicas* 24:275–302.

Fisher, Christopher T., and Tina L. Thurston

2004 Dynamic Landscapes and Socio-Political Process: The Topography of Anthropogenic Environments in Global Perspective. Special section edited by Fisher and Thurston: *Antiquity*. http://intarch.ac.uk/antiquity/landscapeintro.html.

Focacci, Guillermo

1981 Descripción de un Cementerio Inka en el Valle de Azapa. *Chungará Revista de Antropología Chilena* 7:212–216.

Ford, Richard I.

1978 *The Nature and Status of Ethnobotany.* Anthropological Papers 67, Museum of Anthropology. Ann Arbor: University of Michigan.

1985 *Prehistoric Food Production in North America.* Anthropological Papers 75, Museum of Anthropology. Ann Arbor: University of Michigan.

Frame, Mary, Daniel Guerrero, Maria del Carmen Vega, and Patricia Landa

2004 Un Fardo Funerario del Horizonte Tardío del Sitio Rinconada Alta, Valle del Rimac. *Arqueología de la Costa Central del los Períodos Tardíos. Bulletin de l'Institut Français d'Etudes Andines* 33(3): 815–860.

Frye, Kirk L.

2006 The Inca Occupation of the Lake Titicaca Region. In *Advances in Titicaca Basin Archaeology — 1*, edited by Charles Stanish, Amanda B. Cohen, and Mark S. Aldenderfer, 197–208. Los Angeles: Cotsen Institute of Archaeology, University of California.

Fuller, Dorian Q.

2003 Indus and Non-Indus Agricultural Traditions: Local Developments and Crop Adaptations on the Indian Peninsula. In *Indus Ethnobiology: New Perspectives from the Field*, edited by Steven A. Weber and William R. Belcher, 343–396. Lanham, Md.: Lexington Books.

Gallardo, Francisco, Mauricio Uribe, and Patricia Ayala

1995 Arquitectura Inka y Poder en el Pukara de Turi, Norte de Chile. *Gaceta Arqueológica Andina* 24:151–171.

Gallardo, Francisco, and Flora Vilches

2001 Rock Art during the Inka Domination of Northern Chile. In *The Footsteps of the Inka in Chile*, edited by Carlos Aldunate and Luis Cornejo, 34–37. Santiago: Museo Chileno de Arte Precolombino.

Garcilazo de la Vega, Inca
1960 [1609]   *Comentarios Reales de los Incas.* Vols. 133–135. Madrid: Atlas.

Giddens, Anthony
1979   *Central Problems in Social Theory.* London: Macmillan.
1984   *The Constitution of Society: Outline of the Theory of Structuration.* Cambridge: Polity Press.

Gifford, Chad, Samuel Connell, and Ana Lucia Gonzalez
2002   "Y el Inga Guayna Capac Derribado": Difficult Encounters in Pambamarca, Ecuador. Paper presented at the 21st annual Northeast Conference on Andean Archaeology and Ethnohistory, University of Pittsburgh.

Gifford, Clarence H.
2003   Local Matters: Encountering the Imperial Inkas in the South Andes. Ph.D. diss., Columbia University. Ann Arbor, Mich.: University Microfilms.

Godoy, F.
1945   Estudio Químico de la Calandrinia Discolor. Licenciatura thesis, Universidad de Chile, Santiago.

Gondard, Pierre, and Freddy López
1983   *Inventario Arqueológico Preliminar de los Andes Septentrionales del Ecuador.* Quito: MAG. PRONAREG and ORSTOM.

Góngora Marmolejo, Alonso de
1960 [1575]   *Historia de Chile desde su Descubrimiento hasta el Año de 1575.* Vol. 131. Madrid: Biblioteca de Autores Españoles, Ediciones Atlas.

González, Alberto Rex
1980   Patrones de Asentamiento Incaico en una Provincia Marginal del Imperio: Implicaciones Socioculturales. *Relaciones de la Sociedad Argentina de Antropología* 14(1): 63–82.
1983   La Provincia y la Población Incaica de Chicoana. In *Presencia Hispánica en la Arqueología Argentina*, edited by Eldo S. Morresi and Ramón Gutierrez, 633–674. Chaco: Instituto de Historia, Facultad de Humanidades, Universidad Nacional del Noreste.

González, Alberto Rex, and Pío Pablo Díaz
1992   Notas Arqueológicas sobre la Casa Morada, La Paya, Pcia. de Salta. *Estudios de Arqueología* 5:11–61.

Gordillo, Jesús
2000   Desde Tiwanaku hasta la Ocupación Inka en el Valle Medio del Río Caplina, Tacna-Peru. *Cultura y Desarrollo* 2:83–108.

Grosboll, Sue

1993   . . . And He Said in the Time of the Ynga, They Paid Tribute and
            Served the Ynga. In *Provincial Inca: Archaeological and Ethnohis-
            torical Assessment of the Impact of the Inca State*, edited by Michael
            A. Malpass, 44–76. Iowa City: University of Iowa Press.

Guamán Poma de Ayala, Felipe

1956 [1613] *La Nueva Crónica y Buen Gobierno. I Parte*. Lima: Editorial
            Cultura.

1993 [1613] *Nueva Crónica y Buen Gobierno*. Lima: Fondo de Cultura
            Económica.

Gudemos, Monica L.

1998   Campanas Arqueológicas de Metal del Noroeste Argentino.
            Anales del Museo de América 6:111–145.

Guerrero, Daniel

1998   Algunos Alcances Sobre las Ocupaciones Tardías en el Valle del
            Rimac. Paper presented at the Primer Coloquio de Arqueología
            del Valle del Rimac durante el Período Intermedio Tardía, Lima.

Guevara, Tomás

1929   *Chile Prehispano*. Santiago: Historia de Chile.

Gyarmati, Janos, and András Vargas

1999   *The Chacaras of Wari: An Inca State in Cochabamba Valley, Bo-
            livia*. Translated by Magdalena Seleanu. Budapest: Museum of
            Ethnography.

Habermas, Jürgen

1987   *Theory of Communicative Action. Lifeworld and System: A Critique
            of Functionalist Reason*. Vol. 2. Boston: Beacon Press.

Hanihara, Tsunehiko

1996   Comparison of Craniofacial Features of Major Human Groups.
            American Journal of Physical Anthropology 99:389–412.

Harris, Olivia

1997   Los Límites como Problema: Mapas Etnohistóricos de los Andes
            Bolivianos. In *Saberes y Memorias en los Andes. In Memorian Thi-
            erry Saignes*, edited by Thérèse Bouysse-Cassagne, 351–373. Lima:
            IHEAL-IFEA.

Hassig, Ross

1985   *Trade, Tribute, and Transportation: The Sixteenth-Century Political
            Economy of the Valley of Mexico*. Norman: University of Oklahoma
            Press.

1992   *War and Society in Ancient Mesoamerica*. Berkeley: University of
            California Press.

Hastings, Charles Mansfield
1985   The Eastern Frontier: Settlement and Subsistence in the Andean
            Margins of Central Peru. Ph.D. diss., University of Michigan.
Hastorf, Christine A.
1990   The Effect of the Inka on Sausa Agricultural Production and Crop
            Consumption. *American Antiquity* 55:262–290.
1993   *Agriculture and the Onset of Political Inequality Before the Inka.*
            Cambridge: Cambridge University Press.
Hayashida, Frances
1995   State Pottery Production in the Inka Provinces. Ph.D. diss., Uni-
            versity of Michigan.
1998   New Insights into Inka Pottery Production. In *Andean Ceramics:
            Technology, Organization and Approaches*, edited by Izumi Shi-
            mada, 313–335. Philadelphia: University of Pennsylvania Museum
            of Archaeology and Anthropology.
1999   Style, Technology and State Production: Inka Pottery Manu-
            facture in the Leche Valley, Peru. *Latin American Antiquity*
            10:337–352.
Helmer, Marie
1955–1956   La Visitación de los Yndios Chupachos: Inca et Encomendero,
            1549. *Travaux de l'Institut Francais Andiens* 5:3–50.
Herrera Wassilowsky, Alexander Charles
2005   Territory and Identity in the Pre-Columbian Andes of Northern
            Peru. Ph.D. diss., University of Cambridge.
Heyerdahl, Thor, Daniel H. Sandweiss, and Alfredo Narváez
1995   *Pyramids of Tucumé: The Quest for Peru's Forgotten City.* New York:
            Thames and Hudson.
Hidalgo, Jorge, and Alan Durston
1998   Reconstitución Étnica Colonial en la Sierra de Arica: El Cacicazgo
            de Codpa, 1650–1780. *Actas del IV Congreso Internacional de Etno-
            historia* 2:32–75.
Hidalgo, Jorge, and Guillermo Focacci
1986   Multietnicidad en Arica, Siglo XVI. Evidencias Etnohistóricas
            y Arqueológicas. *Chungará Revista de Antropología Chilena*
            16–17:137–147.
Hidalgo, Jorge, and Calógero Santoro
2001   El Estado Inca. In *Pueblos del Desierto. Entre el Pacífico y los Andes*,
            edited by Calógero Santoro, Eliana Belmonte, Vivien G. Standen,
            Juan M. Chacama, Jorge Hidalgo, Luis Briones, Liliana Ulloa,
            and Héctor González, 73–84. Arica, Chile: Universidad de
            Tarapacá.

Hoffmann, Adriana E.

1979   *Cactáceas en la Flora Silvestre de Chile.* Santiago: Ediciones Claudio Gay.

Howard, George D., and Gordon Willey

1948   *Northwest Argentine Archaeology.* New Haven, Conn.: Yale University Press.

Howe, Ellen, and U. Petersen

1994   Silver and Lead in the Late Prehistory of the Mantaro Valley, Peru. In *Archaeometry of Pre-Columbian Sites and Artifacts: Proceedings of a Symposium Organized by the UCLA Institute of Archaeology and the Getty Conservation Institute, Los Angeles, CA, March 23–27, 1992,* edited by D. A. Scott and P. Meyers, 183–198. Malibu, Calif.: Getty Conservation Institute.

Howells, W. W.

1973   Cranial Variation in Man: A Study of Multivariate Analysis of Patterns of Difference among Recent Human Populations. *Papers of the Peabody Museum of Archaeology and Ethnology 67,* Harvard University.

Hyslop, John

1976   An Archaeological Investigation of the Lupaca Kingdom and Its Origins. Ph.D. diss., Columbia University.

1977   Chulpas of the Lupaca Zone of the Peruvian High Plateau. *Journal of Field Archaeology* 4:149–170.

1984   *The Inka Road System.* New York: Academic Press.

1988   Las Fronteras Estatales Extremas del Tawantinsuyu. In *La Frontera del Estado Inca,* edited by Tom D. Dillehay and Patricia J. Netherly, 35–57. Oxford: BAR International Series 442.

1990   *Inka Settlement Planning.* Austin: University of Texas Press.

1993   Factors Influencing the Transmission and Distribution of Inka Cultural Materials throughout Tawantinsuyu. In *Latin American Horizons: A Symposium at Dumbarton Oaks,* edited by Don Rice, 337–356. Washington, D.C.: Dumbarton Oaks Research Library and Collections.

Ibarra Grasso, Dick E.

1944   Ensayo sobre la Arqueología Boliviana. *Relaciones de la Sociedad Argentina de Antropología* 4:133–150.

1960   *Prehistoria de Potosí, Revista del Instituto de Investigaciones Históricas, Vol. 1 Arqueología.* Potosí, Bolivia: Universidad Tomás Frías.

1973   *Prehistoria de Bolivia.* La Paz–Cochabamba, Bolivia: Los Amigos de Libro.

Iriate Brenner, Francisco

1960   Algunas Apreciaciones sobre los Huanchos. In *Antiguo Peru: Espacio y Tiempo,* 259–263. Lima: Librería Editorial Juan Mejía Baca.

Isaacson, John S.

1982   Informe Preliminar: Proyecto Tulipe. Manuscript. Museos del
             Banco Central del Ecuador, Quito.

Isbell, William H.

1997   *Mummies and Mortuary Monuments.* Austin: University of Texas
             Press.

Jacob, Cristian

1999   Combatiendo la Corrosión: Arqueometalurgia en el Valle
             Calchaquí Norte. *Libro de Resúmenes del XIII Congreso Nacional
             de Arqueología Argentina* 1:264.

Jara Velástegui, Holguer

n.d.   Excavaciones Arqueológicas y Restauración de las Piscinas de
             Tulipe. Manuscrito Inédito. Quito: Museos del Banco Central
             del Ecuador.

Jijón y Caamaño, Jacinto

1951   *Antropología Prehispánica del Ecuador.* Quito: La Prensa
             Católica.

Jimenez Borja, Arturo

1988 [1973]   *Puruchuco.* Lima: Biblioteca Nacional del Perú.

Joseph, H. Claude

2006 [1930]   *Platería y Vivienda Araucana.* Valdivia, Chile: Serindigena
             Ediciones.

Joyce, Barry

1997   Finding the Spirit of Place in Detail. *British Archaeology* 25.
             www.britarch.ac.uk/ba/ba25/BA25INT.HTML.

Julien, Catherine J.

1983   *Hatunqolla: A View of Inka Rule from the Lake Titicaca Region.*
             Publications in Anthropology Vol. 15. Berkeley: University of
             California Press.

1985   Guano and Resource Control in Sixteenth-Century Arequipa.
             In *Andean Ecology and Civilization,* edited by Shozo Masuda,
             Izumi Shimada, and Craig Morris, 185–231. Tokyo: University
             of Tokyo Press.

1987   How the Inca Decimal Administration Worked. *Ethnohistory*
             35(30): 257–297.

1987–1989   Las Tumbas de Sacsahuaman y el Estilo Cuzco-Inca. *Ñawpa
             Pacha* 25–27:1–125.

1993   Finding a Fit: Archaeology and Ethnohistory of the Incas. In
             *Provincial Inca: Archaeological and Ethnohistorical Assessment
             of the Impact of the Inca State,* edited by Michael A. Malpass,
             177–233. Iowa City: University of Iowa Press.

1995   Oroncota entre Dos Mundos. In *Espacio, Ètnias, Frontera: Atenuaciones Políticas en el Sur del Tawantinsuyu, Siglos XV–XVIII*, edited by Ana María Presta, 97–160. Sucre, Bolivia: ASUR 4.

1997   Colonial Perspectives on the Chiriguaná (1528–1574). In *Resistencia y Adaptación Nativa en las Tierras Bajas Latinoamericanas*, edited by María Susana Cipolleti, 17–76. Quito: Abya-Yala.

Kauffman-Doig, Frederico

1983   *Manual de Arqueología Peruana*. 8th ed. Lima: Ediciones Peisa.

Kaulicke, Peter

2002   Nota Editorial. *Boletín de Arqueología, PUCP* 6:5–10.

Keatinge, Richard W., and Geoffrey W. Conrad

1983   Imperialist Expansion in Peruvian Prehistory: Chimú Administration of a Conquered Territory. *Journal of Field Archaeology* 10(3): 255–383.

Kendall, Ann

2000   Una Red de Caminos Prehispánicos: Rutas de Comercio en el Distrito de Ollantaytambo, Cuzco, Peru. In *Caminos Precolombinos: Las Vías, los Ingenieros y los Viajeros*, edited by Marianne Cardale de Schrimpff and Leonor Herrera, 221–242. Bogotá: Instituto Colombiano de Antropología e Historia.

Knapp, A. Bernard, Vincent Pigott, and Eugenia W. Herbert

1998   *Social Approaches to an Industrial Past: The Archaeology and Anthropology of Mining*. London: Routledge.

Kohn, Luci A. P., and James M. Cheverud

1991   The Effects of Cradleboarding on the Cranial Base and Face. *American Journal of Physical Anthropology* 12:106.

Krapovickas, Pedro

1983   Las Poblaciones Indígenas Históricas del Sector Oriental de la Puna (Un Intento de Correlación entre la Información Etnohistórica y la Etnográfica). *Relaciones de la Sociedad Argentina de Antropología* 15:7–24.

La Lone, Darrell E.

1994   An Andean World-System: Production Transformation under the Inka Empire. In *The Economic Anthropology of the State*, edited by Elizabeth M. Brumfiel, 17–41. New York: University of America Press.

La Lone, Mary, and Darrell E. La Lone

1987   The Inka State in the Southern Highlands: State Administrative and Production Enclaves. *Ethnohistory* 34:47–62.

Latcham, Ricardo E.

1928   *La Alfarería Indígena Chilena*. Santiago: Sociedad Impresora y Litografía Universo.

1936   *La Agricultura Precolombiana en Chile y los Países Vecinos*. Santiago: Ediciones de la Universidad de Chile.

Lechtman, Heather

1976   A Metallurgical Site Survey in the Peruvian Andes. *Journal of Field Archaeology* 3:1–42.

1984   Andean Value Systems and the Development of Prehistoric Metallurgy. *Technology and Culture* 25:1–36.

Lecoq, Patrice

1999   *"Uyuni Préhispanique": Archéologie de la Cordillère Intersalar (Sud-Ouest Bolivien).* Oxford: BAR International Series 798.

2003   La Ocupación en los Valles de Yura y los Alrededores de Potosí durante los Períodos Intermedio Tardío e Inka, a la Luz de Nuevos Descrubimientos Arqueológicos. *Textos Antropológicos* 14(2): 105–132.

Lecoq, Patrice, and Ricardo Céspedes

1996   Nuevas Investigaciones Arqueológicas en los Andes Meridionales de Bolivia. *Revista de Investigaciones Históricas* 8:183–267.

1997   Nuevas Investigaciones Arqueológicas en los Andes Meridionales de Bolivia: Una Visión Prehispánica de Potosí. *Revista de Investigaciones Históricas* 9:111–152.

Leibowicz, Iván

2007   Espacios de poder en La Huerta, quebrada de Humahuaca. Estudios Atacameños. *Arqueología y Antropología Surandinas* 34:51–69.

Lennstrom, Heidi A., and Christine A. Hastorf

1992   Stores and Homes: A Botanical Comparison of Inka Storehouses and Contemporary Ethnic Houses. In *Inka Storage Systems*, edited by Terry Y. LeVine, 287–326. Norman: University of Oklahoma Press.

LeVine, Terry Y.

1992   *Inka Storage Systems.* Norman: University of Oklahoma Press.

Lima Tórrez, María del Pilar

2000   ¿Ocupación Yampara en Quila Quila? Cambios Socio-Políticos de una Sociedad Prehispánica Durante el Horizonte Tardío. B.A. thesis, Universidad Mayor de San Andrés, La Paz.

2008a   Interculturalidad como Estrategia de Control Político: La Relación de los Inkas con los Grupos Locales del Sur del Lago Poopó. In *Arqueología de las Tierras Altas, Valles Interandinos y Tierras Bajas de Bolivia: Memorias del I Congreso de Arqueología de Bolivia*, edited by Claudia Rivera Casanovas, 131–144. La Paz, Bolivia: IIAA-PIEB.

2008b   La política imperial Inka en el norte de Chuquisaca: El Caso de la Capital Yampara de Quila Quila. In *Arqueología de las Tierras Altas, Valles Interandinos y Tierras Bajas de Bolivia: Memorias del I Congreso de Arqueología de Bolivia*, edited by Claudia Rivera Casanovas, 265–276. La Paz, Bolivia: IIAA-PIEB.

Lippi, Ronald D.

1998   *Una Exploración Arqueológica del Pichincha Occidental, Ecuador.* Quito: Museo Jacinto Jijón y Caamaño de la Pontificia Universidad Católica del Ecuador y el Consejo Provincial de Pichincha.

2003   Some Clues to the Prehispanic Expansion of Barbacoan Populations in Northwestern Ecuador. Paper presented at the symposium "Breaking Down Boundaries in the Intermediate Area: Toward a New Macro-Chibchan Synthesis," at the 68th annual meeting of the Society for American Archaeology, Montreal.

2004   *Tropical Forest Archaeology in Western Pichincha, Ecuador. Case Studies in Archaeology.* Belmont, Calif.: Thomsom/Wadsworth.

Lippi, Ronald D., and Tamara L. Bray

2003   The Pucara de Palmitopamba: An Inca Fortress in Northwestern Ecuador's Subtropical Rainforest. Paper presented at the 43rd annual meeting of the Institute of Andean Studies, Berkeley, Calif., and (in slightly revised form) at the 31st Annual Midwest Conference of Andean and Amazonian Archaeology and Ethnohistory, Chicago.

Lizárraga, Reginaldo de

1928   *Descripción Colonial.* Vols. 1–2. Buenos Aires: Biblioteca Argentina.

Llagostera, Agustín

1976   Hipótesis sobre la Expansión Incaica en la Vertiente Occidental de los Andes Meridionales. In *Homenaje al R. P. Gustavo Le Paige S.J.,* edited by Hans Niemeyer, 203–218. Antofagasta, Chile: Universidad del Norte.

Locke, Leland

1923   *The Ancient Quipu or Peruvian Knot Record.* New York: American Museum of Natural History.

Looser, Gualterio

1943   Chenopodium Quinoa: Un Cultivo que Desaparece de Chile. *Revista Argentina de Agronomía* 10(2): 111–113.

1945   Cultivos de Quinoa en Chile. *Revista Argentina de Agronomía* 13(4): 285–286.

Lorandi, Ana María

1980   La Frontera Oriental del Tawantinsuyu: El Umasuyu y el Tucumán. Una Hipótesis de Trabajo. *Relaciones de la Sociedad Argentina de Antropología* 14(1): 147–164.

1988   Los Diaguitas y el Tawantinsuyu: Una Hipótesis de Conflicto. In *La Frontera del Estado Inca,* edited by Tom D. Dillehay and Patricia J. Netherly, 215–234. Oxford: BAR International Series 442.

1997   *De Quimeras, Rebeliones y Utopías. La Gesta del Inca Pedro Bohorques.* Lima: Pontificia Universidad Católica del Perú, Fondo Editorial.

Lorandi, Ana María, and Roxana Boixadós

1987–1988   Etnohistoria de los Valles Calchaquíes en los Siglos XVI y XVII. *Runa* 17–18:263–419.

Loyola, Rodrigo, Calógero Santoro, and Álvaro Romero

2000   Socioeconomic Inferences from Analysis of Late Intermediate and Late Period Spindle Whorls of the Lluta Valley, Northern Chile: Informe Proyecto Fondecyt 1970597. Archivo en Poder de los Autores.

Luttwak, Edward

1976   *The Grand Strategy of the Roman Empire from the First Century A.D. to the Third.* Baltimore: John Hopkins University Press.

Lynch, Thomas

1993   The Identification of Inka Posts and Roads from Catarpe to Río Frío, Chile. In *Provincial Inca: Archaeological and Ethnohistorical Assessment of the Impact of the Inca State*, edited by Michael A. Malpass, 117–142. Iowa City: University of Iowa Press.

MacCormak, Sabine

1998   Time, Space, and Ritual Action: The Inka and Christian Calendars in Early Colonial Peru. In *Native Traditions in the Postconquest World*, edited by Elizabeth Hill Boone and Tom Cummins, 205–343. Washington, D.C.: Dumbarton Oaks Research Library and Collection.

Mackey, Carol

1970   Knot Records in Ancient and Modern Perú. Ph.D. diss., University of California, Berkeley.

2003   La Transformación Socioeconómica de Farfán Bajo el Gobierno Inka. In *Boletín de Arqueología PUCP, No. 7*, edited by Peter Kaulicke, Gary Urton, and Ian Farrington, 321–353. Lima: Pontificia Universidad Católica del Perú.

2006   Elite Residences at Farfán: A Comparison of the Chimú and Inka Occupations. In *Palaces and Power in the Americas: From Peru to the Northwest Coast*, edited by Jessica Joyce Christie and Patricia Joan Sarro, 313–352. Austin: University of Texas Press.

Mackey, Carol, and César Jaúregui

2001–2003   *Informes Preliminares del Proyecto Arqueológico Farfán.* Lima: Instituto Nacional de Cultura.

Mackey, Carol, Hugo Pereyra, Carlos Radicati, H. Rodriguez, and Oscar Valverde

1990   *Quipu y Yupana.* Lima: Consejo Nacional de Ciencia y Tecnología.

Makowski, Krzysztof

2002   Arquitectura, Estilo e Identidad en el Horizonte Tardío: El Sitio
            de Pueblo Viejo-Pucará, Valle de Lurín. *Boletín de Arqueología,
            PUCP* 6:137–170.

2003   The Highland Presence on the Central Coast of Peru during Late
            Pre-Hispanic Times: A Case Study from the Lomas of the Lurín
            Valley. Paper presented at the 23rd annual meeting of the North-
            east Conference of Andean Archaeology and Ethnohistory, New
            Haven, Conn.

Malpass, Michael A.

1993   *Provincial Inca: Archaeological and Ethnohistorical Assessment of
            the Impact of the Inca State.* Iowa City: University of Iowa Press.

Mann, Michael

1986   *The Source of Social Power.* Vol. 1, *A History of Power to A.D. 1760.*
            Cambridge: Cambridge University Press.

Martin, Alexander C., and William D. Barkley

1973   *Seed Identification Manual.* Berkeley: University of California
            Press.

Massone, Claudio

1980   Los Tipos Cerámicos del Complejo Cultural Aconcagua. Licen-
            ciatura thesis, Universidad de Chile.

Medina, José Toribio

1952 [1882] *Las Aborígenes de Chile.* Santiago: Fondo Histórico y
            Bibliográfico.

Menzel, Dorothy

1959   The Inca Occupation of the South Coast of Perú. *Southwestern
            Journal of Anthropology* 15(2): 125–142.

Meyers, Rodica

2002   Cuando el Sol Caminaba por la Tierra: Orígenes de la Interme-
            diación Kallawaya. La Paz, Bolivia: Plural Editores.

Millaire, Jean-Francois

2004   The Manipulation of Human Remains in Moche Society: De-
            layed Burials, Grave Reopening and Secondary Offerings of
            Human Bones on the Peruvian North Coast. *Latin American
            Antiquity* 15:371–388.

Miller, Daniel, Michael Rowlands, and Christopher Tilley

1989   *Domination and Resistance.* London: Routledge.

Minc, Leah

2006   Preliminary Report on the Analysis of Inca Pottery from Ecuador
            using INAA, Project RC1780. Manuscript on file, Oregon State
            University Radiation Center, Corvallis.

Mix, Robert L.

2004   *Vieja de la Inundación/Hag of the Flood. Mitos de los Tsáchilas.* Guaya-
        quil, Ecuador: Museo Antropológico, Banco Central del Ecuador.

Molina, Juan Ignacio

1776   *Compendio de la Historia Civil del Reyno de Chile.* Vol. 26. Madrid:
        Colección de Historiadores de Chile.

Montes de Oca, Ismael

1989   *Geografía y Recursos Naturales de Bolivia.* 2nd ed. La Paz, Bolivia: Aca-
        demia Nacional de Ciencias de Bolivia.

Moragas, Cora

1995   Desarrollo de las Comunidades Prehispánicas del Litoral Iquique-
        Desembocadura Río Loa. *Revista Hombre y Desierto* 9:65–80.

Moreno Yáñez, Segundo, and Udo Oberem

1981   *Contribución a la Etnohistoria Ecuatoriana. Colección Pendoneros (20).*
        Otavalo, Ecuador: Instituto Otavaleño de Antropología.

Morris, Craig

1967   Storage in Tawantinsuyu. Ph.D. diss., University of Chicago.

1972   State Settlements in Tawantinsuyu: A Strategy of Compulsory Urban-
        ism. In *Contemporary Archaeology,* edited by Mark P. Leone, 393–401.
        Carbondale: Southern Illinois University Press.

1982   The Infrastructure of Inka Control in the Peruvian Central High-
        lands. In *The Inca and Aztec States, 1400–1800: Anthropology and
        History,* edited by George A. Collier, Renato I. Rosaldo, and John D.
        Wirth, 153–170. New York: Academic Press.

1992   The Technology of Highland Inka Food Storage. In *Inka Storage Sys-
        tems,* edited by Terry Y. LeVine, 237–258. Norman: University of Okla-
        homa Press.

1995   Symbols to Power: Styles and Media in the Inka State. In *Style, Society
        and Person, Archaeological and Ethnological Perspective,* edited by
        Christopher Carr and Jill E. Neitzel, 419–433. New York: Plenum
        Press.

1998   Inca Strategies of Incorporation and Governance. In *Archaic States,* ed-
        ited by Gary M. Feinman and Joyce Marcus, 293–309. Santa Fe, N.M.:
        School of American Research Press.

2007   The Inka Transformation of the Chincha Capital. In *Variations in the
        Expression of Inka Power,* edited by Richard L. Burger, Craig Morris,
        and Ramiro Matos Mendieta, 135–164. Washington, D.C.: Dumbarton
        Oaks Research Library and Collection.

Morris, Craig, and Donald E. Thompson

1985   *Huánuco Pampa: An Inca City and Its Hinterland.* New York: Thames
        and Hudson.

Mösbach, Ernesto W. de
1992 [1955]   *Botánica Indígena de Chile*. Santiago: Editorial Andrés Bello.
Mothes, Patricia
2003   Report for Ron Lippi on the Two Ash Samples and One Chemical Analysis Taken from the Tulipe [*sic*] Archaeological Area. Unpublished report. Quito.
Muñoz, Iván
1989   Perfíl de la Organización Económica Social en la Desembocadura del Río Camarones. Períodos Intermedio Tardío e Inca. *Chungará Revista de Antropología Chilena* 22:85–112.
1998   La Expansión Incaica y su Vinculación con las Poblaciones de los Valles Occidentales del Extremo Norte de Chile. *Tawantinsuyu* 5:127–137.
Muñoz, Iván, and Juan M. Chacama
1988   Cronología por Termoluminiscencia para los Períodos Intermedio Tardío y Tardío en la Sierra de Arica. *Chungará Revista de Antropología Chilena* 20:19–45.
1993   El Inca en la Sierra de Arica. Actas del XII Congreso Nacional de Arqueología Chilena. Vol. 1. *Boletín Museo Regional de la Araucanía* 4:269–284.
2006   *Complejidad Social en las Alturas de Arica: Territorio, Etnicidad y Vinculación con el Estado Inca*. Arica, Chile: Ediciones Universidad de Tarapacá.
Muñoz, Iván, Juan M. Chacama, and Gustavo Espinosa
1987   El Poblamiento Prehispánico Tardío en el Valle de Codpa: Una Aproximación a la Historia Regional. *Chungará Revista de Antropología Chilena* 19:7–61.
Muñoz, Iván, Juan M. Chacama, Gustavo Espinosa, and Luis Briones
1987   La Ocupación Prehispánica Tardía en Zapahuira y su Vinculación con la Organización Social y Económica Inca. *Chungará Revista de Antropología Chilena* 18:67–90.
Muñoz, Iván, Juan M. Chacama, and Mariela Santos
1997   Tambos, Pukaras y Aldeas, Evidencias del Poblamiento Humano Prehispánico Tardío y de Contacto Indígena-Europeo en el Extremo Norte de Chile: Análisis de los Patrones Habitacionales y Nuevas Dataciones Radiométricas. *Diálogo Andino* 16:123–190.
Murillo, Adolfo
1889   Plantes Medicinales du Chili. Paper read at Exposition Universelle de Paris, Section Chilienne, Paris.

Murra, John V.

1958   On Inca Political Structure. In *Systems of Political Control and Bureaucracy in Human Societies*, edited by Frederick Ray Verne, 30–41. Seattle: University of Washington Press.

1960   Rite and Crop in the Inca State. In *Culture in History: Essays in Honor of Paul Radin*, edited by Stanley Diamond, 393–407. New York: Columbia University Press.

1962   Cloth and Its Functions in the Inca State. *American Anthropologist* 64:710–728.

1972   El Control Vertical de un Máximo de Pisos Ecológicos en la Economía de las Sociedades Andinas. In *Visita a la Provincia de León de Huánuco en 1562*, edited by John V. Murra, 429–476. Huánuco, Peru: Universidad Hermilio Valdizán.

1978   Los Olleros del Inka: Hacia una Historia y Arqueología del Qollasuyu. In *Historia, Problema y Promesa: Homenaje a Jorge Basadre*, 415–423. Lima: Pontificia Universidad Católica del Peru.

1980   *The Economic Organization of the Inka State*. Research in Economic Anthropology, Supplement. Greenwich, Conn.: JAA Press.

1982   The Mit'a Obligations of Ethnic Groups to the Inka State. In *The Inca and Aztec States, 1400–1800: Anthropology and History*, edited by George A. Collier, Renato I. Rosaldo, and John D. Wirth, 237–262. New York: Academic Press.

1983   La Mit'a al Tawantinsuyu: Prestaciones de los Grupos Étnicos. *Chungará Revista de Antropología Chilena* 10:77–94.

2002   *El Mundo Andino, Población Medio Ambiente y Economía*. Lima: Instituto de Estudios Peruanos.

Navas, Luisa E.

1976   *Flora de la Cuenca de Santiago de Chile*. Vol. 2. Santiago: Ediciones de la Universidad de Chile.

1979   *Flora de la Cuenca de Santiago de Chile*. Vol. 3. Santiago: Ediciones de la Universidad de Chile.

Nelson, Andrew J.

1998   Wandering Bones: Archaeology, Forensic Science and Moche Burial Practice. *International Journal of Osteoarchaeology* 8:192–212.

Nelson, Andrew J., Christine S. Nelson, Luis Jaime Castillo, and Carol J. Mackey

2000   Osteobiografía de una Hilandera Precolumbina: La Mujer detrás de la Máscara. *Íconos* 4(2): 30–43.

Netherly, Patricia J.

1977   Local Level Lords on the North Coast of Peru. Ph.D. diss., Cornell University.

Newman, Marshall T.
1943   A Metric Study of Undeformed Indian Crania from Peru. *American Journal of Physical Anthropology* 1:21–45.

Nielsen, Axel E.
1996   Demografía y Cambio Social en Humahuaca (Jujuy, Argentina) 700–1535 D.C. *Relaciones de la Sociedad Argentina de Antropología* 21:307–385.

Nielsen, Axel E., and William Walker
1999   Conquista Ritual y Dominación Política en el Tawantinsuyu. El Caso de Los Amarillos (Jujuy, Argentina). In *In Sed non Satiata. Teoría Social en la Arqueología Latinoamericana Contemporánea*, edited by Andrés Zarankin and Félix Acuto, 153–169. Buenos Aires: Ediciones Del Tridente.

Niemeyer, Hans
1963   Excavaciones en un Cementerio Incaico en la Hacienda Camarones (Provincia de Tarapacá). *Revista Universitaria* 48:207–233.

Niles, Susan
1987   *Callachaca Style and Status in an Inca Community.* Iowa City: University of Iowa Press.
1992   Inca Architecture and Sacred Landscape. In *The Ancient Americas: Art from Sacred Landscapes*, edited by Richard F. Townsend, 346–357. Chicago: Art Institute of Chicago.
1999   *The Shape of Inca History: Narrative and Architecture in an Andean Empire.* Iowa City: University of Iowa Press.

Núñez, Lautaro
1992   *Cultura y Conflicto en los Oasis de San Pedro de Atacama.* Santiago: Editorial Universitaria.

Oberem, Udo
1969   La Fortaleza de Montaña de Quitoloma. *Boletín de la Academia Nacional de Historia* 114:196–204.
1986   Complejos de Fortalezas en el Área Andina. *Miscelánea Antropológica Ecuatoriana* 6:103–116.

Ocaña, Diego de
1969   *Un Viaje Fascinante por la América Hispana del Siglo XVI.* Madrid: STVDIVM Ediciones.

Ogburn, Dennis E.
2001   The Inca Occupation and Forced Resettlement in Saraguro, Ecuador. Ph.D. diss., University of California, Santa Barbara. Ann Arbor, Mich.: University Microfilms.

Osorio, Alfonso, and Calógero Santoro
1988   Trasvase Prehispánico Vilasamanani — Socoroma, Norte de Chile. *Idesia* 10:37–43.

Ovalle, Alonso
1969 [1646]   *Histórica relación del Reyno de Chile.* Santiago: Instituto de
              Literatura Chilena.
Pärssinen, Martti
2003   *Tawantinsuyu: El Estado Inca y su Organización Política.* Lima:
              IFEA.
Pärssinen, Martti, and Ari Siiriäinen
1997   Inka-Style Ceramics and Their Chronological Relationship
              to the Inka Expansion in the Southern Lake Titicaca Area
              (Bolivia). *Latin American Antiquity* 8:255–271.
1998   Cuzcotoro and the Inka Fortification System in Chuquisaca,
              Bolivia. *Baessler-Archiv* 46:135–164.
2003   Andes Orientales y Amazonía Occidental: Ensayos entre la
              Historia y la Arqueología de Bolivia, Brasil y Perú. *Colección
              maestría en Historias Andinas y Amazónicas,* Vol. 3. La Paz,
              Bolivia: Producciones CIMA.
Pauketat, Timothy
2001   Practice and History in Archaeology: An Emerging Paradigm.
              Anthropological Theory 1(1): 73–98.
Pearsall, Deborah M.
1989   Adaptation of Prehistoric Hunter-Gatherers to the High Andes:
              The Changing Role of Plant Resources. In *Foraging and Farm-
              ing: The Evolution of Plant Exploitation,* edited by D. R. Harris
              and G. C. Hillman, 318–332. One World Archaeology 13. Lon-
              don: Unwin-Hyman.
Pease G.Y., Franklin
1982   The Formation of Tawantinsuyu: Mechanisms of Colonializa-
              tion and Relationship with Ethnic Groups. In *The Inca and Aztec
              States, 1400–1800: Anthropology and History,* edited by George A.
              Collier, Renato I. Rosaldo, and John D. Wirth, 173–198. New
              York: Academic Press.
Pietrusewsky, Michael
1996   Multivariate Craniometric Investigations of Japanese, Asian and
              Pacific Islanders. In *Interdisciplinary Perspectives on the Origins
              of the Japanese: International Symposium,* edited by Omoto Kei-
              ichi, 65–104. Kyoto: International Research Center for Japanese
              Studies.
Planella, María Teresa
1988   La Propiedad Territorial Indígena en el Valle de Rancagua a
              Fines del Siglo XVI e Inicios del Siglo XVII. Master's thesis,
              Universidad de Chile, Santiago.

Planella, María Teresa, and Rubén Stehberg
1994   Etnohistoria y Arqueología en el Estudio de la Fortaleza Indígena de
        Cerro Grande de La Compañía. *Chungará Revista de Antropología Chi-
        lena* 26:65–78.
Planella, María Teresa, Rubén Stehberg, Hans Niemeyer, Blanca Tagle, and
        Carmen Del Río
1991   La Fortaleza Indígena del Cerro Grande de la Compañía (Valle de
        Cachapoal) y su Relación con el Proceso Expansivo Meridional
        Incaico. *Actas del XII Congreso Nacional de Arqueología Chilena*,
        403–421.
1992   El Complejo Defensivo Indígena del Cerro Grande de La Compañía
        (Valle del Cachapoal). *Clava* 5:117–132.
Platt, Tristán
1982   *Estado Boliviano y Ayllu Andino: Tierra y Tributo en el Norte de Potosí.*
        Lima: Instituto de Estudios Peruanos.
1988   Pensamiento Político Aymara. In *Raíces de América: El Mundo Aymara*,
        edited by Xavier Albó, 365–443. Madrid: Alianza America/UNESCO.
1999   Imagined Frontiers: Recent Advances in the Ethnohistory of the
        Southern Andes. *Bulletin of Latin American Research* 18(1): 101–110.
Platt, Tristán, Thérèse Bouysse-Cassagne, and Olivia Harris
2006   *Qaraqara-Charka: Mallku, Inka y Rey en la Provincia de Charcas (Siglos
        XV–XVII).* La Paz, Bolivia: IFEA.
Plaza Schuller, Fernando
1976   *La Incursión Inca en el Septentrión Andino Ecuatoriano: Antecedentes
        Arqueológicos de la Convulsiva Situación de Contacto Cultural.* Serie
        Arqueológica No. 2. Otavalo, Ecuador: Instituto Otavaleño de
        Antropología.
1977   *El Complejo de Fortalezas de Pambamarca: Contribución al Estudio de
        la Arquitectura Militar y Prehispánica en la Sierra Norte del Ecuador.*
        Serie Arqueológica No. 3. Otavalo, Ecuador: Instituto Otavaleño de
        Antropología.
Pollard, Gordon
1981   The Bronze Artisans of Calchaquí. *Early Man* 33:27–33.
1983   Nuevos Aportes a la Prehistoria del Valle Calchaquí, Noroeste Argen-
        tino. *Estudios de Arqueología* 3–4:69–92.
Presta, Ana María
2000   *Encomienda, Familia y Negocios en Charcas Colonial (Bolivia): Los Enco-
        menderos de La Plata, 1550–1600.* Lima: Instituto de Estudios Peruanos.
Protzen, Jean-Pierre
1993   *Inca Architecture and Construction at Ollantaytambo.* Oxford: Oxford
        University Press.

Raffino, Rodolfo A.

1981   *Los Inkas del Kollasuyo.* La Plata, Argentina: Editorial Ramos Americana.

1983   Arqueología y Etnohistoria de la Región Calchaquí. In *Presencia Hispánica en la Arqueología Argentina*, edited by Eldo S. Morresi and Ramón Gutierrez, 817–861. Chaco: Instituto de Historia, Facultad de Humanidades, Universidad Nacional del Noreste.

1988   *Poblaciones Indígenas de la Argentina.* Buenos Aires: Editorial TEA.

1993a   El Dominio Inka en el Altiplano de Bolivia. In *Inka, Arqueología, Historia y Urbanismo del Altiplano Andino*, edited by Rodolfo A. Raffino, 169–212. Buenos Aires: Ediciones Corregidor.

1993b   *Inka Arqueología, Historia y Urbanismo del Altiplano Andino.* Buenos Aires: Ediciones Corregidor.

Ramirez, Susan

1996   *The World Upside-Down: Cross Cultural Contact and Conflict in Sixteenth-Century Perú.* Stanford, Calif.: Stanford University Press.

Rasnake, Roger

1988   *Domination and Cultural Resistance: Authority and Power among an Andean People.* Durham, N.C.: Duke University Press.

Reich, Karl

1901   *Los Productos Vegetales Indígenas de Chile.* Santiago: Imprenta Cervantes.

Reinhard, Johan

2002   A High Altitude Archaeological Survey in Northern Chile. *Chungará Revista de Antropología Chilena* 34:85–99.

Rivera Casanovas, Claudia

2002   Inka Domination and Local Sociopolitical Dynamics: A Vision from Cinti. Paper presented at the 67th meeting of the Society for American Archaeology, Denver, Colorado.

2004   Regional Settlement Patterns and Political Complexity in the Cinti Valley, Bolivia. Ph.D. diss., University of Pittsburgh.

2005   Sociedades Prehispánicas Tardías en los Valles Interandinos del Suroeste de Chuquisaca, Bolivia. *Nuevos Aportes* 3:76–92.

2008   Proyecto Arqueológico San Lucas: Trayectorias Evolutivas Locales y Sistemas de Territorialidad Discontinuas Prehispánicas y Coloniales en San Lucas, Chuquisaca. Report submitted to the Instituto de Investigaciones Antropológicas y Arqueológicas, Universidad Mayor de San Andrés, La Paz.

2008   Aproximación Inicial a la Explotación Minera y Metalurgia
              Prehispánica en la Región de San Lucas, Chuquisaca. In *Minas
              y Metalurgias en los Andes del Sur, entre la Época Prehispánica y el
              Siglo XVII*, edited by Pablo Cruz, and J.-J. Vacher. Lima, Perú:
              Institutó Francés de Estudios Andinos.

Rodriguez, Arturo, Ramón Morales, Carlos González, and Donald Jackson
1993   Cerro La Cruz: Un Enclave Económico Administrativo Incaico,
              Curso Medio del Aconcagua (Chile Central). *Actas del XII Con-
              greso Nacional de Arqueología Chilena* 2:201–222.

Romero, Álvaro
2002   Cerámica Doméstica del Valle de Lluta: Cultura Local y Redes
              de Interacción Inka. *Chungará Revista de Antropología Chilena*
              34:191–213.
2003   Chullpas de Barro, Interacción y Dinámica Política en la Pre-
              cordillera de Arica, durante el Período Intermedio Tardío. *Textos
              Antropológicos* 14(2): 83–103.

Romero, Álvaro, and Luis Briones
1999   CO-37: Estado y Planificación Inca en Collahuasi. *Estudios Ata-
              cameños* 18:141–154.

Romero, Álvaro, Calógero Santoro, and Mariela Santos
1998   Asentamientos y Organización Sociopolítica en los Tramos Bajos
              y Medios del Valle de Lluta. *Actas III Congreso Chileno de An-
              tropología* 2:696–706.

Romero Sánchez, Rodrigo
2004   El Tawantinsuyu en Aconcagua (Chile Central). *Chungará Re-
              vista de Antropología Chilena* 36:325–336.

Rosales, Diego de
1877 [1674]   *Historia General del Reino de Chile*. Valparaíso, Chile: Imprenta
              del Mercurio.

Rossen, Jack
1994   Food for the Frontier: The Archaeobotany of the Inca Fortress of
              Cerro Grande de La Compañía, Central Chile. Paper presented
              at the 12th annual meeting of the Northeast Conference on An-
              dean Archaeology and Ethnohistory, Ithaca, N.Y.
1997   Quinoa in Central Chile: Ethnographic Survival and Archaeo-
              logical Question. Paper presented at the annual meeting of the
              Society for American Archaeology, Nashville, Tenn.

Rostworowski de Diez Canseco, María
1953   *Pachacutec Ynca Yupanqui*. Lima: Imprenta Torres Aguirre.
1970   Mercaderes del Valle de Chincha en la Época Prehispánica. *Re-
              vista Española de Antropología Americana* 5:135–177.

1972   Breve Ensayo Sobre el Señorío de Ychma. *Arqueología* 13:37–51.

1975   Pescadores, Artesanos y Mercaderes Costeños en el Perú Prehispánico. *Revista del Museo Nacional* 38:250–314.

1977   *Étnia y Sociedad: Ensayos Sobre la Costa Central Prehispánica*. Lima:
Instituto de Estudios Peruanos.

1978   *Señorios Indígenas de Lima y Canta*. Lima: Instituto de Estudios
Peruanos.

1988a   *Conflicts Over Coca Fields in XVIth-Century Peru*. Vol. 4. Memoirs
of the Museum of Anthropology No. 21. Ann Arbor: University of
Michigan.

1988b   *Historia del Tahuantinsuyu*. Lima: Instituto de Estudios Peruanos.

1990   Las Macroetnias en el Ámbito Andino. *Cusco: Instituto de Pastoral
Andina: Allpanchis* 22(35–36): 3–28.

1999   *History of the Inca Realm*. Translated by Harry B. Iceland. New York:
Cambridge University Press.

Rowe, John H.

1944   *An Introduction to the Archaeology of Cuzco*. Vol. 27. *Papers of the Peabody Museum of American Archaeology and Ethnology* 27(2), Harvard
University.

1946   Inca Culture at the Time of the Spanish Conquest. In *Handbook of
South American Indians*, Bureau of American Ethnology Bulletin
No. 143, edited by Julian H. Steward, 183–330. Bureau of American
Ethnology, Washington, D.C.

1948   The Kingdom of Chimor. *Acta Americana* 6(1–2): 26–59.

1982   Inca Policies and Institutions Relating to the Cultural Unification of
the Empire. In *The Inca and Aztec States, 1400–1800: Anthropology and
History*, edited by George A. Collier, Renato I. Rosaldo, and John D.
Wirth, 93–118. New York: Academic Press.

Rydén, Stig

1947   *Archaeological Researchers in the Highland of Bolivia*. Göteborg, Swe-
den: Elanders Boktryckeri Aktiebolag.

Salomón, Frank

1980   *Los Señores Étnicos de Quito en la Época de los Incas*. Colección Pendoneros No. 10. Otavalo, Ecuador: Instituto Otavaleño de Antropología.

1986   *Native Lords of Quito in the Age of the Incas: The Political Economy
of North Andean Chiefdoms*. Cambridge: Cambridge University
Press.

1997   *Los Yumbos, Niguas y Tsáchila o Colorados durante la Colonia Española:
Etnohistoria del Noroccidente de Pichincha, Ecuador*. Quito: Ediciones
Abya-Yala.

Salomón, Frank, and George L. Urioste
1991   The Huarochirí Manuscript: A Testament of Ancient and Colonial Andean Religion. Austin: University of Texas Press.

Sánchez, Rodrigo
2004   El Tawantinsuyu en Aconcagua. Chungará Revista de Antropología Chilena 2:325–336.

Sanguinettei, N.
1975   Construcciones Indígenas en el Cerro Mercachas (Departamento de los Andes, Provincia del Aconcagua). Anales del Museo de Historia Natural de Valparaíso 8:129–139.

Santoro, Calógero
1983   Camino del Inca en la Sierra de Arica. Chungará Revista de Antropología Chilena 10:47–55.
1995   Late Prehistoric Regional Interaction and Social Change in a Coastal Valley of Northern Chile. Ph.D. diss., University of Pittsburgh.

Santoro, Calógero, Sheila Dorsey-Vinton, and Karl J. Reinhard
2003   Inka Expansion and Parasitism in the Lluta Valley: Preliminary Data. Memórias de Instituto Oswaldo Cruz 98(1): 161–163.

Santoro, Calógero, Jorge Hidalgo, and Alfonso Osorio
1987   El Estado Inka y los Grupos Étnicos en el Sistema de Riego de Socoroma. Chungará Revista de Antropología Chilena 19:71–92.

Santoro, Calógero, and Iván Muñoz
1981   Patrón Habitacional Incaico en el Área de Pampa Alto Ramírez (Arica Chile). Chungará Revista de Antropología Chilena 7:144–171.

Santoro, Calógero, Lautaro Núñez, Vivien G. Standen, Héctor González, Pablo Marquet, and Amador Torres
1998   Proyectos de Irrigación y la Fertilización del Desierto. Estudios Atacameños 16:321–336.

Santoro, Calógero, Álvaro Romero, and Mariela Santos
2001   Formas Cerámicas e Interacción Regional durante los Períodos Intermedio Tardío y Tardío en el Valle de Lluta. In Segundas Jornadas de Arte y Arqueología, edited by José Berenguer, Luis Cornejo, Fernando Gallardo, and Carol Sinclaire, 15–40. Santiago: Museo Chileno de Arte Precolombino.

Santoro, Calógero, Álvaro Romero, Vivien G. Standen, and Amador Torres
2004   Continuidad y Cambio en las Comunidades Locales, Períodos Intermedio Tardío y Tardío, Valles Occidentales del Área Centro Sur Andina. Chungará Revista de Antropología Chilena 1:235–247.

Santoro, Calógero, and Liliana Ulloa
1985   Culturas de Arica. Santiago: Ministerio de Educación.

Sapp, William D. III

2002   The Impact of Imperial Conquest at the Palace of a Local Lord in the Jequetepeque Valley, Northern Peru. Ph.D. diss., University of California, Los Angeles.

Scattolin, C., and Veronica I. Williams

1992   Actividades Minero Metalúricas en el N.O. Argentino. Nuevas Evidencias y Significación. *Bulletin de l'Institut Français d'Études Andines* 21(1): 59–87.

Schaedel, Richard P.

1988   Comentario: Las Fronteras del Estado Inca. In *La Frontera del Estado Inca*, edited by Tom D. Dillehay and Patricia J. Netherly, 261–272. Oxford: BAR Internacional Series 442.

Schauer, Matt

2007   Warfare and Defensive Architecture on the Inca Northern Frontier. Paper presented at the 35th annual Midwest Conference on Andean and Amazonian Archaeology and Ethnohistory, Carbondale, Ill.

Schiappacasse, Virgilio

1999   Cronología del Estado Inca. *Estudios Atacameños* 18:133–140.

Schiappacasse, Virgilio, Victoria Castro, and Hans Niemeyer

1989   Los Desarrollos Regionales en el Norte Grande (1000 a 1400 d.c.). In *Culturas de Chile, Desde la Prehistoria hasta los Albores de la Conquista*, edited by Jorge Hidalgo, Virgilio Schiappacasse, Hans Niemeyer, Carlos Aldunate, and Iván Solimano, 181–220. Santiago: Andrés Bello.

Schiappacasse, Virgilio, and Hans Niemeyer

1989   Avances y Sugerencias para el Avance del Conocimiento de la Prehistoria Tardía de la Desembocadura del Valle de Camarones (Región de Tarapacá). *Chungará Revista de Antropología Chilena* 22:63–84.

1997   Continuidad y Cambio Cultural en el Poblado Actual de Pachica, Quebrada de Camarones. *Chungará Revista de Antropología Chilena* 29:209–247.

2002   Ceremonial Inca Provincial: El Asentamiento de Saguara (Valle de Camarones). *Chungará Revista de Antropología Chilena* 34:53–84.

Schjellerup, Inge

2005   *Incas y Españoles en la Conquista de los Chachapoya*. Lima: Fondo Editorial Pontificia Universidad Católica del Perú and Instituto Francés de Estudios Andinos.

Schmidt, Peter

1996   *The Culture and Technology of African Iron Production*. Gainesville: University Press of Florida.

1997   *Iron Technology in East Africa: Symbolism, Science and Archaeology*. Bloomington: Indiana University Press.

Schreiber, Katharina J.

1987   Conquest and Consolidation: A Comparison of the Wari and
            Inka Occupations of a Highland Peruvian Valley. *American Antiq-
            uity* 52:266–284.

1992   *Wari Imperialism in Middle Horizon Peru.* Anthropological Papers
            87, Museum of Anthropology. Ann Arbor: University of Michigan.

1993   The Inca Occupation of the Province of Andamarca Lucanas,
            Peru. In *Provincial Inca: Archaeological and Ethnohistorical Assess-
            ment of the Impact of the Inca State,* edited by Michael A. Malpass,
            77–116. Iowa City: University of Iowa Press.

Schutz, Alfred, and Thomas Luckmann

1973   *The Structures of the Life-World.* Evanston, Ill.: Northwestern Uni-
            versity Press.

Shimada, Izumi

1991   Pachacamac Archaeology: Retrospect and Prospect. In *Pachaca-
            mac and Pachacamac Archaeology,* edited by Max Uhle and Izumi
            Shimada, 16–58. Philadelphia: University of Pennsylvania Mu-
            seum of Archaeology and Anthropology.

1994   Pre-Hispanic Metallurgy and Mining in the Andes: Recent
            Advances and Future Tasks. In *Quest of Mineral Wealth: Ab-
            original and Colonial Mining and Metallurgy in Spanish America,*
            edited by Alan Craig and Robert C. West, 37–73. Baton Rouge:
            Department of Geography and Anthropology, Louisiana State
            University.

Siiriäinen, Ari, and Martti Pärssinen

2001   The Amazonian Interests of the Inca State (Tawantinsuyu).
            Baessler-Archiv 49:45–78.

Silva, Osvaldo

1985   La Expansión Incaica en Chile: Problemas y Reflexiones. *IX Con-
            greso Nacional de Arqueología Chilena* 1:321–344. La Serena.

1986   Los Promaucaes y la Frontera Meridional Incaica en Chile. *Cua-
            dernos de Historia* 6:7–17.

1992–1993   Reflexiones Acerca del Dominio Incaico en Tarapacá (Chile).
            Diálogo Andino 11–12:77–93.

1993   Reflexiones Sobre la Influencia Incaica en los Albores del Reino
            de Chile. *Actas del XII Congreso Nacional de Arqueología Chilena,*
            1:285-92. Boletín del Museo Regional de Araucania 4, Temuco.

Silverblatt, Irene

1987   *Moon, Sun and Witches. Gender Ideologies and Class in Inca and
            Colonial Peru.* Princeton, N.J.: Princeton University Press.

1988   Imperial Dilemmas, the Politics of Kinship, and Inca Reconstructions of History. *Comparative Studies in Society and History* 30:83–102.

Spalding, Karen

1984   *Huarochirí: An Andean Society under Inca and Spanish Rule.* Stanford, Calif.: Stanford University Press.

Speakman, Robert J., and Michael D. Glascock

2003   Instrumental Neutron Activation Analysis of Ceramics and Clays for the Palmitopamba Archaeology Project, Ecuador. Report prepared for Ronald Lippi and Tamara Bray at the Archaeometry Laboratory of the Missouri University Research Reactor, Columbia, Missouri.

Spurling, Geoffrey E.

1992   The Organization of Craft Production in the Inca State: The Potters and Weavers of Milliraya. Ph.D. diss., Cornell University. Ann Arbor, Mich.: University Microfilms.

Standen, Vivien G., and Bernardo T. Arriaza

2000   Traumas in the Preceramic Coastal Populations of Northern Chile: Violence or Occupational Hazards? *American Journal of Physical Anthropology* 112:239–249.

Standen, Vivien G., Bernardo T. Arriaza, Calógero M. Santoro, Álvaro Romero, and Francisco Rothhammer

2009   Perimortem Trauma in the Atacama Desert and Social Violence during the Late Formative Period (2500–1700 years BP). *International Journal of Osteoarchaeology.* Published online July 6, 2009 in advance of print. http://ww3.interscience.wiley.com/journal/122485452/abstract.

Stanish, Charles

1997   Nonmarket Imperialism in the Prehispanic Americas: The Inka Occupation of the Titicaca Basin. *Latin American Antiquity* 8:195–216.

2001a   Formación Estatal Temprana en la Cuenca del Lago Titicaca, Andes Surcentrales. *Boletín de Arqueología, PUCP* 5:189–215.

2001b   Regional Research on the Inca. *Journal of Archaeological Research* 9(3): 213–241.

2005   Migration, Colonies and Ethnicity in the South-Central Andes. In *Us and Them: Archaeology and Ethnicity in the Andes,* edited by Richard Martin Reycraft, 226–232. Los Angeles: Cotsen Institute of Archaeology, University of California.

Stehberg, Rubén

1976   *La Fortaleza Chena y su Relación con la Ocupación Incaica de Chile Central.* Publicación Ocasional No. 23. Santiago: Museo Nacional de Historia Natural.

1995   *Instalaciones Incaicas en el Norte y Centro Semiárido de Chile*. Colección Antropología 2. Santiago: Centro de Investigaciones Diego Barros Arana, Dirección de Bibliotecas, Archivos, y Museos.

Stehberg, Rubén, María Teresa Planella, and Hans Niemeyer

1997   Complejidad Arquitectónica de las Ruinas Prehispanas de Chada en la Antigua Ruta entre los Ríos Maipo y Cachapoal. *Xama* 6–11:6–7.

Stojanowski, Christopher M., and Michael A. Schillaci

2006   Phenotypic Approaches for Understanding Patterns of Intracemetery Biological Variation. *Yearbook of Physical Anthropology* 49:49–88.

Strathern, Andrew

1994   Keeping the Body in the Mind. *Social Anthropology* 2(1): 43–53.

Sutter, Richard C.

1997   Dental Variation and Biocultural Affinities among Prehistoric Populations from the Coastal Valleys of Moquegua, Peru, and Azapa, Chile. Ph.D. diss., University of Missouri, Columbia.

2000   Prehistoric Genetic and Culture Change: A Bioarchaeological Search for Pre-Inca Altiplano Colonies in the Coastal Valleys of Moquegua, Peru, and Azapa, Chile. *Latin American Antiquity* 11:43–70.

2005   A Bioarchaeological Assessment of Prehistoric Ethnicity among Early Late Intermediate Populations of the Azapa Valley, Chile. In *Us and Them: Archaeology and Ethnicity in the Andes*, edited by Richard Martin Reycraft, 183–205. Los Angeles: Cotsen Institute of Archaeology, University of California.

Tabachnick, Barbara G., and Linda S. Fidell

2001   *Using Multivariate Statistics*. Boston: Allyn and Bacon.

Tabio, Ernesto E.

1965   Una Tumba Tardía de Puruchucu, Lima. In *Excavaciones en la Costa Central del Perú*, 91–106. Havana: Academia de Ciencias, Departamento de Antropología.

Tarragó, Myriam

1977   La Localidad Arqueológica de las Pailas, Provincia de Salta, Argentina. In *Actas del VII Congreso de Arqueología de Chile* 2:499–517.

2000   Chakras y Pukara. Desarrollos Sociales Tardíos. In *Los Pueblos Originarios y la Conquista, Nueva Historia Argentina, Tomo I*, edited by Myriam Tarragó, 257–300. Buenos Aires: Editorial Sudamericana.

Tarragó, Myriam, Luis González, and Javier Nastri

1997   Las Interrelaciones Prehispánicas a través del Estilo: El Caso de la Iconografía Santamariana. *Estudios Atacameños* 14:223–42.

Téllez, Eduardo

1990   De Inca, Picones y Promaucaes. El Derrumbe de la "Frontera Salvaje" en el Confín Austral del Collasuyo. *Cuadernos de Historia* 10:69–87.

Thomas, Nicholas

1997   Partial Texts. In *On Oceania: Visions, Artifacts, Histories,* edited by
                Nicholas Thomas, 23–49. Durham, N.C.: Duke University Press.

1999   The Case of the Misplaced Ponchos: Speculations Concerning
                the History of Cloth in Polynesia. *Journal of Material Culture* 4(1):
                5–20.

Thompson, Robert G.

2003   Phytolith Analysis of Selected Sherds from La Mesa and Palmito-
                pamba, Highland Ecuador. Report prepared for Ronald Lippi and
                Tamara Bray. Minneapolis: University of Minnesota.

Topic, John R., and Theresa Lange Topic

1997   Hacia una Comprensión Conceptual de la Guerra Andina. In *Ar-
                queología, Antropología e Historia en los Andes: Homenaje a María
                Rostworowski,* edited by Rafael Varón Gabai, Javier Flores Espi-
                noza, and María Rostworowski de Diez Canseco, 567–590. Lima:
                Instituto de Estudios Peruanos.

Torres-Rouff, Christina

2005   Violence in Times of Change: The Late Intermediate Period in
                San Pedro de Atacama. *Chungará Revista de Antropología Chilena*
                37:75–83.

Towle, Margaret A.

1961   *The Ethnobotany of Pre-Columbian Peru.* Viking Fund Publica-
                tions in Anthropology 39. New York: Wenner-Gren Foundation.

Trimborn, Hermann, Otto Kleemann, Karl Narr, and Wolfgang Wurster

1975   *Investigaciones Arqueológicas en los Valles de Caplina y Sama
                (Depto. Tacna, Perú).* Studia Instituti Anthropos No. 25. Tacna:
                Editorial Verbo Divino.

Tschauner, Hartmut

2001   Socioeconomic and Political Organization in the Late Pre-
                hispanic Lambayeque Sphere, Northern North Coast of Peru.
                Ph.D. diss., Harvard University.

Ubelaker, Douglas H.

1984   *Human Skeletal Remains: Excavation, Analysis, Interpretation.*
                2nd ed. Washington, D.C.: Tarazacum.

Uhle, Max

1991 [1903]   *Pachacamac: A Reprint of the 1903 Edition. Archaeology.* Philadel-
                phia: University of Pennsylvania Museum of Archaeology and
                Anthropology.

Uribe, Mauricio

1999–2000   La Arqueología del Inka en Chile. *Revista Chilena de Antropología*
                15:63–97.

2004   El Inka y el Poder como Problemas de la Arqueología del Norte
             Grande de Chile. *Chungará Revista de Antropología Chilena*
             36:313–324.

Uribe, Mauricio, and Leonor Adán
2004   Acerca del Dominio Inka, Sin Miedo, Sin Vergüenza. *Chungará Re-
             vista de Antropología Chilena* 36:467–480.

Uribe, Mauricio, Viviana Manríquez, and Leonor Adán
2000   El Poder del Inka en Chile: Aproximaciones a Partir de la Arque-
             ología de Caspana (Río Loa, Desierto de Atacama). *Actas del III
             Congreso Chileno de Antropología* 2:706–722.

Valarezo G., Ramón
1987   *La Resistencia Andina: Cayambe, 1500–1800.* Quito: Centro Andino
             de Acción Popular.

Valenzuela, Daniela, Calógero Santoro, and Álvaro Romero
2004   Arte Rupestre en Asentamientos del Período Tardío en los Valles
             de Lluta y Azapa, Norte de Chile. *Chungará Revista de Antropología
             Chilena* 36:421–437.

Van Buren, Mary
1996   Rethinking the Vertical Archipelago: Ethnicity, Exchange and
             History in the South-Central Andes. *American Anthropologist*
             98:338–351.
2003   Un Estudio Etnoarqueológico de la Tecnología de Fundición
             en el Sur de Potosí, Bolivia. *Textos Antropológicos* 14(2):
             133–148.
2006   The Material Record and the Political Moment: Encounters be-
             tween Archaeological and Documentary Data in the Andes. Paper
             presented to the fourth Congress of the Bolivian Studies Associa-
             tion, June 21–25, Sucre.

Van Buren, Mary, and Barbara Mills
In press   Huayrachinas and Tocochimbos: Traditional Smelting Tech-
             nology of the Southern Andes. *Latin American Antiquity*
             16:3–25.

Van de Guchte, Maarten
1999   The Inca Cognition of Landscape: Archaeology, Ethnohistory
             and the Aesthetic of Alterity. In *The Archaeologies of Landscapes:
             Contemporary Perspectives,* edited by Wendy Ashmore and Bernard
             Knapp, 149–168. Oxford: Blackwell.

Verano, John W.
1987   Cranial Microvariation at Pacatnamu. Ph.D. diss., University of
             California, Los Angeles. Ann Arbor, Mich.: University Microfilms.

1997   Physical Characteristics and Skeletal Biology of the Moche Population at Pacatnamu. In *The Pacatnamu Papers*, Vol. 2, edited by Christopher B. Donnan and Guillermo A. Cock Carrasco, 189–214. Los Angeles: UCLA Fowler Museum of Cultural History.

2001   The Physical Evidence of Human Sacrifice in Ancient Peru. In *Ritual Sacrifice in Ancient Peru*, edited by Elizabeth P. Benson and Anita Gwynn Cook, 165–184. Austin: University of Texas Press.

2003   Human Skeletal Remains from Machu Picchu: A Reexamination of the Yale Peabody Museum's Collections. In *The 1912 Yale Peruvian Scientific Expedition Collections from Machu Picchu: Human and Animal Remains*, edited by Richard L. Burger and Lucy C. Salazar, 65–118. New Haven, Conn.: Yale University Publications in Anthropology.

Verano, John W., and Michael J. DeNiro
1993   Locals or Foreigners? Morphological, Biometric and Isotopic Approaches to the Question of Group Affinity in Human Skeletal Remains Recovered from Unusual Archaeological Contexts. In *Investigations of Ancient Human Tissue: Chemical Analysis in Anthropology*, edited by Mary K. Sandford, 361–386. Langehorne, Pa.: Gordon and Breach.

Vicuña Mackenna, Benjamín
1881   *La Edad del Oro en Chile.* Santiago: Imprenta Cervantes.

Vignale, Pedro J., and Dick E. Ibarra Grasso
1943   Culturas Eneolíticas en los Alrededores de Potosí. *SUR* 1:79–119.

Vilches, Flora, and Mauricio Uribe
1999   Grabados y Pinturas del Arte Rupestre Tardío de Caspana. *Estudios Atacameños* 18:73–87.

Vitry, Christian
n.d.   Los Incas y el Pasaje: Organización Geopolítica y Religiosa del Territorio Prehispánico. Museo de Antropología de Salta, Argentina. http://www.antropologico.gov.ar-incas.htm.

Von Hagen, Victor Wolfgang
1959   *The Incas of Pedro de Cieza de León.* Norman: University of Oklahoma Press.

Von Nordenskiöld, Erland
1917   The Guaraní Invasion of the Inca Empire in the Sixteenth Century: An Historical Indian Migration. *Geographical Review* 9:103–121.

Wachtel, Nathan
1982   The Mitimaes of the Cochabamba Valley: The Colonization Policy of Huayna Capac. In *The Inca and Aztec States, 1400–1800: Anthropology and History*, edited by George A. Collier, Renato I. Rosaldo, and John D. Wirth, 199–235. New York: Academic Press.

Wallerstein, Immanuel

1976   *The Modern World-System: Capitalist Agriculture and the Origins of the European World-Economy in the Sixteenth Century.* New York: Academic Press.

Walter, Heinz

1959   Die Ruinen Pucara de Oroncota (Sudost-Bolivien). *Baessler-Archiv,* N.F. Vol. 7: 333–341.

Weber, Steven A.

2003   Archaeobotany at Harappa: Indications for Change. In *Indus Ethnobiology: New Perspectives from the Field,* edited by Steven A. Weber and William R. Belcher, 175–198. Lanham, Md.: Lexington Books.

Wernke, Steven A.

2006   The Politics of Community and Inka Statecraft in the Colca Valley, Peru. *Latin American Antiquity* 17:177–208.

Wiessner, Polly

1990   Is There a Unity to Style? In *The Use of Style in Archaeology,* edited by Margaret W. Conkey and Christine A. Hastorf, 105–112. Cambridge: Cambridge University Press.

Williams, Verónica I.

1999   Organización de la Producción de Cerámica Inka en los Andes del Sur. *Arqueología* 9:71–111.

2000   El Imperio Inka en la Provincia de Catamarca. *Intersecciones en Antropología* 1:55–78.

2004   Poder Estatal y Cultura Material en el Collasuyu. *Boletín Arqueología, PUCP* 8:209–245.

2005   Poder y Cultura Material en el Kollasuyu, Tercera Parte. In *Identidad y Transformación en el Tawantinsuyu y en los Andes Coloniales. Perspectivas Arqueológicas y Etnohistóricas.* Boletín de Arqueología PUCP 8 (2004), edited by Peter Kaulicke, Gary Urton, and Ian Farrington, 204–245. Lima: Pontificia Universidad Católica del Perú.

Williams, Verónica I., and Terence N. D'Altroy

1998   El Sur del Tawantinsuyu: Un Dominio Selectivamente Intensivo. *Tawantinsuyu* 5:170–178.

Williams, Verónica I., Calógero M. Santoro, Álvaro L. Romero G., Jesús Gordillo, Daniela Valenzuela, and Vivien G. Standen

2009   Mecanismos de Dominación Inka en los Valles Occidentales y Noroeste Argentino. *Andes (Boletín del Centro de Estudios Precolombinos de la Universidad de Varsovia)* 7:615–624.

Williams, Verónica I., María Paula Villegas, María Soledad Gheggi, and María
     Gabriela Chaparro
2006   Hospitalidad e Intercambio en los Valles Mesotermales del Noroeste
     Argentino. *Boletín de Arqueología, PUCP* 9:335–372.

Zanolli, Carlos
2003   Los Chichas como Mitimaes del Inca. *Relaciones de la Sociedad Argen-
     tina de Antropología* 28:45–60.

Zuidema, Tom
1964   *The Ceque System of Cuzco: The Social Organization of the Capital of the
     Inca.* Translated by Eva M. Hooykaas. International Archives of Eth-
     nography, Supplement to Vol. 50. Leiden: E. J. Brill.

Index